WORK 3.0

Celebrating 35 Years of
Penguin Random House India

PRAISE FOR THE BOOK

'While many companies and leaders are grappling with the "Future of Work", the pandemic disrupted the playbook many were already struggling to put together. Since then, things have taken 180-degrees turn. A kick-ass office is no longer a magnet when people prefer to work remotely. Combined with the great resignation and quiet quitting, leaders are at a loss of what to do and where to begin. This book is an excellent start to help you make sense of the evolving players at work and aid you in reflecting how to best navigate them'—Adrian Tan, podcast host, Channel NewsAsia

'We live in uncertain, unpredictable times. The disruptions of a technology-driven ecosystem have been further accelerated by the pandemic and raised fundamental questions about the worker, workplace and work in the future. Chanda and Bandyopadhyay address these questions in a multi-pronged way, combining multidisciplinary academic research, official reports and data, business case studies and their real-life applications in the workplace, expert interviews and anecdotal evidence to arrive at tangible, implementable recommendations. *Work 3.0* is a concerted thought leadership that focuses on the subject from the standpoint of the Indian ecosystem—and my sense is that it will continue to be one of the most impactful, for years to come'—Anuradha Kedia, co-founder, The Better India

'*Work 3.0* is an absolute must-read for leaders looking to provide vision and stability in our fast-changing, turbulent and evermore interconnected world. The book provides a unique and needed perspective, bringing together wide-reaching research with a crucial focus on India as a world powerhouse of the innovative industries. Especially for leaders seeking a global perspective, this book will change the way you think about the future and how the past and present still shape it'—Aubrey Blanche, senior director of equitable design, product & people, Culture Amp, and founder-CEO, The Mathpath

'The future of work, workers and the workplace is not what it used to be. Much of what was being talked about before 2020 has undergone a radical change as we view the path ahead with the pandemic having radically rearranged the landscape. Chanda and Bandyopadhyay have given us a roadmap to help workers, managers and organizations think about the new skills needed, how work may be organized and these might mean for assembling a productive "office". This book is where the Fourth Industrial Revolution meets the Third Work Revolution meets the First Inner Revolution'—Bhaskar Chakravorti, dean of global business, The

Fletcher School of Law & Diplomacy, Tufts University; chairman of Digital Planet and former Partner, McKinsey and Company

'The COVID-19 pandemic has brought a paradigm shift in the way one envisages the workforce, workplace and the nature of work itself. It has opened many opportunities and curtailed others. In this ambitious project, Avik Chanda and Siddhartha Bandyopadhyay have taken a multidisciplinary approach, to analyse how pandemic-induced shocks have disrupted the system and offer recommendations on how they can be successfully mediated. This is a prodigious work that is lucid, astute, thought-provoking, and with a tremendous breadth in its allusions and insights. One should definitely read *Work 3.0*'—Bibek Debroy, chairman of Economic Advisory Council to the Prime Minister

'In their insightful and informative book, Sid Bandyopadhyay and Avik Chanda address some of the most important issues facing us today. Trying to make sense of the future of work requires both articulate argument and thinking outside of the box. The authors succeed in both here whilst getting to grips with the wicked problems that underpin our future including new technologies, skills, mental health and inequalities. Bandopadhyay and Chanda have produced a must-read account for readers who wish to either familiarise themselves with these debates, or develop their understanding much further'—Catherine Cassell, professor, executive dean, Durham Business School

'To my knowledge, *Work 3.0* is the most comprehensive discussion of the present and future of labour in the contemporary world. Focusing on India and on the losers and winners of its contemporary transformations, but with a critical analysis that might well be applied to countries of the global north, the book is an indispensable guide on global technological metamorphosis at the dawn of the "end of history". Well written and documented, it will become a reference point for any analysis of capital accumulation'—Clara Mattei, The New School, author of *The Capital Order: How Economists Invented Austerity and Paved the Way to Fascism*

'The "New Normal" has rewritten the rules of the future of work and it's just the beginning. *Work 3.0* shares solid insights covering depths and breadths of technology and its impact across industries and stakeholders with historical references. With interesting references and data combined, *Work 3.0* takes you through a journey on rewriting the rules in this new world and staying ahead of the curve by embracing technology and keeping innovation at the core to drive this change in the twenty-first century'— Daniel Nath, Google, *Forbes* 30 Under 30 Asia, Global Shaper, World Economic Forum, former founder, Cybersecurity SaaS venture

'This timely and engaging book provides a brilliant analysis of why the nature of work is changing and where it is headed. Its focus on skills gaps and the need for AI and automation-driven workplaces, to continue to remain responsible and ethical—will resonate with many. A key feature of the book is its abiding human-centricity. Therefore, even discussions on the role of the state and industry are formulated in relation to their impact on the individual worker. Combining in-depth research with a style that is highly readable, Bandyopadhyay and Chanda's book offers new directions to the most challenging issues related to the workplace'—David Lloyd, police and crime commissioner for Hertfordshire

'Avik Chanda and Sid Bandyopadhyay present an extensively-researched, nuanced and objective analysis of the key issues around the emergent workplace globally, with a special focus on India. The authors balance their discussions of emergent technologies, domains, jobs and skills with an investigation into other aspects such as inequality and climate change. *Work 3.0* is a book that informs, provokes and empowers the reader'—Dipesh Chakrabarty, Lawrence A. Kimpton Distinguished Service professor of history, South Asian languages and civilizations, and the College, University of Chicago, Winner of the Arnold Toynbee Prize

'As we ease out of the global pandemic, what's next, especially in the world of work? Co-authors Chanda and Bandyopadhyay have written the perfect guide to help us navigate this new era, which they label "work 3.0". Their book initially tracks the evolution of this phenomenon from work 1.0 starting in the 1950s to work 2.0 in the 1990s to work 3.0 since the pandemic. Though their primary focus is India, there is some reflection on how these trends can apply to other countries. It isn't easy to make judgments about the future, but the authors leverage everything from surveys and interviews to secondary research to make some very nuanced judgements. What tech trends will shape this decade? How will mental health impact the way we work? How will the startup ecosystem change going forward? *Work 3.0* is a must-read for anyone—employee or employer—who wants to be better prepared for what's next in the world of work. Highly recommended to help you figure out how to reshape your career goals this decade'—Dr Maha Hosain Aziz, NYU MA IR professor and author of *Future World Order* (2020) and sequel *Global Spring: Predictions for a Post-Pandemic World* (2022)

'As the world recovers from COVID-19, mental ill-health of the worker has come into greater focus. The book covers this as well as how the transformations that were taking place in the workplace have been affected by the pandemic. A joint product of an academic with a policy bent (Bandyopadhyay) and a management consultant and bestselling author

(Chanda), it is sweeping in scope while being accessible and insightful. A rare combination of rigour and readability'—Eddie Kane, professor and director, Centre for Health and Justice, Nottingham University

'A wise book! It strikes a nice balance between optimism and pessimism about the future of work, the worker and the workplace. It is clear-headed, sound and coherent. And always compassionate, caring for the vulnerable'—Gurcharan Das, author and former CEO, Procter & Gamble India

'Much is being said around the world, about the future of work. In this book, the authors offer a perspective that is multidisciplinary, imaginative and uniquely their own. Consequently, they are able to connect the dots from seemingly disparate threads into a coherent narrative, gleaning new interdependencies and insights, in the process. From technological and behavioural competencies to the future of globalisation and the blurring of boundaries between the virtual and the real, *Work 3.0* is a tour de force of research and original intellectual thought. Essential reading for our times!'—Hisham Mehanna, professor of head and neck surgery; deputy pro-vice chancellor (interdisciplinary research); director of The Institute for Global Innovation (I.G.I.) and the Institute for Advanced Studies (I.A.S), University of Birmingham.

'Avik Chanda and Siddhartha Bandyopadhyay have researched and written a comprehensive review of the many economic and psychological trends that are shaping the evolution of work and its possible future. An important read for all leaders'—Jim Harter, chief scientist of workplace management and wellbeing at Gallup

'Sid Bandyopadhyay and Avik Chanda have produced an informative and insightful text which helps the reader start to make sense of the complex issues faced in dealing with the future of work. Their wide ranging and highly readable book is based on extensive research—it is, quite simply, a must-read for those wanting to deepen their understanding in this area'—Joanne Duberly, professor of organisational studies; deputy pro-vice chancellor (equality, diversity and inclusion), University of Birmingham

'*Work 3.0* offers a comprehensive account of both the challenges and opportunities that lie ahead for the work, worker and workplace of the future. For company leaders, amidst the gloomy predictions of so many narratives, this book is particularly refreshing and empowering. Identifying and nurturing emergent skills, developing organizational resilience, enhancing the effectiveness of DEI initiatives, improving psychological safety at work, and creating value through CSR in wholly new and meaningful ways—the authors offer implementable solutions for the most pressing work-related issues of our times. *Work 3.0* is a book that leaders should read, go back to, and follow'—Joey Uppal, director of Global Faculty Network at EMERITUS Executive Education

'Bandyopadhyay and Chanda, global experts in their respective domains, offer an extensively researched and lucid answer to one of the most pressing questions of our times: what would the future of work look like? The book covers all that one would usually expect and plus some concerns around technology, the skills gaps, mental health and growing inequality are seamlessly woven into discussions of the Metaverse and ethics in the new workplace. A highly original take on a topic that is everyone's business'— Jon Parry, head of research, Skills for Justice Research

'*Work 3.0* offers new thinking for a new age. As the world emerges from the pandemic, workers settle into hybrid working and digital meetings, coaching and working all sit centre stage, how should workers, managers and leaders respond. Chanda and Bandyopadhyay, thought leaders, provide ideas on how we can thrive in this new world of work'—Prof. Jonathan Passmore, Henley Business School, and SVP Coaching, CoachHub, the digital coaching platform

'For anyone looking for a concise, evidence-based compendium of the core issues associated with the future of work, this is an essential read. *Work 3.0* covers all the critical areas of the future of work from general labour demands and the gig economy to AI and the metaverse. It considers the opportunities and challenges raised with digitization, particularly which skills which will be needed for the future, and those which will be subsumed into the digitization. Whilst the book focuses on what this means for India, it draws on evidence and examples globally, making it relevant wherever you are in the world. With a light touch and a little humour, this is an informative and accessible read'—Kate Field, Global Head Health, Safety and Well-being at British Standards Institution

'*Work 3.0* is a carefully woven exposition that takes us on a journey above and beyond the workplace, its origins and future. Existential in nature, we are forced to question and confront countless possibilities, each one distinct, yet entwined inextricably, to paint a rich and vivid picture—a grand synthesis of where we are, our current predicament and the shape our future will take. This treatise is a sweeping reconstruction of ideas and ideologies of this thing that we call "work", of influence and thought, and indeed of human evolution itself, free of angles, while all the time examining the singularity of each "melodic phrase"! I am reminded of the music of Bach—polyphonic, didactic in nature, contrapuntal in style, with harmonic clarity, melodic poise, rhythmic stability and unbelievable versatility.

Work 3.0 is an invaluable resource that uncovers and re-discovers the perplexing world of modern corporations through a variety of disciplines. As we meander through a labyrinth of social, business, political and economic history, through science, industrialisation, automation and technology, through intellectual history, the behavioural sciences, cognitive evolution, literature and philosophy, we are compelled to examine and re-examine our perspective of civilisation itself, and our place in it. *Work 3.0*, skilfully unleashes and evokes a sea of ideas, a panorama, a state of consciousness, as it tells a human story, more complex than the twenty-first century itself'—Khursheed N. Khurody, chairman of Shivia Livelihoods Foundation and managing committee member of Seva Sadan Society

'Authors Avik Chanda and Sid Bandyopadhyay find the future of work and the workplace already upon us, representing *Work 3.0*, deriving from previous milestones in 1947 and 1991. Their focus is on India, but with universal relevance, embracing the ever-expanding nation-state, threats posed by global warming and other exogenous shocks. Evolution has become revolution, with automation and impermanence of jobs, widening the digital divide and human inequality. The characteristics of this anti-human-centric change-process are speed, unpredictability and transformative effect, whose challenge must be countered through an inner revolution. In laying out what this comprises, the authors warn against cast-iron answers or permanent solutions. They have produced a visionary book; one the public would do well to heed'—Krishnan Srinivasan, former foreign secretary of India

'This book is what we need to take stock of where we are and start thinking about where we can go. What I appreciated most was the practical blueprint of what the emerging sectors and roles are and more importantly, what their corresponding skills appear to be. Being able to determine where one's interest lies and then charting out an action plan to fill the skill gap is so powerful. This promise of both awareness and action excited the career coach in me. More so, the idea conveyed that while several agents such as the government, entrepreneurs etc. need to come together to make the picture of the future of work attractive, the onus is ultimately on each one of us. The book is a must-read for every professional designing a workplace and/or their own individual future of work'—Krusha Sahjwani Malkani, director of Sociabble; co-founder The Pink Thread, LinkedIn 2022 Top Voice

'This book has been a tour de force on everything connected to work today. The authors, Avik Chanda and Siddhartha Bandyopadhyay, have done a fabulous job analysing how current events and technology are changing the way we work. They have created a one-stop resource for anyone interested in knowing more about the future of work. The authors have deeply researched various aspects of history, technology, psychology and public policy (including the New Education Policy) to let readers know which jobs and skills will be in demand. This book is a must-read for nearly everyone—employers, educationists, students, parents, etc. The authors have taken an enormous amount of data aggregated from a diverse set of literature and research and made it available in one place for the first time'—Luis Miranda, chairman of Indian School of Public Policy, Centre for Civil Society, CORO India, and Senior Advisor, Morgan Stanley

'Avik Chanda and Sid Bandyopadhyay have prudently put together the concepts in a critical and analytical way of the present situation and future challenges of this era of the 4.0 Industrial Revolution. The wealth of information is stimulating and thought-provoking, parallel to Harari's work. Worldwide, institutions dealing with human workforce will greatly benefit of this read. The global innovation has brought the world together but at the same time it has created new challenges and a wake-up call, like, increasing disparity and poverty. The stepwise analysis of these challenges with proposed solutions to enrich human lives—for example, investment in retraining, is a ray of hope to mitigate these. The future of Man with Machine, Databiology, including Metaverse, information is exhilarating. Wellness is a central theme in the present era and how best this can be nurtured at the workplace is well focused. This book will continue to enrich human lives for generations to come'—Mohan S. Gundeti, professor of paediatric urology (surgery) and MFM (Ob/Gyn) and paediatrics, the University of Chicago Medicine and Biological Sciences, Director Pediatric Urology, Comer Children's Hospital

'Perhaps the most common question in the post pandemic is—how will that look in the future workplace? Nobody can predict the future until they live it, and while many predictions about the future of work have been made, they have less to do with providing the readers with a broad perspective on business and people, as well as thoroughly researched data. Written by two leading experts, Avik Chanda, a bestselling author and Dr Siddhartha Bandopadhyay, an UK-based economist, Work 3.0 is the most comprehensive book that covers almost every aspect of business, post pandemic workforce, current and future trends in workplace, accelerated digital transformation, power AI and automation, workplace resilience and productivity, etc. This book is a great resource for your business planning and implementation. Work 3.0 is ground-breaking—for helping entrepreneurs, CEOs, senior managers, HR/OD, and other business leaders develop motivating and implementable mid-and long-term strategies for their organizations'—Ng Hooi, author, president of Malaysian Association of Certified Coaches

'Work 3.0 is a book that is rich in research, insights and recommendations, to successfully navigate the world of work in the post-pandemic scenario. Its focus on the issues around inequality, through analysis and in-depth interviews, is commendable. The answer it arrives at—that NGOs, private industry, government agencies and start-ups should also work cohesively to uplift the condition of the underprivileged—is the need of the hour. This is a book that resonates not only in corporate boardrooms but also with socially conscious professionals and entrepreneurs looking to make a difference on the ground'—Paul Abraham, president of Hinduja Foundation, board member, former COO of IndusInd Bank

'Bertrand Russell once said that with mechanization, we would be a happier lot—we could produce the same output with fewer hours of work put in by its workers—that technology would make us happier. This unfortunately never happened, and this is what Chanda and Bandyopadhyay bring out so well when they talk about the gig economy, the startups, associated disruptions and emerging chasms of inequality. The book rightly states that its role isn't to define the future—the word "future" itself is premised on being fluid and at best can be captured as the "unknown" error variable in a mathematical equation. We come across tables, data and interpretation that make for objective study. Read this book if you like Gurcharan Das but more conversant to a younger, albeit impatient audience. Read this book if you like Ramachandra Guha and his recount of Indian history but fast-forwarded 50 years for its anecdotes, and technological case studies. Most of all, read this book, for it captures works of other greats, economists, philosophers, and gives you a flavour about the future of work, based on the authors' own deep reading and insights'—Prerna Mukharya, founder of Outline India, Fortune 40 under 40, Chevening fellow

'Being a founder of a Web 3.0, Metaverse start-up, I was intrigued after reading Work 3.0. The book talks not just about the present digital era, but also emphasizes how the transformation happened in the past and why it is happening faster now, with relevant data points. It's a must-read for all the career aspirants who are entering the emerging industry of opportunities like web 3.0, Blockchain, Metaverse . . .'—Pushpak Kypuram, co-founder and director at NextMeet®, India's First Metaverse for Meetups

'This is a must-read for anyone looking at building new age digital workplace. It's a blueprint that will help you handcraft the Workplace 3.0 for your organization. The beauty of this masterpiece is, it's relevant to organizations of all sizes, be it a start-up or a multi-billion enterprise'—Raghavendra Hunasgi, Global Shaper, World Economic Forum; chief adviser, UN; TED speaker; bestselling author and branding leader

'Authors Chanda and Bandyopadhyay cut through the clutter to paint a picture of how the future is unfolding, the trade-offs and what we might do to navigate our way through. A great read. A thoroughly researched work that entitles them to be heralded as the futurists of our times'—Ram Gopal, chief executive officer at Barclays Bank India

'Chanda and Bandyopadhyay have taken on the challenge of the post-pandemic workplace and work life in *Work 3.0* with a wide-ranging view of the dynamics affecting our traditional view of work. They provide a robust overview of the drivers, challenges, and potential considerations for India's future with pathways towards both individual and collective actions as we prepare for what lies ahead'—Rick Smith, professor and vice dean of education and partnerships, Carey Business School, Johns Hopkins University; former partner and managing Director, Accenture Singapore

'In this book, business adviser and prolific writer Avik Chanda teams up with globally renowned economist, Sid Bandyopadhyay, to give the reader a fascinating glimpse into what the future of work will look like. The book seamlessly integrates academic research, industry reports, and expert interviews with original analysis to present a gripping narration of how work, the worker and the workplace in India are dramatically transforming. Read this book if you are an employer, professional, academic, policymaker or a student. Most of all, read it if you care deeply about the future of India and want to be ready to meet it when it's here'—Rudra Sensarma, professor of economics and former dean, Research, Innovation and Internationalization, IIM Kozhikode

'*Work 3.0* is a great read for anyone—whether you're already in the workforce and thinking about how to future-proof your skills or if you're someone that wants to take a data-driven approach as you create your roadmap to enter the future workforce. This book will make you think and appreciate the different forces driving the future of work. And it will also help you develop your own perspective on no-regret moves you can make today to not only survive by building resilience to the changes yet to come, but also thrive by acting on the opportunities that will present themselves'—Sachin Lulla, EY principal and Americas Consulting Sector leader

'*Work 3.0* takes a holistic perspective on the future of work: what will work, worker and workplace of the future look like? To address these questions, the book divides its discussions into various themes, for example, technology and employment, emergent sectors, jobs, domains, skills, behavioural skills, workplace imperatives, such as DEI and mental health, and the emergent world of the metaverse, and its underlying cutting-edge technologies. In a departure from many future of work accounts that are obsessed with technology, in this book the authors dedicate a separate chapter to discuss the relationship between education, pedagogy, research, innovation and productivity, list the challenges faced on this front, and through a series of analyses and interviews, arrive at some concrete recommendations. Combining academic research with reports on industry applications, business case studies, expert interviews and anecdotes, Chanda and Bandyopadhyay have produced a book that is highly ambitious in scope, rich in analytical detail, and far-reaching in its conclusions'—Sanghamitra Bandopadhyay, director of Indian Statistical Institute, Padma Shree Awardee

'Work 3.0 is a very interesting read—a book through which Avik and Siddhartha reinforce Heraclitus that "Change in the only constant in life". The book is a testimony to how changes in the workplace have taken place at different junctures in the history of India and how that has changed the way India has been propelled into higher orbits of development and economic wellbeing. And how the rate of change has increased with every new phase of development. While the book is distinctly about India, yet the authors have done a remarkable job of linking the same to global issues and changes, thus highlight both similarities and dissimilarities between the India story and the global story. The wonderful thing about Work 3.0 is that it encompasses all aspects of life and not just business—thus while it expectedly spans the economy and economic developments, it also brings into its folds issues pertaining to the changing dynamics in public policy, social structure, health care, law and order, climate changes, etc. What is most heartening is the importance that innovation gets in the development of the narrative.

The book is a must-read for all and helps one adapt to the changing environment that we all live in and more importantly, equip ourselves to embrace the rapidly changing environment and thus remain relevant and in some sense ahead of the curve'—Sankarshan Basu, dean of Ahmedabad University; former Professor at IIM-Bangalore

'The way we work is shifting, and this book helps us figure out how to navigate the changes. Work 3.0 addresses the emerging global trends and the forces that created them. Work plays a major role throughout our lives, but we don't often critically analyse it. Well researched and nuanced, this book pushes people to think about the future and question how technology is transforming and accelerating innovation. This is an important book for leaders who want to build companies that can adapt quickly and be relevant for years to come'—Sarah Nadav, behavioural economist, senior strategist, World Economic Forum Expert Network; LinkedIn Top Voice

'The future of work is definitely to one's imagination, but COVID has left a few footprints. Vertical organizations will start rethinking hierarchy; people supply chains will need to look like concentric circles of permanent employees, contract staff, apprentices, temporary hires, consultants and gig-workers; fixed costs will need variabalization as outcomes are no longer guaranteed; resilience will become as important as productivity; continuous upskilling will provide the competitive edge; employees will demand flexibility of time and space. The book takes an interesting dig into several aspects of the Future of Work and will be an interesting read for entrepreneurs and will add value to business executives too'—Shantanu Rooj, founder, TeamLease Edtech

'Work 3.0 tackles one of the most complex questions of the present times: what will the worker, workplace and work itself, look like in the future? To address this, authors Chanda and Bandyopadhyay have combined academic research with business case studies and expert interviews into a rich book with multi-disciplinary insights. This is an important book, with insights that are both timely and urgent'—Soumitra Dutta, Peter Moores dean and professor of management, Saïd Business School, University of Oxford

'Today we face seismic shifts in the world of work, never seen before. If we are to move forward successful, it's critical we face these changes and challenges with as broad an awareness of our circumstances as possible. Work 3.0 accomplishes this task—it is the ultimate Future of Work Preparation Guide that begins with a chapter that essentially says "You are Here", as if you have stepped into a new environment for the first time and need guidance, and then proceeds to walk you through the entire landscape of work in great detail'—Steve Cadigan, LinkedIn's first CHRO; PeopleHum Top 200 Global Thought Leader; Future of Work Keynote Speaker; author

'Work 3.0 provides what all of us need the most today, a glimpse of the future of work and how we can prepare to excel as individuals and companies. Insights and recommendations based on research and views of experienced professionals are not only enriching but also provide a certain path to navigate the future and make a positive difference for people around us. A must-read for all'—Subir Verma, head HR, T&D Companies, Tata Power and Author of the bestselling book Job Search Secrets

'The challenge with accounts that offer "a glimmer of hope" about the future of work is that they tend to lapse into wishful thinking. This is where *Work 3.0* is markedly different. Using a wide range of research publications across disciplines, official statistics, industry think-tank studies and extensive illustrations from the workplace, the authors offer compelling frameworks to negotiate the vagaries of the future. Chanda and Bandyopadhyay show how it is possible to remain positive in these uncertain times—but using logic, data and science'—Sudipto Banerjee, professor and chair of the Department of Biostatistics, UCLA and 2022 president of the International Society for Bayesian Analysis

'This book is about work, the nature of work and the future of work. It takes up disparate patterns and data besides tech trends, to weave them into multi-disciplinary frameworks, for greater ease of understanding. The book is a must-read for professionals who wish to understand work, skills, the talent gap and the way forward'—S.V. Nathan, chief people officer, Deloitte India, and national president of the National HRD Network

'We are in a strange era of global politics and economics, when predicting anything is difficult. Well established models are coming under question and policymakers are at a loss to find the right models relevant in a post pandemic world. Despite all this, one fundamental is unchanged—we humans will need to work to survive and make this world a better place. This book has focused on the very topic of what that "future of work" looks like and how we need to re-program seven billion of us to brighten that future. This is also a grand collaboration between bestselling author and thought leader, Avik Chanda and well-known multidisciplinary economist, Sid Bandyopadhyay, to produce a research-backed and thought-provoking output that will inspire every intellectual who wants to leave this world a little better place than they found it'—Tanmay Bandyopadhyay, senior vice president, technology and digital, AmerisourceBergen (US Fortune 10 Healthcare Delivery Corporation)

'This is a magnificent work. It is always difficult to write about the present, and the changes we are living through, with the eye of a historian. On the other hand, everyone, from the journalist to the politician, sees the present as a great moment in history. The authors have avoided such "clutter" and linked the present and the future with history, and not short-changed history in the process. What makes the book distinctive is a strong humanist tenor in the whole text, and especially the conclusion, a call to balance technologies that engulf us in "metaverse" with sentiments, capacities, and potentials, that is not only wholesome but also suggestive of how one should reorganize lives in the future'—Tirthankar Roy, professor of economic history, London School of Economics

'A masterpiece . . . Ingenious and thought-provoking. This book makes you rethink the way you work. After reading *Work 3.0*, I feel I have a whole new perspective on life. This book not only talks about technological advancements but also about inculcating behavioural skills in the workplace. Highly recommended for Business leaders and entrepreneurs'—Vikash Dash, *ET* 40 under 40; *Fortune* 40 under 40; Britannica 20 under 40; World Financial Review's Top 10 Financial Inclusion Heroes Globally; World Economic Forum Global Shaper

WORK 3.0

AVIK CHANDA

SIDDHARTHA BANDYOPADHYAY

PENGUIN
BUSINESS

An imprint of Penguin Random House

PENGUIN BUSINESS

USA | Canada | UK | Ireland | Australia
New Zealand | India | South Africa | China

Penguin Business is part of the Penguin Random House group of companies
whose addresses can be found at global.penguinrandomhouse.com

Published by Penguin Random House India Pvt. Ltd
4th Floor, Capital Tower 1, MG Road,
Gurugram 122 002, Haryana, India

First published in Penguin Business by Penguin Random House India 2023

Copyright © Avik Chanda and Siddhartha Bandyopadhyay 2023

All rights reserved

10 9 8 7 6 5 4 3 2

ISBN 9780670093489

Typeset in Adobe Caslon Pro by Manipal Technologies Limited, Manipal
Printed at Replika Press Pvt. Ltd, India

www.penguin.co.in

To all our teachers . . .

FIRST LORD
What time o' day is't, Apemantus?
APEMANTUS
Time to be honest.

—William Shakespeare, *Timon of Athens*

Contents

Dialogue

Late July 2021. The authors Avik Chanda (AC) and Siddhartha Bandyopadhyay (SB) meet online, in keeping with the times, sitting in Kolkata, India and Birmingham, UK, across the shadow lines of evening and afternoon, darkness and light.

What follows is an excerpt from their conversation, a raw transcript.

After two years of remote logins, online meetings and calls, dear reader, you must be well-equipped to interpolate the attendant sights and sounds of their meeting: an occasional blip in the audio, the routers flickering tenuously, a smile frozen awkwardly for a moment on the screen, and—seeing that it is monsoon in India—the incessant chorus at one end of the dull, brooding monotone of rain.

AC: I don't know if you see it quite the same way, but for the longest time, I've felt there's something fundamentally constraining about book titles.

SB: What do you mean?

AC: Well, the fact that each book, any book, is stuck with just that one title. To my mind, this robs it of other possibilities. Yes, many books these days, especially in the business/non-fiction category, also carry a tag line—but that's more of an embellishment rather than something empowering. Ideally, I think a book should have around five to six titles that it's free to choose between at any given point in time. And each of these individual appellations can then mean different things to different readers, certainly making for whole new spheres of potential experience, presumably resulting in a longer shelf life for the book.

SB: Fine, let's imagine that's the case, at least with this book. What would have been some of your other options? We couldn't have *Future Shock*, *The End of Work*, *Pandemic 2.0* or even *The Year of Dreaming Dangerously*—not that I think our dreams have bordered on the dangerous. These titles are all taken.

AC: No, I was thinking more along the lines of *Homo Infirmus*.

SB: I get the obvious riff on *Homo Deus*. What's your larger point, though?

AC: Right! In *Homo Deus*, Harari's starting point is that in the twenty-first century, we have overcome the three problems that have hitherto accompanied human civilization—wars, plagues and famine. Which then prompts him to ask: what now? And take us on a journey towards that ultimate goal of humans—immortality. But the global COVID-19 pandemic has turned that premise pretty much on its head, so that human civilization, as we speak, is continually retrogressing towards an earlier, almost atavistic state of vulnerability, sickness, fear. Hence, *Homo Infirmus*.

SB: Hmm. But I have a somewhat different take on this. I feel that Harari's premise may have been shaken, possibly even stirred, as a result of the pandemic—but not broken.

AC: Interesting choice of words! But go on!

SB: So, here's how I view it. Underlying Harari's narrative is the slew of industrial and technological advancement, an incessant process, that has allowed humans to come up to this point, where they can dream of achieving immortality. I think his premise of progress, of development, holds good even in these pandemic times. For instance, it's this tremendous pace of technological advancement that has made it possible for multiple companies across the world to independently research and devise the vaccines that are efficacious against the virus, as well as to produce them by the tens of millions, all of this in less than a year. Two or three decades ago, such a feat would have been unthinkable. In other words, what I'm trying to say is that the pandemic may have deflected the ambition of the human race momentarily from its quest for immortality to seeking sheer survival. But the final goal hasn't really wavered. What that means is, immortality has just become a more distant goal, the road to it longer, more arduous and fraught with potholes.

AC: I think 'fast-forward' is a term suited for the effects of the pandemic. You talk about the unheard-of speed and efficiency in vaccine production. Think of the automation of operational processes, increased use of AI, data analytics and algorithms across all sectors—all of these have been part of a trend for, say, a decade now? But they've been accelerated by the pandemic, at a pace that would have been unimaginable in a pre-COVID, business-as-usual paradigm.

SB: It's as if the pandemic has suddenly turned the entire global ecosystem into a single giant lab. Consequently, any disruption, innovation, technological or operational leap that might have taken years to come into being, is now taking months, if not weeks! While many organizations such as those in healthcare or logistics, are having to undertake the experiments as a matter of exigency, others are doing it precisely because this is a less risky time to innovate in the workplace.

AC: The problem is that the ability to conduct such experiments needs to be matched, at least to some measure, by social responsibility. This may certainly be the case for vaccine manufacturers across the world. But when I look at all the companies that are on a spree of mechanization and overhauling of their existing processes, I have some serious concerns. I commend the energy and urgency, the frenetic level of activity. But when it comes to executive decisions, such as declaring a permanent work-from-home mode of operations for entire departments, or accelerating use of algorithms and robotics to displace job roles . . . how many organizations are thinking carefully through the longer-term ramifications?

SB: Yes, that's very disturbing. Sadly—and this is likely the case not just in India but in other economies too—there's the same sense of 'fast-forwardness' in areas where the pandemic is setting us back. We notice as soon as we start sifting the data the rising inequality, lower labour share of income, greater digital divide, a further gulf in opportunities between the rural and urban populations, rising domestic violence and abuse, and a mental health crisis on a truly macro-economic scale . . . the list can go on. These are not just India's problems but ones that echo globally. One hopes that some of these phenomena may be temporary and reversible. However, there's another worrying discovery, and I'm not so sure how reversible that is. This refers to a study, specific to the UK, which found that the younger generation (those born in the 1980s—younger than us, I mean!) is no better off in real-income terms than those ten years ago, for the first time since at least the Second World War. In fact, the pay is worse for those in employment, taking into account the larger numbers that constitute the present workforce. And wealth-wise, they are actually worse off!

AC: Of course, we need to examine if that's true for India, which, by corollary, might also make it likely for a large majority of developing economies. But I want to get back to one of the other things you mentioned—the mental health pandemic. For a country like India, this is critical on so many different levels, starting with the obvious. There was a report published midway through 2020, and I have the figures here with me . . . at that point, India had 9000 psychiatrists, 2000 psychiatric nurses, 1000 clinical psychologists and 1000 psychiatric social workers. But, taking into account the mental health problems induced by the pandemic, it was estimated that the country needed an additional 30,000 psychiatrists, 37,000 psychiatric nurses, 38,000 psychiatric social workers and 38,000 clinical psychologists.

SB: There's a challenge at an even broader level. The pandemic has hastened the need for inculcating a whole range of behavioural competencies. Flexibility and adaptability, resilience and grit, emotional intelligence, future-mindedness, optimism, and so on. I mean, every think tank, analyst, research or consulting firm worth its salt has been talking about this, right? Which brings me to my hypothesis. I don't live in India, so tell me if you don't think this is true—but I suspect that neither academia nor industry are equipped right now, either methodologically, or in terms of infrastructure, tools and the scale of human expertise that are needed, to build these skills across the board.

AC: Oh, I'm convinced that's totally the case. In fact, I alluded to that in a previous book I co-wrote back in 2017, *From Command to Empathy: Using EQ in the Age of Disruption.* The scale of the behavioural or psychological problem is truly staggering!

SB: More so, considering that on this particular front, the situation has only become worse over the past year— especially in the wake of the deadly second wave of the pandemic in India.[1] And my sense is that all these effects are exacerbated for the marginalized, the disadvantaged, the millions of people working as farm hands, or the hundreds of thousands of migrant workers . . . these people have minimal access to vaccine centres and diagnostic clinics. And we're talking about access to clinical psychologists and counsellors! Know what I'm saying? I think this is an important aspect, because with our usual urban, white-collar lenses, there's a tendency on our part to either disregard the existence of the 'other' or believe that mental health issues are elitist or first-world problems that don't affect the rural poor. Do you agree with me?

AC: Yes.

SB: It's just that you seem to have gone very piano, suddenly.

AC: There's so much here that's of concern, things can really get overwhelming. For a moment, I was thinking of all this from the reader's standpoint. He or she has enough problems on his or her plate, and the last thing such a person would want is a tome that's on a mission to list every last pitfall in the future of work, the very reading of which becomes a depressing, burdensome experience. Therefore, I think it's important for us to balance out the challenges and concerns, critical as they are, with an exploration of the silver linings, the new opportunities that the pandemic is presenting to us.

SB: Agreed.

AC: I suppose it all boils down to what questions we really want to examine in the book.

SB: Exactly! You know, a few days back I was watching an interview of Richard Baldwin, author of *The Globotics Upheaval: Globalisation, Robotics and the Future of Work*. Something quite interesting took place. The interviewer was Rob Johnson—from the Institute for New Economic Thinking—and at the outset, before he got to any of the main themes in the book, he said: 'choosing the questions is 90 per cent of the way there' . . . or words to that effect.

AC: Well, I think this conversation has given us some food for thought to do just that.

SB: To the questions, then!

AC: And the future!

Introduction

This book is a response to tomorrow having arrived prematurely, abruptly, and, in some respects, menacingly. What was an evolution in the workplace became a revolution, with big changes forced on us at an incredible speed. In the process, the future has become the present.

For several years now, we had already been living in a VUCA (volatile, uncertain, complex, ambiguous) world.[1] From new electronic modes of currency to virtual assistants, the pace of technological changes has been dizzying. Information is now available at our fingertips, yet we do not have the time to screen through the often-contradictory messages across the multitude of TV, radio and internet channels and social media forums, all vying for our ever-shrinking attention. We've become spoilt for choice, and at the same time feel overwhelmed at the magnitude and range of our options.

In the workplace, we've come to learn that a growing number of jobs across several sectors can be automated. Many organizations have embraced large-scale automation of their business processes, which obviates the need to worry about employee well-being, bonuses and commissions, sick leave, investment in health insurance plans and pension funds, or the need to sit down across the table, to solve 'people problems'. But for the people, state-of-the-art automation has come at the cost of job security and fear of retrenchment. For the first time since at least the Second World War, the UK reports that the current labour market entrants will be worse off than those of the previous generations, and the United States is also recording a slowdown in both life satisfaction and consumer spending.[2] Developing nations, while acknowledging that some automation as inevitable, are still struggling to arrive at the precise employment implications of these changes. For an increasing number of us globally, there has been a growing sense of the impermanence of jobs, the tenuousness of living and the fragility of human relationships.

But even the staggering sum total of all these experiences paled in comparison to the jolt delivered worldwide by the COVID-19 pandemic in the first quarter of 2020. The smug self-assuredness of thriving economies and societies was replaced overnight by a desperate bid for sheer physical survival. During the early days of the pandemic, countries were trying to put on a game face, but as the true scale of the crisis unravelled, spirits swiftly dampened. The opportunity of the Great Reset[3] that was to mark the close of the second decade of the twenty-first century had become the Great Implosion—the world hurtling into a bottomless abyss.[4] Lives were lost and livelihoods destroyed, on the scale of a global war. The richest and most powerful nations were rendered as helpless as the poorest, at least initially, in stemming the spread of the virus. The devastation wrought by the pandemic was intensely personal. We lost friends and family members and were not able to pay our last respects to them. Festivities and funerals were observed remotely, in a state of house arrest or of solitary confinement.

Slowly, amid the shock, disbelief and trauma, we then began to reorient ourselves to the way we come to live and think and work, now and in the future. When it comes to work and the workplace, especially in countries such as India, during those interminable, extending lockdowns and enforced social distancing, we've sometimes felt as if all operations—let alone future planning and advancement—have come to a grinding halt. In many sectors, such as travel, tourism and hospitality, this was literally true. The year 2020 was particularly hard for smaller businesses. At least a third of the micro, small, and medium enterprises (MSME), contributing a third of the nation's gross domestic product and employing over 110 million people, was impacted. The indication at that point was that nearly 60 per cent of enterprises in this sector would scale down, close operations or sell out. Given the absence of any financial relief package from the government during the initial period of the pandemic, coupled with reduced investments and the drying up of cash reserves, India's hitherto burgeoning start-up ecosystem received a similar blow. By October 2020, although one still hoped for a strong recovery, it was estimated that 40 per cent of all Indian start-ups had been hit.[5]

And yet, throughout these very same debilitating, mutating waves of the virus, tremendous advancements were also continuously taking place. Essential services such as healthcare, law and order, transportation and logistics, banking services and technology support . . . all reoriented themselves hastily, to continue operating under the unexpected, curfew-like conditions. With travel and in-person meetings put on hold, enterprises in India and the world over adapted by switching to operations in a remote, virtual mode. Think tanks, research laboratories, technologists and innovators focused on devising swift, safe, technology-driven means of producing and transporting goods. In a span of less than a year, manufacturers in different parts of the globe had researched, developed and started to produce vaccines on a scale that would suffice for a substantial proportion of the world population.

Although the breathtaking pace of these innovations was a testimony to mankind's enterprise, not everyone benefited.

The developed countries surged ahead in terms of vaccination, leaving behind much of the world. The massive and coerced use of technology widened the digital divide and increased inequalities between the most privileged and most marginalized sections of society. For example, school closures led to education being delivered almost exclusively online for a long time in most parts of the world. In India, the period of closure was particularly long, second only to Uganda's, according to a UNESCO report.[6] This particularly hit the poorest sections, who do not have adequate and reliable access to the internet.

Coming out of the shadow of the pandemic to reclaim the future, a basic question faces us—what does such a future hold, especially in the context of the workplace?

The problem with trying to understand the future of work is not that there's inadequate information, but that there's a surfeit of it. Over the past three years, bloggers, columnists, authors, journalists, coaches and self-styled pundits have all aired their opinions and come up with their own predictions— add to this the range of surveys, studies and reports from global and regional think tanks, analysts and experts with proven track records of producing comprehensive trends and market analysis. The cumulative effect of all of this is numbing.[7]

In this book, we cut through the clutter and the noise to glean the broad patterns and movements that we think will typify the nature of work as well as of the workplace in the future.

The centre of our focus is India. In terms of sheer scale and complexity—whether it is in the magnitude of its vaccine drive and the challenges associated with it, the number of people displaced and impoverished in the wake of the pandemic, or the range of new opportunities available due to technological innovation—there are few parallels elsewhere in the world. But with regard to the global experience at the emotional and psychological levels, and the efforts, measures and innovations undertaken to find solutions and relief in an otherwise bleak world, the arguments, findings and suggestions presented by us in this book may strike a familiar chord with readers around the world. This book is not about the pandemic. It's about the trend of disruptions set in motion earlier but accelerated by the pandemic, and about what these disruptions mean to individuals, organizations and institutions—in the context of work—and how they can be navigated.

WHY US AND WHY NOW?

This book was started as a solo venture by Avik Chanda in 2019. He began hesitantly, through a protracted, amorphous period of indecisiveness, endless self-interrogation and the self-consciousness of having taken on an 'important' project. The book was going to be all about the future of work in the foreseeable future. But which should be the key sectors on one's radar, and why? How best could one bring the key findings to life? Should the book concentrate on organizations or the individual, or both? Even more fundamentally— what were the key questions that the book was going to answer? Eventually, work began: some secondary research was undertaken, a few experts interviewed, and sections of chapters drafted in urgent haste.

Right then, the pandemic struck.

And in the grip of that initial overwhelming period, Avik quickly came to the realization that not just the book he was writing, but life itself was unravelling before one's eyes. Suddenly, the relevance of those initial readings, interviews and insights became a giant question mark in their entirety. Avik's initial thought was that the book could perhaps wait a few months, to be resumed when the worst was over. But the death toll kept rising, lockdowns were extended, markets tumbled, migrant workers—retrenched from daily wage jobs and evicted by their landlords—took to the road, escalations began along India's border with China, and the daily fresh incidence of COVID-19 cases in India approached the 1,00,000-mark. Writing a book on the future when the here and now itself was so volatile seemed like an impossibility.

During this period, Avik reconnected with his old friend Siddhartha (Sid) Bandyopadhyay in the UK, the distance between them not being an issue as the whole world had moved online. In one of their conversations, Sid commented on how the forced WFH (work from home) mode was disrupting the social networks at work. His point was that this new mode of functioning would end a lifeline for many, with the unwitting consequence being a rise in violence within the household and a growing number of people becoming trapped in high-conflict situations. Avik realized that Sid's ongoing research on what was unfolding during the pandemic in the UK and other societies, in particular his work straddling academia and the policy world, could breathe new life into the stalled book project. These chats turned into co-authored newspaper articles, and soon afterwards, Sid joined the project as co-author.

The two of them were now faced with a basic problem of choice with regard to the timelines for the book. As the onslaught of the particularly destructive COVID-19 second wave continued through the first half of 2021, one option was to wait out this period of the pandemic, however long that might take. That might mean pushing back the writing to, say, 2023, by which time the dust of the storm would finally have settled. At that point, the total life cycle of the pandemic and its aftermath—economic, social, political, cultural, technological— could all be analysed and discussed more objectively, as a collection of events that had occurred in the past, through the cauterized, hermeneutically sealed prism of 'history', however recent and scarring. A cautious, 'wait and watch' approach clearly had its merits, particularly in these turbulent times.

The alternative was to work within the melee of the ongoing storm, to somehow keep focusing on the here and now, plunge into events and evidence as they unfolded and surfaced, and attempt to derive patterns from them. This second option, doubtless more exciting, came with its problems. With no advantage of hindsight, one would have to continually keep turning back the pages for almost everything—primary and secondary data, published metrics and contested ones, anecdotes and newly born archetypes, patterns and predictions—and keep questioning them. While the big questions would remain the same, our hypotheses might need calibration, as well as our inferences, as new evidence emerged. Even with our best efforts, some findings might remain inchoate even as the book went into print.

Yet, without the slightest hesitation, both of us chose the second option. The reason for this was simple. The future of the workplace and its unfolding are impacting each and every one of us, at every moment. The subject is too urgent to wait for the cold certainty of hindsight. Like the challenges surfacing from the pandemic, the opportunities too are emerging continuously, and it would be a waste not to take advantage of them. We're aware that certain facts and statistics quoted by us might become obsolete by the time you read this book. But we believe that many of the insights will still hold good.

In his introduction to *Future Shock*, Alvin Toffler writes: 'The inability to speak with precision and certainty about the future, however, is no excuse for silence . . . In dealing with the future, at least for the purpose at hand, it is more important to be imaginative and insightful than to be one hundred percent "right".'[8] Our decision to work through the pandemic, through extended periods of sickness, professional anxieties and personal bereavement, has largely been guided by this position.

WHY WE'VE CALLED THE BOOK 'WORK 3.0'

Choosing a name for the book has left us with a bit of buyer's remorse: would the names we did not choose have been better? But we ultimately chose *Work 3.0*, as in our view the current period represents a third wave for India in its post colonial history. There are distinct global parallels as well. We appreciate that any attempt to box in and explain periods of history through timelines and labels is, in some measure, ultimately arbitrary and idiosyncratic. The very term 'Work 3.0' presupposes earlier versions or stages where the constructs, processes and practices of work were less evolved. And it also anticipates upcoming, presumably 'improved' versions in the future. In setting the timelines for these different stages, we've adopted the following approach: We've homed in on specific years where global happenings or policy decisions taken by the government resulted in a clear break with the past, with regard to the form and scope of and opportunities at the workplace, in India and beyond.

When Karl Polanyi wrote his magnum opus *The Great Transformation*, the key time frame was the nineteenth century, during which the rapid development of the market economy had resulted in a society so deeply divisive he felt it couldn't sustain on its own, in the longer term. Eric Hobsbawm, on the other hand, proposed very specific timelines in his celebrated series of books, *The Age of Revolution* (1789–1848), *The Age of Capital* (1848–1875), *The Age of Empire* (1875–1914) and *The Age of Extremes* (1914–1994), the last in the series marking what he called 'The Short Twentieth Century'.[9]

In our formulation, for Work 1.0 we've taken our 'ground zero' timeline as starting off from 1947. This is the year India won independence from the British and came into its own as a sovereign nation, though with a terribly impoverished economy. From a global standpoint, 1945 might be the more appropriate marker, both victor and vanquished nation-states emerging from the debris of the Second World War to view their realities afresh. While the models and technologies were often vastly different, the programme of reappraisal and economic reconstruction in India and elsewhere around the world was broadly consistent, during this period. The way we see it, Work 1.0, which began in India in 1947, continued for roughly three and a half decades, until 1991.

This is not to say that during this entire period India witnessed no changes. But the period nonetheless represents a certain acceptance of a type of economic policy. The socialist models favoured by Jawaharlal Nehru and given mathematical shape by Prashanta Mahalanobis by way of five-year planning, had segued into a protectionist regime, replete with bureaucratic tethers. This came to be known as the License Raj—the system of licences, regulations and accompanying red tape in the setting up and running of businesses in India between 1947 and 1990.

Of course, there were changes taking place everywhere— from fashion trends in attire and hairdos to land reforms and improvement in agricultural techniques through the Green Revolution, from a steady increase in migration of people from the countryside to the cities, to the growth of an urban-based middle class, with its attendant rise in consumerism, TV sets and cars becoming widely available and more affordable. But all these shifts and developments, were—to borrow a phrase from the late, great Clayton Christensen—'sustaining' in nature, and not 'disruptive'.[10]

The clean, sweeping break from the past came in 1991, marking the beginning of Work 2.0. The changes that followed were a direct result of the landmark liberalization policy, announced by the finance minister of the time, Manmohan Singh, under the Congress government of Narasimha Rao, ushering international markets into the Indian workplace and catapulting India on its journey as a global economy. Liberalization exposed the country and its workforce to the tugs and pushes of the global financial markets and the vagaries of foreign economies, and not everybody was happy. But, over the next two decades, a great many positive changes were witnessed. The services segment, not traditionally buoyant, really took off the runway. Young students and professionals trained in the then newly crafted 'science technology engineering maths' (STEM) methodology, honed their coding, testing and data management skills, which were hugely in demand. Multinationals invested heavily in setting up offices and operations in India, leading to a massive surge in domestic job creation, unprecedented since Independence. In the two decades that followed, India became the back end—according to many, the backbone—of the world's IT and business process outsourcing industry.

Globally, the year 1990, very close to our own start date for Work 2.0, is one that is widely accepted as the beginning of the Information Technology Revolution. That year, IBM introduced its 9345 hard-disk drive, the first ever to use magneto-resistive heads. This was also the year when magneto-optical disks, which could be rewritten up to a million times, were introduced. Intel came up with its supercomputer prototype, Touchstone Delta, used for a range of purposes, from real-time processing of satellite images to simulation of molecular models in AIDS research. Microsoft deployed Windows 3.0, the first truly successful version of Windows, in the global market. Television and public-access stations shifted from legacy video-editing systems to the Video Toaster. And by Christmas of 1990, the prototype of the World Wide Web was born.

As for Work 3.0, few would argue with the dateline of 2020.

This book aims to provide insights into what the future worker, the future workplace and the nature of work itself will look like in the post-pandemic paradigm. To do so requires us to understand the underlying socio-economic-demographic forces that will determine the demand and supply mechanisms in the marketplace for goods, services and ideas, going forward. Underlying these are frictions—in institutions or technology—that cause mismatches between the forces of demand and supply. We need to understand these frictions and the means to smooth them. Delving into them brings up questions around alternative normative frameworks. For firms, would all objectives start and end with profits, or would an increasing number of them begin to address larger, societal concerns?

Besides industry, two other key factors play a role. That the ever-expanding state accounts for a large part of all economic activity certainly merits attention. The other is the environment—the ever-closer threats posed by global warming will affect the world as we know it. The manner in which we respond to this will impact the future of work.

Finally, the global pandemic has brought into focus the precariousness of our world when it comes to external shocks. It has, as we noted, accelerated some changes that were inevitable while bringing new degrees of uncertainty for which different sections of society are unequally prepared. Therefore, the pandemic's role in transforming work is part of our analysis.

The key questions in the book are therefore linked to the interactions of three strategic actors—individuals (both as consumers and producers), firms (as producers) and the government, through its expansive role. While India remains our focus, we also step back to look at these interactions globally, to analyse how they are disrupted by shocks to the system and how they can be subsequently mediated.

THE WORK BEHIND 'WORK 3.0'

Any book requires preparation, more so when the subject is both topical and complex. What was particularly challenging in our case was that we had to contend with competing ideas, from which we had to frame a cohesive narrative. There's a disquieting atonal music to our times. What start out as neatly crafted antiphonic ideas devolve rapidly into antagonistic skirmishes, and then into all-out war between opposing camps. Evidence of this is ubiquitous. Think of the proponents and opponents of lockdowns, vaccine apostles and anti-vaccine lobbyists, anti-technology luddites and futurists who swear by AI, automation and embrace cutting-edge technologies, free-market evangelists and die-hard protectionists. While debates between opposing camps have often been vigorous, the fight now is not just about opinions but facts—but competing narratives and sets of data, that are presented as facts.

Right at the outset, we recognized this danger with polemics. We have, therefore, made a conscious effort to put forward the premises and arguments of opposing factions objectively, regardless of our personal leanings. In many cases, we are aware that there's no clear, single truth. In such instances, the answer depends on a host of uncertain factors—here, readers may disagree on the proposed solutions and draw their own conclusions.

In order to address the far-reaching and complex questions before us, we have viewed them through a multi disciplinary prism. Our reading for *Work 3.0* has been eclectic. We've consulted books and journal articles across economics, statistics, medicine, political science, philosophy, cognitive psychology, sociology, history and the environmental sciences. We've pored over government policy documents and census tomes, reports by think tanks and analysts, sifted through charts and statistics, and interviewed a number of experts. We've scanned dailies and business magazines, looking for examples and counter-examples relevant to our key themes. In our bid to stay 'current', we've referenced trends and trendsetters operating in the avant-garde phalanxes of AI and automation. At the same time, we've also braved cobwebs and spider caresses to dig out volumes of Marx and Marcuse, unopened since our student days, layered with the dust of neglect, and read the old, prescient passages again, rediscovering their continuing relevance to issues, such as the effect of automation on employment.

THE DILEMMA OF THE PRESENT CONTINUOUS

Things around us are changing at an ungraspable speed. While some of the changes may prove to be irrevocable, many others are transitory fluctuations. Underlying both sets of changes, however, are forces and directions of change that we believe are more definite. The data for the book has been collated over several months, and in each instance the figures we've relied on were those that were 'current' or the 'latest' at that particular point in time. These 'current' figures became the 'past', and 'dated', within a matter of months, if not weeks.

So, from the point they were first referenced to when you're reading this book, a remarkably vast range of metrics would have changed, from GDP (gross domestic product) growth figures, market valuations, currency exchange rates, labour share of income, labour-force participation rates, rural-urban migration, net effect on employment as a result of technological innovation, projections of automation on employment, projected adoption rate of emergent technologies, and the sectoral share of the labour force. Likewise, the demand for goods and services in certain sectors and for associated job roles and skills, the ranking of nations across various indices—such as innovation and happiness, rates for COVID positivity and fatalities, population growth, incidence of crime, domestic violence, and suicides—would also have changed. Some of these, materially.

By and large, we've avoided the addictive (and potentially infinite!) loop of updating and re-updating the data throughout the course of writing this book. Instead, our approach has been to look at diverse strands of data across sources, modes of collection, disciplines and domains, and glean from them common patterns and trends, and their implications for Workforce 3.0. While the data figures and metrics would have changed, it's our belief that the underlying causes, direction and pace of change, as well as the attendant concerns, impact of these changes, challenges, opportunities and recommendations, would still remain fundamentally unaltered, and relevant.

The same applies to the case studies, anecdotes and examples you'll come across in the pages that follow. In the meantime, companies would have launched their IPOs and new start-ups would have joined the mythical club of unicorns, and once-mighty corporations have taken a tumble, and still others gone out of business. Consequently, the examples we've worked through in the book should be viewed in terms of what they symbolize or hint at, rather than their individual specificities. Whether you're studying the data sheets or examples, it'll be helpful to view them not as permanent markers of any kind, but as being symbolic of broader directions of change.

Semantically, this book has presented us with the same challenge faced by anyone writing about the future. Ideally, each argument, prediction or projection in the chapters that follow ought to have been accompanied by a string of caveats and riders. But this would leave no room for any conjecture or hypothesizing, however logical or well-informed. The reading experience, too, would no doubt suffer. So, across the fault line of semantic caution and leniency, we've leaned on the side of the latter. Which means that every free flourish of 'will' and 'shall' in this book should be supplanted by 'in most likelihood, as far as we can gauge at this particular time' while reading it.

A quick, final word about how to make use of this book. The chapters below are arranged thematically, in line with the key questions we've examined, detailed in Chapter One. But they're also arranged in clusters of what, to some extent, are stand-alone essays, addressing the concerns of the three principal agents in any economy—institutions, industries and individuals. While we certainly believe you'd profit from reading this whole book, cover to cover, you could also use the premise of Chapter One to branch out and read on specific themes of your interest.

CHAPTER 1

Charting the Future of Work

The nature of work is continuously changing, and innovation in technology and processes constantly drives old skills out while creating demand for new skills. This constant tendency of economies, particularly capitalist economies, has long been noted by scholars. For example, in his celebrated book *Capitalism, Socialism and Democracy (1950)*, Joseph Schumpeter asserted that a gale of 'creative destruction' described the 'process of industrial mutation that continuously revolutionizes the economic structure from within, incessantly destroying the old one, incessantly creating a new one'.[1]

While displacing certain types of labour and rendering some skills obsolete, innovation also opens up new opportunities. This process, which is bound to be particularly painful for countries where people have no access to unemployment benefits or a strong social safety network, has nevertheless come to be considered a pre requisite for progress among captains of industry. But it has its detractors. From at least the time of the 'machine breakers' or Luddite movement of the early nineteenth century,[2] concerns around technology or automation displacing labour have been voiced in outrage, as successive waves of labour-displacing technologies enter industry. Even among today's technology optimists, some concede that rapid automation can produce both winners and losers.

In India too, such worries are not new. When mass-scale computerization began in 1985, the use of computers was greeted with suspicion by the general population and politicians. Looking back across almost four decades now, it is easy to see that some low-skill, low-paying jobs—such as those of typists[3]—were lost, several times more jobs were created, and the initial pessimism of the naysayers proved to be unfounded. However, the recent pace of change has been so rapid it warranted a new era: Industry 4.0 or the Fourth Industrial Revolution. This term represents the fourth age of revolution in manufacturing and industrial practices.[4] The First Industrial Revolution started the mechanization of production through the use of water and steam power, the Second owed its impetus to the discovery of electricity, allowing for assembly line production, while the Third was marked by automated production and the IT revolution. One can argue that the Fourth Industrial Revolution builds on the third, but both in its rate of change and in the way it connects machine to man as well as to other machines, it represents a distinct phase. This involves machine-to-machine communication and other forms of 'smart automation' that reduce the need for human intervention at many points in the production process.

In its advances in genetic engineering and use of artificial intelligence (AI), this new era creates disturbing possibilities of the designing of superior intelligence antithetical to the human species. It is not quite a dystopian fantasy that humans might become serfs of this genetically engineered super-being, or that humans will become cyborgs. This second possibility is far less laughable than it sounds at first. At a basic level, any organism that relies on technology to enhance its capabilities is a cyborg. By this token, a person living with an implanted pacemaker is, in a sense, a cyborg. In this particular case, of course, no one is worried that the Terminator might step out of the screen and into one's home, and the patient himself is much relieved at having been granted a second lease of life. However, the challenge is that the reach of enhanced technological capabilities does not end there. As Yuval Noah Harari puts it, if one cyborg could retrieve the memory of another, and minds become a sort of collective, basic human concepts such as self and gender identity themselves tend to get blurred, if not lose their meaning.[5]

Even leaving aside such possibilities, the impact of unbridled technological advancement on the workplace, as well as the type and numbers of workers in demand, is worrying enough by itself. Globally and in India, for hundreds of millions employed in jobs and/or poised to join the workforce, perhaps the most terrifying thought is that of being rendered unemployed as a result of superior technology. This scenario and, more broadly, the relationship between technological advancement and employment, is discussed in Chapter Two. As we shall see there, some, such as the political thinker and sociologist Herbert Marcuse in his landmark book *One-Dimensional Man*, have gone so far as to suggest that technology would displace almost all conventional jobs. The final, logical conclusion of such a scenario would be the state of creative destruction that Schumpeter pessimistically predicted, following Marx, where the entire capitalist system of production would break down as a result of the unprecedented scale and speed at which old skills lost their value. And, while history suggests that such an alarmist scenario is unlikely to occur, there have been serious warnings about what this may mean for several categories of workers even in the absence of a total capitalistic implosion.

As Brynjolfsson and McAfee warn in their book, *The Second Machine Age*:

> Rapid and accelerating digitization is likely to bring economic rather than environmental disruption, stemming from the fact that as computers get more powerful, companies have less need for some kinds of workers. Technological progress is going to leave behind some people, perhaps even a lot of people, as it races ahead. As we'll demonstrate, there's never been a better time to be a worker with specialist skills or the right education, because these people can use technology to create and capture value. However, there's never been a worse time to be a worker with only 'ordinary' skills and abilities to offer, because computers, robots, and other digital technologies are acquiring these skills and abilities at an extraordinary rate.[6]

DRIVERS OF LABOUR DEMAND

A theme that runs through the course of our book is that the potential and rewards for the 'right kind of skills and education' are enormous, but those without these evolved skills will be increasingly marginalized unless active steps are taken to stop this. We will show that the implications of this potential inequality are enormous and far-reaching, going beyond impacting only the current workforce.

There are three drivers of the ubiquitous change in the kind of labour that is in demand. While technology is often considered the main driver of change, two other drivers have impacted the nature of work and the workplace. One is globalization. While some of the impact of globalization is tied with technological advancement, globalization is conceptually distinct. Globalization is often narrowly understood as trade and investment flows across countries. More widely, it encompasses the idea that economies, people, and even cultural norms, are connected worldwide. Certainly, some of this has been enabled by technology, which has interlinked the world. But technology can also be used to create barriers, for instance, to shut down or to censor information or to impede the free flow of goods.

A universal concomitant of globalization has been widespread use of electronic and social media, connecting common people across the world. We are all aware of repression, when governments shut down social media platforms or, more insidiously, censor posts, boost or dampen traffic on posts and programmes, and manipulate social media outreach, powered by state-of-the-art technology and algorithms. At the same time, we've seen how media, both partisan and critical of regimes, have played a part in recent geopolitical events of global proportions, be it the 2021 US elections or the Russia–Ukraine conflict. As Deepak Ajwani, editor at the *Economic Times*, puts it:

> Media is not just the purveyor of information and a channel of communication; now with social media in play it also facilitates interconnection and cross pollination of ideas and thoughts. It thus plays a vital role, more so in the digital age, wherein information travels in split seconds, and misinformation or wrong facts get perpetuated leading to an environment of falsehood. Hence, it is critical to believe in trusted media channels and brands that have a check mechanism on what is put out in the public domain and how.

In its most productive and enriching form, globalization has led directly to a 'weightless economy'[7], where work is no longer tied to its place of demand. The implications of such an economy are tremendous. It meant that the work of whole business departments, information and data analysis, and technical programming of business processes and reports began to be outsourced to locations tens of thousands of miles away—a big reason why the Indian economy was able to reinvent itself as the IT and business process outsourcing (BPO) back end of the world. A weightless economy, driven by knowledge and enabled by ICT (information and communications technology), potentially allows everyone with a good business idea to find a global market for it.

Creativity, knowledge, individuality and the power of impactful ideas have come to the fore as never before in human economic history. From the garrets of Silicon Valley to Tel Aviv cafes and bedroom offices in Bengaluru, start-ups have mushroomed, giving rise to not only company valuations unheard of in the pre-start-up era, but also to a whole new taxonomy of classification of start-ups themselves: A Pony with a valuation of $10 million, a Centaur that boasts of $100 million in valuation, a Unicorn with its mammoth $1 billion in valuation, and market-defining Decacorns and Hectacorns at valuations of $10 billion and $100 billion, respectively.[8] This new spate of growth and wealth creation in new domains continued even through the pandemic. In the decade preceding the COVID-19 crisis, India saw the entry of eighty-four start-ups in the Unicorn club, against forty-two new Indian start-ups accorded Unicorn status in 2021 alone.[9]

Globalization has allowed goods and services to flow to where demand for them is highest, or, to use Adam Smith's words, 'to its highest valued use'. It has attracted capital flows to countries needing it, with the net impact of free mobility of goods and factors of production (labour and capital) being a fall in the overall prices of goods, by concentrating production where there is comparative advantage for it. While the economic benefits of globalization are enormous, there are equally wide-ranging ramifications when it becomes the dominant mode of operations between economies around the world. For instance, it naturally deepens the legitimacy and effectiveness of global bodies such as the United Nations (UN), the International Monetary Fund (IMF) and the World Bank.

However, when it comes to jobs in fields like technology, globalization is a mixed blessing. While it increases the total number of jobs, a look at where and how these jobs are distributed presents a more complex picture. Globalization creates winners and losers as some jobs shift away from one country to another that has comparative advantage in a certain kind of production that is in demand. This job churn, much like creative destruction, may lead to the level of overall wealth increasing in the latter economy, but leaves many people worse off than before, as their skills are no longer required. This scarring effect of unemployment has an enormous impact on these 'displaced' individuals and increases inequalities between and within regions.[10] This has far-reaching consequences in terms of social unrest and has been, at least partly, responsible for kindling the rise of expansionism or nationalism in multiple countries, Russia being the most prominent of them at present. The cost of unemployment is evaluated in economic terms, as loss of GDP or as the quantum of social benefits required to keep the displaced, especially those in the poorest sections, at a minimum subsistence level. The huge mental and emotional costs, however, are mostly disregarded or simply not mentioned at the macroeconomic level. We shall focus on these, and other associated problems, in Chapter Six.

The third and final driver of labour demand is policy-driven. This may take the form of taxes and subsidies to encourage or discourage production, quotas on exports or imports, or even outright bans on production of certain goods. Indeed, some form of protectionism from free trade is seen even in the most 'free trade' nations. This is often driven by a desire to protect a sector from international competition. Whether such protectionist policies are wise has been a matter of much debate. Most economists are sceptical of such restrictions unless it is to correct a specific labour-market anomaly, but such policies no doubt affect the demand and supply of labour. This, of course, is not a new phenomenon, except that now the variables that shape the scope of regulation in a free market have changed.

One form of regulation has found a fair degree of support, even among otherwise market-friendly economists. This is the set of legislation and compliance measures driven by worries around global warming. Given that the impact of an individual's action on the environment is negligible, individual incentives to act for the social good are considered insufficient, necessitating the need for regulation. This is the so-called classic 'tragedy of the commons', where individuals do not consider the social impact of polluting the environment through their actions. This has led to several forms of price and non-price incentives to lower individual consumption that is harmful for the environment. This has a consequent impact on the workplace, since it changes the relative attractiveness of products whose supply chain involves more or less pollution.

The Climate Change Conference of the Parties (COP26), which concluded in November 2021, was the first conference since the Paris Climate Conference (or COP21) in 2015 where all 196 participating countries were expected to make further changes in their policies to combat climate change. The conference did reach agreement, but not before India and China insisted on last-minute changes, with the language around 'phasing out coal' being replaced with one around 'phasing down coal'. Not the most natural of allies, the two countries faced criticism from other nations (not to mention the ire of climate-change activists), but they nonetheless agreed to make the concessions necessary for an agreement to be reached. But there were other nations that supported India and China, with the defence that developed countries were as much to blame for the watered-down agreement, with oil and natural gas being excluded from it, making the impact fall disproportionately on developing nations such as India and China.

While the question of what more could have been done is beyond the purview of this book, the nature of regulation of activities and parameters that affect our global climate has implications for work and for the sectoral composition of jobs. The last-minute controversy in COP26 notwithstanding, governments across the board are bringing in regulatory mechanisms (though of different degrees of stringency) and corporations have been setting out environmentally considered policy (often above and beyond the minimum requirements). While often dismissed by activists as 'too little, too late', or worse still, as 'window-dressing', this, by itself, has implications both for the type of industries that are being phased out and for the type of new industries that have sprung up to support the regulatory regime or to work with corporations to implement their voluntary regimes.

That this is not purely window-dressing seems to be borne out by an International Labour Organization (ILO) publication, the World Employment and Social Outlook Report, which estimates that by 2030, at least 24 million green jobs will be created.[11] It is expected that at least some of this will come at the expense of oil and gas. Meanwhile, WEF (World Economic Forum) reports that in 2015, LinkedIn data showed the ratio of US oil/gas jobs to renewables/environment jobs at 5:1, but by 2020 this had fallen to 2:1.[12] Indeed, while they may have been decades late in rising to the challenge, corporations have, through a mix of moral coercion, enlightened self-interest, or because of regulatory pressure, taken cognizance of the polluting effect of their production processes.

Fortune-500 companies are taking a number of steps that involve climate targets. These take three main forms: (i) becoming carbon neutral, where a company offsets its greenhouse gas emissions, (ii) use of 100 per cent renewable energy, and (iii) reduction of emissions, in line with the need to keep global warming below 2 degrees Centigrade. The size and extent of these actions is debated, with activists claiming this does not, by any measure, go far enough. But the current trend nonetheless favours industries that can help corporations achieve these targets, which accords with ILO's World Employment and Social Outlook Report, mentioned above. More sombrely, the same report predicts 72 million full-time jobs could be lost by 2030 because of heat stress. Thus, like it or not, our very existence may require a move to sustainability and, consequently, the rise of green jobs.

EMERGING AND DECLINING DEMAND FOR LABOUR

Keeping in mind these technological, global and institutional drivers of change in the demand for labour, we will try to understand the trends in the Indian and global labour markets, looking not just at projected net demand but also commenting on the distributional consequences (i.e., who gains and loses), as the demand for labour shifts. Who are these workers with 'specialist skills' or the 'right education', who can harness new technologies? And who are the 'ordinary' workers for whom the next decade is not so propitious?

It is helpful to start with a few projections. Every year, the WEF and other institutions publish a list of emerging and declining industries, indicating how demand for labour (in the broadest sense) is shifting. These projections are useful, showing the trends in changes in labour demand across sectors, though some of the projections may need adjustment because of the workplace transformation that occurred directly or indirectly because of COVID. It is still instructive to look at some trends and projections from before COVID to see the direction of change.

The table below provides a snapshot projection of emergent and displaced jobs globally and in India for 2022 and 2025; the variation in the estimates notwithstanding, both projections in the WEF reports suggest a net increase in jobs.

Table 1.1: Projections of Emergent and Displaced Jobs

Source (Projection year)	Emergent Jobs in Millions (Global)	Displaced Jobs in Millions (Global)	Net Jobs in Millions (Global)	Emergent Jobs in Millions (India)	Displaced Jobs in Millions (India)	Net Jobs in Millions (India)
WEF (2022)	133 million	75 million	58 million	Not available	Not available	Not available
WEF (2025)	97 million	85 million	12 million	Not available	Not available	Not available
MGI (2016-2030)	20 to 50 million	400 to 800 million	380 to 750 million	114 million	60 million	54 million
MGI (2018-2030)	Not available	Not available	Not available	Not available	53.5 million	Not available

Source: The data in this table is taken from WEF (2018), WEF (2020), MGI (2017) and MGI (2021)

Interestingly, another report by the McKinsey Global Institute (MGI) presents a slightly different picture. While acknowledging that up to 800 million jobs may be lost due to technology, it predicts job growth spurred by rising income, more jobs in healthcare to address an ageing population, more jobs from investments in infrastructure and from green sectors. Thus, it argues that technology will displace labour, but that as income increases, consumers with higher income will spend more on durables, telecommunication, healthcare, education and leisure. Thus, MGI suggests that while technology drives out jobs by raising standards of living, it creates more demand for products, leading to new jobs. This would have given some cause for cautious optimism, until the COVID-19 pandemic struck. As the figures above pre-date COVID-19, they don't reflect the massive global upheaval in employment, reducing the number of ways in which consumers could spend their income and nearly decimating sectors such as travel and hospitality. Globally, it is estimated that working-hour losses were 8.8 per cent, which is equivalent to 255 million FTE (full time equivalent) jobs. Out of this, forgone job growth amounted to 30 million (26 million FTE jobs), employment loss for 144 million people (98 million FTE jobs) and reduction of working hours equivalent to 131 million FTE jobs. Out of the population that lost employment, 81 million consisted of those that went out of the labour force and stopped working, and the remaining 33 million people remained unemployed.[13]

Some of these losses are likely to be long-lasting, while in other sectors the losses may be transient. As the threat of new variants of the virus looms, it may render all of these projections meaningless. Yet, in the way people have tried to go back to how they lived during off-and-on periods of normality during the course of the pandemic, we hope the pre-COVID-19 trends give us some insights as to how the future will look, even if that gets delayed by a few years. Before the COVID-19 disruptions, the net picture seemed to be one of *increased overall demand for labour*. However, the key point is not whether the overall demand increased but how the demand for labour will change as a result of technological changes and their consequent social impact. The true fear around technology displacement is not one of contraction of overall labour demand, as has often been simplistically portrayed, but around the distributional consequences. In other words, the critical question is what happens when some skills become obsolete and news skills are demanded.

To see this, we need to look at not just the broader macroeconomic patterns but at the sectoral ones too. In many industries, there is a rise in demand for specialists. The biggest demand is for data scientists, IT and security specialists, which subsumes demand for AI and machine learning specialists as well as data analysts and internet of things (IOT) specialists. Demand for those who do routine jobs (including those who may be considered specialist, like accountants and auditors) which can be easily automated, is declining. But data and IT specialists are not the only people in demand. Those who can supervise complex projects or help business to develop, including advising on behavioural skills, are also needed. Chapters Three and Four investigate these trends in greater detail and glean insights around specific combinations of sectors, domains and associated skill sets that are likely to be in greater demand in the future.

DEMAND, SKILLS, WAGES, GENDER GAP

Given the change in skills that would be in demand in the future, it might seem obvious that focused interventions are needed to upgrade and match people's skills with the demands emerging in the workplace. However, not everyone agrees on this. Standard neoclassical economists argue that temporary fluctuations aside, over a longer period, markets adjust to remove any mismatch in demand and supply of labour. This view suggests that people respond to incentives by acquiring skills to match the emerging demand for skills, whether the demand is brought about by the pace of change of technology, globalization, or by regulatory regimes. They do not deny that rapid automation poses its own problems, but they argue that upskilling workers with the right skills and education will necessarily happen. They place trust in the incentives of the market to cause such upskilling to take place. Essentially, they argue for an inverted form of Say's Law, which has been paraphrased as: 'Supply creates its own demand.'

Now, the 'inverted' form of Say's Law would mean that demand, in this case, for labour, will create its own supply. Proponents of the neoclassical school argue that market forces, in the form of higher prices for the skills in demand, are enough of an incentive for demand to begin to keep pace with supply. Just as prices go up when a good is scarce, incentivizing supply while tempering demand, the same will happen in the case of newly emerging skills in demand. Thus, in this world, people will just invest in the skills that are needed in emerging industries while moving out of declining industries. This sounds plausible, but how long does it take for market incentives to work? The reality is that labour markets can be quite sluggish, though differences of opinion exist as to how long it takes for supply to catch up with demand. We will revisit Say's Law again in Chapter Two.

On one point, though, there is fairly broad consensus among experts. The key challenge globally, and for India, is not whether the anticipated overall demand for labour is rising (there is ample evidence that it is), it lies in matching this increased demand with supply. Here too there is some acceptance that there is a skills gap at present, not just at the junior level of professionals but at the managerial and leadership levels as well. Looking at the emerging and waning industries, it is not difficult to see a sharp rise in demand for data and information specialists, and a decline in demand for routine, repetitive work which can be easily automated.

It would be unrealistic to expect people to make a swift and seamless transition from declining industries and skills to emerging ones. For instance, it is rather unlikely that the office secretary or factory worker can become a successful data analyst naturally through the incentive of higher wages. The process of transition will take time, and many will struggle to successfully make the transition on their own. To be truly effective, such a project needs the concerted effort of government bodies, industry associations and firms working in unison. In the later chapters of the book, we look at the initiatives taken in other economies and offer recommendations for the Indian context.

One may argue that India seems to be following in the footsteps of industrialized nations where the movement away from low-skilled to high-skilled industries is at least partly fed by automation and has left a large sector of the population unemployed, as retraining was either inadequate or not feasible. But the skills gap seems more global. For instance, in the UK, the skills gap has left one in four jobs unfilled, as reported by the UK Commission for Employment and Skills, a trend that has not changed much between 2015 and 2019.[14] A more recent report by Monster, published in April 2022, found that 87 per cent of UK employers across all sectors were struggling to fill positions, while 63 per cent of employers have on occasion actually failed to fill positions on account of skills shortages.[15] A Deloitte survey found that 71 per cent of CEOs anticipate that the skills and labour shortage will be 2022's biggest business disrupter.[16] The problem is not just UK-centric.

Reports in the US show that approximately 74 per cent of hiring managers agreed that there are skill gaps still, with almost 50 per cent of them stating that most candidates did not meet the requirements for even the jobs they were applying for.[17] In

2019, over 7 million jobs in the USA remained unfilled due to non-availability of people with the right skills. Furthermore, a study by McKinsey found that the pandemic has speeded up adoption of technologies by several years. While this may be good news to many, we argue that this may cause the skills gap to increase further and widen existing inequalities.[18]

A key reason for the skills gaps to increase because of COVID-19 is that the pandemic tended to widen the digital divide where it already existed. In India, there are significant differences across socio-economic-demographic groups, both in terms of digital access and capabilities. Indeed, concerns have already been expressed around this, with even vaccine access being affected by how digitally savvy one is.[19] This digital divide is in fact ubiquitous. Of particular concern is how this has been playing out in the education sector during the pandemic, significantly affecting children from less well-off families who have limited access to computers or the internet. This has enormous inter-generational consequences, as poorer children are shut out from the potentially levelling-up effects of education. Inequalities in access to education will widen the skills gap, accelerating wage inequalities and magnifying the already serious issue of income inequality in India.[20]

In India, the skills gap is significant. NCSDE (National Council for Skill Development and Entrepreneurship) reports that 53 per cent of Indian businesses were unable to recruit in 2019 because of a skills shortage. In spite of India having a younger population than most countries of the world, Indian schools do not seem to provide a curriculum that would be useful for the modern job market, and firms do not compensate for this through adequate training. Alarmingly, at the current rate, the skills gap is projected to rise until it reaches 75–80 per cent.[21]

The urban–rural disparity in technological facilities and usage also has the potential to increase the rural–urban divide. In the absence of barriers to migrating, one would expect to see increased rural–urban migration in India, given the continued decline of the agricultural sector's share in the GDP, which has slipped below 20 per cent, though reaching just over 20 per cent in 2020–21 due to better growth than in other sectors that year.[22] However, rural–urban migration has never been anywhere near as high as one would have predicted. There are a number of plausible reasons for this. For example, well-functioning informal insurance networks (for example, lending and borrowing within the rural community, or availability of assistance when needed) have allowed people to stay in their villages even when they have lost their jobs. On the other hand, the lack of formal insurance markets, combined with the dearth of state safety nets, has meant that migration away from their current informal networks is risky for people. So, even with the substantial rural–urban wage gap in India, reported migration levels are far lower than what one would predict in a market without any barriers to migration.[23]

Rural employment programmes, while not bridging the wage gap, lead to even less incentives for people to leave their villages as there has been a basic improvement in their quality of life. This is a significant factor in the continued low rates of migration, even in the face of a declining share of agriculture as a provider of employment. The pandemic has reduced rural–urban migration even further. Part of this may have to do with the difficulties people faced when they were stranded in 'no-man's lands' during the first lockdown, but part of this can be attributed to local job availability under the guaranteed employment scheme, the Mahatma Gandhi National Rural Employment Guarantee Act (MGNREGA),[24] and better infrastructure in the villages. Indeed, this adds further reasons for people not to migrate.

The trends indicate that labour demand in India, and globally, will continue to rise at the same time as the rate of vacancies is also rising. However, even at the pre-COVID-19 pace of technological transformation, the skill sets needed to take advantage of the opportunities offered by emerging industries were often missing. A continuing skills gap may push firms towards labour-displacing technologies, with consequences for societal inequality. However, the world of technology has left other parts of the economy with a skills deficit.

For example, the rapid pace of technology changes affects not just the worker but also has implications for the consumer, whose skill sets may need updating as well. Most financial products (such as banking, bill payment products, etc.) have now moved online. Thus, for a consumer, not being tech savvy is becoming increasingly costly. For example, many offers and discounts on products may only be available online and not in the retail store. Further, the full range of products may only be available on online menus. The combination of the technology skills shortage among the workforce and the consumer's inadequacy of knowledge to safely navigate the internet comes with important security implications.

Consumers in India are becoming increasingly comfortable shopping online, yet a sizeable portion of them does not appear to be aware of the associated risks. A survey by McAfee found that 29.5 per cent of Indians shop online frequently (3–5 times weekly) but 15.7 per cent have no awareness of cyber risks and only 27.5 per cent use security solutions. This is encouraging on the one hand, as it indicates there is no technological gap preventing consumers in urban areas from switching their mode of purchase. However, on the other hand, it highlights an alarming 'knowledge gap' with regards to online security.[25]

What is the impact of forced digitalization in a country where many consumers do not understand the risks of online transactions and firms do not offer adequate protection either? The impact of such a digital transformation will be skewed, to say the least. While the proliferation of online shopping is a boon to the tech-savvy consumer, the reduction in offline facilities for shopping, as well as the digitalization of the banking industry is adversely impacting the elderly, who are often less tech savvy. Looking at cybersecurity from an organization's perspective, most large companies are, or plan to be, on the path of digital transformation. However, the vast majority of firms in the MSME, start-up and social entrepreneurship sectors have neither the imperatives nor the resources to focus on data and cybersecurity. During the pandemic, as many struggled merely to stay afloat, they became susceptible to cyberattacks. At the same time, the threat of data theft and cyberhacking opens up business and employment opportunities in the IT security sector.

From the perspective of consumers, the elderly are the most susceptible to cybercrime. There are still woefully few studies focusing on the scale of cybercrime against the elderly in India, though some qualitative work has identified some reasons why they may be victimized. Their risk of victimization has been magnified by the pandemic as it has forced them to rely heavily on digital technology, which is susceptible to cybersecurity breaches.[26] The combination of increased cyber-usage with relatively low levels of cybersecurity is a potent one, and we need to gauge the level of cyber-vulnerability in different segments of the population and address how best to protect the vulnerable. Research in the UK points to socio-economic and regional divides in cyber-vulnerability. Building vulnerability matrices, mapping the population cohorts most at risk and the type of transactions that increase the risk, is the first step to prevent cyber-victimization in India. Predictive data analytics can then mine the information collected from cyber-transactions to understand patterns that can pinpoint which groups are most at risk, and where they are located. This, in turn, could pave the way for more sharply focused regulation and targeted campaigns to raise security awareness. For instance, in response to a sharp rise in cybercrime during the initial months of the pandemic, a National Cyber Security Strategy was launched in 2020 in the UK by the National Security Council.

What are the social implications of such rapid changes in technology? We've already seen that these rapid changes may lead to different forms of inequality. Whether entirely emanating from a skills gap or not, inequality in India has been an issue for a long time, and the pandemic appears to have increased it. This mirrors global trends and also possibly outstrips them. An Oxfam India Supplement 2021 report titled The Inequality Virus notes that the wealth of Indian billionaires increased by 35 per cent during the extended lockdowns in 2020, and by 90 per cent since 2009. The report argues that the fourth tranche of the government's relief package benefited many of the already super-rich, further deepening the inequality divide between the rich and the poor. The digital divide meant that closure of schools and educational institutes disproportionately affected the poor, where only 8.9 per cent have access to the internet and 2.7 per cent access to computers. Coupled with the glaring health inequalities, also highlighted in the report, the medium-term outlook may also continue to be affected adversely.[27]

From a gender perspective, COVID-19 has negatively affected India's already low female labour-force participation. India slid twenty-eight places to rank 140th (out of 156) in the 2021 Gender Gap Index. Whether this is a blip or not, much more needs to be done to improve female labour-force participation rates. The World Inequality Report 2022 provides further bad news for India, pointing out that 'India stands out as a poor and very unequal country with an affluent elite'. India's female-labour share of income, of 18 per cent, is low even by Asian standards, which stands at 21 per cent. Among Asian economies, the big exception is China, which in 2021 recorded a 44.51 per cent female labour-force participation.[28]

THE GIG ECONOMY

Another disruptive force the world over relates to the nature of contracting and employer–employee obligations. While there has always been a demand for flexible working, it is only in recent times that technology has made it mainstream. Going forward, chances are that this will become the norm in many sectors. From a mere speck on the horizon as late as in 2000, there were close to 800 digital labour platforms, according to ILO and the Crunchdatabase 2021, with this number expected to keep growing. These platforms serve as matchmakers, giving rise to a gig economy that is unprecedented in its growth. No longer a niche way of earning, this accounts for the income of over a third of US workers. This is in no way restricted to the developed world and, as we shall see in this book, the gig economy is fast gaining currency across different sectors in India.

It comes as no surprise that the maximum growth in the gig economy is in technology and BPO and in the services sector. For the first time in the history of the organized sector in post-Independence India, we have a new form of worker. This professional carries out his tasks without the obligation of being a 'full-time employee' with an enviable degree of autonomy and puts in 'full-time' hours but without job security or benefits such as Employee Provident Fund, gratuity, house rent allowance, medical insurance, medical expenses or leave travel allowance, which a large section of the middle-class urban Indian has been accustomed to. At the low end of the spectrum, for instance, among gig workers in the market for deliveries, this insecurity can be particularly challenging and increase economic uncertainty. Indeed, much has been written about the insecurity of low-end gig workers, about their long working hours and depressed wages, particularly in the delivery and transport sector. However, it is a form of working that is increasingly proving to be robust and self-sustaining, and so longer-term solutions are required, focused on how to sustain the flexibility accorded by gig work while safeguarding workers against the inherent insecurity it brings.

Globally, the prominence of this form of working has been accelerated by COVID-19, truly creating a borderless workforce globally. Workers, and sometimes governments, pressure digital labour platforms and employers into embracing some kind of corporate social responsibility.[29] In India, the New Labour Codes of 2019 define and include a gig worker and, for the first time, the Code on Social Security 2020[30] extended social security benefits to gig workers. These are important initial steps in acknowledging what will be one of the most dominant forms of working in the current era. However, neither of these codes provides details of the scope, nature, minimum goals, and (most importantly) funding mechanism for operationalizing the protections mentioned for gig workers.

The twin features of gig working and a weightless economy are closely related, and together form part of a global, interconnected system. It represents a major structural change as regards the nature of work. For many jobs, workers are not tied to their physical location. This has been correlated with many of the (same) workers no longer being tied to a firm. However, Industry 4.0 is bringing about the culmination of a change that has been long in the making. A key element of Industry 4.0 is that, thanks to cutting-edge technology, work may no longer need a worker. For a long time, it was axiomatic that workers would follow work opportunities. There may be friction in the process, but where there was need for work to be done, there would be demand for workers. Not until recently has the concept of some types of work occurring without direct human guidance been more than the métier of twentieth-century science fiction. Yet, from guiding spaceships to investigating the contents of shopping trolleys, the concept of workerless work is no longer a fantasy. Hence, while we will continue to talk about work and workers in the subsequent chapters, distinguishing between the two is not just a matter of semantics any more.

This divorce of work from worker may well be a culmination of the technological revolution, where work may occur without human direction. Not only do we see this shift, with technology taking the place of workers in assembly lines, today's technological revolution is also a data revolution. This particular revolution achieves more getting tasks done that a human would have done otherwise. It means that non-human computational mechanisms make decisions that affect our life course. For the greater part of two decades at least, mathematical models or algorithms (we will use the two terms interchangeably) pervade decision-making in domains unseen.

From deciding who gets loans and at what rate of interest, which defendant gets bail or which prisoners are released early, who gets admitted to which school, using models that are impenetrable to all but a few, algorithms make decisions in what were usually the domain of human beings. Such data-driven or algorithmic decision-making is ubiquitous. Whether these algorithms are neutral and reduce human bias or, to use Cathy O'Neil's expression, are 'weapons of math destruction' that scale up existing inequalities, they pose a number of challenges around accountability, which require careful thought.[31] We will examine two key questions in the next section: who is accountable for the decisions made by these models, and why are some people excited and others worried about the use of these models?

WHOSE DECISION IS IT ANYWAY?[32]

If important tasks that involve decision-making can be fulfilled without human intervention, the next logical question is: who should be liable for the impact of such decision-making? There have been well-informed debates on this, the possibility of driverless cars, for instance, provoking questions around who would be liable if a decision goes wrong, e.g., if the driverless car meets with an accident. The topic assumes some urgency when we realize that, going forward, an ever-increasing proportion of our interactions with the world will be guided by outcomes determined by algorithms. While many such applications are already operational in the Indian ecosystem, let's consider the example of the criminal justice system, where the use of algorithms in the future may speed up decision-making and operational efficiencies but also create some new challenges.

We draw on the global use of algorithms in policing in the Western world to understand both its rationale and the challenges posed by it, considering what the implications would be for India and the developed world. Algorithms in the world of criminal justice started with benign intentions, mirroring, to an extent, the earlier adoption of these methods by healthcare. There are several reasons for their adoption. The first had to do with the increasing availability of data, through manual and automated collection processes, which makes the use of sophisticated algorithmic techniques, such as machine learning (ML), both possible and less tedious.

The second coincided with the growing pressure on police departments to combat a rise in criminal behaviour without a commensurate increase in resources. In this context, using models to decide where to focus resources seemed a smart option. Algorithms, it was felt, would guide the best use of scarce policing resources. It would exploit the ability of computational techniques to process vast quantities of information which could not be processed manually, allowing a consideration of information beyond the capabilities of humans.

The third reason arises from the use of predictive tools in the hope of pre-empting crimes or to identify vulnerable individuals and proactively prevent their exploitation. While this alarmed many, who saw this as a real-life version of the movie *Minority Report* playing out, their effectiveness was soon demonstrated on the ground. A great example is 'hotspot policing', which facilitates deployment of personnel, resources and strategies to where crime is concentrated or most likely to occur, and so results in optimal use of law-enforcement resources.

Fourth, there has been a rise of new forms of crime, such as cybercrime, which can only be combated using algorithmic methods. This includes, for example, responding to cyber-attacks or monitoring cybercrimes, such as sexual exploitation of children. Finally, there is a case to be made for the position that algorithmic methods using large data sets are more robust and relatively unbiased, acting as a neutral judge while also saving resources. There are substantial counterarguments to such a view, both with regard to the quality of the data as well to the biases or deficiencies that may be inherent in the algorithms themselves.

For all their speed and efficiency, algorithms present their own particular ethical, moral and practical issues that are not easily resolvable or involve difficult trade-offs. To begin with, the way data is collected, classified and organized may itself be subjective and therefore prone to bias.[33] For example, data containing the details of location, ethnicity or community of people may influence judgements in unintended ways.

Imagine a situation where people in poorer neighbourhoods exhibit a higher rate of economic crime because they lack job opportunities. Suppose also that some ethnic groups are poor because of job discrimination arising out of historical bias. There may be over-policing of such neighbourhoods, given their high correlation with past crimes. Consequently, more crimes are discovered, including petty crime or recreational drug use, which would never have been discovered or investigated in another neighbourhood that was not so well policed. This has a cascading effect, with more people, often young, getting a criminal record, which damages their future employment prospects, which in turn propels them down the path of criminality. In this case, the model is clearly 'validated', even though some of the push to criminality has been created by the over-policing arising from reliance on the model in the first place.

There are simpler ways in which data can give false predictions, creating what Cathy O'Neil calls a 'pernicious feedback loop'. Let's extend the example above. Suppose police historically believed that people of a certain ethnicity are more crime-prone and investigated them disproportionately through, say, stop and search. As a result, more crimes are recorded against a certain ethnicity because they have been investigated more even if their crime rate is the same as another less-policed ethnic group. However, a model built on such biased data will flag people of that ethnicity as more crime-prone and cause them to be policed more, again leading to more crimes being discovered as a result. This perpetuates the initial bias in the data. Simply put, flawed data gives rise to flawed predictions. If flawed or biased data is used to build the model, any subsequent decision-making undertaken by the algorithm will also be skewed, reflecting those biases. There could also be measurement error. If crime is over-reported in certain areas and under-reported in others, any model that does not allow for this may not be measuring the distribution of crime accurately.

Such biases are often present where algorithms may suggest automated paths of action or assessment. In such cases, outcomes purely based on the model's evaluation may be self-fulfilling in many ways and will lack reflective or reactive information that could inform decisions. Thus, in this case, there is a need for an 'unbiased' programme, say, through a historical analysis of whether certain areas were over- or under-policed. Instances of self-fulfilling prophecies may also rise from focusing on crimes that are more amenable to solution by algorithmic methods, leading to a bias against the people charged and brought to court and, in turn, convicted. For example, if there is a belief that petty thefts can be solved more easily using algorithmic methods, then there may be a greater focus on them, leading to the data on solvable crimes being skewed towards thefts. As a result, models based on historical data that targets investigation based on solvability will target resources towards such crimes.

The question of algorithmic error becomes doubly tricky when the companies creating them do not reveal the workings used to design the algorithms. This 'black box' approach can lead to concerns about lack of transparency. In many circumstances, the processes leading to a decision are non-transparent and separated from the decision-maker, making scrutiny and challenge of the decision difficult. Such systems, where the inputs and operations are not visible to the user or other interested parties, are essentially impenetrable. Errors can go unnoticed until they cause significant problems. This can result in unfairness and the undermining of public confidence and legitimacy.

Algorithmic methods intrude upon privacy. This is self-evident, given that these methods must inevitably rely on data that one could argue should remain private. For example, in identifying and disrupting criminal gangs, extraction of mobile phone data may be needed, as telephonic exchanges often reveal vital information about the plans and whereabouts of individuals. In this case, intrusion of privacy has beneficial effects for society. But in many other instances, algorithms may have an adverse impact on issues related to human rights. For example, where methods involve the use of personal data extracted without the knowledge or consent of the person involved, this would go against human rights and against data-protection legislation meant to protect our privacy. This becomes especially problematic when the means of gathering the evidence is not made public, ostensibly in the interests of security.

This previous discussion has focused on the criminal justice sector, where there is a continuing debate about the use of algorithmic decision-making. This has not yet taken off in India or in most developing countries. Yet, in a country where the backlog in the criminal justice sector is enormous, the temptation to use algorithmic models is great.

The use of algorithms influences almost every aspect of our lives. The use of algorithms by companies to micro-target consumers has come under much scrutiny. At one end of the spectrum are the advertisements that Google, Amazon, Facebook and other tech companies target us with, based on our online footprints. This supposedly makes our lives better, directing our attention only to products that are likely to be of interest to us. At the other end of the spectrum are the targeted political advertisements, based on data that has been illegally harvested—for example, when Facebook sold its data to Cambridge Analytica, which used it illegally even when asked by Facebook to stop doing so. As a result, consumers were sent specific, tailored messages on one particular issue, which was given a particular slant. Consumers were also able to interact with 'birds of the same feather', meeting people who shared their specific views. The inevitable result of such micro-targeting is to increase political polarization, creating information bubbles that confirm our existing biases and also helping the spreading of 'fake news'.[34]

We suggest a nuanced approach to assessing the use of algorithms, being conscious of the dangers they pose, while at the same time appreciating their benefits and, in many cases, their possible superiority over more manual approaches to decision-making. For example, in an environment where increasingly large quantities of data are being collected and processed, it is clear that purely manual approaches are unlikely to be feasible if the data gathered is to be put to proper use. Algorithms that are used to merely organize data in this way should not be controversial. However, when algorithms have substantial predictive content that can lead to substantive decisions, we need to be most careful and develop safeguards in its use as we discuss below.

Issues of fairness and accountability must also be borne in mind, especially when recommendations are made for increasing the reach and scope of algorithmic methods. Algorithms must be transparent, allowing the citizen whose life is affected to understand and challenge the rationale behind them. Otherwise, through their pernicious feedback loops, they can indeed become a 'weapon of math destruction', amplifying existing societal inequalities. Any non-transparency in modelling will give rise to a general distrust in data and scientific methods, creating deep divisions in society, something we have seen play out (e.g., between vaccine evangelicals, to whom the data speaks of the efficacy of vaccines, and vaccine sceptics, who distrust the data because they do not trust either the data or the models generated by the data). Without safeguards in place, the sustained adoption of 'black box AI' (i.e., an artificial intelligence system where the system does not explain how it reaches its conclusion—hence the phrase 'black box') may ultimately precipitate a situation where data is perceived as an ugly word, undoing its role in advancing human civilization, particularly over the last two centuries.[35]

CONCERNS ABOUT INDUSTRY 4.0

The speed of change in this Fourth Industrial Revolution has been incredible. Technology has largely made the worker redundant when it comes to most routine tasks, while globalization has meant that many workers no longer need to be geographically tied to the workplace. For economic, political and humanitarian reasons, a labour surplus in less affluent nations means they continue to employ labour in place of machines, but even these economies have felt the definite direction of change. The effect of technological advancement isn't unidirectional—it almost certainly creates jobs at the same time as it displaces others. The new jobs could include those created by raising income levels and inducing demand in sectors as disparate as consumer goods and healthcare. The real problem lies in the skills gap it creates and the fact that there will be resultant winners and losers from the process, which can exacerbate inequalities.

Skills mismatch is an old problem. No one has ever argued that the process of creative destruction is painless. However, three features of this current revolution make this a change that has mammoth social implications. The first is that the divorce of the worker from the workplace has immediate and tangible repercussions for the well-being of the worker. While the choice of WFH allowed many to continue to function during the pandemic, many workplaces no longer kept this a choice but made it an operational norm for employees in the post-pandemic scenario. For a considerable part of the workforce, this cuts them off from a natural support network, with grave implications for the most vulnerable, for whom support from peers is vital. We shall explore in Chapter Six how a forced model of WFH has functioned as a global laboratory where its effect on the physical and mental well-being of the workforce can be studied.

The second important feature is the rise of data-driven models that make substantive decisions affecting major aspects of our life. This doesn't just replace man with machine, but with a machine that makes decisions, affecting real people. Properly constructed, algorithms and data decision-making can perform better than biased humans. Yet they may well create a new kind of inequality—algorithmic inequality—based on the logic they are set on, the rules of interpretation and the resultant decisions. Such inequalities can be hard to undo because of the opaqueness about how algorithms make their decisions. Being able to micro-target specific sections of society, they can also create pernicious information bubbles, exacerbating social inequalities and political polarization. But data science can help us detect a child at risk of abuse or disrupt networks of criminal gangs too. It can also free us from tedious, repetitive work and cut back on errors.

The third feature, and to many the most terrifying, is the possibility that advances in science and technology are robbing us of our personhood and we may even end up creating an intelligent being that usurps our primacy in the world. What, then, does the future hold for humanity? Is the world edging towards a technological dystopia, where the human race will no longer have either use or even existence? Or are we on the threshold of advances that free up our time, prolong our lives and take us to the cusp of immortality? Our aim here in this book isn't to delve into philosophical questions about our nature and being. Instead, in the subsequent chapters, we will explore how work, the worker and the workplace are all undergoing a change in Industry 4.0, and discuss what we need to do to navigate its challenges and take advantage of the opportunities it offers.

CHAPTER 2

Technology and Employment

At first blush, the subject of the effect of technology—powered by AI and automation—on employment may appear to be a minefield. The public domain is deluged with information, consisting of opinion pieces, vlogs, debates, articles, books carrying an array of divergent viewpoints on different sectors, job roles and skills. The total effect of all this can be quite overwhelming, increasing the general sense of uncertainty and, for salaried employees, their sense of job security. This may not actually be warranted. This surfeit of information, far from bringing any clarity on the topic, only adds to the confusion. Our aim in this chapter will be to cut through the fog and noise engulfing this subject, dispel some common misconceptions, glean insights from the existing data on the subject and provide an anecdotal flavour of the AI and automation-based advances taking place across sectors of the economy.

In the section that follows, we show that in truth there isn't a multitude of positions and opinions on the subject but two principal schools of thought. One consists of those that are enthusiastically in favour of technological advancement and adoption. We'll call them the 'Optimists'; and the other consists of those who have grave reservations about the same, who we shall term the 'Pessimists'. 'Luddites' and 'Marxists' are among other appellations given to the second category, but we will keep to 'Pessimists'. We shall chart the development of these opposing schools and the mutations they've undergone over time. Our intention isn't to side with one position or the other, or even to strike a compromise. We will outline, compare and contrast their arguments, helping you apply them to situations as they continue to unfold in the future.

Next, we take up the question of the impact of automation-led technological advances on employment in the Indian ecosystem—a topic that has been the subject of much debate and controversy in recent years. We shall examine how the alarmist projections that began in 2017 have played out in the subsequent years up to the pandemic period. However, as we shall see, the pandemic has also forced us to view other aspects of technological advancement in a far clearer light, including the misconceptions that many still cling to. We will list and review these items, demonstrating why they are myths, and in the process reveal the concerns, hopes, beliefs and apprehensions that lie at their root.

Later in the chapter, we shall provide examples of technological advances across key sectors of the economy in India that show a trend of 'catching up' with the practices and processes in vogue globally. We shall be taking up the emergent skills in demand in these sectors, especially behavioural competencies, in the subsequent chapters. Note that the examples of specific companies and situations mentioned in the sections that follow should not be taken as an end in themselves but as milestones along a particular route, as patterns pointing in a certain direction.

Finally, we shall sketch a picture of the imprint of technology on non-routine, creative pursuits or activities that require highly evolved skills, from indoor games to music and the fine arts. In all of these cases, the underlying technologies have been available for years. Our argument is that these innovations are no longer curiosities but workable prototypes on the cusp of being launched commercially in the market. The right combination of unit costs, ease of scalability and a sustainable market for them in the future can, at any point, provide the trigger for their widespread market launch.

WHOSE TRUTH IS IT ANYWAY?

We'll start with the Pessimists. In industrialized societies, instances of 'machine breaking' go all the way back to the 1760s, though the main thrust of opposition to mechanization and technology was witnessed during the first half of the nineteenth century. As late as in 1844, when the power of steam had become a fait accompli, the nature-loving Wordsworth was writing to the *Morning Post*, protesting against the introduction of railways in the Lake District in northern England.[1]

There were no mills and quarries there, he argued, the main economic rationale for locomotives. But his own objection was aesthetic. The railways, and in their wake, crowds of people and establishments, Wordsworth said, would disfigure the scenic beauty of the region.

Arthur, Duke of Wellington, famous for his victory over Napoleon at the Battle of Waterloo in 1815, was also a strong opposer of railways. An intricate, affordable network meant that the poor commonfolk could roam about at will all over the country, something that aggrieved his supercilious, aristocratic way of thinking. The only domain of technological advancement he wholly supported was, of course, that of arms and armaments. Wellington's equally famous and flamboyant contemporary, Lord George Gordon Byron, adopted a humane, 'socialist' view. He deplored the inhuman working and living conditions of factory workers and their families as mills sprung up continually. In the prevalent upper crust of British society, his was a lone voice that rang out in defence of the 'machine breakers'—or the Luddite movement.

The movement, which took its name from Ned Ludd, a weaver from Anstey, near Leicester, involved handloom and workshop owners in Nottingham, England, at the beginning of the nineteenth century, the halcyon days of the Industrial Revolution. New-age capital-rich manufacturers had recently introduced machines that produced textiles at an astonishing speed, consistent in quality and low in cost, which traditional handlooms simply couldn't compete with. When these looms closed down and the workers went to look for employment in the textile factories, they found the going tough. The automated technology in these factories needed fewer workers to produce a much greater output of goods. The handloom owners and their job-hands lost their livelihoods.

The simmering sense of injustice erupted into open protest, and then rioting. Between the night of 11 March 1811 in Arnold, Nottingham, and early 1812, when there were such incidents in West Riding of Yorkshire, and a year later in Lancashire, handloom owners and workers raided local mills and smashed their stocking and cropping frames. Mill owners retaliated by arming themselves and shooting at the machine breakers. But the Luddites had no national organization, and before the riots could spread further, the British government of the time swung into action, brutally quashing them. Throughout 1812, 12,000 troops were deployed to this end. That same year, the Frame Breaking Act 1812 made the rioters' offence punishable with the death penalty under the law. A show trial followed in York in

January 1813, where, out of the sixty men charged, several were executed or punished by penal transportation. Although sporadic instances continued to take place, the Luddites had no way of stopping the deployment of labour-displacing technologies.[1]

But fifty years after the last Luddite act of opposition, their struggle finally found a voice—and with it, lasting political and intellectual legitimacy. Today, Karl Marx is most popularly known for *The Communist Manifesto*,[2] which he co-wrote with Friedrich Engels and which was published in 1848, and the monumental *Capital*, published in 1867. But between these two milestones, i.e., between 1857 and 1858, Marx filled in seven notebooks with dense, upwardly sloping written text, a labyrinthine manuscript over 800 pages long, which he titled *Grundrisse*—in English, *Outlines of the Critique of Political Economy*. It was here, in the chapter on 'Capital', that he first examined the phenomenon of technological unemployment. In his vision, as larger industries continued to develop, creation of wealth would depend progressively less on the time that workers put in and more on the progress of technology and its application in production. Naturally, this would lead to a severe imbalance between labour and the capital-intensive process of production.[3]

The logical end point of this would be ominous. From being the chief agent of production, the worker would become an overseer, or worse, a mere bystander. Neither his effort nor his time would be relevant to production and wealth, which was now appropriated by technology and capital. In Marx's formulation, this trait of capitalism would prove to be self-consuming and eventually lead to its downfall. As labour continued to be marginalized, wealth and capital would come to be concentrated in the hands of ever fewer capitalists, till a point came when labour's share in the production process came down to zero. At this juncture, with labour having no purchasing power, goods and commodities would cease to have any exchange value or price, and capitalism as a superstructure would collapse.

Through all the great turbulence and wars in the first half of the twentieth century, Marxism survived—in fact, thrived, in intellectual circles as well as practice on the ground. As the Cold War deepened through the 1950s and 1960s, Marxist thinking became the dominant mode of intellectual opposition to the capitalist system, led, ironically, by scholars living in the heart of the Western capitalist societies. One of the most influential books to critique the burgeoning capitalist miracle of the 1960s was Herbert Marcuse's *One-Dimensional Man: Studies in the ideology of advanced industrial society*, published in 1964. Marcuse described the prevalent human condition as one where the individual was being continuously subjected to a new kind of totalitarianism. Man was being swallowed up by the apparatus of consumerism and mass media, but so subtly and imperceptibly that he himself was unaware of it, or at any rate helpless to change it. This new system was itself a form of oppression, which not only denied the possibility of change but also all contradiction, dissidence, protest and, finally, the spirit of inquiry, for any free-thinking individual.

According to Marcuse, man was reduced to being 'one dimensional' because he no longer bore any trace of imagination and the questions, contradictions and conflicts that made him multi-dimensional. True to his Marxist allegiance, Marcuse called for forms of resistance that radically opposed the dominant capitalist system. He maintained that Western democracies in the 1960s were not genuinely democratic because their people had been prevented, craftily, from thinking critically, and instead coaxed into making choices that always remained within the control of the system.

Particularly interesting in today's context was his vision for a mechanized, automated future workplace. Marcuse envisaged rapid establishment-robotization. He felt that underlying all things mass-produced, from nuclear weapons and space satellites to automobiles and TV dinners, was a level of technological maturity capable of liberating the world from poverty and misery. However, instead of liberating the worker, factory owners would use technology to produce more with progressively fewer workers, with those same displaced workers wooed by advertising to buy up the very same products that they no longer made by hand. In his gloomy prognosis: 'The negative features of automation are predominant: speed-up, technological unemployment, strengthening of the position of management, increasing impotence and resignation on the part of the workers. The chances of promotion decline as management prefers engineers and college graduates [over low-skilled wage earners].'[4]

Marxist intellectuals and academics were by no means the only ones studying this problem. The same year that Marcuse published *One-Dimensional Man*, the ILO held a conference in Geneva, producing a publication under the title *Employment Problems of Automation and Advanced Technology: An International Perspective*. In Chapter 6 of that document, 'Perspectives of Employment Under Technical Change', author Otto Eckstein expressed his apprehensions about the effects of automation in mechanized environments. In his analysis, semi-skilled workers were the ones most at risk from automation. He identified mass-production industries, such as automobile, meat-packing and rubber, as well as continuous-process industries, e.g., steel, chemicals and petroleum refining, as areas where the brunt of labour displacement would be felt. When semi-skilled workers in these sectors lose their jobs, Eckstein noted, it was often a year or longer before they secured employment again, sometimes at a pay cut of 40 per cent. This was due to the fact that the skills they had acquired in their earlier assembly lines had very little transferable value. There would, the author predicted, be many plants closing and partial layoffs.[5]

Three decades on, Jeremy Rifkin's *The End of Work*, published in 1995, sounded a similar clarion call against impending mass-scale displacement of labour by technology, which would send us hurtling into widespread global unemployment. Rifkin's thesis was that unlike the two earlier industrial revolutions where technologies replaced human labour, the third revolution (the information age), focused on developing computer-based technologies that operated as thinking machines. Parallel processing, artificial intelligence and robots would make a large number of white-collar workers redundant. For Rifkin, '. . . computers that can understand speech, read script, and perform tasks previously carried out by human beings foreshadow a new era in which service industries come increasingly under the domain of automation'. Rifkin's solutions included a thirty-hour week, wherein employees would take a small pay cut but do only 75 per cent of the work they did earlier. Some of their 'free time' could be invested in volunteering for childcare, hospitals, churches and other initiatives in the social sector. The government could encourage such activities by offering a 'shadow wage' or compensation in the form of a deduction on income taxes for volunteer hours.[6]

In more recent years, the books by Silicon Valley computer engineer Martin Ford have captured the public imagination. The first of these, *The Lights in the Tunnel: Automation, Accelerating Technology and the Economy of the Future*, published in 2009, asked two fundamental questions. What will the economy of the future look like? And, where will advancing technology, job automation, outsourcing and globalization lead? Ford employed an interesting thought experiment: an imaginary 'tunnel of lights' to visualize the emergent ecosystem. New lights turning on represented new sectors and jobs, and the ones being extinguished represented jobs supplanted by technology. The rapid darkening of the tunnel over time, in his experiment, was a clear indication of how accelerating technology would disrupt the economy. Ford's main purpose was to highlight the dangers of rapidly advancing technology and stress on the need for countering such exigencies through far-sighted planning and inclusive public policy.

His subsequent book, *Rise of the Robots: Technology and the Threat of a Jobless Future*, published in 2015, takes the argument further. Here he stated that globalization, the decline of unions and the capture of government by special interests had collectively contributed to a rise in economic inequality, and that a broken political system would be unable to fix the problem. The usual prescription of enhancing education to keep workers ahead of robots and automation didn't impress him. Such an approach was bound to be self-defeating, according to Ford, since it would mean ever larger numbers of people fighting for ever-smaller numbers of jobs. In the pyramid of skilled jobs, there was a physical limit to how far the base could be expanded, and scant space at the top. Ford insisted on the need for a fundamental restructuring of the current economic rules. The villain of the piece was a rather pernicious twenty-first-century capitalism, intent on multiplying profits and surplus, concentrating the proceeds in the hands of a shrinking minority, to the point of self-destruction.[7]

Not everyone shares the somewhat dystopian future that the Pessimists paint. We now view the rosier portraits of the future, moving on to our sketch of the Optimists.

In 2005, when American inventor Ray Kurzweil published *The Singularity Is Near*, much of its contents read like science fiction. Singularity, according to Kurzweil, was the imminent point in the future when the pace of technological change would be so rapid, its impact so deep, that human life would be irreversibly transformed. At this juncture, the boundary between human and machine, biological and non-biological, would dissolve. By 2025, he predicted, humans would create machines smarter than themselves. Machines would be able to learn and improve by themselves, speeding up the rate of change further. Besides IT and neuroscience, three fields would lead in bringing about such a singularity: genetics, nanotechnology and robotics (GNR). Doctors would be able to make repairs to the body such as reversing predisposition towards heart disease. Eventually, nanotechnology would enable people to redesign their bodies completely. Immortality would be within one's grasp.

Kurzweil's solution to poverty, hunger and lack of healthcare was likewise infused with optimism. Through cloning, scientists would develop mass-scale disease-resistant plants and animals for distribution to people in need. Meat would also be cloned. Raw materials that speeded up manufacturing, slashing transportation and power costs, would be created. As all mechanical processes became more efficient, energy transmission would improve via the use of carbon nanotubes, and energy storage would become more sophisticated. Energy use would plummet, and manufacturing would not only become energy-neutral but even generate energy, not just products. However, the question of creation of new jobs in this emergent economy, or the steps that could be taken to counter technological unemployment, was not an area of focus in his book.[8]

Six years later, in 2011, author and fellow optimist Michio Kaku, professor of theoretical physics at the City University of New York and doyen of the string field theory, published his *Physics of the Future*. By this time research labs had created humanoid robots that could walk and talk but could not navigate around furniture. Kaku's work was a synthesis of interviews of leading scientists in various fields of research, and his own insights. The common opinion that emerged was that AI would perform sluggishly. Computers of the future would still lack common sense and more evolved sensibilities, allowing humans to continue to handle creative and analytical tasks. Kaku's interviewees laid great stress on electronic, computational and nanotechnological advances: from internet-enabled contact lenses, ubiquitous computer screens connected to the internet, facial and name recognition, unmanned vehicles that consume little fuel and electromagnetic vehicles that didn't touch the ground or rails.[9] While Kaku enumerated the means by which life in the future would get better, he didn't directly address the question of unemployment.

Experts have predicted that by 2050, cyberspace and the physical world would merge, and by 2100 scientists would discover how to slow down or even reverse the process of ageing, life spans reaching 150. The use of nanotechnology would extend to manufacturing; common devices could be shrunk or expanded at will. Manufacturers could craft 'claytronic atoms' or computer chips the size of a grain of sand. Metal would become as supple as clay. The very rubric of consumer behaviour would change, users preferring to purchase software to upgrade existing products instead of repeatedly buying new products.

A quick aside on the rate of technological change: through the second half of the twentieth century, Moore's Law stood as a kind of truism, as a descriptor and also as an index of technological progress. Gordon Moore, founder of Intel, noticed in 1965 that the number of transistors on integrated circuits was doubling roughly every two years. Generalizing from this, Moore's Law says that we can expect the speed and capabilities of our computers to double every couple of years, while costs would remain the same or even decrease. For forty years, this prediction has held.

In *Abundance: The Future Is Better than You Think*, published in 2012, serial entrepreneur and CEO of XPRIZE, Peter Diamandis, and bestselling journalist and author Steven Kotler argued that the phenomenon of 'convergence' witnessed in recent times had disrupted Moore's Law, exponentially speeding up the rate and scale of technological change. The 'technological shock waves' would bring multiple benefits, including time savings, easier access to capital through avenues such as crowdfunding, a shift towards more demonetized ways of doing business, new business models, an explosion in the platforms and quantum of information exchange, and increase of the human life span to well over 100 years.

For Diamandis and Kotler, in the future, technology would help humanity deal with the planet's biggest challenges, primarily environmental, including climate change, species extinction and access to clean water. Threats might also emerge from technology that humanity cannot control. Picture nanotechnology running wild, genetically modified organisms taking over ecosystems. In their view, humanity must bolster its capacity for long-term thinking with three elements: a clear-sighted long-term vision, planning ahead for preventive measures, and a highly focused and concerted ecosystem of governance across the globe.[10]

The premise of Steven Kotler's 2015 book *Tomorrowland: Our Journey from Science Fiction to Science Fact*, closely echoes the ethos of Yuval Noah Harari's *Homo Deus*. The era of Homo Sapiens, as we knew it over the ages, is drawing to a close, through the many ways in which science and technology are fundamentally altering our bodies—bionic soldiers, conscious bringing about of epigenetic change, stem cell research, use of steroids and psychedelic drugs to prolong life, engaging of a synthetic-biology (synbio) community to preempt synbio-based terrorist attacks, use of genetics to combat disease—malaria, dengue, cancer and HIV—which, combined, claim millions of lives each year. Safe reactors could herald a 'backyard nuke' revolution, bringing up to 300 megawatts of clean power to remote sites. Humans might even be able to mine asteroids for precious metals such as gold and platinum. For Kotler, technology isn't itself the Master, but rather the promise of hope and possibilities that it brings.[11]

Predicting the technological advances of the future isn't exclusively a twenty-first-century phenomenon. Jules Verne's second novel, *Paris in the Twentieth Century*, written in 1863 but not discovered until 1994, contains a host of prescient images. Though Verne was critical of the so-called progress of human civilization, he envisaged an explosion in suburban living, the shopping culture, mass-scale higher education, working women, synthesizer-driven electronic music with a recording industry to sell it, metropolises of elevator-equipped skyscrapers, electrically illuminated all-night, gas-powered cars and service stations, subways, magnetically propelled trains, fax machines, a communication system not unlike the internet, the electric chair and weapons of mass destruction.[12]

Adam Smith (1723–1790), considered the father of economics, was of the firm belief that self-interested individuals doing business with each other would nevertheless bring about economically and socially beneficial outcomes, guided by what he termed the 'invisible hand', a metaphor for market forces. This has often been used to argue that governments should leave their populace alone to transact business among themselves. This theory influenced thinkers of successive generations, among them the French economist and businessman Jean-Baptiste Say (1767–1832). Say postulated that production of a good indicates that there is demand for it, which in turn generates demand for other commodities. Famously summarized by Keynes as 'supply creates its own demand', it seems to suggest that supply of different types of labour should be matched by a demand for them. By corollary, an economy would be close to full employment most of the time. Any unemployment that existed would be temporary and not structural, and indeed could be exacerbated by a government's tinkering with its economy.[13]

It is true that there are critical differences between the eighteenth-century Optimist-economists and their modern-day successors. For one, in discussions on tax concessions, cost reductions and public policy, modern-day Optimists, unlike Adam Smith and Jean-Baptiste Say (keeping in mind that they themselves had more nuanced views) with their laissez-faire prescriptions, underscore both governments' responsibilities and accountability towards the well-being of their citizens. But with regard to their general spirit and the conviction, undaunted by floods, wars and pestilence, that 'things will work out fine', there is a fairly unbroken intellectual tradition between these two lots of economists.

Our purpose here has been to present the debate objectively. The Pessimists focus their attention on displacement of jobs because of technology. Their underlying assumption is that the overall employment market is stagnant, if not shrinking— an assumption that may not hold for sectors witnessing unprecedented growth and increased demand for human workers, not just for robots and technology. The Optimists, on the other hand, advocate technology as a 'good' in itself, expounding on the ease and the comforts it brings to life, in general. This overlooks the frictions inherent in technology-driven unemployment, whatever its scale, and the psychological impact of gadgetization and technology-led operations, e.g., alienation, lack of self-worth, apathy and dejection.

ALARM BELLS AND EXIGENCIES

Serious research-based projections of the impact of technology in general, and of computerization in particular, on employment, have been around in the West for over a decade. In 2013, Oxford University researchers Carl Benedikt Frey and Michael Osborne undertook a study to examine how susceptible jobs were to computerization, taking the US as their arena. Their approach was not to arrive at absolute numbers but to estimate the likelihood of computerization of 702 well-documented occupations in the US, categorizing them into high-, medium- and low-risk occupations. Their findings, published in what was to become a much-cited paper since—'The Future of Employment: How Susceptible Are Jobs to Computerisation?'—were nothing short of dramatic.[14]

According to their estimates, 47 per cent of all jobs in the US were in the high-risk category, i.e., those that could be replaced by automation in the next decade or two. Most workers in transportation and logistics, the bulk of office and administrative personnel, and workers in production, were all at risk. A substantial share of jobs in service occupations, where the most growth in jobs in the US had occurred through the past decades, were also highly susceptible to computerization. The study also provided evidence that wages and educational attainment exhibited a strong negative correlation with the likelihood of computerization. The implication is unambiguous: as technology disruptions continued, low-skill workers would need reallocation to jobs less susceptible to computerization, for instance, those requiring creative and social intelligence. Such a shift would only be successful if these workers were able to acquire the required creative and social skills. The emergent skills of the future are examined in detail, in Chapter Three of this book.

When it came to addressing the same question in India, alarm bells began ringing in earnest in the early months of 2017. The trigger was a report by the consulting firm McKinsey & Company, estimating that a total of 6,00,000 (6 lakh) people working in IT services firms across the country might lose their jobs by the end of 2020,[15] averaging an alarming 2 lakh jobs lost per year, to automation. McKinsey urged IT companies to explore new hybrid models of man-and-machine working, and reskilling of employees with emerging technologies. The report sent shock waves throughout the economy. Analysts were quick to point out that the real impact on employment would be far more debilitating than what these bare figures indicated, given that some of the people displaced would become permanently unemployed. According to industry estimates in vogue at this time, 30 per cent to 40 per cent of the current workforce could not be readily reskilled.

If industry leaders and think tank analysts were praying for a silver lining, their hopes were soon to be dashed. McKinsey's prediction was supported by a report published only a few months later, by US-based research firm HFS Research. Their analysis included the once-flourishing BPO sector and IT, and considered a slightly larger time scale. According to HFS, a total of 7,50,000 'low-skilled' professionals across both these sectors in India could lose their jobs to automation and AI by 2022. The agency posited, though, that during this same period, 3,00,000 new mid-to-high-skilled jobs would be created in India.[16]

More grim news was to follow. Whereas McKinsey and HFS had focused on IT and BPO, the results of a third report, published by TeamLease, spelt retrenchment doom for India's manufacturing sector. Their survey-based analysis found that the routine and repetitive processes employed in the sector made the jobs in it relatively simple to automate, which would lead to displacement of assembly-line workers. According to them, as much as a third of the total existing workforce in the sector was at risk of being replaced by automated processes or technology within three years. A case in point was the textile major, Raymond. Between 2017 and 2020, the company was planning to cut 10,000 of its 30,000 personnel across sixteen manufacturing plants, replacing them with robots and advanced technology. The media erupted over this news. For journalists and industry leaders claiming that the figures seemed quite unrealistic, there was a simple answer. Between 2000 and 2010, the US manufacturing sector lost 5.6 million jobs—a matter of indisputable, recorded fact, not a projection. Why was it so inconceivable, then, that the Indian experience would be very different?[17]

There is one fundamental challenge in trying to gauge the extent to which these projections were borne out by live data on the ground in 2020–2022. The effects of the COVID-19 pandemic and its immediate aftermath have been so drastic that any notion of 'things continuing as per their existing course' has become meaningless. Statistical projections and models such as the ones reviewed did not take into account the possibility of massive and unexpected systemic shocks. In statistical language, a structural break has occurred, rendering the earlier forecasting prone to large errors. Over time, one may be able to forecast a new trend, but at this present moment we can only make certain informed conjectures.

Taking IT as an illustration, we see that multiple forces have been at work. There's the employment reduction that might have occurred through technological advances and automation, even without the pandemic. However, the pandemic has hastened and deepened the use of labour-supplanting business processes and technology and has increased demand for new technological skills in the sector. Disentangling the temporary from the permanent is problematic.

Macroeconomically, in April 2020, unemployment across India had peaked to 23.5 per cent and remained at 21.7 per cent even the following month, thereafter falling sharply to 10.18 per cent; and while it has fluctuated, it showed a slow downward trend all through mid-2021. The unemployment rate, overall, for 2020 was 7.11 per cent, a steep rise from 5.27 per cent in 2019, according to the Centre for Monitoring Indian Economy (CMIE) and a report by Centre for Economic Data and Analysis (CEDA) based on the ILOSTAT database of ILO. To go further back in time, India saw its unemployment rate rise between 2008, when it was 5.36 per cent, and 2010, when it became 5.65 per cent. It maintained a downward trend between 2013 and 2019, when it came down from 5.67 per cent to 5.27 per cent. But the nation witnessed the toughest lockdown globally, starting in March 2020, with highly stringent restrictions on mobility and economic activity,[18] sending unemployment soaring.

This staggering rate of unemployment could be broken down under the following heads: jobs lost in the MSME and informal sectors, mass-scale retrenchment in the organized sector, and the almost complete freeze in recruitment by companies across the board. Clearly, all these factors are traceable to a single cause—the COVID-19 pandemic. Conversely, the biggest trigger for economic recovery would have been indications that either the worst phase of the pandemic was behind us, or that the authorities, industry and civic society were collectively better prepared to tackle future outbreaks of the virus. This was as much a matter of genuine economic performance as of public sentiment—the perception that a phased opening-up of the economy would occur, from essential services, from essential services to shops and establishments, places of entertainment and worship, and finally, local trains, schools and colleges.

In September 2021, TeamLease EdTech published a report focusing on the propensity of employers to hire freshers. Culling data from July to December 2021 across eighteen sectors and fourteen cities, their paper indicated that 17 per cent of employers surveyed were keen to hire freshers through the course of the financial year 2021. Pitted against the estimated global hiring rate of freshers, which was a mere 6 per cent, this relatively rosy projection once again made scribes and experts spout superlatives about the Indian economy.[19]

The drastic break from the past forced upon the economy by the pandemic certainly makes it more difficult to disentangle the precise apportionment of unemployment witnessed throughout the period to its constituent factors.[20] But the hastening in the use of capital or technology-intensive processes has brought into sharper relief some typical myths around modes, factors and impacts of technological change at the workplace. Why do these misconceptions still exist? For all of us, the experience of the protracted pandemic period has been nothing short of traumatic, in both the personal and professional spheres. On the work front, regardless of the appellation we choose—Next Normal/ Emergent Workplace—there is a need for the mind to return to a semblance of stability, order and predictability. And in searching for even a proxy for normalcy, it is natural and easier to converge to the memory of things and ideas prior to the pandemic, which indicate a state of relative stability, rather than hypothesize about the future. Nevertheless, they are myths in the post-pandemic paradigm, and we'd do well to dispel them.

1. **In the workplace, work = permanent jobs.** In India, many companies still tend to view workers as only those employees

who are on their permanent payroll, whereas in the UK and US, for several years, there has been a definite shift towards a 'gig economy'. Here, individuals pursue several alternative modes of earning concurrently from multiple organizations, on a retainership or freelance basis. The contract and 'temp' mode of working, already mature in advanced economies, was further accelerated by the pandemic.

According to experts, this is the natural progression of how careers will come to be shaped, even in India. Abhijit Bhaduri, leadership coach and author, has a term for this—Career 3.0. Career 1.0 took place as professionals discovered the freedom to change employers, but typically still restricted themselves to their own sector or industry. As opportunities opened up, Career 2.0 came into being. Workers would change jobs or even professions, moving beyond their initial domains or sectors, bankers turning authors, marketing and technical specialists turning entrepreneurs, and so on. Career 3.0, in comparison, according to Bhaduri, will be about the bulk of the workforce becoming gig workers and operating outside the payroll of an employer. This multi-skilled workforce, approaching multiple buyers, would be paid at different rates depending on their level of proficiency.[21] Career 3.0 will require a suite of behavioural skills that are quite distinct from what earlier career avatars demanded. This is a topic we examine in the subsequent chapters.

2. **Retrenchment in any sector is primarily caused by automation**. This too, as we have already seen, is a specious argument. A slowdown in the market, leading to a recruitment freeze and retrenchment in companies, sometimes has little to do with automation. During the pre-pandemic period, a slowdown did happen, but that had more to do with geopolitical factors, such as restrictions on offshoring, restrictions on H1B visas and protectionist

measures in the US and other advanced economies. As these conditions relax, the demand for people will pick up. This has happened time and again. The COVID-19 pandemic that has ravaged the world from the first quarter of March 2020 onwards, has permanently put paid to any lingering doubts that automation is the only or even primary source of mass-scale unemployment.

3. **Impact of automation and AI is limited to the IT sector.** This is a legacy of the 2017 McKinsey report. While it's true that the IT sector will continue to be affected by automation, it is by no means the only sector that will be affected. There are irrefutable signs that skills such as assessment of reports, filing of documents, financial accounting and bookkeeping, and those required in customer service, call centres and help desks, as well as general administration, may all fall in demand in the future, under the anvil of automation.

4. **Only workers with low-skilled, repetitive jobs are at risk.** While the impact on those at the base of the workplace pyramid is most noticeable, they're not the only ones at risk. Fewer staff means fewer managers to oversee them. With advances in the analytical ability of machines, computers and machine-based reasoning, fewer analysts are needed to sift through and interpret large volumes of data. Our traditional hierarchy of managers and junior personnel might undergo a huge implosion, giving rise to a fresh set of questions and challenges. Erstwhile managers across industries would need to revisit their core competencies and ascertain how best to put them to use in the emergent workplace.

5. **The only emergent skills in demand are technical.** Technical skills are only one piece of the bigger picture. The World Economic Forum Future of Jobs 2020 report

shows that two distinct streams of skills and attributes are coming into greater demand as automation deepens across industries. Jobs involving a high degree of mathematical and technical ability will be limited in number compared to the scope for programmers and testers in the earlier ecosystem. Also, professionals are limited in their ability to upskill themselves suitably to the required level, in the emergent workplace. At the same time, there's a growing need for a range of skills along the human dimension, including creativity, imagination, innovation, design thinking and, increasingly, empathy. Expertise in these attributes greatly increases the chances of sustained work for individuals, even in a largely automated workplace.

EMPLOYMENT TRENDS IN INDIA AND COVID-19[22]

In this section, we take a step back from the question of the technological impact on employment to explore the effect of the COVID-19 pandemic on employment, with a focus on India. We shall begin with the urban sector, along with the caveat that the data from the main source used here—the Periodic Labour Force Survey (PLFS)—comes with a lag. The quarterly PLFS urban sector data dates from March 2021, and the annual PLFS data from 2019–20. Additional indicators, e.g., subscriptions to the Employees' Provident Fund Organization (EPFO) scheme and demand for work under MGNREGA, have been included for analysis of the employment situation across urban and rural sectors. Labour force participation rate (LFPR) is defined as the percentage of population in the labour force. The labour force comprises persons who were either working (employed) or seeking work (unemployed). Worker population ratio (WPR) is defined as the percentage of employed persons in the total population. Unemployment rates (UR) is defined as the percentage of unemployed persons in the labour force.

Prior to the COVID-19 pandemic, the urban labour market had shown signs of improvement in terms of LFPR, WPR and UR. However, the nationwide lockdown imposed in late March 2020 had a severe adverse impact on the urban labour market. In the first quarter of 2020–21, the unemployment rate for the urban sector rose to 20.8 per cent. The LFPR and WPR for the urban sector also declined significantly during this quarter, as seen from the table below, which is based on quarterly PLFS data.

Table 2.1: Labour Market Indicators for Urban Sector (Age: 15 & above) at CWS, as Percentage

Survey Year	Quarters	LFPR	WPR	UR
2019–20	July–Sept. 2019	47.3	43.4	8.3
	Oct–Dec. 2019	47.8	44.1	7.8
	Jan–March 2020	48.1	43.7	9.1
	April–June 2020	45.9	36.4	20.8
2020–21	July–Sept. 2020	47.2	40.9	13.2
	Oct–Dec. 2020	47.3	42.4	10.3
	Jan–March, 2021	47.5	43.1	9.3

Source: Taken from the Periodic Labour Force Survey (PLFS), 2019–20 and 2020–21

As the economy showed signs of revival in the subsequent quarters of 2020–21, all three labour market indicators showed recovery. The UR gradually declined during this period, to touch 9.3 per cent in Q4 of 2020–21. The UR for males as well as females, aged fifteen and above, recovered to the pre-pandemic levels. Both LFPR and WPR for males as well as females, aged fifteen and above, neared their pre-pandemic levels during Q4 of 2020–21.

We now move on to some of the key PLFS annual data. Between 2018–19 and 2019–20, around 4.75 crore additional workers had joined the workforce, three times more than the number of jobs created between 2017–18 and 2018–19. The rural sector, adding 3.45 crore people, contributed to this expansion in a major way, relative to the urban sector, where the incremental workforce was 1.30 crore. Of the new entrants, 2.99 crore were females (63 per cent), while about 65 per cent of those who joined in 2019–20 were self-employed. A massive 75 per cent of female workers who joined as self-employed constituted 'unpaid family labour', while 18 per cent of the new entrants were 'casual labourers' and another 17 per cent 'regular wage/salaried employees'. Further, the number of unemployed persons in 2019–20 also decreased, by 23 lakhs, constituting largely males from the rural sector.

Although not very recent, PLFS data gives us a good idea of formal vs. informal employment as it was developing across both the organized and unorganized sectors in the period leading up to the pandemic. Of the additional workers who joined in 2019–20, close to 90 per cent were in the informal nature of employment, and more than 98 per cent were in the unorganized sector. About 91 per cent of the additional workers were in the unorganized informal sector.

Table 2.2: Formal-Informal Employment across Organized and Unorganized Sectors (in crores)

Type of Employment	Organized	Unorganized	Total
2017–18			
Formal	4.43	0.28	4.70
Informal	4.62	37.79	42.43
Total	9.05	38.07	47.13
2018–19			
Formal	4.91	0.45	5.35
Informal	4.55	38.87	43.43
Total	9.46	39.32	48.78
2019–20			
Formal	5.09	0.80	5.89
Informal	4.46	43.19	47.64
Total	9.55	43.99	53.53

Source: Periodic Labour Force Survey (PLFS)

The data on industry-wise employment for the same period shows that out of the workers added in 2019–20, more than 71 per cent were in the agriculture sector. Among these new workers, females accounted for a good 65 per cent. The trade, hotel and restaurant sector accounted for a little over 22 per cent of the new workers, in line with the previous year's trend, where the sector represented more than 28 per cent of the new workers. As we know, this sector was to be among the worst affected as a result of the pandemic. The share of manufacturing in 2019–20, compared to the previous year, showed a decline—from 5.65 per cent of new workers added in 2018–19 to about

2.41 per cent added in 2019–20. Construction, too, recorded a decline, from 26.26 per cent to 7.36 per cent.

Next, we consider the data from EPFO, covering workers in medium and large enterprises in the organized sector. The net addition in EPFO subscriptions indicates the extent of formalization of the job market, with social security benefits accruing to its workforce. This figure turned negative in April–May 2020, indicating a net exit from the scheme. With the easing of restrictions, the subscriptions recovered, touching 12.2 lakh in September 2020. There was a decline again, during the second wave of COVID-19 (April–June 2021), though less in magnitude than that witnessed during April–May 2020. More recently, the net addition in EPF subscribers reached 13.95 lakh in November 2021, showing a 109.21 per cent growth from November 2020, and in fact higher than even the corresponding months in 2019, the year before the pandemic. This points to formalization of the job market as well as new hiring.

To conclude this section, we take a brief look at the findings from the data under the Mahatma Gandhi National Rural Employment Guarantee Scheme (MGNREGS), an indicator of rural labour markets. The MGNREGS data suggests the following:

i.   MGNREGS employment peaked during the nationwide lockdown in 2020
ii. The demand for MGNREGS work has stabilized after the second COVID wave
iii. Aggregate MGNREGS employment is still higher than the pre-pandemic level

During the nationwide lockdown, the overall demand for MGNREGS work across the economy peaked in June 2020 and has stabilized since. During the second COVID-19 wave, the demand for MGNREGS employment reached the maximum level of 4.59 crore persons in June 2021. At the time when this chapter was being revised, in July 2022, the demand for MGNREGS work at an aggregate level still appeared to be above the pre-pandemic levels of 2019, though for a few states, e.g., Andhra Pradesh and Bihar, the demand had reduced to below pre-pandemic levels.

We will now resume our discussion of the big technology-specific questions.

ARE WE HEADING TOWARDS A 'TECHNOLOGICAL WATERWORLD'?

The term 'Technological Waterworld', as we've coined it, has dual allusions. The first is a nod to Hollywood, to the 1995 post-apocalyptic film *Waterworld*, starring Kevin Costner. In distant 2500, sea levels have risen over 8000 metres and every continent on the planet is submerged. Human civilization is reduced to a few clusters of individuals who live in makeshift floating communities known as atolls, with no living memory of life on land. There is, however, widespread belief in the myth of a 'Dryland' existing somewhere in the ocean, and there is a relentless quest to find it.

Our second, and deeper, allusion is to the way MIT scientist and author Max Tegmark has characterized the growing imprint of computer advancements into areas of core human abilities in his book, *Life 3.0: Being Human in the Age of Artificial Intelligence*, published in 2017. Drawing from the metaphor of Hans Moravec, it illustrates a landscape of human competencies, complete with seas and bays, lowlands, plains, valleys and snow-peaked mountains. The competencies in the sea are those where computers have firmly overshadowed human abilities, the lowlands are areas being taken over, computers surpassing human intelligence, and the peaks are the deeply creative or intuitive skills that largely remain in the human domain. The technological sea level is rising continuously, and as time passes the speed at which it rises also increases.[23]

According to Tegmark, somewhere along the inexorable technological sea-level rise is a tipping point. Up until then, humans improve machines. Beyond it, with machines learning, improving and reinventing themselves, their pace of progress is exponential—and we're in the realm of Singularity. We shall see that Tegmark's illustration is no elevated intellectual exercise but a reality where AI, automation and robots are playing an increasing part across sectors in India in the post-COVID-19 scenario. Besides, even today there exists technology that can submerge the mountain peaks of human ability in many areas.

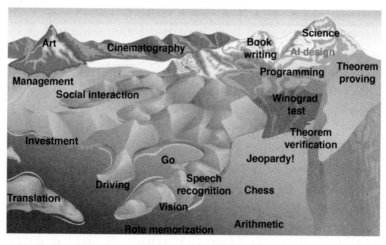

Source: Illustration by Max Tegmark of Hans Moravec's 'landscape of human competence', where elevation represents difficulty for computers, and the rising sea level represents what computers are able to do. Max Tegmark, 'Chapter 2', *Life 3.0: Being Human in the Age of Artificial Intelligence*, Vintage, 2018

A PwC analysis published in 2018, after studying the impact of AI across industries and user groups, concluded that AI in India was no mere hype but a soon-to-be-lived-in reality. The study surveyed both business stakeholders and employees, the responses across the two cohorts presenting an interesting contrast. A high 68 per cent of stakeholders felt AI would help businesses by boosting productivity and generating growth, outweighing employment concerns. In comparison, 60 per cent of employees felt that AI would reduce the time it takes to get answers to routine work-related queries, and a substantial 45 per cent expressed fears about job losses. The study also examined the respondents' views on AI Adviser across a range of managerial tasks. While 75 per cent of stakeholders felt they could rely on AI for effective and unbiased decision-making, an even higher 85 per cent still preferred to meet a fellow human for feedback, reviews and recommendations for promotion.[24]

We now present a snapshot of the tremendous pace of technology-driven innovations, globally and in India, across six key sectors.

MANUFACTURING

For decades, the shift towards automation has been pronounced in the manufacturing sector, from heavy engineering and automobiles to electronics and computer-aided production of garments. The diminished demand for goods and the periods of factory shutdown during the pandemic have further accelerated this trend, globally as well as in India, as automation saves on fixed labour costs when labour demand is low. Customization of product design, product development, optimization of logistics and the use of 'digital twins'—or online, digital avatars of physical persons—are the biggest areas of technology adoption. The following table provides a sketch of some of the key areas of usage of automation internationally, which sooner rather than later are likely to be replicated in India.[25]

Table 2.3: Examples of Technology Innovation in Manufacturing

Application	Features & Functionality
AI-powered equipment failure prevention	An example is Schneider Electric, which uses Microsoft's Azure ML platform to monitor and configure oil pump settings remotely. Anomalies in temperature and pressure are flagged as potential issues, to prevent failure.
Deep learning-powered quality control	By integrating high optical resolution cameras and GPUs with image classification, object detection and instance segmentation algorithms, data engineers create a precise AI-enabled inspection system to detect manufacturing defects, obviating the need for human intervention. Examples include Google Cloud ML Engine and Amazon ML.
Deep learning-driven product design	All feasible product design options are created by a deep learning model, using attributes such as weight, size and materials. The most suitable design is selected and put into production. General Motors, along with Autodesk, created a seat belt bracket prototype, 40 per cent lighter and 20 per cent stronger than the existing one by this means.
Smart energy consumption	ML models predict future energy consumption by processing and analysing historical data. This provides a deeper understanding of energy consumption at facilities and optimizes manufacturing processes. For example, Swiss Corporation, ABB, offers manufacturers an AI-driven platform to minimize peak-time energy costs.

HEALTHCARE

Here, technological advancement in areas such as robotic or computer-aided surgery has been flourishing not just globally but in India too, for decades. To cite only a couple of landmark cases: in 1998, doctors from Escorts Heart Institute and Research Centre (EHIRC) used a robotic arm to fix a hole in a patient's heart, and in 2002, Dr Naresh Trehan at EHIRC deployed a robotic arm equipped with an endoscopic camera which could provide 3D imaging of organs. Since its launch in 2015, IBM has partnered with medical institutes, e.g., Manipal Hospital, to deploy their AI and NLP (natural language processing)-powered bot, Watson. The sector is seeing a host of new solution providers, such as ASIMOV Robotics, Intuitive Surgical and Stryker, gaining eminence. In its 2018 report, think tank NITI Aayog put healthcare at the top of the list of domains that they felt needed focus in AI. The ministry of health and family welfare (MoHFW) had focused on greater digitization of the sector under the aegis of National eHealth Authority (NeHA) and other initiatives, including the Integrated Health Information Program (IHIP), Electronic Health Records Standards for India and MHealth.

The pandemic, which compelled medical and support personnel to become 'COVID warriors' in the fight against the virus, also helped accelerate tech-led innovation around disease detection and diagnostics, patient-facing applications, including touchless diagnostic tools, ventilators, medical and surgical devices, besides process optimization. Robotics, previously limited to complex surgical procedures, took to the ward floors. Delhi's AIIMS (All India Institute of Medical Sciences) began using a humanoid robot to spray floor disinfectant in its COVID-19 wards, while Fortis Hospital, Bengaluru, deployed an interactive robot to screen patients and medical staff entering the premises for the virus.

Despite all the trauma and disruptions of the pandemic, the boost it has provided to technological start-ups in the healthcare sector has been incredible. A comprehensive list of all the organizations in this area and their innovations is beyond our purview. Here, we only provide an anecdotal flavour of the range and scale of advancements taking place. The pace of change being particularly exponential, by the time you're reading this, many of the innovations and offerings listed here may have become dated.[26]

Table 2.4: Examples of Technology Innovation in Healthcare

Start-up	Innovations & Offerings
Niramai Health Analytics	Founded in 2016, Bengaluru-based Niramai focuses on early detection of breast cancer. The company uses AI and thermal analytics in its 'Smile Tool', a real-time cloud-based diagnostics tool for breast cancer screening.
Sigtuple	Founded in 2015, the company provides a data-driven, machine-learnt, cloud-based solution for detecting anomalies and improving the accuracy and efficiency of disease diagnosis. It deploys an ML platform, Manthan, to predict the chances of particular diseases from medical diagnostic images. Its peripheral blood smear analyser solution, Shonit, provides image processing-based solutions for differential blood count and for screening of diseases and conditions such as malaria and anaemia.
Qure.ai	Founded in 2016, Mumbai-based Qure.ai has devised an AI-based clinical decision support tool for analysing diagnostic images and giving insights to the doctor. Its radiology solution can diagnose disease from CT scans, MRIs and X-rays as well as outline and quantify regions of interest, such as tumours or lung disease patterns. The company also offers a digital pathology solution which can distinguish malignant from benign biopsies and grade a variety of tumour types.
TriCog	Founded in 2015, the Bengaluru-based company provides an online platform connecting heart patients and doctors and providers of ECG devices and doctors. Patients can search for doctors with ECG devices in their clinics, and intimate them about their arrival. Doctors get a notification of the bookings and connect to the TriCog network to access the patients' medical history.

Start-up	Innovations & Offerings
Healthplix	The company provides an electronic medical record solution for chronic care management, with features such as e-prescription generation, lab management, billing and dashboards providing AI and machine learning-based insights related to finance, marketing, testing of clinical hypothesis, and tracking of patient records.
Perfint Healthcare	Founded in Chennai in 2005, Perfint Healthcare has developed diagnostic equipment for the oncology space. Its products are Robio EX (CT & PET-CT guided robotic positioning system), Robio EZ (robotic, mobile stand-alone system with 5 DOF for needle placement during CT scan) and Maxio (image-guided, physician-controlled stereotactic accessory device for a CT system). Its image-guided equipment uses medical image processing and robotics to help clinicians plan and execute CT-guided cancer biopsies, drug delivery and ablation of small tumours. Maxio is their FDA 510(k)-approved device, which won the Department of Biology-Biotechnology Industry Research Assistance Council (DBT-BIRAC) Innovation Award in 2012.
Innovaccer	Founded in 2014, with centres in San Francisco and Noida, Innovaccer provides a cloud and AI-based patient health data analytics platform for population health management. The company offers a data activation cloud-based platform to collect, analyse and provide insights on patient health. The company's offerings are InNote, InConnect, InGraph and InCare, with solutions like virtual care networks, remote patient monitoring, social determinants of health (SDOH) management and others. Other offerings include surgery optimization, customer relationship management (CRM) and referral management.
DocTalk	Founded in 2016, the Mumbai-based company offers a virtual assistant programme to streamline the healthcare industry in India. Its app enables patient interactions with their physicians, while medical reports and photos are saved on the cloud.

Start-up	Innovations & Offerings
FitCircle	Founded in Mumbai in 2014, FitCircle provides AI-powered fitness training and diet coaching apps, creating daily workout challenges and enabling users to track their activities through their smartphones. Nutrition advice and meal plans are available based on Ayurvedic concepts, with Zi, its AI-based chatbot, providing advice and feedback on fitness training and nutritional plans.
Wysa	The Bengaluru-based company has crafted an AI-based chatbot for managing mental health. It measures the emotions expressed by the user and uses evidence-based cognitive-behavioural techniques (CBT) and micro-actions to help the user feel better. It uses machine learning to understand the emotional state of the user and proactively reaches out to the user to help as and when required.

BANKING

Throughout the COVID-19 pandemic, banking, like IT, joined the ranks of essential services. The rising incidence of infection among employees forced these sectors to seek ways of working remotely and of ensuring greater safety for their personnel. Robotic process automation (RPA) emerged as the single largest measure of adoption. Worldwide, significant efficiencies have been reported by the sector: consumer loan-processing time slashed by 66 per cent, elimination of data transcription and other errors during the opening of a new account, faster customer verification, more effective fraud detection and prevention, regulatory compliance, and wealth management and mortgage processing. Indian banks have closely mirrored the wide-scale technology adoption witnessed across the globe.[27]

Table 2.5: Illustration of Technology Innovation in Banking

Bank	Features & Functionality
State Bank of India	SBI Intelligent Assistant (SIA), an AI-powered smart chat assistant, developed by Payjo, with a capacity to handle around 10,000 customer inquiries per second.
HDFC	'Eva', a chatbot developed by Bengaluru-based Senseforth AI Research, works with Google Assistant across a range of Android devices and has completed over 5 million user queries (by 2021), with more than 85 per cent accuracy.
ICICI	Software robotics across multiple business processes, addressing 2 million transactions daily, i.e., 20 per cent of its overall volume.
Axis Bank	AXAA, a multilingual IVR system; the bank has also set up an innovation lab to expedite AI solutions for the banking sector.
Bank of Baroda	Assisted Digital Interaction (ADI), AI-based chatbot for customer service; in 2018, the bank had set up an Analytics Centre of Excellence (ACoE).
Andhra Bank	AI interactive assistant, 'ABI Ii', developed by Floatbot, integrated with the Core Banking Servers (CBS) of Andhra Bank, automating customer support for 50 million account holders.
Kotak Mahindra Bank	AI-enabled bilingual chatbot, Keya, integrated with the bank's phone banking helpline service.
YES Bank	Partnered with Gupshup, a bot platform, to launch 'YES mPower'—a banking chatbot for its loan product. Another AI product, YES ROBOT, is equipped to answer consumers' banking-related queries any time, anywhere, without the hassle of their having to wait for on-call or searching online.
IndusInd Bank	'IndusAssist', with Alexa, Amazon's virtual assistant, to conduct financial and non-financial banking transactions.

PROFESSIONAL SERVICES

This includes a wide range of offerings, from IT, BPO and KPO (knowledge process outsourcing) to customer services, learning and development, financial and legal services. But all of these offerings have two things in common. First, they are human-centric and knowledge-based industries. Second, they all generate a huge quantum of management reports, data analytics, compliance and other documentation, significantly more than many other sectors. One of the key ways in which the sector has responded to the pandemic is through the enhanced use of AI and automation. The table below lists a few examples.[28]

Table 2.6: Examples of Technology Innovation in Professional Services

Application	Features & Functionality	Benefits
Review and correction of invoices	Compares invoice text against client billing guidelines and approval procedures, flags issues and discrepancies	Speed, accuracy, time savings
Improving accuracy of financial forecasts	Compares expenses (and earnings) of projects of similar team size, timelines, scope of work and complexity, competitor data and figures from previous years, to arrive at more informed financial forecasts	Realistic project costs and earnings, estimates of legal costs
Spotting irregularities and ensuring compliance	Checks reported figures against norms and guidelines, identifies inconsistencies, categorizes in terms of severity/criticality, and report findings	Risk management, preemption of potential compliance issues, cost savings

Application	Features & Functionality	Benefits
Analysis of legal contracts	Checking of specific instances of a particular issue or problem in a database of cases, identification and tagging of documents that are a fit; interpreting, annotating and presenting results	Time savings, accuracy of findings
Screening and selection during recruitment	Algorithm-based mechanism of matching, screening out and shortlisting candidates, based on hiring guidelines and benchmarks	Better fitment of new hires to company values and culture, expedited recruitment
AI Adviser—role fitment, decision management and promotions	Matching of skills, competencies, attributes and benchmarks required to current scores; evaluation and presenting of recommendations	Better fitment to roles and responsibilities
'Conversational AI'	Digital HR assistants/bots, handling employee queries, walk-through of common processes around benefits, providing updates around employee policies and enterprise-level decisions	Greater accuracy, effort and costs savings
Process mapping and workflow automation	Automate business processes, to minimize time-consuming tasks and eliminate human intervention—useful for customized, non-repeatable tasks as well	Greater accuracy of data, faster business processes, time and costs savings

HOSPITALITY, TRAVEL & TOURISM

Hospitality, travel and tourism have been among the worst affected sectors during the pandemic. Throughout 2020, and beyond, retrenchment and wage cuts have been rife in this industry, and establishments struggled to stay afloat as extended lockdowns and debilitating waves of the virus outbreak ravaged the country, forcing the populace indoors and severely curtailing takeaway and home-delivery orders. The industry has responded through the use of technology to address two major imperatives that emerged as a result of the pandemic: how to provide high quality of service in a contactless and risk-free mode, and how to keep costs to a minimum, without compromising customer experience. The features below illustrate some of the technology-driven solutions that are transforming the sector.[29]

Table 2.7: Examples of Technology Innovations in Hospitality, Travel & Tourism

Application	Features & Functionality	Benefit
Smart rooms and digital concierge	App-based room-unlock, control of room features and appliances, customer service, ordering of meals, payments, experience reviews	Minimized risk of infection, without compromising on service quality
AI-powered housekeeping	Cloud-based platforms of applications, e.g., customer alerts and messaging, task assignment, inspections, room cleaning, interdepartmental communication and reporting	Lower payroll and overheads, improved profitability and guest experience
Travel desk bookings	Billing profile creation through third parties (to ensure payment card industry [PCI] compliance), integrated with online reservation booking and payment	Cost reduction, errors minimized, increased responsiveness
Fraud detection	Customized ML model to predict and detect fraud	Prevention of fraud
Loyalty and sentiment analysis	Analysis of customers' preference for specific loyalty programme features, customized recommendations	Greater customer satisfaction

Application	Features & Functionality	Benefit
Upselling/remarketing	Using previous data to understand purchase behaviour and preferences, personalizing the stay experience and creating new revenue opportunities	Greater customer satisfaction, increased earnings
Various contactless solutions	Non-touch control panels in elevators, digital menus scanned via QR-code, online check-ins	Improved efficiency of operations, better guest experience
Virtual reality tours	App and web-based experience of tours to exotic locations	Safe, albeit vicarious, experience of travel and tourism

LOGISTICS & TRANSPORTATION

The COVID-19 pandemic heightened the need for flexibility, agility and non-human-centric modes of transportation and delivery. Logistics providers across the globe have taken advantage of AI-enabled offerings to transform their businesses. Supply planning, demand forecasting, automated warehousing, accurate inventory management, enhanced safety and reduced costs of operations, warehouse robotics, inspection and damage detection, predictive maintenance, self-driven vehicles, autonomous delivery drones, freight management and automated back-office processing, have emerged as major areas of technology adoption. AI investment and adoption in supply chain management has been highest for retail, followed by telecom and high-tech. The table below sketches some of the advances fast becoming the norm across sectors.[30]

Table 2.8: Examples of Technology Innovation in Logistics and Transportation

Application	Features & Functionality
Neural networks for supply chain management	Use of demand-forecasting methods to optimize logistics processes and routes. The German automotive supplier Continental is a case in point. The company uses an AI-based solution to predict the optimal points for tyre changes for commercial fleets, to optimize the inventory of tyres, increase uptime and reduce maintenance costs.
AI-enabled predictive capabilities	DHL is a preeminent example. The company analyses fifty-eight different parameters of internal data to create a machine learning model for air freight. This allows freight forwarders to predict how the average daily transit time could change, up to a week in advance.
Robotics	The Netherlands-based start-up Fizyr automates logistics globally, through the extensive use of robotics. It incorporates deep learning algorithms into robotics, with autonomous decision-making for identifying, analysing, counting, picking and placing goods. In particular, the company has devised a solution that enables the robot to identify package type—in less than 0.2 seconds—and move the item to the desired location.
Cleansed & big data-based forecasting	Since the sector is complex and dynamic, cleansing of data is as important as the analysis that follows. For instance, when companies have incomplete shipment data, AI algorithms can systematically go through past shipments to create sophisticated estimates about the missing shipment data. UPS, the global leader in package delivery, saves 10 million gallons of fuel annually by optimizing its routes.

Application	Features & Functionality
Computer vision	IBM Watson had earlier been programmed to identify damaged train wagons. When cameras were installed along train tracks to gather images of the wagons, the robot's visual recognition capabilities improved to an accuracy rate of more than 90 per cent. Likewise, Amazon utilizes computer vision systems that can help to unload a trailer of inventory in only thirty minutes against the hours that manual effort takes without using such systems.
Autonomous & electric vehicles	Improved driving systems allow trucks to drive in formation, saving fuel consumption. Vehicles are going electric and enhancing their distance capabilities. Tesla's Semi Truck will be able to drive as far as 800 kilometres on full battery and an additional 600 kilometres with just thirty minutes of charging. Tesla, Einride, Daimler and Volkswagen are all in the process of developing fully autonomous solutions.

An aside on media and communications. We spoke to Deepak Ajwani, editor at the Economic Times online, about the increasing use of emergent technologies in media. He said: 'AI and ML have already stepped in, helping digital media decide the form and character, as well as predicting content choices of readers. AI has also taken over some repetitive tasks being done in operations to help free up time and bandwidth to allow focus on human effort on tasks that matter, and those that require human intelligence. With so much data being made available, future media roles will be more about understanding platforms, decoding reader/viewer and content patterns and their engagement metrics. These roles will be critical to shape content and understand media consumption trends.'[31]

While AI remains the cornerstone of technological advancement for many sectors,[32] many disruptions are led by robotics, which has made huge inroads in India, in terms of both industry and personal use. A survey of the range of robotics deployed across the nation is beyond our purview. What we'll do instead is present a snapshot of the affordable robots available in the Indian market since mid-2021. The examples below are anecdotal (and are no endorsement!), and our usual caveat applies: by the time you're reading this, things would have moved much further afield.[33]

Table 2.9: Examples of Advances in Robotics

Robot/ Company	Function	Area of Usage
DJi RoboMaster S1 (2nd Gen.)	Interactive classroom sessions with robots, for a more exciting learning experience	Education
Penguin Engineering	Order taking and delivery of food and refreshments; other services include washing, cooking and cleaning	Hotels, restaurants, food courts, hospitals
Comp-point Systems Private Limited	Multi-function humanoid robot branded as the 'perfect mate for a naughty child'	Children's entertainment
MarvelMind	Electric-powered motorized device for delivery of goods and products	Warehousing and delivery
iRobot	Robotic vacuum cleaner with cleaning sensors, robotic drives and programmable controls	Floor cleaning
UBTECH/ Lynx	Home applications, e.g., communication via an avatar, remote control of appliances, surveillance and flash updates	Home applications
RH-P12-RN-UR	Robotic hand for welding, gripping, spinning and other associated tasks	Industrial/shop floor

Robot/ Company	Function	Area of Usage
ECHEERS/ Spaceman Robot	Playing music, reading bedtime stories, dancing	Entertainment
Hong RC Intelligent Early Education Electric Robot Dog Toy	Robotic dog equipped with voice recognition, various touch sensors, LED lights, RF sensors and Bluetooth speakers	Children's entertainment

In the next section, we see how purely intuitive and creative abilities, the mountain peaks of talent in the Tegmark–Moravec framework, can be submerged in the imminent future.

THE MASTER OF GO, 'BRUTUS' AND AI REMBRANDTS

In his celebrated novel *The Master of Go*, the Japanese Nobel Laureate Yasunari Kawabata chronicled a championship match of Go, an ancient and traditional board game. Two players take turns, placing black and white stones over a 19 X 19 grid, the winner decided by who controls the most territory. In each move, a player has 200 options, compared to the twenty-odd in chess. In the story, the game takes place in pre-Second World War Japan, between an elderly, frail and clearly ailing aristocrat, Honnimbo Shusai, the 'Master of Go', and a much younger, brash challenger, Otake. The epic contest takes over a year to reach its outcome and entails a schedule of full-day games calling for extreme physical and psychological stress. Neither man has an advantage over the other until very late in the contest, when the Master makes a crucial play that the challenger is able to exploit, defeating him. The Master dies only a few weeks later, his death and the progression of the game itself, in Kawabata's masterly elegy, symbolizing the passing of an era in Japanese culture.[34]

An upset of a different kind occurred in May 2017, when AlphaGo, a computer-generated programme developed by AlphaGo, Google's AI arm, defeated the nineteen-year-old Chinese Go prodigy and world champion, Ke Jie. The AI program had previously defeated several other grand masters, forcing players to learn from and even mimic the unorthodox moves made by it, challenging a tradition going back millennia. AlphaGo's spokesperson viewed this victory as the promise of new technologies to perform complex tasks in the imminent future, from driving cars to drafting legal documents and fuelling the conduct of research on rare or incurable diseases. The event had serious analysts pondering over what to do when computers routinely replaced humans in the workplace. And for the boy genius Ke Jie, the defeat was traumatic. 'Everyone can see from today's match—it actually made no mistakes . . .,' he said shortly after the match. 'It is so calm that you can hardly feel any hope of winning, not even a little hope. I am suffering, really suffering.'[35]

This was the denouement of a trend set in motion decades ago. Through the 1990s, IBM was developing DeepBlue, a chess-playing computer that relied on machine-driven memory and computational abilities. Early versions were clumsy; the moves made by the computer were clearly laughable and human grand masters defeated it with ease, and even a little disdain. The unthinkable happened in 1997, when DeepBlue overpowered the prevalent reigning world champion and chess legend, Gary Kasparov. Likewise, IBM's computer, Watson, unseated the human world champion in the popular quiz show Jeopardy!, by dint of its 'superhuman' memory and speed of processing. Technology's journey of victories from 1997 to

2017 is significant: from mastery of memory and computational skills to that of learning on its own, not only from the vast database but incrementally, from its own experience, move by winning move.

Our purpose here is not to produce a litany of machine-over-man tales, but to underscore the fact that over and above the routine, mundane and repetitive tasks, machines and algorithms have developed the capability of special creative talent, to the point of genius. DeepBlue, AlphaGo and the couple of other instances that follow aren't by any means isolated ones. For instance, research in machine models of music goes back at least three decades, during which time advancements have taken the shape of predictive modelling, making music interactive.[36] Our aim here is to familiarize you with some of the advancements in creative technologies and invite you to reimagine possible futures, in terms of how we view, appreciate and engage with art and creativity.

BRUTUS is arguably one of the world's top storytelling computer programs. The tales it generates are credible, intriguing, and sometimes even manage a sense of mystery. Needless to say, they spin the narrative using sentences that are all syntactically correct. How does BRUTUS achieve this feat, repeatedly? First, BRUTUS was programmed to build up an impressive database of thematic knowledge, comprising four important aspects of information: a general domain knowledge of the social, economic and political settings for the stories, linguistic knowledge pertaining to construction of sentences into a narrative, literary knowledge around rhetoric, styles, turns of phrase and, finally, a special level of Literary Augmented Grammars (LAGs), bringing the rhetorical knowledge of the literary knowledge level to bear on the syntax controlled by the linguistic level. In creating a story, it uses all of these to first set the thematic context or 'stage', generate a plot, expand the structure of the story and finally produce the sentences and paragraphs constituting the tale by leveraging its linguistic and literary knowledge database.[37]

Here is a typical AI-driven story generated by BRUTUS:

Betrayal in Self-Deception*

Dave Striver loved the university. He loved its ivy-covered clocktowers, its ancient and sturdy brick, and its sun-splashed verdant greens and eager youth. He also loved the fact that the university is free of the stark unforgiving trials of the business world—only this isn't a fact: academia has its own tests, and some are as merciless as any in the marketplace. A prime example is the dissertation defense: to earn the Ph.D., to become a doctor, one must pass an oral examination on one's dissertation. This was a test Professor Edward Hart enjoyed giving.

Dave wanted desperately to be a doctor. But he needed the signatures of three people on the first page of his dissertation, the priceless inscriptions which, together, would certify that he had passed his defense. One of the signatures had to come from Professor Hart, and Hart had often said—to others and to himself—that he was honored to help Dave secure his well-earned dream.

Well before the defense, Striver gave Hart a penultimate copy of his thesis. Hart read it and told Dave that it was absolutely first-rate, and that he would gladly sign it at the

---

* Selmer Bringsjord and Dave Ferrucci, 'Brutus and the Narrational Case Against Church's Thesis', Extended Abstract, School of Computer Science, Carnegie Mellon University, https://www.cs.cmu.edu/afs/cs/user/michaelm/www/nidocs/BringsjordFerrucci.pdf

defense. They even shook hands in Hart's book-lined office. Dave noticed that Hart's eyes were bright and trustful, and his bearing paternal.

At the defense, Dave thought that he eloquently summarized Chapter 3 of his dissertation. There were two questions, one from Professor Rodman and one from Dr. Teer; Dave answered both, apparently to everyone's satisfaction. There were no further objections.

Professor Rodman signed. He slid the tome to Teer; she too signed, and then slid it in front of Hart. Hart didn't move. "Ed?" Rodman said. Hart still sat motionless. Dave felt slightly dizzy. "Edward, are you going to sign?"

Later, Hart sat alone in his office, in his big leather chair, saddened by Dave's failure. He tried to think of ways he could help Dave achieve his dream.

Finally, and with all due apologies to Paul Valery, let's talk about painting. The Dutch bank ING, along with Microsoft, Tu Delft and the Mauritshuis museum, teamed up to create a new computer-generated painting as it would have been executed by the seventeenth-century Dutch master Rembrandt. To distil the artistic DNA of Rembrandt, an extensive database of his paintings was built and analysed, pixel by pixel. Next, 346 of his paintings were studied, to arrive at the subject, in this case a portrait of a man, between thirty and forty years of age, and with facial hair, facing the viewer. To generate the features of the 'male sitter', a software program was designed, which utilized Rembrandt's style, such as his colour palette and light-and-shade schema, to form the features. The process involved over 500 hours of rendering. In order to bring the painting to life, the 2D image that had been produced was augmented by a height map, mimicking the brushstrokes used by Rembrandt.

The eventual product was a 3D print on a paint base, with the textures of brushstrokes and the glisten of thick impasto paint.[38]

Source: https://www.nextrembrandt.com/

The instances presented in this chapter make two things undeniably clear. First, technological capabilities globally are rapidly reaching a point of maturity—Singularity, if you prefer that term—when the full range of tasks, from the menial and repetitive to the creative and intellectually elevated, can be accomplished either wholly or to a very large extent, through technological means and without the need for human intervention. And second, we see the trend for an increasing number of these applications to scale up and sweep the market. By definition, all such technological advances improve the effectiveness, accuracy and efficiency of the businesses they cater to. To a large extent, they displace the manual effort of workers previously engaged to do the tasks. On its own, the implications for technological unemployment are indeed alarming.

However, to arrive at a more comprehensive picture, this issue needs to be viewed in conjunction with other key questions. Is the effect of technological advances on employment unidirectional, or will new job opportunities open up as a result, at the same time that existing ones are replaced by AI, robotics and automation? If the latter, what skills and competencies, technical, domain and behavioural, would be needed in order for people to become successful in these new jobs of the future? To what extent is the existing structure of educational institutions and learning facilities at work equipped to build and nurture these skills? To what extent can the new skills be developed in the workplace, and how?

These are the questions we take up in the subsequent chapters.

3

Sectors, Domains, Skills in Flux

In Chapter One, we discussed Schumpeter's view of creative destruction: obsolescence of particular skills and domains due to the decline of certain sectors, and emergence of others to meet the demands of a changed economy. We also noted broad trends in the way demand for labour has been shifting, on the whole. But the devil, as they say, is in the details. Within a single overall trend there are sometimes significant sectoral variations, with skill demand in certain sectors not matched by the availability of those competencies. The 'skills gap' that results has largely been caused by the astonishing pace of technological change, human upskilling struggling to keep pace with it. Two years of the pandemic have further accelerated that process, deepening the skills gap, at least in the short term. In this chapter, we take a deeper look at this particular matter. We explore not only these sectoral changes but also the resultant shifts in key domains of work and the skills that they embody. While the demand for technological skills continues to predominate many sectors, e.g., IT, BPO/KPO, product companies, the need for specific behavioural skills too has emerged as being almost as important. The latter come into use for managing a workforce that deploys a greater proportion of gig workers, and also more hybrid—and for certain departments, remote—modes of operations, on a long-term basis.

Specifically, we shall examine the situation unfolding in what we call the 'Emerging & Waning Sectors'. By this, we mean the sectors where demand for workers and specific skills is on the rise and expected to remain so in the near term, and those that are declining, respectively. We shall look at this picture from the perspective of the Indian ecosystem as well as from the global perspective, noting patterns of convergence. From sectors, we then shift our focus to domains (broadly defined job roles), to investigate the same question. Following this, we then explore how these dual shifts are translating into a changing demand for skills.

For several years now, the nature of work and jobs has been undergoing a transformation. A definite trend can now be observed—a shift from generalist roles in the workplace towards greater specialism of job roles and associated competencies. In fact, we see three distinct areas of specialism. The first two of these focus on technological, domain and industry expertise, especially all manner of technical competencies, and on competencies that emphasize more evolved behavioural, human-centric skills. The third area of specialism has emerged in response to the ecological crisis worldwide, and involves skills relating to the emergence of the 'green economy', and correspondingly, new job opportunities. A fourth has been a shift in demand for health and healthcare, driven by ageing populations in many parts of the world.

Within the ambit of behavioural skills, globally and in India, we will show that a clear bifurcation has emerged in the context of specialization. On the one hand are analytical abilities, complex problem-solving, and the cluster of attributes commonly clubbed under IQ, and on the other are attributes such as mindfulness, empathy, resilience and grit, which can be clubbed under the EQ category. This second category of behavioural skills and competencies, and their application in the workplace, are discussed in detail in Chapter Four. But over and above the emergent behavioural skills there are also two specific kinds of specialization, driven by demographic changes and ecological crises. The demographics component looks at the demand for greater healthcare facilities and services in light of ageing populations across many economies in the world, including, eventually, in countries with younger populations such as India. At the same time, there is the emergence of 'green jobs' resulting from ecological concerns. We will examine how this new sector can create growth and employment opportunities while leading to a better quality of life for future generations.

From sectors, domains and associated job roles, we then turn our attention to the nature of jobs itself. There has been tremendous disruption in the workforce in recent years. Retrenchment aside, globally we are witnessing what has come to be dubbed the Great Resignation or Great Attrition. This has led to a major shift in the way employers hire, nurture and retain the 'right talent'. In this context, we shall examine to what extent there is a shift towards the gig economy, globally as well as in India, gleaning from current research what the implications are for workers and organizations. In our current times, especially, in the wake of the Great Resignation, the employee value proposition (EVP) has assumed fresh importance among company leaders. Simply put, EVP is what an organization can do or offer to make itself more attractive to its employees; this can include a range of aspects, from compensation to employee policies, organizational culture, work practices, commitment to society and the environment. Now, with freelance or 'gig' work on the ascendant, is there a case to be made for an analogous gig value proposition (GVP)? If so, what specific factors are likely to be attractive for gig workers, and what should an effective GVP entail? We conclude the chapter by exploring this question.

EMERGING & WANING SECTORS

Let's start with some pre-pandemic projections. The figure below summarizes a large-scale Global Index study conducted by McKinsey in 2017,[1] envisioning the world of work in 2030. Here, the changes in the demand for labour are seen along two categories, first a 'trendline scenario', based on current spending observed across economies, and second a 'step-up' scenario, based on additional investments expected in some key areas.

Figure 3.1: Potential Jobs Created from 7 Categories of Labour Demand, McKinsey Global Institute, 2017

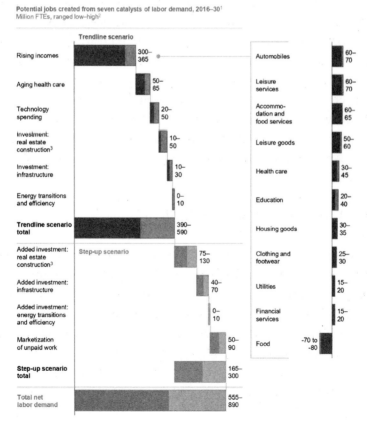

Source: MGI (2017)

Six different catalysts of demand for labour emerge from this picture:

- **Rising incomes**

Rising incomes, most naturally, are expected to contribute the most to labour demand by 2030. Higher incomes generate higher spending on consumer goods and services, health and education. More specifically, they lead to an estimated 1 billion people in emerging economies becoming consumers, and driving most of the projected growth. Besides the labour demand created locally by sectors such as manufacturing, accommodation, retail and food services, additional demand is also expected from economies that export goods and services to these emerging countries. Due to increasing GDP per capita, accelerating healthcare and education expenses, access to healthcare and gross enrolment rates would also increase, especially in India and other fast-emerging economies. The McKinsey report had projected that labour demand could go up by as much as 26 million to 43 million because of increased access to healthcare providers, and by up to 37 million jobs in education.

- **Ageing populations and healthcare**

Similar to a higher standard of living, demographic changes also play a key role. Given that the global population is projected to reach 8.5 billion by 2030, the population of the aged (sixty-five years and older) is projected to reach 300 million by 2030, with 25 per cent of them being from Germany, China, Italy and Japan. Though not immediately significant for an economy such as India, with its youthful population, given the population's greatly improved longevity it may likely find itself in a similar situation after a couple of decades. An ageing population demands an increase in healthcare and medical facilities, leading to higher expenditure in that sector. Consequently, jobs in healthcare that are focused on the aged, including personal care, nursing and home health assistance, will also see a natural increase. The report projected that this factor alone could create between 10 per cent and 15 per cent of the net new labour demand in economies such as China and Japan.

- **Technology**

Technology advancements can also trigger demand for labour for its continuous development, deployment, maintenance and upgradation. As we have seen, increasing incomes lead to higher consumer spending, and much of it can be routed to tech products. Larger outlays by businesses that are big adopters of technology would also result in increased spending on IT services, creating labour demand. Some of these services, e.g., computer support services, will remain largely local, while demand for tech hardware and software will be largely served by global players such as India, China, Germany, the US and the Netherlands. McKinsey projected that more than half of global jobs would be created in China and India—13 million and 6 million, respectively.

The above three are drivers of demand in a 'trendline' scenario. The study also estimated projections in a 'step-up' scenario, where new investments are expected.

- **Investment: infrastructure/real estate**

If measures are taken to close the infrastructure gap across many economies, a significant number of new jobs is likely to be created. With continuous investment in infrastructure, buildings and real estate, following the usual pattern observed, spending would increase as countries develop economically, and create new jobs. Additional spending involving investment over and above what is needed by countries to close their investment gap and at the very least reach levels of commercial and residential real estate investment comparable to those in the United States (as envisaged in the so-called step-up scenario in the report) would increase this labour demand even further, especially for middle-wage jobs highly affected by automation. As the infrastructure gap begins to get bridged, infrastructure and building spending would subsequently be much higher, to sustain the now higher level of infrastructure stock and investment. Similar to education and healthcare, this job creation will depend on allocations made to both the private and public sectors. Around 30 per cent to 40 per cent of this demand could be created in India—but this has not taken place as yet, as a result of current underinvestment and high rates of urbanization. It would likely remain labour intensive in other countries, such as Indonesia and Nigeria, due to the relatively slow pace of technology adoption there.

- **Energy transitions and efficiency**

Labour demand from investments in new energy sources will also depend on whether it follows the current trends (trendline) or the accelerated trend (step-up), as targets set by countries in the future become more ambitious, to meet the goals outlined in the Paris Accord. Investment in renewable energy, such as wind and solar-based power, which are becoming relatively cheaper, is on the rise. State-of-the-art technologies, e.g., internet of things and smart electrical meters, are transforming both production and consumption of resources. Sources of energy-efficient fuel will also be on the rise. Both trendline and incremental step-up scenario jobs will be created from the increase in employment in the power sector as a result of GDP per capita growth.

- **Marketization of unpaid work**

Some household work, such as cleaning and caring for the young, could be shifted to becoming paid employment through day care, kindergarten, etc. This would be stimulated by a higher female labour-force participation rate globally, if governments decide to push in a lot of investments in this sector, both through improving pay and conditions, as well as by subsidizing families with children. The report projected that in moving these jobs into the labour market, the labour demand for them would also record a natural increase.

It is interesting to note that none of the six factors outlined above has diminished in importance in the aftermath of the pandemic experience. On the contrary, technology and healthcare have both received unprecedented attention, along with innovations. We now turn to a more recent McKinsey study, conducted in the midst of the pandemic, in 2021.[2] Here, McKinsey used a new methodology to examine job growth and projections. Both pre-COVID and post-COVID scenarios were examined, by first incorporating the latest projections of real GDP growth from Oxford Economics and labour-force growth projections from the UN and ILO for the pre-COVID scenario, as well as current modelled trends.[3] Then, building on it, the study included three additional trends,[4] accelerated by the pandemic, that would likely affect labour demand and work at the post-COVID global workplace.[5]

According to this new report, globally, the shifts in the mix of occupations could be larger than before. Displacement of workers could rise by 10 per cent to 35 per cent. The jobs most likely to be in this category are those involving high levels of people-to-people proximity and human interaction, e.g., those of cashiers, food service attendants and store representatives. As companies seek efficiencies through automation, large displacements may occur among office support workers. Hybrid work will reduce demand for office facilities as well as maintenance jobs, such as those of custodians, receptionists and security guards. These same trends, though, might accelerate job growth in other occupations. For instance, even as jobs in stores are displaced, new jobs could be opening up in warehousing and delivery. Similar to the pre-COVID scenario, ageing populations will require more healthcare services. Hence, jobs in nursing and other health support services will increase. Increased adoption of automation and AI would also drive demand for engineers, computer scientists and programmers to create and maintain technology-driven solutions.

With regard to India, there might be relatively less impact from the pandemic because of the nature of the country's demographics and its economic development. Jobs are expected to grow as a result of its growing population, with the labour force expected to increase by 70 million over the coming decade. And more than 20 million workers might transition from agriculture to manufacturing and construction, in addition to moving to retail trade and transportation, in the coming decade. Thus, the proportion of total labour could go up in both manufacturing and construction. On the other hand, the proportion of labour working on agriculture would diminish significantly, as seen in the table below.[6]

Table 3.1: Pre-and Post-COVID Employment, by Occupation

Occupation	Differences in estimated net employment[7] between pre-COVID and post-COVID scenarios[8]		Estimated change in share of total employment, post-COVID-19 scenario[9]	Employment (2018)[10]
	In %[11]	Million	In %	Million
Health aides, technicians and care workers	2.3	0.2	1.0	5.8
Health professionals	2.8	0.3	0.5	2.9
Creatives and arts management	0.0	0.0	0.5	2.8
STEM professionals	5.0	0.5	0.8	5.3
Managers	-3.8	-0.4	0.6	8.4
Transportation services	3.2	0.3	0.4	16.6
Business and legal professionals	-4.6	-0.5	0.8	10.8
Community services	1.1	0.1	0.2	5.6
Builders	10.5	1.1	1.0	46.6
Educators & workforce training	0.3	0.0	0.7	13.8
Property maintenance	2.8	0.3	-0.4	23.8
Food service	-12.0	-1.2	0.7	11.9
Customer service and sales	-1.8	-0.2	0.3	34.4
Mechanical installation and repair	1.1	0.1	0.5	15.7
Office support	-6.9	-0.7	0.3	15.8
Production and warehousing work	-18.1	-1.8	1.0	54.2
Agriculture	18.0	1.8	-8.9	189.6

Source: McKinsey Global Institute (2021)

So far, our focus has been on traditional industries and occupations. We now turn to job creation in the new renewable energy sector. In this context, we shall be looking at two sets of projections, based on different scenarios. These projections, for job creation in 2030 and 2050, respectively, come from work undertaken by the ILO, using original projections by IRENA.[12] ILO adopted two scenarios in the estimations, the Planned Energy Scenario (PES) and the 1.5°C Scenario (1.5-S). The PES provides a perspective on energy system developments based on governments' current energy plans and other planned targets and policies, including nationally determined contributions (NDCs) under the Paris Agreement. On the other hand, the 1.5-S looks at an energy pathway aligned with the 1.5°C climate ambition—that is, to limit global average temperature increase by the end of the present century to 1.5°C, relative to pre-industrial levels.

Several views are shown in the data tables below. First, the projected jobs in the renewable energy sector, by type of technology used; next, the projections, by segment of the value chain; third, projections in the overall energy sector, based on educational requirements and overall energy sector job projections; and finally, projections across the energy sector, sectors of energy transition and fossil fuels.

Some clear indications emerge from the data:

- First, both scenarios show a steady growth in renewable jobs. However, the 1.5-S shows a far more rapid acceleration in renewable jobs. For example, there is a more-than-three fold increase by 2030 and a nearly four fold increase by 2050.
- While the degree of projected change differs across the two scenarios, both PES and 1.5°C show a rise in jobs

between 2030 and 2050 as regards biofuel, operation and maintenance, as well as in construction and installation, but a fall in this same time period for manufacturing.

- Interestingly, the educational requirements show an increase in jobs for those who have primary as well as secondary education, between 2030 and 2050. However, in both scenarios, the figure shows a sharp drop in demand from 2030 to 2050 for workers with tertiary education. One clear inference from this is that as time passes, jobs in the renewable sector will start to get more complex and sophisticated, warranting a higher level of education.

- The main point of difference between the two scenarios appears to be with regard to sector-specific jobs. While PES projects a slight increase in jobs across all three sectors, in 1.5°C, the jobs actually go down across all sectors. As the world moves progressively towards renewable forms of energy, a decline in the number of jobs might be expected in both fossil fuel and transition-type sectors. But the 1.5°C scenario shows a decline in jobs for some types of renewable energy (wind and geothermal) as well. It may be envisaged that for this scenario, the level of labour-displacing automation and mechanization is very high.

Table 3.2: Projected Renewable Energy Jobs, by Technology (in millions)[13]

TECHNOLOGY	2021	PES[14]		1.5°C	
		2030	2050	2030	2050
Solar	5.52	7.31	10.26	17.32	19.90
Bioenergy	5.34	5.09	5.95	11.11	13.67
Wind	1.98	2.52	3.37	5.57	5.48
Hydro	3.52	2.9	2.65	3.32	3.70
Geothermal	0.14	0.18	0.21	0.30	0.23
Tidal/Wave	0.002	0.18	0.06	0.18	0.37
Total		18	22.5	37.8	43.4

Source: ILO (compared with data from original source, IRENA)

Table 3.3: Projected Renewable Energy Jobs by Segment of Value Chain (in millions)

SEGMENT	2021	PES		1.5°C	
		2030	2050	2030	2050
Biofuel	4.6	4	4.1	9.4	11.2
Operation and Maintenance	3.1	3.9	6.3	5.4	9.3
Manufacturing	4.3	4.8	3.1	11.0	8.7
Construction and Installation	4.5	5.3	9.1	12.0	14.2

Source: ILO (compared with data from original source, IRENA)

Table 3.4: Projected Overall Energy Jobs by Educational Requirement (in millions)

	2021	PES		1.5°C	
		2030	2050	2030	2050
Primary	24.1	38.9	59.7	47.3	60.7
Secondary	37.8	26.2	40.3	34.8	44.8
Tertiary	29.1	45.7	14	54.5	16.2

Source: ILO (compared with data from original source, IRENA)

Table 3.5: Projected Energy Sector Jobs (in millions)

	2021	PES		1.5°C	
		2030	2050	2030	2050
Energy Sector	91.0	110.7	113.8	136.5	121.8
Transition-Related	52.5	66.7	67.5	106.5	95.8
Fossil-Fuels	37.9	43.3	45.8	29.4	25.8

Source: ILO (compared with data from original source, IRENA)

EMERGING & WANING JOBS

Before focusing on the changes in labour demand with regard to specific sectors, let us examine job roles across some of the major sectors. In this section, our aim is to first explore if there is a pattern to the increase and decrease in job roles in India and across the world, regardless of the sectors they feature in. For this, we have made use of the World Economic Forum's Future of Jobs Report 2020 and multiple other publications on the subject.[15, 16]

Some clear insights emerge from this:

- In India as well as globally, there's an undeniable shift towards specialism in job roles across sectors and industries.
- The specialism occurs along two dimensions; most of the specialism occurs along the technical and technological front; however, with roles such as business development professionals and project managers, we catch a glimpse of the behavioural or human-centric nature of the jobs.
- There is a strikingly high synergy between the emerging jobs globally and in India; this synergy is at least in some part a reflection of the breadth, depth and pace of technology adoption in Indian companies, across sectors.
- For predominantly human-centric roles, such as those of project manager (#6), India, in fact, seems to have stolen a march on the global trend, where project manager ranks at #11.

Table 3.6: Top 10 Emerging Jobs, Globally and in India (World Economic Forum 2020)

SR#	EMERGING DEMAND FOR ROLES–GLOBAL	EMERGING DEMAND FOR ROLES–INDIA
1	Data analysts and scientists	AI and machine learning specialists
2	AI and machine learning specialists	Data analysts and scientists
3	Big data specialists	Information security analysts
4	Digital marketing and strategy specialists	Internet of things specialists
5	Process automation specialists	Big data specialists
6	Business development professionals	Project managers
7	Digital transformation specialists	Fintech engineers
8	Information security analysts	Digital marketing and strategy specialists
9	Software and applications developers	Software and applications developers
10	Internet of things specialists	Business development professionals

Comparing the jobs that are rapidly diminishing in demand, globally as well as in India, we again have some interesting findings:

- Similar to the top ten jobs that are increasing in demand, here too the similarities between the global decline and the decline in India are remarkable.
- Jobs that are essentially human-centric or labour intensive and can be easily automated are on the way out. This covers a range of jobs, from low-level clerical jobs to what were considered personalized services, such as client information and customer services.

- The decline of jobs in the latter category can be attributed to the rise in websites for self-search and easy comparison of various attributes, such as price, quality and associated risks of products and services, as well as the ability of bots to answer routine customer inquiries.[17, 18]

Table 3.7: Top 10 Declining Jobs, Globally and in India (World Economic Forum 2020)

SR#	DECLINING DEMAND FOR ROLES – GLOBAL	DECLINING DEMAND FOR ROLES – INDIA
1	Data entry clerks	Administrative and executive secretaries
2	Administrative and executive secretaries	General and operations managers
3	Accounting, bookkeeping and payroll clerks	Assembly and factory workers
4	Accountants and auditors	Accounting, bookkeeping and payroll clerks
5	Assembly and factory workers	Data entry clerks
6	Business services and administration managers	Accountants and auditors
7	Client information and customer service workers	Architects and surveyors
8	General and operations managers	Human resources specialists
9	Mechanic and machinery repairers	Client information and customer service workers
10	Material recording and stock-keeping clerks	Business services and administration managers

As mentioned earlier, we shall explore the specialism of behavioural skills and its implications for the workplace in Chapter Four. Right now, we take a deeper look at the shift towards technology-related specialism. The first data we examine are on the specific technologies that companies are likely to be adopting the most. We've taken global and Indian projections for 2022 and 2025, from World Economic Forum studies. Comparative figures are not available for the exhaustive list of technologies across the two studies, for the time frames in question. A case in point is robotics. The following table is therefore limited only to those technologies where we have comparative figures. The numbers below show the percentage of companies likely to adopt the corresponding type of technology as part of their business operations.

Some clear indications emerge:

- There is a large consonance between the India and global figures, for both years.
- At a broad sweep, companies across the board are quite likely to adopt technologies around data, analytics and IOT.
- However, adoption of newer-age technologies, such as blockchain has already come up in a big way and is likely to be accelerated in the coming years.
- In areas such as cloud computing, encryption and IOT, adoption by Indian companies actually exceeds the global projection.

PROJECTED TECHNOLOGIES[19] (GLOBAL AND IN INDIA), COMPARING 2022 AND 2025[20] PROJECTIONS (IN %)[21]

Table 3.8: Top 10 Emerging Jobs, Globally and in India (World Economic Forum 2020)

	Global (2025)[22]	India (2025)[23]	Global (2022)[24]	India (2022)[25]
User and Entity big data analytics	87	88	85	89
Internet of things	84	90	75	77

	Global (2025)[22]	India (2025)[23]	Global (2022)[24]	India (2022)[25]
Machine learning	82[26]	81[27]	73	75
Cloud computing	89	98	72	72
Digital trade	61[28]	73[29]	59	64
Encryption	83	95	54	57
Distributed ledger (blockchain)	56	75	45	48
Non-humanoid land robots	62[30]	77	33	40

Source: WEF (2018, 2020)

We round up this section by taking a look at the specific technologies that are most likely to be adopted globally by each of the fourteen key sectors shown in the next table. The table below culls data from the WEF Future of Jobs 2020 report. While this presents a global macroeconomic view, one can use this data to draw similar inferences about the Indian economy, given the close parallels in technology advancement and adoption between the global and Indian ecosystems. The broad pattern that emerges is that across sectors, AI, cloud computing, encryption and cybersecurity have the highest likelihood of mass-scale adoption, with up to 95 per cent of sectors adopting them by 2025. Adoption of technology on the whole is expected to be significantly high across all sectors, the lowest being the use of encryption and cybersecurity in agriculture, an aspect of the limited use of technology in that sector.

This also enables you, at an individual level, to make a note of the leading technologies in your sector, with the aim of upskilling yourself.

Table 3.9: Top 5 Projected Technologies Likely to be Adopted Globally by Sector, by 2025 (in %)[31]

Technologies/sector	AGRI	AUTO	CON	DIGICIT	EDU	ENG	FS	GOV	HE	MANF	MIM	OILG	PS	TRANS
Artificial intelligence	62	76	73	95	76	81	90	65	89	71	76	71	76	88
Big data analytics	86	88	91	95	95	76	91	85	89	81	90	86	86	94
Cloud computing	75	80	82	95	95	88	98	95	84	92	87	86	88	94
Encryption and cybersecurity	47	88	85	95	86	88	95	95	84	72	83	71	78	75
Internet of things and connected devices	88	82	94	92	62	94	88	79	95	84	90	93	74	76

Source: WEF (2020)

Where: AGRI=Agriculture, food and beverages; AUTO=Automotive; CON=Consumer; DIGICIT=Digital communications and information technology; EDU=Education; ENG=Energy utilities & technologies; FS=Financial services; GOV=Government and public sector; MANF=Manufacturing; MIM=Mining and metals; OILG=Oil and gas; PS=Professional services; TRANS=Transportation and storage

FROM WANING TO EMERGING SECTORS & DOMAINS

We now turn to the immediate impact of increased technological specialism on working professionals as well as the nature of jobs in the emerging workplace. We base our analysis on the findings in the WEF 2020 report. The diagram below can seem a bit daunting at first glance, so it would be useful to break it down, by component, to glean specific insights. Using the basic terminology of set theory, we can think of the large cluster on the left-hand side of the diagram as the Domain. This cluster represents the superset of jobs existing at present or in the recent past, across sectors and domains. Similarly, we can think of the significantly smaller cluster on the right-hand side as the Range. This is the set or 'family' of jobs that are most likely to be in demand in the near-term future. The 'mapping from Domain to Range' from left to right across the diagram represents the shift from the type of jobs that professionals are currently engaged in to the jobs of the future. Some highly impactful findings emerge from the picture:

- First, it is obvious that the Domain of skills is much larger than the Range. Leaving aside the emerging green economy and the job opportunities that come with its rise, this means that for the more traditional sectors, specialism leads to a shrinkage of the different types of job roles in the future workplace.
- Even though the types of job roles, overall, may be coming down in a super-specialized future workplace, for certain occupations the opportunities actually increase. For instance, those working in IT can choose a future innings

in cloud computing, engineering, data and AI, as well as in product development.

- Going by education, skills and relevance of experience, we also see that it is easier or more natural for certain shifts to take place in the economy. For instance, it is more natural for professionals working in engineering (in the Domain) to focus on a career in cloud computing, data and AI, as well as product development, with a significantly lower proportion choosing to continue with traditional engineering (in the Range).

- For most job roles in the Domain, there is the possibility of mapping to multiple roles in the Range. This is true for a very large set of jobs, including operations, business development, support, quality assurance, research, programme and project management, education, finance, arts & design, and of course, all manner of entrepreneurship.

- However, for some of the major Domains, there is either no shift or a simple one-to-one mapping from Domain to Range. Professionals working in marketing and sales are most likely to continue doing so, even though the tools, technology and data they use may undergo a sea change. Similarly, as traditional HR tasks get more streamlined and automated, professionals working in this domain shift to people and culture, an area for which they are best suited, given their background and experience in HR.

Figure 3.2: Transitions into Jobs of the Future (World Economic Forum 2020)[32]

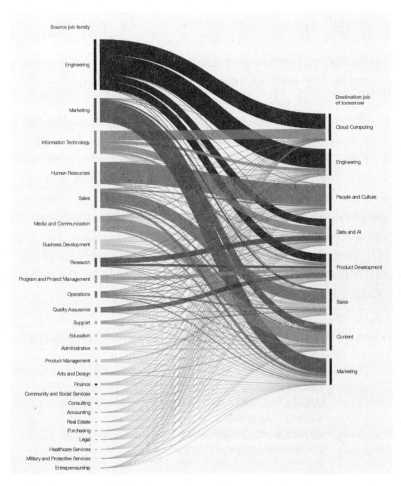

Source: WEF (2020)

The above analysis, while providing some key insights, also opens up some big questions. If a shift is the order of the day, for which types of jobs is the shift likely to be largest, and for which the smallest? Which are the job roles where one's occupation itself undergoes a change, and to what extent? And what does the transition mean, in terms of acquisition of new skills and applicability of existing ones? In other words, for which occupations will the skills across the earlier and new jobs be similar, and for which will they be dissimilar?

Using the findings from the WEF 2020 report, let us now briefly examine each of these questions.

First, consider the type or nature of the job. As the table below shows, the similarity between earlier and emergent jobs is the most for professionals working in people and culture/HR, and engineering, where, technological adoption notwithstanding, the underlying goals, principles and primary processes undergo relatively little change. The other end of the spectrum features product development as well as data and AI, where technological advancements frequently change the very rubric of the work process and, by corollary, the nature of the job.

Figure 3.3: Job Pivots by Job Family of Source Occupation[33]

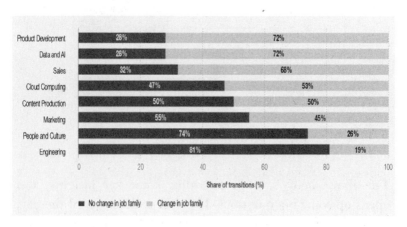

Source: WEF (2020)

Next, picture the transition occurring for the various occupations and job clusters. Two findings appear in this regard, as seen in Figure 3.4. First, the overall level of transition across all occupations is really high. For even the lowest transition among these, as in data and AI, the transition is still around the 50 per cent mark. For others, such as sales, the transition projected at close to 80 per cent, is endemic. The direct implication is the level of flexibility and preparedness that a professional must develop, depending on the occupation/job role he or she is in. For example, a present-day sales executive in the manufacturing sector needs to be prepared to make a shift to doing sales for an IT company, or a product start-up, or in the renewable energy sector, or perhaps even in social entrepreneurship, securing funds for a worthy cause.

Figure 3.4: Transitions by Occupation and Job Cluster[34]

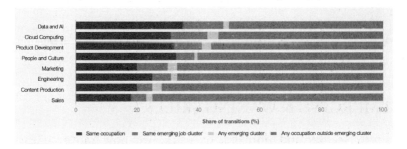

Source: WEF (2020)

And now, as we conclude this section, let us look at shifts in one's original occupation. As the figure below shows, there is wide divergence in the extent of change in the nature of one's job, depending on whether it is a traditional occupation or one that has emerged more recently in the ecosystem. Those in traditional occupations, such as those relating to people and culture/HR and engineering, can continue to see a 56–60 per cent similarity in the nature of their jobs after they transition out into their new jobs. For others, such as those in cloud computing or data and AI, the nature of their jobs in the future may be unrecognizable, compared to what they are today. As with the transition in occupation and job clusters seen above, this too has a direct implication for the level of adaptability and love of learning for people in these sectors, where the transition is drastic.

Figure 3.5: Job Pivots by Skills with Source Occupation[35]

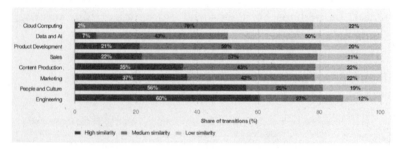

Source: WEF (2020)

EMERGING & WANING SKILLS

From sectors and domains of work, we now move to the specific skill sets that are in demand globally and in India. The comparative table below, culled from the findings of the WEF 2020 report, presents a clear picture on many fronts. First, as with sectors and domains, the similarities between India and the global ecosystem across the entire set of emerging skills is striking. Second—and by now this comes as no surprise—all of these relate to areas of specialism, and none around skills that are routine, repetitive, and can therefore be automated. Within specialism itself, there are two distinct categories, specialism in evolved cognitive, behavioural and human-centric skills, and specialism in data science/IT and technology skills.[36]

Table 3.10: Top 15 Emerging Skills Globally and in India

SR#	Global [37]	India [38]
1	Analytical thinking and innovation	Analytical thinking and innovation
2	Active learning and learning strategies	Complex problem-solving
3	Complex problem-solving	Active learning and learning strategies
4	Critical thinking and analysis	Critical thinking and analysis
5	Creativity, originality and initiative	Resilience, stress, tolerance and flexibility
6	Leadership and social influence	Technology design and programming
7	Technology use, monitoring and control	Emotional intelligence
8	Technology design and programming	Creativity, originality and initiative
9	Resilience, stress, tolerance and flexibility	Leadership and social influence
10	Reasoning, problem-solving and ideation	Reasoning, problem-solving and ideation
11	Emotional intelligence	Technology use, monitoring and control
12	Troubleshooting and user experience	Service orientation
13	Service orientation	Troubleshooting and user experience
14	System analysis and evaluation	Systems analysis and evaluation
15	Persuasion and negotiation	Persuasion and negotiation

Source: WEF (2020)

The need for human-centric skills, like the need for technological advancement, has been accentuated by the pandemic experience. And as Figure 3.6 shows us, within this cluster of skills too, a definite pattern has emerged. Those around physical abilities and core literacy skills, for instance, show a decrease in importance, while skills such as problem-solving, critical thinking and analysis are unambiguously increasing in importance. The implication is clear: there is a definite and continuing shift towards more evolved, higher-order skills and attributes in the emergent workplace.[39]

Figure 3.6: Relative Importance of Different Skill Groups

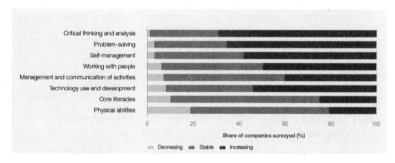

Source: WEF (2020)

Before concluding this section, let us look at the demand for specific skills in the post-pandemic workplace in India. For this, we have used the McKinsey 2021 report. Its findings, summarized in the table below, offer some striking insights:

- The increase in demand for technological skills (ranging from 26 per cent to a whopping 171 per cent) on the whole far outweighs the increase in demand for social and emotional skills, as well as for higher cognitive skills, in the post-pandemic world.

- Within technological skills, basic abilities will likely see the maximum rise in demand. This implies far more widespread basic computational, word-processing, presentation and communication-related tasks for a greater proportion of the workforce, regardless of sector and domain, and job role/occupation.
- The demand for social and emotional skills presents an interesting range. While the rise in demand for leadership, advanced communication and negotiation skills is likely to remain modest, that for entrepreneurial abilities, interpersonal skills and empathy will be substantial.
- The situation in the case of higher cognitive skills is similar. While demand for project management, quantitative skills, critical thinking and decision-making will remain unchanged or stagnant, demand for creativity is likely to see a dramatic rise.
- Skill clusters, physical abilities and basic cognitive skills witness little rise in demand, and in some cases, such as inspecting and monitoring, even a decrease in demand. This clearly reinforces what we have seen in the previous sections of this chapter: that repetitive, routine work is increasingly going to be replaced by automation and technology-driven processes.

Table 3.11: Breakdown of Skills in Demand, by Skill Category (Post-COVID-19 Scenario)

Skill	Skill Category	% Change[40]
Technological skills	Basic computer skills	171
	Scientific research and development	71
	Technology design, engineering and maintenance	61
	Advanced IT skills and programming	78
	Data analysis and computational skills	26
Social and emotional skills	Interpersonal skills and empathy	70
	Leadership and managing others	15
	Advanced communication and negotiation skills	10
	Entrepreneurship and initiative taking	37
	Adaptability and continuous learning	32
	Teaching and training others	40
Higher cognitive skills[41]	Creativity	56
	Critical thinking and decision-making	4
	Complex information processing and interpretation	19
	Project management	0
	Quantitative and statistical skills	0
	Advanced literacy and writing	13
Physical and manual skills	Gross motor skills and strength	17
	Fine motor skills	8
	General equipment repair and mechanical skills	9
	Craft and technician skills	12
	General equipment operation and navigation	5
	Inspecting and monitoring	-1
Basic cognitive skills[42]	Basic literacy, numeracy and communication	9
	Basic data input and processing	0
Change in size of workforce due to demographics		14

Source: McKinsey Global Institute (2021)

SKILL DEVELOPMENT INITIATIVES IN INDIA[43]

While all education, research and skill-building is related to growth and new opportunities, it is important to make the distinction between different forms and levels of education. There is higher education, research, innovation and patents, which collectively lead to enhanced human, intellectual and technological capital. This shall be the main subject of our focus in Chapter Five. However, there is also skill-building and vocational training, conducted with the direct aim of building capabilities in particular trades and occupations, and so enhance employability. This second aspect is what we shall focus on in this brief section, with special reference to the initiatives undertaken in recent times by the Indian government.

According to the Periodic Labour Force Survey (PLFS) 2019–20, formal vocational/technical training among both the youth, aged fifteen to twenty-nine, and among the working population, aged fifteen to fifty-nine, has improved in 2019–20, as compared to 2018–19. This improvement in skills has been for males as well as females, and in both the rural and urban sectors. However, formal training for both males and females is lower in rural than in urban areas. Going by the report of April–June, 2021 of the Quarterly Employment Survey (QES)[44], 17.9 per cent of establishments employing at least ten workers in nine major sectors were imparting formal skills training; 29.8 per cent of the IT/BPO companies were imparted skills training, followed by 22.6 per cent of firms in financial services and 21.1 per cent of companies in the education sector. Further, about 24.3 per cent of all establishments were imparting 'on-the-job' training, including 36.1 per cent of the IT/BPO sector and 34.8 per cent of firms in the financial services sector.

Among the skill development efforts made by the government of India, the Skill India Mission, launched in 2015, remains preeminent. This subsumes the Pradhan Mantri

Kaushal Vikas Yojana (PMKVY), the Jan Shikshan Sansthan (JSS) Scheme, the National Apprenticeship Promotion Scheme (NAPS) and the Skill Development Training and Craftsman Training Scheme (CTS). They are briefly described here:

- **Pradhan Mantri Kaushal Vikas Yojana (PMKVY)**—This has two training components, short-term training (STT) and recognition of prior learning (RPL). Between April 2016 and 15 January 2022, under PMKVY, about 1.10 crore persons were trained. Several micro-programmes have also been formulated for artisan clusters to partner with the private sector to enhance employment among artisans. The RPL component aims: (i) to align the competencies of the unorganized workforce of the country with the standardized National Skill Qualification Framework; (ii) to enhance employment opportunities and alternative means of higher education; (iii) to provide opportunities for reducing inequalities. As on 15 January 2022, over 63 lakh beneficiaries have been certified across thirty-seven different sectors.
- **Jan Shikshan Sansthan (JSS) Scheme**—JSS aims to provide vocational skills to non-literate and neo-literate persons with a rudimentary level of education up to eighth standard and to those who have dropped out any time up to twelfth standard, in the age group of fifteen to forty-five. The priority groups are women, SC, ST, minorities, divyangjan and other backward sections of the society.
- **National Apprenticeship Promotion Scheme (NAPS)**— This scheme promotes apprenticeship training and the engagement of apprentices by providing financial support to industrial establishments undertaking apprenticeship programmes under The Apprentices Act, 1961. As on

31 October 2021, 4.3 lakh apprentices were found to be engaged under the scheme.

- **Craftsmen Training Scheme (CTS)**—The objective of CTS is to provide long-term training in 137 trades through 14,604 Industrial Training Institutes (ITIs) across the country. For in the financial year 2020–21, a total of 13.36 lakh trainees were enrolled under this scheme.

Linking these initiatives to the job market is the Aatmanirbhar Skilled Employees Employer Mapping (ASEEM) programme, a digital directory that aims to match the supply of skilled workforce with the market demand. As of 31 December 2021, 1.38 crore candidates have been registered on the portal, including candidates registered on the Skill India Portal (SIP). Around 26.7 lakh migrants' data/profiles are available on the portal, which consists of three AI-based interfaces: A) a job application system for individuals with access to hyper-local jobs using machine learning and automated match, based on persona; B) a demand-and-campaign management system for employers to forecast current and future demand; and C) a management dashboard for analytics and insights.

The India International Skill Centre (IISC) Network caters to the needs of foreign countries where Indian manpower is in demand. It is a fee-based market-driven model, which provides incremental skills training on international standards and assessment of skills for overseas employment, leveraging agreements with Germany, Belarus, the United Kingdom, France, Australia, Japan and Qatar.

There is also the Pradhan Mantri Dakshta aur Kushalta Sampann Hitgrahi Yojana (PM-DAKSH), a national action plan for skilling of marginalized persons, including scheduled castes, backward classes and *safai karamcharis*. During the financial year 2021–22, the government had set a target of providing skill development training to approximately 50,000 persons under this scheme.

WORKERS WITHOUT EMPLOYERS: IS THE GLOBAL ECONOMY GOING GIG?

The term 'gig' appears to have been coined in the second decade of the 1900s by jazz musicians who regularly performed in jazz clubs. Gig, in its original sense, means an event or a show. Today, of course, the term is most prevalently applied to the 'gig economy'—referring to a labour market characterized by short-term contracts or freelance work, as opposed to permanent jobs. The gig economy is not new. Seasonal agricultural workers have been a historical feature in most countries, predating by centuries the use of the term 'gig' to describe their work. Indeed, while the explosion of the gig economy in developed countries may appear to be a relatively new phenomenon, people working in the ubiquitous informal sector in India and in most developing economies meet the definition of 'gig' workers. However, they often do not make it to the official estimates, nor in many cases in their employer's books, nor in the government database for tax returns. Living precariously, often hand-to-mouth, these casual workers nonetheless have been a significant part of the labour force in India and in many other developing countries. As these gig workers are not considered in the international descriptions of the gig economy, we will not discuss them further in this chapter, so as to be able to make consistent international comparisons.

Figure 3.7, from the McKinsey Global Institute, 2021, reveals that between 2019 and 2020 during the pandemic, the share of e-commerce sales through groceries delivery through apps and other online platforms increased between 1.8 and 4.5 times across the countries surveyed, highlighting the increasing relevance of the gig economy. This is part of a growing trend of the gig economy, which we will examine in some detail.[45]

Figure 3.7: Year-over-Year Growth of e-Commerce, as Share of Total Retail Sales

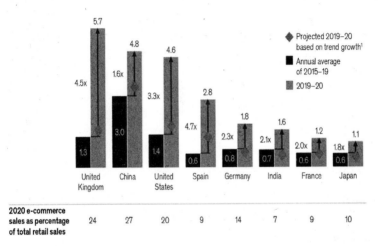

2020 e-commerce sales as percentage of total retail sales	24	27	20	9	14	7	9	10

Source: MGI 2021

It's interesting to see that the rise of the gig economy globally is not wholly made up of an increased workforce undertaking only less skilled job roles. While low-end gig work carries the uncertainties of the informal sector, many high-end jobs requiring specialized skills are also being performed by gig workers or freelancers with highly evolved skills, and for high compensations. As Figure 3.8, from Mad About Growth, shows, growth in the gig economy encompasses three major sectors.

Figure 3.8: Increase in Gig Demand for 3 Work Categories

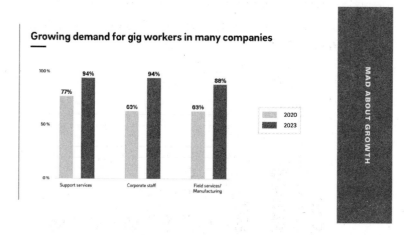

This growth is possibly why recent surveys show that two-thirds of gig workers actually think freelancing is more secure than traditional employment.[46]

Today, a confluence of demand-and-supply factors has made the gig economy manifest itself as the dominant mode of working globally. The demand for gig workers has been accelerated by the pandemic because companies facing uncertain demand are reluctant to offer permanent employee contracts. Interestingly, as the pandemic wanes, these employers see no economic or operational reason to change the new status quo. From a supply-side standpoint too, many workers, especially 'Generation Z' professionals, prefer the flexibility of gig work. Others use the expanding gig economy to do some work in addition to their permanent jobs to supplement their income.

One big reason behind the growing gig economy has been the rise of aggregator platforms. Starting small, some of these platforms, such as Airbnb, have become billion-dollar industries, and ride-sharing platforms (Uber, Ola, Lyft, Bolt) serve millions across the globe. The net effect of this is that the gig economy accounts for around a third of the world's working population,[47] with nearly a quarter of workers across nineteen countries surveyed being full-time gig workers and 9 per cent doing gig work in addition to traditional employment. The volume of gig work was estimated to be over $200 billion in a 2019 study by MasterCard,[48] and it has been estimated to cross the $500 billion mark in five years' time.[49]

As many as 30 per cent of Fortune 500 companies (i.e., 500 of the largest US companies ranked by total revenues for their respective fiscal years) source their work through Upwork, one of the largest US freelance platforms. Some of the big names hiring from freelance platforms include Facebook (Meta), Paladin, BDO, Pepsi, The Axa Group, FedEx, Bank of America and Verizon. Some platforms, such as Toptal and Catalan, focus on high-end talent, while others such as Upwork, Freelancer and 99Designs, match individuals with companies for discrete task-oriented projects; while not at the exclusive end, the work they offer can be specialized and could be to design a logo, or to translate a legal document. In short, the gig economy is now mainstream—and hybrid modes of working will only enable it to grow further.

This worldwide trend has to some extent been replicated in India. In January 2021, the Economic Survey of India 2020–21 stated that India had become one of the largest markets for flexi-staffing in the world, as a result of the widespread adoption of online retailing and e-commerce. Later in the summer, the Associated Chambers of Commerce and Industry of India (ASSOCHAM) estimated that India's gig economy would grow at a compounded annual rate of 17 per cent, reaching $455 billion by 2023. Another report published by Boston Consulting Group (BCG) and Michael & Susan Dell Foundation said India's gig economy is poised to triple in the next three to four years, catapulting from 8 million to 24 million jobs in the non-farm sector. The total number of gig jobs could soar to 90 million in eight to ten years, contributing to 1.25 per cent of the nation's GDP in this longer horizon. As a point of comparison, in March 2021, the organized IT-BPO sector in India employed around 4.5 million professionals.

A study, 'Unlocking the Potential of the Gig Economy in India', conducted jointly by the BCG and Michael and Susan Dell Foundation, said the gig economy in India has the potential to create up to 90 million jobs in the coming years, adding around 1.25 per cent to the country's GDP.[50] The four largest industry sectors—construction, manufacturing, retail, and transportation and logistics—could collectively account for over 70 million of these jobs. The net new jobs would result from a better ability to match demand and supply of skills, greater efficiencies in delivery at lower costs, and growing demand arising out of small increments in consumption.[51]

In terms of legislation, some steps have been taken to address this new demand. One of these is the Code on Social Security,[52] introduced in September 2020 in both houses of Parliament, which cleared it, and which came into force in May 2021. This legislation amends and consolidates the earlier laws relating to social security, with the aim of extending social security to all employees and workers in the organized and unorganized sectors. For the first time in Indian economic history, this brings the unorganized sector, gig workers and platform workers under the ambit of social security schemes such as life insurance and disability insurance, health and maternity benefits, provident insurance, and pension and skill upgradation. The Act, which integrated nine previous legislations relating to social security, also proposed the formation of a social security fund for all workers across different categories.

Taken together, these might suggest that the gig economy is a boon for both workers and employers. This is what Diane Mulcahy[53] seems to suggest in her book on the gig economy. However, not all aspects of the gig economy have been viewed positively. It has come under criticism for the exploitative practices at the low end of the skills spectrum. For instance, during the pandemic, delivery workers in India were frequently asked to deliver in containment zones, increasing their risk of being infected, with no corresponding insurance for days off or payment for treatment.[54] Many Uber and Ola drivers have claimed that because of the reduced amount of work during the pandemic, they could not even pay their instalments against the loans they had taken to purchase their vehicles.[55] This job insecurity is often coupled with a downward-bidding war for non-specialized tasks. A recent report from PayPal suggests that over half of gig workers have not always been paid for work done.[56] This is part of a larger problem—the lack of social security or employment laws covering gig workers, not just in India but in most parts of the world too. A combination of such factors, together with the lack of networks at work, can have a damaging impact on mental health, which we take up in greater detail in Chapter Six.

We round off this section with a quick look at how company stakeholders have been responding to the increasing specialism and shift in demand for skills. The table below shows the responses to shifting skills needs in India (share of companies surveyed). Compared to 2022 projections drawn in 2018 by the WEF, 2025 projections, undertaken in 2020, show that a very large majority of employers expect their personnel to reskill themselves on the job. The emphasis on gig workers has remained relatively high and unchanged. Sixty-two per cent of the employers surveyed stated that they would hire new temporary staff with skills relevant to new technologies, while

56 per cent said they would hire freelancers with skills relevant to new technologies.

Table 3.12: Employers' Expectations of Worker Reskilling

Reskilling needs	2022 projections (in %)[57]	2025 projections (in %)[58]
Look to automate work	83	82
Retrain existing employees	79	92
Hire new permanent staff with skills relevant to new technologies	78	84
Expect existing employees to pick up skills on the job	70	95
Outsource some business functions to external contractors	67	65
Hire new temporary staff with skills relevant to new technologies	62	67
Hire freelancers with skills relevant to new technologies	56	56
Strategic redundancies in staff, lacking the skills to use new technologies	51	59

Source: WEF (2018, 2020)

GIG VALUE PROPOSITION

In India as well as globally, there is fresh interest in how to hire, nurture and retain the best talent that the marketplace offers, especially with regard to professionals who are able to demonstrate the skills of the future. In other words, there is greater focus on employee value proposition (EVP), which refers to the value an employee perceives in being a member of an organization.[60] While compensation is of course important, employees value non-monetary attributes such as work content (Do people have autonomy? Is the work challenging?), career progression (How well is it defined; are there clear pathways to moving up the ladder?) as well as the values of the company (Is it committed to green processes? Does it support charitable causes?). It also includes benefits in a wider sense, including allowing for career breaks and flexibility of working arrangements.[61] Clearly, different individuals will value some of the components differently and companies should design their EVP to attract the kind of employees they would most like to hire and retain. Properly designed, an EVP could potentially make workers feel a sense of belonging and inspire them to give their best to the company. It also has the secondary benefit of creating a brand for the organization, which brings it the benefit of attracting customers who can associate with their ethos.

EVP becomes particularly important at a time when there is a general exodus of people from companies, as seems to be happening currently. Recruiters across organizations are vying with each other to turn the Great Attrition of our times into the Great Retention as the battle for talent intensifies. While this renewed focus on EVP is welcome, company leaders would also be well-advised to also start focusing on its much-neglected sibling—gig value proposition, or GVP, given the shift happening towards the gig economy. Among the many changes wrought by the pandemic in the workplace is the way organizations hire and work with gig—as compared to full-time—workers. While certain characteristics, such as compensation and benefits, may be valued in the same way, how can companies inspire workers who are not wedded to an organization (or for that matter, the organization not wedding to them) is a challenging task.

Crafting a compelling GVP presents an interesting creative challenge. Rehashing the usual EVP offerings would be an obvious mistake. This is because the work practices that make an organization a sought-after employer for full-time workers may not be as attractive to gig workers. Training interventions, offsite retreats and other initiatives clubbed under 'employee engagement' often seem to have an organizational focus, and may not be immediately compelling to gig workers. At the very least, they would need to be revisited. From Provident Fund, house rent allowance and leave travel allowance to gratuity and medical insurance for the family, financial benefits that are par for the course for full-time employees are not extended to gig workers. Meaningful CSR projects and commitment to a 'green footprint' may be appealing to prospective full-time hires, but do they necessarily hold the same importance for a freelancer working on a six-month assignment? A social media strategy that shows the company in a favourable light is imperative, but this brings us right back to the moot question—what sort of social media posts are likely to attract the best gig talent?

The constituents of any compelling GVP would, by definition, need to evolve as the workplace continues to disrupt itself. But the starting point has to be a genuine commitment on the part of employers and managers to dedicate time to such a project, and not cut corners. Here are a few areas where they might wish to focus their energies.

Better work-life integration: In the new 'work from anywhere' (WFA) mode of operating businesses, employees see their normal working hours stretched, at times seeping into the weekend, and are compelled to live with it. Many gig workers, however, are zealously proprietorial about their independence, in particular about their 'me time'. Indeed, part of the reason why they choose not to get a permanent job is because they value the flexibility of non-permanent working conditions. While deadlines and deliverables stand unchanged, leaders and managers must find newer ways of keeping freelancers engaged. Flexible working hours, allowing of adequate breaks during the day, an emphasis on productivity and outcomes over the hours worked, are only some of the ingredients. The traditional micro-managing style of getting work done has undergone a mutation. Currently, managers demand multiple check-in calls and updates during the course of the day, but for any GVP to be effective, this approach will need to take a permanent backseat.

Co-creation of value: The widespread grouse against gig workers globally is that they are lacking in commitment, as well as in what organizations call 'employee loyalty', compared with full-time workers. But the argument works both ways. A purely piecemeal, transactional attitude on the part of employers with regard to gig workers only serves to perpetuate apathy on the part of the latter. The equation changes to the advantage of both parties when the attitude of the employer shifts to one that appreciates the co-creation of value through gig work. Work practices that encourage crowdsourcing of ideas and innovation, and recognize the power of individual contribution, are some steps in the right direction. Gig workers, even if working for a short time for a company, are likely to be more engaged in their work when they know that their individual contributions are appreciated and also experience a sense of shared pride when they feel part of a larger creative, constructive process.

Reimagining talent fitment: Currently, corporates have started to pay considerable attention to the recruitment process, especially the adoption of AI and online assessments to expedite and streamline the screening process and aid in selecting the right candidate. The same imperative applies to hiring of the right gig talent and retaining their services on future assignments. Contrary to the easy, fit-to-order notion around the selection of gig talent, there is a cost associated with hiring freelancers who are a good fit and, based on their performance, earmarking them for future assignments. This cost factor becomes more important over time as the hiring of gig workers intensifies, in turn increasing the need for mechanisms to ascertain gig fitment. Organizations could first arrive at a competency matrix, based on the skills and attributes of gig workers required across assignments, and deploy curated online assessments to evaluate candidates on their fitment for the needed roles.

Infusing 'gigness' into the organizational culture: Organizational culture is so much more than the vision and mission statements published on the company website. It spans an array of attributes, from shared values, attitudes and work practices to the working conditions and environment, policies, procedures, the support, recognition and opportunities that an organization provides to its people. As gig hires increase, the company culture needs to be calibrated to take them into account. Including the modalities of working with freelancers is a good place to start. A provision for rewarding high-performing gig workers in the same manner as employees could be an attractive proposition. Another could be extending the many privileges that high-performing or senior, permanent employees enjoy, whether they are corporate memberships and discounts for services, ranging from cab hires to restaurants, and travel and hospitality. Such an offer, reserved for seasoned gig workers with specialized skills, would provide a clear signal to those professionals about the value of their work in the eyes of the organization.

More generally, just as a good EVP has different aspects that appeal to workers at different stages in their lives and careers, GVP should also signal the attributes of the company to gig workers they would most like to attract. For instance, millennials and Gen-Z workers value work-life integration and may also be attracted by a company's larger mission or ethical values. They are also more likely to be gig workers, and so a GVP should be tailored to the type of worker the organization wishes to attract. The aspects discussed above are far from exhaustive. But it is hoped that they will provide some context and food for thought to company leaders, as they work the gig factor into their overall scheme of business plans and operations.

An aside on what motivates millennials. A Gallup study, 'How Millennials Want to Work and Live', offers some key observations and findings.[62] First, they tend to be unattached, relative to previous generations, to their jobs or to the brands to which they give their money. They are also less likely than other generations to feel pride in their communities or to identify with particular religious or political affiliations. At the same time, they are highly connected with the world around them, through the use of technology and social media. Millennials are unconstrained in pushing for change in the world. They demand that businesses approach them differently and adjust the customer experience to meet their needs. The same goes for employers—millennials want to be free of old workplace policies and performance management standards, and they expect leaders to adapt accordingly. Millennials also tend to be idealistic, in that they believe that life and work should be worthwhile and have a sense of purpose.

The six critical findings on millennials are as follows:

1. *Millennials don't just work for a pay cheque—they want purpose.* For millennials, work must have meaning. They want to work for organizations with a mission and purpose.

Compensation is important and must be fair, but it's no longer the driver. The focus for millennials has switched from the pay cheque to purpose—and so must the organization's culture.

2. *Millennials are not pursuing job satisfaction—they are pursuing development.* Most millennials aren't impressed by the frills in the workplace—a chic cafeteria, indoor games and recreational facilities. These don't enhance job satisfaction for them. What millennials want are purpose and development.

3. *Millennials don't want bosses—they want coaches.* The role of an old-style boss is command and control. Millennials care about having managers who can coach them, who value them as both people and employees, and who can help them understand and build their strengths.

4. *Millennials don't want annual reviews—they want ongoing conversations.* The way millennials communicate is real-time and continuous. This dramatically affects the workplace because millennials are accustomed to constant communication and feedback. Annual reviews no longer work.

5. *Millennials don't want to fix their weaknesses—they want to develop their strengths.* Weaknesses never really develop into strengths, while strengths develop infinitely. Accordingly, organizations should minimize their emphasis on correcting weaknesses and instead maximize strengths.

6. *It's not just my job—it's my life.* Millennials are perpetually asking, 'Does this organization value my strengths and my contribution? Does this organization give me the chance to do what I do best every day?' Because for millennials, a job is no longer just a job—it's a matter of their lives.

In conclusion, we see that the nature of work is changing dramatically. It is easy to ascribe it all to a technological revolution, and indeed the breadth and pace of this revolution has been astonishing. But there is a human side to it, with the need for behavioural, human-centric skills. Further, there are other sectoral shifts, driven by demographic changes. This works in two ways—the increasing proportion of millennials and Gen-Z workers and the implications of that, as discussed above. The second relates to an increased demand in the health and healthcare industry to minister to an ageing population. A big change has been policy-driven—as government regulations and industry response have led to a rise in green jobs.

CHAPTER 4

Behavioural Competencies for the New Age

... What shall we do tomorrow?

'What shall we ever do?'

The hot water at ten.

And if it rains, a closed car at four.

And we shall play a game of chess,

Pressing lidless eyes and waiting for a knock upon the door.

—T.S. Eliot, The Wasteland

What shall we do tomorrow? What shall we ever do?

In these present times, Eliot's eternal questions in *The Wasteland* return to haunt us—in a disturbing new way. That the knock on the door, which promised to rouse us from the dull tedium of our lives and offer something to look forward to, has now mutated into something unnerving that we find ourselves powerless against: prolonged sickness and fatigue, fear of retrenchment, loss of a dear one. So, what can we really do about any of this, especially when it comes to our work and livelihoods? In Chapter Three, we saw how the workplace is undergoing a distinct transformation, from more generalized job roles to specialized ones. In fact, this specialization across both categories is warranted as one moves up the career ladder.

In this chapter, we examine how the behavioural competencies of the future workplace dovetail, enabling us to combat stress, develop long-term resilience and thrive in this age of continued disruption. We will begin by showing how the seemingly eclectic array of skills favoured by experts and think tanks actually converges into a 'heat map' of core behavioural competencies. We then explore the triggers of stress that are so much a part of our lives, and how the cultivation of mindfulness can help to address and reduce it over a sustained period. Next, we delve into resilience, that other buzzword of our times, but in reality, something about which our understanding is still evolving. We then move on from adversity, to the ability to achieve and sustain peak performance by developing a growth mindset, positive emotions and future-mindedness. Finally, we outline a simple approach whereby, starting from sectors and domains, you could converge to a specific combination of skills to focus on in the near future for your career.

We do not claim to have all the answers. But in your quest to negotiate the future workplace through its dark maze of challenges and uncertainty, we hope to cast the modest light of a torch.

THIS TIME IS DIFFERENT

In 2008, at the height of the subprime crisis, the financial COVID of those times, Carmen Reinhart of the University of Maryland and Harvard's Kenneth S. Rogoff published their celebrated work, *This Time Is Different*, in which they surveyed and analysed eight centuries of financial crises, globally. Across the long litany of disasters, they found a common pattern. Serial default was a nearly universal phenomenon, as old-world societies went through the disruption of giving rise to advanced economies. Likewise, the authors noticed that crises frequently emanated from the financial centres and were transmitted via interest rate shocks and commodity price collapses. Viewed through this lens, no new financial crisis, even the subprime debacle, was truly unique. However, because instances of major macroeconomic or global-scale defaults have been spaced decades apart, they've always created an illusion that 'this time is different'.[1]

A similar argument can be made for skills and competencies. From steam engines to the bullet train, from Babbage-style computing to cloud computing, every major break with the past has meant that the skills and competencies required also undergo transformation. Not surprisingly, in many of these instances the disruption witnesses its share of anxiety, professional turmoil, even unemployment among people—a pattern all too familiar to us. Therefore, as regards the need for developing new skills and competencies, surely there's no reason to think that our current experience is unique in history.

Except that this time *really* is different—for multiple reasons.

Many observers argue that Moore's Law, which has been explained earlier, has been hastened by the pandemic. Fascinatingly, we also seem to be witnessing something of a 'Moore's Law of Skills and Competencies'. While the time period for skills obsolescence isn't quite two years, in many technology-driven sectors it is certainly no more than four years. Therefore, at least for these sectors, we can perhaps assert: *Workplace competencies need to be upgraded every four years.*

Next, there is the scale of reskilling that is required. We've noted a clear shift towards a new form of specialism that necessitates both analytical and behavioural skills, left brain as well as right brain. While Daniel Pink's prediction of right brainers ruling the future hasn't come true as yet, an increasing number will be in demand, in the future.[2] It's heartening that development of right-brain competencies is being taken seriously in the arena of corporate budgets and training. This has also entered the curricula of higher education institutes (HEIs), which are taking tenuous steps beyond the STEM mode of learning. After a slow start, there are indications that things are moving in the right direction.[3]

Third, the pandemic has also compelled a shift in focus at the workplace. The subprime crisis of 2008 threw the spotlight on the chief financial officer (CFO), demanding better controls, compliance and legislation. The COVID-19 crisis, essentially human-centric, has brought the office of the chief human resource officer (CHRO) into the limelight. The focus on HR has a cascading impact across processes and culture in a company. HR is typically more open to working with psychologists, counsellors and coaches than other departments. These external experts bring in new perspectives, experiences and ideas across disciplines. New ways of analysing and solving problems, taking a more inclusive view of employees, setting up a culture of candour and being concerned about well-being and mental health in the workplace—all these, and more, then follow naturally.[4]

Finally, there is the convergence of studies, reports and recommendations, from researchers and advisers globally, around the urgency for developing behavioural competencies in the workplace. Combining the insights from these, a certain 'heat map' of skills can be seen to emerge, presented in the diagram below. A few definite skill clusters can be identified:

- The first cluster relates to advanced communication and negotiation skills; this subsumes the range of negotiation skills, frameworks and models needed for effecting successful outcomes in the workplace.
- The second involves the cluster of social and emotional intelligence, empathy, the measure of one's emotional response, especially in stressful or high-pressure situations.
- The third is the set of behavioural skills and attributes required for what is commonly known as a 'growth mindset'—namely, adaptability, curiosity, agility, creativity and ability to innovate.
- Finally, we have the cluster of attributes around collaboration, influence and willingness to trust, all of which assume greater importance as work shifts to gig and hybrid modes.

Figure 4.1: Heat Map of Desired Behavioural Competencies

SR#	SKILL	MCKINSEY	FORBES	ENTREPRENEUR	GARTNER (FOR CHRO)	FORRESTER	EGON ZEHNDER (FOR CXOs)	RUSSELL REYNOLDS (FOR CXOs)	LINKEDIN	CNBC
1	ADVANCED COMMUNICATION/ NEGOTIATION SKILLS	■							■	
2	SOCIAL INTELLIGENCE/ EMOTIONAL INTELLIGENCE/ EMPATHY/ MEASURED EMOTION	■	■		■					■
3	LEADERSHIP/ MANAGEMENT SKILLS/ STRATEGIC ORIENTATION	■		■				■		■
4	ENTREPRENEURSHIP/ INITIATIVE-TAKING/ CREATIVE RISK-TAKING	■							■	
5	TEACHING & TRAINING									
6	ADAPTABILITY/ FLEXIBILITY/ CREATIVITY & INNOVATION/ CURIOSITY/ AGILITY/ GROWTH MINDSET	■		■	■	■			■	■
7	CRITICAL THINKING & ANALYSIS/ COMPLEX PROBLEM-SOLVING	■								■
8	TIME MANAGEMENT/ PLANNING & PRIORITIZING WORK/ PERSONAL PRODUCTIVITY/ FOCUS MASTERY		■							
9	SERVICE ORIENTATION/ CUSTOMER FOCUS						■			
10	STRESS MANAGEMENT				■		■			
11	CHANGE LEADERSHIP/ MANAGEMENT				■		■			
12	CONFLICT MANAGEMENT									
13	STORYTELLING					■			■	
14	COLLABORATION AND/ OR INFLUENCE/ WILLINGNESS TO TRUST	■		■	■	■		■		
15	CULTURAL AWARENESS/ PRAGMATICALLY INCLUSIVE			■				■		
16	DIGITAL LITERACY									
17	PEOPLE & ORG DEVELOPMENT/ EFFICIENT READER OF PEOPLE							■		
18	MARKET KNOWLEDGE									
19	BIAS TOWARDS (THOUGHTFUL) ACTION							■		
20	OPTIMISM/ FORWARD THINKING							■		

The skills a professional would need to develop in the near future are a function of multiple factors, including education, domain, sector, level of expertise, tenure of overall workplace experience and individual aptitudes. However, as we shall see in the final section of this chapter, being able to club together and view skills as clusters can make it easier to plan a programme for self-development. For organizations too, this makes it easier to design more focused learning and development programmes for their teams.

As part of a WEF study on the future of jobs, surveys were conducted across employers in a number of economies, including China, Japan, India, the US, the UK and Spain, to gauge the various strategies adopted by companies in response to the COVID-19 outbreak.

The figures in the table below denote the percentage share of companies against the various factors for which they were surveyed.[5]

Table 4.1: Employer Strategies in Response to COVID-19

Strategy	India	Japan	China	United States	United Kingdom	Spain
Provide more opportunities to work remotely	90.3	83.9	82.1	86.4	91.4	85.7
Accelerate digitization of work processes (e.g., use digital tools, video conferencing)	87.1	61.3	92.3	91.5	94.3	92.9
Accelerate automation of tasks	58.1	48.4	53.8	57.6	57.1	64.3

Strategy	India	Japan	China	United States	United Kingdom	Spain
Accelerate digitization of upskilling/ reskilling (e.g., education technology providers)	51.6	93.5	53.8	54.2	65.7	78.6
Accelerate implementation of upskilling/ reskilling programmes	48.4	38.7	41	44.1	48.6	50

Source: WEF (2020)

There is a pattern emerging here as well. The highest emphasis was on enabling work through remote modes, followed by greater digitization of work processes, automation, and reskilling of personnel on emergent processes and technologies. Initiatives to develop skills other than those immediately needed for operations, in comparison, clearly took a backseat during the initial phase of the pandemic. As the crisis waned, it became important once again for company stakeholders to focus on these human-centric skills.

STRESS, MEDITATION AND THE MINDFULNESS REVOLUTION

In our times, few things are as immediately relevant as stress and its impact on focus, motivation and productivity. The debilitating experience of the pandemic has kept stress at the forefront of discussions in HR and other industry fora. As its antidote, mindfulness has once again come to the fore. Research on mindfulness and its applications, in areas from clinical treatment to the workplace, particularly in the West, have been around for over four decades. The literature on mindfulness is both vast and varied. Here, we shall limit ourselves to outlining the two predominant schools of thought that have emerged out of Western academia with regard to mindfulness.[6]

One of these owes its fame to Jon Kabat-Zinn. After a brilliant Ph.D. in medicine at MIT, Kabat-Zinn turned his attention to yoga, meditation and other ancient Indic practices. Over time, he was able to infuse these with the empirical rigour of scientific research. Consequently, he developed his method for teaching mindfulness, enabling people to cope with stress, anxiety, pain and illness in a more effective and meaningful way. The mindfulness-based stress reduction (MBSR) programme created by Kabat-Zinn, offered by a large number of medical centres, hospitals and health-solution organizations globally, is described in his book, *Full Catastrophe Living*. His subsequent books, such as *Wherever You Go, There You Are*, and *Mindfulness Meditation*, expanded on his original ideas, bringing the practice of mindfulness to the lives of millions across the world.[7]

Kabat-Zinn's work was one of the first to help explain why we humans are neurologically wired for a fight/flight/freeze reaction to stressful situations. The answer lies in internal and external stressors, and in our reaction to them. Internal stressors are factors arising within oneself, viz., emotions, as well as thoughts and feelings that are hurtful, such as pain, depression, rejection, loneliness, injustice or humiliation. External stressors, on the other hand, include extremes of heat or cold, hunger, thirst, abuse, being subject to physical threat and other hurtful factors originating outside one's body and mind. Our typical reaction to stress is accompanied by psychological hyper-arousal, alertness, strong feelings or emotions, and copious release of stress hormones, such as adrenaline, noradrenalin and cortisol.

Neuro-scientifically, any stress creates a 'conflict' between different parts within the human brain. The prefrontal cortex, the seat of intellect and analytical thinking, processes and internalizes the stressor, viewing its urgency within the overall scheme of things. But the amygdala, which harks back to the age of dinosaurs, sees every stressor as critical, triggering the fight/ flight/freeze reaction within a fraction of a second. A more mindful response to stress involves momentary hyper-arousal, tempered by a greater awareness of the experience of stress and acceptance of the situation. So, a 'reaction' to stress is likely to be impulsive, split-second, knee-jerk, and typically powered by the amygdala. But a 'response' to stress means that the brain has had a few extra seconds to process and analyse the stress, giving the poised prefrontal cortex a chance to have its say.

The diagram below presents these two contrasting impacts of stress. The left-hand side represents the typical fight/ flight/freeze reaction, while the right-hand side shows a more measured, mindful response to a stress trigger.

Figure 4.2: Mindful and Non-Mindful Response to Stress

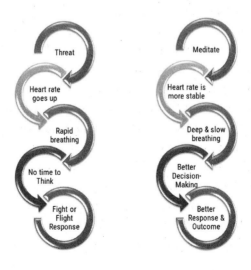

At its core, Kabat-Zinn's work is steeped in the tradition of the Buddhist masters. One of his gurus was the revered Vietnamese monk Thích Nhất Hạnh, whose life, according to many around the world, has had as much of a calming influence on his followers as the Dalai Lama's on his. Thich Nhất Hạnh successfully built a network of monasteries and retreat centres in France, the US, Australia, Thailand, Vietnam and Hong Kong. The author of over 100 books, including *Zen Keys*, *The Miracle of Mindfulness*, *Being Peace*, *The Heart of Understanding*, *Living Buddha, Living Christ* and *No Death, No Fear*, he also offered the world many recorded meditation practice sessions, discussions and dharma talks.[8]

Mindfulness, according to him, is all about inhabiting the present moment, and meditation the practice that anchors one in the present moment. Its opposite is forgetfulness and inability to stay focused in the present moment, because the mind is either leaping ahead into the future, with its deadlines and anxieties, or mired in sadness and regrets about the past. Our restless, incessantly active mind takes us away from the present moment, which is really the only time available to us, to experience life. Reversing centuries of European intellectual thought that had been grappling with the problem of the body-mind duality, Thích Nhất Hạnh declared: 'I think, therefore I am not alive.'

The literature on meditation and the scientific evidence of its benefits would fill many a library shelf, and cannot possibly be reviewed here at any great length. But here are some of the benefits. The first relates to the effect of sustained practise of meditation over several weeks on the regulation of blood pressure in the body. Kabat-Zinn and his associates found that there was a discernible, stabilizing influence of meditation on blood pressure, both in clinical patients suffering from chronic mental health conditions and in regular people seeking to address stress in their daily lives. The diagram below provides a snapshot of the blood-pressure changes among participants following a meditation retreat.

Figure 4.3: Effect of Meditation on Blood Pressure

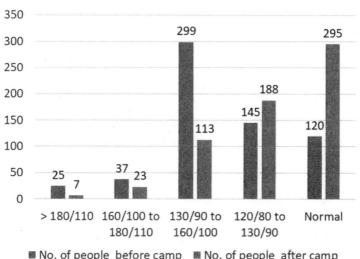

The second impact of mindfulness is its rewiring of our neuro-circuits, pruning away the least used connections and strengthening the ones we exercise most. It increases the volume and density of the hippocampus, which is crucial for memory. Meditators have robust connections between different regions of their brain, facilitating synchronized communication between them. They develop a particularly wrinkly cortex, which is the site of the most sophisticated mental activities, such as abstract thinking and introspection. Such people have scored higher on tests on attention and working memory. The calming effect of meditation can also be seen in brain EEG or electroencephalograms, which provides evidence of spontaneous activity in meditators, as seen in the diagram below.

Figure 4.4: Effect of Meditation on Level of Brain Activity

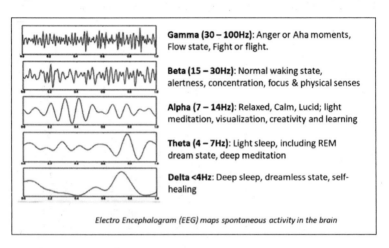

Gamma (30 – 100Hz): Anger or Aha moments, Flow state, Fight or flight.

Beta (15 – 30Hz): Normal waking state, alertness, concentration, focus & physical senses

Alpha (7 – 14Hz): Relaxed, Calm, Lucid; light meditation, visualization, creativity and learning

Theta (4 – 7Hz): Light sleep, including REM dream state, deep meditation

Delta <4Hz: Deep sleep, dreamless state, self-healing

Electro Encephalogram (EEG) maps spontaneous activity in the brain

Our most common EEG state is beta, where waves are at a frequency of 15–30 Hz. This is our normal waking state, associated with alertness, concentration and focus. The alpha state is a relaxed and calm state, which we experience when we wake up and when we are about to fall asleep. The theta and delta states are associated with light and deep sleep, respectively. Meditators show an alpha state during light meditation and a theta state during deep meditation. So, during deep meditation, brain activity is similar to that of light sleep, and even during light meditation the brain experiences a relaxed and calm state, typically associated with creativity and learning.

This has clear implications when it comes to how stressors affect us. A seasoned meditator is less susceptible to the 'now or never' pressures from the amygdala. The longer-term effect of meditation is to resituate the 'default setting' of the brain's activity level to a less manic, theta state. This means that when a stress trigger occurs, it takes that much more time—and more provocation—for the brain to fly into a gamma state of anger or panic.

We conclude this section by briefly discussing the alternative, non-meditation-based school of thought on mindfulness. This is traced back to the pathbreaking work of Dr Ellen Langer who, in 1981, became the first woman ever to be tenured as a professor of psychology at Harvard University. Over the past four decades, Professor Langer has studied the illusion of control, decision-making, ageing and mindfulness theory. Her hugely influential work, *Counterclockwise*, published in 2009, answers the question of ageing from her extensive research, and hugely increased interest in the subject. But it is also with good reason that she is admiringly described as the 'mother of mindfulness'. Her many books, including *Mindfulness*, *The Power of Mindful Learning*, and *The Art of Noticing*, have made available to the general public the findings and insights of over 200 published research papers and around forty years of research.[9]

Mindfulness, in Professor Langer's view, is the process of actively noticing new things. When we do that, it situates us immediately in the present. It makes us more sensitive to context and perspective. It's the essence of engagement. Professor Langer feels this is energy-begetting, not energy-consuming. The problem is, people mistakenly assume this is stressful and exhausting—all this thinking. However, what's actually stressful is the mindless negative evaluations we make, the worry that we'll find problems and not be able to solve them. Perhaps the biggest challenge of all, according to Prof. Langer, is the fact that most of us are in a state of mindlessness most of the time, without being aware of it.

The practice of mindfulness offers tangible rewards—better creativity, focus and performance being only some of them. Professor Langer also upends commonly believed notions of workplace norms and practices. For instance, when it comes to a particular task or deliverable, leaders and managers often say: 'This is the way to do it'. But such an approach indicates inflexibility and deprives people of the opportunity to think creatively and of new ways of accomplishing the task, which may be more effective than the one that worked in an earlier ecosystem, where the conditions were different. She also believes in 'work-life integration', as opposed to the more popularly used term 'work-life balance'. 'Balance', by definition, she feels, suggests that the two constituent elements are in opposition and have nothing in common. Which, of course, is not true.

A key aspect of Professor Langer's work is the measurement of mindfulness. The Langer Mindfulness Scale, developed by her and her associates at Harvard University, is a comprehensive psychometric scale, validated across multiple populations, and in several languages. Higher Overall Mindfulness Scores are associated with greater physical and psychological well-being (e.g., better health, quality of life), more positive social relationships, greater job satisfaction, more learning and creativity).[10]

Table 4.2: Components of the Langer Mindfulness Scale

Factor	Description	Interpretation
Novelty-seeking	Looking for newness, perceiving each situation as an opportunity to learn something new	Higher Novelty Seeking Scores are associated with the ability to seek out new attributes in people and situations, as well as more open attitudes
Novelty-Producing	Generating new information in order to learn more about the current situation	Higher Novelty Producing Scores are associated with the ability to find new and positive ways to view the world, as well as creativity in everyday life

Factor	Description	Interpretation
Engagement	Scoring high in engagement means a person is likely to notice more details about his or her specific relationship with the environment	Higher Engagement Scores are associated with the ability to fully engage at different levels of a situation, as well as higher self-esteem
Flexibility	Welcome a changing environment rather than resisting it	Higher Flexibility Scores are associated with the ability to take multiple perspectives in situations, and also the ability to recognize one's own and others' emotional states

Source: Ellen Langer's 'Langer Mindfulness Scale—21 Items'

Mindfulness has a tremendous effect on the emotional and mental health of people, and in all spheres of life. Some key workplace initiatives involving mindfulness, undertaken by companies globally, are discussed in Chapter Six.

RESILIENCE IN THE WORKPLACE

Unlike in the case of mindfulness and meditation, or emotional intelligence (which we shall take up in the next section), our awareness of resilience is more recent. Research on this subject and its application in the workplace began much later in the day, as compared to, say, study of mindfulness. But the global COVID-19 outbreak, which has disrupted life so much, has also forced a new sense of urgency for developing resilience at individual, organizational and industry levels, as a means to effecting economic recovery. Analysts and institutional thought leaders, such as Accenture, PwC and Egon Zehnder, have undertaken surveys and published reports underscoring the importance of resilience, with prescriptions and frameworks to enhance it in practice.[11]

But a few important aspects need to be appreciated before we can proceed to workplace interventions. The first relates to our understanding of the concept of resilience itself. Resilient individuals and teams are those that cope well with adversity, show perseverance throughout, and *are able to recover from the disruptive events* by employing adaptive processes. There are clearly two parts to this construct. Yet, in the common perception, the emphasis is squarely on the first part—of coping and persevering—which is arduous, taxing and unpleasant. The fact is that if focused interventions are to be truly effective, they'd need to focus equally on the italicized words above—a process that requires hope, optimism and positivity. Without this, the experience of skill-building will continue to be fraught with the stress and anxiety that is already present in people's lives, and will not lead to respite from them.

The understanding that resilience inherently contains complexities and nuances leads to some fundamental questions. For instance, what is the conceptual relationship between individual-level and team-level resilience? What is the relationship between behaviours, organizational resources and processes? Can processes in the workplace, and not just people, be resilient? What individual factors are associated with resilience at the team level? And finally, what does resilience in the workplace entail, at the individual level?

In April 2020, a team of researchers headed by Angelique Hartwig at the Alliance Manchester Business School in England undertook a systematic review seeking answers to these questions. Their much-needed study provides a deeper, multilevel understanding of resilience, taking into account a dynamic view of team resilience and the interdependencies between team and individual resilience.[12]

There are nine key insights that emerge from the study:

1. The resources of individual team members, e.g., team orientation, expertise and communication skills, are positively correlated with resilient team processes. As the latter are calibrated to give a fillip to employee trust, confidence and resilience, the former, too, get a boost.

2. Team resilience is positively linked to resilient team processes, and this relationship also holds at the individual level.

3. Team-level resources, e.g., interpersonal relationships between team members, as well as team culture, are positively related to resilient team processes.

4. Transformational leadership, wherein a leader engages with teams to identify the changes required, guides the teams by inspiring them and implements the required change in close coordination with the teams, is positively related to resilient team processes.

5. Resilient team behaviour consists of core team processes, including cooperation, coordination and communication, as well as minimizing or managing adverse impact, and behaviours that facilitate mending or healing, during as well as in the aftermath of adverse events.

6. Resilient team processes, e.g., minimizing, managing and mending behaviours, are positively correlated with post-adversity team functioning. The more deeply integrated and effective these processes are prior to a crisis, the smoother will be the team's ability to bounce back later on, and the faster it is likely to do so.

7. Team-level attributes, such as team identity, shared views and mental outlook, team trust, collective efficacy, cohesion and psychological safety, are all positively related to resilient team processes—minimizing, managing and mending behaviours.

8. Resilience at the team level is demonstrated by a team's trajectory following exposure to an adverse event—including its persistence under pressure, its pace and extent

of recovery, improvement in functioning, performance or health, following the crisis.

9. Team resilience is positively and reciprocally related to individual resilience. Therefore, while it's possible for two individuals within a team, each high on resilience, to be at loggerheads with each other, at an aggregate level the resilience level of the team tends to be higher, the greater the level of resilience at an individual level.

By definition, resilience of any kind is contextual. Even so, the study shows that in general, the degree of deterioration in functioning as a result of a crisis, as well as the time needed to recover from adversity, are both important indicators of team resilience. Thus, the measure of resilience becomes a metric on a continuous scale, along which teams vary. The more time a team needs to recover from adversity, the less resilient it's likely to be. Similarly, the more that team functioning is disrupted by an adverse event, the less resilient it is likely to be against its impact.

The table below shows the various factors constituting resilience in the workplace.[13]

Table 4.3: Elements of Workplace Resilience

Factor	Description
Living authentically	Knowledge of one's personal values, and holding on to them, deploying personal strengths, and having a good level of emotional awareness and regulation. Higher scores are associated with the ability to be one's own true self rather than an imitation of what one would like to be, or as others expect one to be. It also fosters closer harmony between one's actions, words and behaviour on the one hand, and beliefs, values and convictions on the other.

Factor	Description
Finding your calling	Seeking work that has purpose brings a sense of belonging and is a fit with one's core values and beliefs. Higher scores are associated with the discovery and pursuance of one's true interests and passion, as well as a greater likelihood of finding real purpose in one's work.
Maintaining perspective	The capacity to reframe setbacks, maintain a solution focus, and manage negativity. Higher scores are associated with the ability to look at the bigger picture and advise others, along with the ability to demonstrate experience and wisdom.
Managing stress	Using work and life routines that help manage everyday stressors, maintain work-life balance and ensure time for relaxation. Higher scores denote the ability to control one's own emotions and maintain composure in situations of stress and crisis, the ability to respond maturely rather than react in a knee-jerk manner to stress, and to achieve better work-life integration.
Interacting cooperatively	A workplace work style that includes seeking feedback, advice and support as well as providing support to others. Higher scores are associated with the ability to look for support and feedback from others, as well as the ability to be supportive to others, including giving praise wherever due.
Staying healthy	Maintaining a good level of physical fitness and a healthy diet. Higher scores are associated with better overall level of physical health and immunity, better consciousness of the importance of maintaining good health, and taking tangible steps in that direction.
Building networks	Developing and maintaining personal support networks, which might be both within and outside the workplace. Higher scores are associated with the ability to connect and engage fully with strangers, beyond the immediate circle of family, friends and colleagues, along with the ability to develop rapport and build trusting relationships with people.
Internal locus of control	Belief that one has control over their life and work environments and events, and so will base one's success or failure on one's own work. Higher scores are associated with belief in one's ability to determine one's own life events and outcomes, and being able to attribute successes and failures to one's own actions.

Factor	Description
External locus of control	Belief that external forces such as fate or luck determine events, so one will attribute one's success or failure to outside influences. Higher scores are associated with the belief that one is not in control of one's life events and outcomes, and success or failure is attributed to outside forces.
Overall workplace resilience	Higher scores on all factors, except external locus of control, indicate higher overall workplace resilience. Higher Overall Resilience Scores are associated with physical and psychological ability to endure adversity and hardship, and ability to bounce back from adversity, and from negative and unpleasant circumstances.

Source: NUVAH Behavioural Test for Workplace Resilience

One thing becomes immediately apparent. Different elements of resilience will come to the fore, depending on the trigger. In a sudden pandemic-like situation, stress management would no doubt seem all-important. But, as that immediate storm passes, maintaining perspective, strengthening networks and interacting cooperatively with stakeholders assume greater importance.

It's now natural to ask: can resilience really be *taught* in the workplace, across demographic groups, from Gen-Zers and Millennials to the older generation of the workforce? The answer to this is a qualified 'yes'. We should note that our understanding of the nuances of resilience is still evolving, as are the methodologies, tools and artefacts required for training interventions in this field. But the signs so far have been positive.

In 2015, a study conducted by Robertson, Cooper, Sarkar and Curran examined a set of fourteen different studies across industry sectors in order to investigate the impact of resilience training on resilience at the individual level. Four categories of dependent variables came to the fore: (1)

Outcomes around mental health and subjective well-being; (2) Psychosocial outcomes; (3) Physical/biological outcomes; and (4) Performance outcomes. Their findings show that resilience training can improve personal resilience as well as psychological well-being among employees.[14] More recently, in 2020, Liu, Ein, Gervasio, Battaion, Reed and Vickers undertook a fresh analysis of various interventions aimed at enhancing resilience in the workplace. They focused on factors such as age, gender, duration of intervention and the approach adopted. A total of 268 studies, with 1584 independent samples, were included in the meta-analysis. This multilevel meta-analysis too indicated that resilience-promoting interventions yielded a statistically significant overall effect.[15]

We now turn to a highly innovative approach to competency and skills development. Imagine that building resilience at the organizational level didn't involve vast expenses, entailing a series of interventions right down to the level of each individual employee. Imagine instead, that resilience could be built, ground up, without really having to focus on it at all, that it could be achieved on its own, organically, as a by-product, and that the entire process, far from involving surgical pain, would be positive, pleasant, even inspiring. If this sounds too good to be true, that is precisely what over two decades of research by positive psychologist Barbara Fredrickson and her associates indicates.[16]

Fredrickson's pathbreaking 'broaden and build theory' makes two remarkable assertions. First, that positive emotions broaden an individual's set of momentary actions in response to thoughts. Thus, joy gives rise to the urge to play, to interest—to explore things beyond the quotidian—and to contentment—to savour and integrate—and love sparks a recurring cycle of these urges within a sphere of safe and close associations. The second, even more powerful hypothesis, is that positive emotions (i) broaden people's attention and thinking; (ii) undo the lingering of negative emotions in people; (iii) fuel psychological resilience; (iv) build consequential personal resources; (v) trigger upward spirals towards greater well-being in the future, and (vi) even pave the way for one's flourishing.

That's not all. Subsequent empirical studies by Fredrickson and Losada seem to have hit upon a single magic ratio that by itself could determine whether, beginning with a certain state of mind, we are likely to languish, slide into despair, or experience that elusive upward spiral of well-being, buoying oneself and one's organization into a state of flourish. That special ratio is the proportion of positive to negative emotions, as experienced by people. It has been found that a ratio of 2.3:1 of positive to negative emotions is something of a threshold. Anything below it, and one has the tendency to lapse into despair. If this ratio is sustained, at best this still maintains only the status quo of well-being. But if, on average, the ratio of positive to negative emotions experienced, say, over a month, is 3:1, individuals may indeed achieve a sort of 'terminal velocity' of optimism and self-sustained high levels of focus, motivation and productivity. At this point, external stressors and incentives play only a very minimal role in their state of well-being. This in turn propels them into a trajectory of flourishing.[17]

For Fredrickson and her associates, everything boils down to positive emotions. From a workplace standpoint, this could mean a wide range of feelings, such as joy, contentment, a sense of bonding and camaraderie, or eager anticipation of coming into work at the beginning of the week. But how can positive emotions be generated in the workplace and sustained over time? Delving into the following questions might help. Can employee policies and processes be curated for optimal empowerment and autonomy, while not compromising on compliance and data security? Can we make employee engagement genuinely effective in the emergent hybrid workplace? Can the emotional and psychological fallouts of an extended work-from-home routine be addressed? Can we learn to be more adaptive to changing circumstances, on a continual basis? Can we avoid the tendency to co-opt every new scenario that we manage to come to terms with—for instance, work from home, or a new form of hybrid work model—and turn it into a comfort fort that we're then reluctant to leave?

Increasingly, leaders and managers must support mental health and cultivate resilience among their employees—not just increase their engagement and performance. Based on more than 100 million Gallup global interviews, *Wellbeing at Work*, authored jointly by Jon Clifton and Jim Harter, explores the five key elements of well-being—career, social, financial, physical and community—and how organizations can help employees and teams thrive in those elements. The book also offers practical suggestions and action items to company leaders, to help employees use their innate talents and strengths to thrive in each of the elements of well-being. Clifton's more recent book, *Blind Spot*, published in 2022, reinforces this idea, pointing out that global leaders, be that of countries or large corporates, focus too much on economic figures, and hardly at all, on the well-being and happiness of their people.[18]

Given that remote/hybrid work will continue to be the dominant mode of operations, at least in the foreseeable future, it is useful to summarize some proven practices and findings. Gallup advocates a four-part approach for leaders, to successfully devise and implement a WFH strategy:[19]

- **Organizational considerations:** Examine your organization's business needs, consider your organizational culture and determine the potential impact on customers when making remote-work decisions. Along with financial risks and opportunities, leaders need to consider culture-related questions in the matter of consistency, clarity and authenticity.

- **Role considerations:** Leaders should evaluate a role's optimal fit for long-term at-home work, based on its task definition and the employee's ability to work independently and effectively in the role outside of the traditional workplace. It is found that an optimal remote work role meets three criteria: a) Employees can perform their duties outside of an on-site workplace; b) Most of the role's tasks and processes are well-defined; and c) The role does not require highly interdependent work for success.
- **Team considerations:** 55 per cent of managers say they will allow their employees to work remotely more often than they did before COVID-19. Given this, consider the interdependency of team members, the dynamics of team member contributions, team engagement and trust.
- **Individual considerations:** More than half of at-home workers say they would prefer to continue working remotely as much as possible even after restrictions on businesses and school closures are lifted. Therefore, managers who want to create successful work-from-home plans for their team members need to evaluate the following criteria for each person on their team: readiness and comfort, life circumstances, performance and strengths.

New forms of employee engagement become crucial in remote and hybrid modes of working. Another Gallup global study has found that highly engaged teams were more resilient than their peers during the 2001–02 and 2008–09 recessions. Favourable job attitudes have a stronger relationship to organizational outcomes in bad economic times than in normal or good times. By developing a culture of employee engagement, leaders can forge strong, resilient organizations, teams and individuals.[20]

EQ, EMPATHY AND THE INDIAN WORKPLACE

Like mindfulness and meditation, emotional intelligence—or EQ, as it's more commonly known—has gained much currency in the workplace in recent years. A growing number of corporate leaders, organizational psychologists and executive coaches globally have been advocating its implementation on the ground, but with at best middling effect, particularly in India. The COVID-19 pandemic, which is at its heart a deeply human crisis, has once again renewed the urgency for leaders, managers and supervisors to be more considerate and empathetic, and to put themselves, emotionally and psychologically, in the shoes of their employees.

In this section, we shall not attempt any in-depth exploration of the relationship between emotional intelligence and focus, productivity, innovation or camaraderie in the workplace, or of the fallouts of absence of empathy, or why, on the demographic dimension, when working with millennials and Gen-Zs, EQ assumes even greater importance. Of the two authors of this book, one has already co-written a book on the subject, *From Command to Empathy: Using EQ in the Age of Disruption*.[21] So, after a quick overview of the framework and factors of EQ, we focus on how the Indian workplace has fared in terms of being empathetic, the reasons behind its bleak performance in the past, the fallout of low EQ, and current opportunities.

Much of our present scientific understanding of EQ can be traced back to Professor Daniel Goleman and his associates at Harvard University. The first thing that strikes one about Goleman's framework is its elegant simplicity. The five skills that, taken together, make up emotional intelligence, according to him, can be clubbed under two competencies—personal competence and social competence. Personal competence is about (a) knowledge of ourselves (self-awareness); (b) the ability to manage ourselves (self-regulation); and c) intrinsic drive and conviction, sustained over time (motivation). Social competence comprises (a) our knowledge of others' feelings and emotions (social awareness); and (b) the ability to manage relationships with others (relationship management, or empathy).

Self-awareness

Self-awareness means having a deep understanding of one's own strengths, weaknesses, needs, drives and emotions. This attribute helps people to become more realistic about and honest with themselves and others. Self-awareness makes them more comfortable discussing both their strengths and what they perceive as the areas they need improvement in. Consequently, they are more willing to learn and are humble enough to ask for constructive criticism. People with a high degree of self-awareness understand how their feelings affect themselves as well as other people around them. Self-awareness extends to an understanding of values, beliefs, needs and fears. In the process, people tend to stay more 'true' to their own values, and this helps in better ethical decision-making. For instance, they could turn down a higher paying job for another which is better aligned with their interests and passion. Overall, higher self-awareness leads to higher self-confidence.

Self-regulation

It is one thing to be conscious of our emotions and to be in touch with them, but managing them is quite another.

Sometimes we find this challenging as our emotions can be quite overwhelming. At the same time, a life devoid of emotion and passion would be boring. And this is where the challenge lies—the human brain is designed in a way that often leaves us with little control over when we will be swept away by emotions or what those emotions will be. The saving grace is that we do have some control over how long they last. Self-management is thus like an ongoing inner conversation, freeing us from being prisoners of our own feelings. People with higher self-management skills do have bad-mood days and emotional impulses, just like everyone else, but they are able to control them better and sometimes to even channelize them in positive ways. It enables them to better cope with ambiguity and change and to also be able to say no to impulses that can end up harming them.

Motivation

Intrinsic motivation is the drive, the passion, to fulfil one's own inner needs and goals. The pursuit of these goals may result in financial gain, acclaim and social recognition, but the motivation that sustains this effort goes beyond them. Those who excel in this area are action-oriented; they set goals, have a high need for achievement and are always looking for ways to do better. They also tend to be very committed and are great at taking initiative. A highly motivated individual demonstrates initiative and commitment to complete a task, as well as perseverance and tenacity in the face of adversity, delays and setbacks. Motivation leads to a state of being where one is perfectly in tune with an activity, and this can lead to peak experiences that feel almost magical. We shall discuss this in more detail, in the next section.[22]

Social Skills

An individual with evolved social skills is often termed a 'people person'. Such individuals are trustworthy team players and confident communicators—as good at listening to other people as they are at speaking themselves. They are likely to make excellent leaders, inspiring and motivating colleagues, managing change and resolving conflict effectively, and giving praise where it's due. In displaying high social skills, a person is actively applying an understanding of his own emotions to communicate and interact with others on a day-to-day basis. Social skills include active listening, highly conscious and honed verbal communication skills as well as non-verbal communication skills, leadership skills, and the ability to persuade, negotiate and develop rapport with others.

Empathy

In a way, empathy is a natural consequence, if not the cumulative effect, of the garnering of the other dimensions of EQ. The more self-aware we are, the more skilled we become at recognizing the feelings of others. Those who can read others' feelings are certainly better adjusted and sensitive, if not more well-liked. Empathy is particularly important today as a key leadership trait, given the demanding and disrupting effects of multiple teams, globalization, the hunt for better talent and the constantly rising standards of professional efficiency.

An empathetic leader is able to sense any dissonance in the viewpoints of the members of the team and across teams, without getting influenced by any particular individual or group. Globalization raises the challenge of cross-cultural dialogue, resulting in higher chances of misunderstanding. Leaders high on empathy are able to develop and retain good people through coaching and mentoring. Instinctively, they sense the best way to give feedback and, very importantly, when to give it. They know when to push and when to hold back, thereby demonstrating empathy in action.

There has been tremendous development in our understanding of empathy over the years. We've come to know that empathy is not a monolith, but a nuanced set of three categories of attributes: cognitive empathy, affective empathy and compassionate empathy. Cognitive empathy is the ability to understand how a person feels and what they might be thinking. People who have this are better communicators than those who don't because their cognitive ability helps them transmit information in a way that is likely to be best received by the other person. Emotional empathy, also known as affective empathy, is the ability to share the feelings of another person. This form of empathy helps a person build emotional connections with others. Finally, there is compassionate empathy, which is also called empathetic concern, which goes beyond simple understanding of another to sharing his or her feelings. This moves a person to take action and help in the best way she can.

It has in fact been posited that, neurologically, all humans are hard-wired for empathy. The brain contains mirror neurons, what the neuroscientist Dr V.S. Ramachandran terms 'Gandhi neurons', which demonstrate the deep connectedness of human consciousness. Therefore, emotions witnessed in others tend to trigger a 'mirror reaction' in ourselves. Dr Simon Baron-Cohen, professor of psychology and psychiatry at Cambridge University and director of Cambridge's Autism Research Centre, has conducted research on social neuroscience for over two decades. His studies, which include extensive MRI scanning, reveal that empathy doesn't reside in a single brain region; there are at least a dozen different regions associated with empathy, including the amygdala (subcortically), the ventromedial prefrontal cortex and the inferior frontal gyrus.

At this point, let us take a step back and review the different factors of EQ mentioned in this section. If we now compare them with those in the heat map we discussed earlier in this chapter, we can see that a good number of the behavioural skills that will be in greater demand in the emergent workplace have directly to do with emotional intelligence. It's therefore clear that EQ and empathy have re-established themselves as important facets of corporate behaviour. With this background, we can ask some questions related to the workplace. How can empathy be measured at the organizational level? How do Indian corporations fare on this front? And, if their performance in the past has been poor, what have been the underlying reasons and how can we learn from them?

For individuals, there are impactful measures of emotional intelligence and empathy, e.g., those developed by Goleman and Baron-Cohen. For comparative evaluations at the organizational level, a different approach is warranted. Belinda Parmar, CEO of the Empathy Business, based out of the UK, has developed a Global Empathy Index for large corporations across economies, with a focus on UK, US and Indian companies. The index was created by breaking down empathy into categories: ethics, leadership, company culture, brand perception, social media-driven messaging and ecological footprint. Studies using the Global Empathy Index, published in *Harvard Business Review* in 2015–16, offered some striking insights. It was observed that the value of the top ten companies increased more than twice as much as those of the bottom ten and generated 50 per cent more earnings. The correlation between departments with higher empathy and those with high performers was a staggering 80 per cent.

But a shock lay in store for both analysts and large corporations waiting to see how Indian companies fared on this index. The study found that six of the ten least empathetic companies listed in the Global Empathy Index were from India. And also, that it was not limited to a particular industry or sector—the six giants spanned oil and gas, pharmaceuticals, finance, telecom, technology and infrastructure. There was quite a furore when the results of the Global Empathy Index study were published. Every publication of note in India carried the news. Given that the companies were listed very clearly meant that a certain element of 'naming and shaming' was present as well in the reportage. But by the time the embers died down, it became evident that barring a few forward-thinking organizations, for whom this was a wake-up call, the large majority of companies in India simply moved on with their targets for the year. Empathy might have found its way into press articles, think tank conferences and occasionally the boardrooms, but its implementation on the ground remained minimal.[23]

The pandemic has delivered a fresh jolt to the modes in which companies have run business. As we have seen in Chapter Three and in the heat map earlier in this chapter, there is now renewed emphasis on emotional/social intelligence and empathy. Before training initiatives for nurturing empathy within the organization receive a new impetus, however, a basic question must be answered. *For employers, what is the return on investment (ROI) on empathy?*

The following aspects of empathy for an organization help to shed some light:[24]

- **Innovation:** Be it a new product, business line or innovative new service, breakthrough ideas typically stem from a deep and genuine understanding of customer pain points, backed by a passion for helping customers resolve those pain points. Infusing empathy into the very fabric of a company's culture encourages employees to view the business and their own work from an outside-in perspective, incorporating new insights and ideas drawn from the needs and goals of customers, partners and even competitors. This also empowers employees to build technology that's more personal, predictive, and tailored to customers' unique needs.

- **Sales and service:** An empathetic approach to sales or customer service entails an intimate understanding of a particular prospect or customer need, embracing it as one's own and working collaboratively to address it. This proactive, action-oriented form of empathy encourages trust and greater openness in communication, allowing employees to solve objections swiftly and also build long-term relationships.
- **Employee engagement:** Empathy is seen to be a powerful critical success factor when it comes to the 'internal customers'. Engaging and empowering a team starts with understanding their day-to-day experiences, committing to make them better and opening lines of communication to continuously test how the organization is doing. For instance, as part of the recruitment process, understanding a candidate's career objectives and exploring how the organization can support them would be a thoughtful and empathetic step, which can define the trajectory of an employee's growth and success.

Emotional intelligence can be seen as a consequence of various other attributes—mindfulness, patience, listening skills, genuine interest in other people and in the world around us, and a facility for that somewhat vital but disregarded skill—the art of conversation. The big question remains: how can organizations and working professionals be equipped to welcome the conditions of greater understanding and collaboration? One answer is to work with industry experts, coaches and/or psychologists, to curate a set of interventions, with behavioural assessments, debriefing, role-play sessions and documenting of learnings that can be undertaken in a corporate workplace set-up.

But a more creative, if unconventional, approach comes from the conversations curated by Theodore Zeldin and his associates at the Oxford Muse Foundation. Zeldin is a globally renowned historian, philosopher, academic and author of pathbreaking books, such as *A Brief History of Humanity*. An understanding of life and the human condition through meaningful conversations has long been at the heart of his approach. Gleaning insights from his vast, multidisciplinary expertise, the Oxford Muse One-Day Conversations aim to improve professional, personal and intercultural relationships between organizations, between departments within organizations, between different specialities, and between institutions in the process of merging, and also between suppliers, clients and customers. The desired outcomes are arrived at through conversations specifically aimed at stimulating the following:

- **Imaginative thinking:** An exploration of how people can go one stage further, beyond the acquiring of information, specialization and competence, and discover new avenues for their thinking, through conversations with both innovating and traditionalist people in many branches of human activity.
- **Expanding knowledge:** Unlike training in communication skills, which teaches techniques without improving the content of what is spoken, the emphasis here is on substance—the ideas, research, discoveries and thinking processes—out of which memorable conversation is

created. The aim is not to make participants fast talkers but to expand their range of knowledge and awareness of past experiences on which they base their judgements and their vision of the future.

- **Integrating personal and professional life:** The conversations point to ways in which one's private life can contribute to enhancing the rewards of work, instead of being in competition with it. They give couples and families maps for endless exploration so that they never again say they have nothing to say to one another.
- **New sources of encouragement:** Going beyond introspection and the 'personal development' of talents already within the individual, the programme encourages the broadening of these talents through interaction with others, and the cultivation of new sensitivities and curiosities.[25]

'FLOW': CREATIVITY, FOCUS, MOTIVATION IN THE WORKPLACE

A couple of things inevitably happens to most people as they go up the career ladder. First, as you progress, new dimensions, and with them expectations, get added to your job role, quite speedily in certain sectors. Second, the level of complexity along these dimensions also increases (and more expectations), over time. Together, these two aspects call for a highly evolved and growing portfolio mix of skills and competencies.

There is a dual challenge in achieving this. Academia in India, until now, have not really equipped students with the intrinsic skills for such an intensive, lifelong learning experience. The most well-intentioned of organizations too cannot provide personalized guidance beyond a point, to say nothing of the majority of companies that still view their employees as 'headcount'. This means that for most working professionals, their sense of higher purpose, deeper engagement at work, buoyed by an intrinsic motivation sustained over time . . . all of these have to come from within themselves. How does one make this happen? Unlike a machine part that can be replaced or software that can be upgraded, in the case of humans, continuous pressure of upskilling will lead to stress and burnout. Upskilling can be sustained only through something inherent in oneself, and through the firm conviction or belief that what one is doing is relevant, meaningful and important. This in turn leads us to the question: *What makes for a more meaningful life, an excellent life?*

Much of what we know today on this subject comes from the work of Hungarian-born positive psychologist Mihaly Csikszentmihalyi and that of his associates for over the past four decades. His life work—development of the theory, practice and application of 'Flow'—has been so influential that it has entered the parlance of our everyday conversations—as in the phrase 'go with the flow'. His research began when Csikszentmihalyi asked himself the question—what makes a person creative, intrinsically motivated and able to sustain a high level of productivity over years, even decades? Thus began a series of insightful interviews with writers and painters, musicians and composers, filmmakers, award-winning actors, industry tycoons, renowned politicians, Olympic athletes and tennis champions, Nobel laureate physicists . . . in short, a wide range of individuals who were all leading lights in their own fields.

Going through the transcripts of reams of written and typed pages, here was the big discovery that Csikszentmihalyi made. As different from each other as many of these eminent people were, a common pattern nevertheless emerged, underscoring the surprisingly same way they felt, thought and wished for outcomes while in a state of 'Flow'. One of these was the quality of becoming totally engrossed and immersed in one's activity, to such an extent that one person tended to lose track of time and didn't feel hunger, thirst, minor discomfort or pain during this period, which often lasted several hours at a stretch, at times more. Equally prominent was the sense of being outside or beyond everyday reality, a heightened inner clarity and self-awareness—of knowing exactly how well one was doing, and of also knowing that while the activity was doable, it summoned all of one's skills and concentration in order to accomplish it. A large majority of the interviewees also reported experiencing a sense of serenity, of going beyond one's worries and even the boundaries of one's ego. Another interesting aspect was that the act of performing that activity gave the person instant and very tangible feedback. And, perhaps for this reason, the activity was autotelic or self-rewarding—requiring, at least during that specific time, no external validation, feedback or support.

The previous paragraph might have made you stop for a moment and say: 'I too have had such an experience, though perhaps not frequently. Was I in a state of "Flow" then, and if so, what could I do to get back into it, and possibly extend its duration?' This was precisely what Csikszentmihalyi focused on next. Having found commonalities among super-achievers from diverse fields, he and his associates spent the next few decades exploring whether regular, ordinary people also experienced 'Flow', and if so, what caused it, why it was usually so short-lived and what measures, if any, could induce 'Flow' to be extended or sustained. The research led to some highly interesting insights, which can be summarized in the diagram below.

Figure 4.5: The Science of 'Flow'

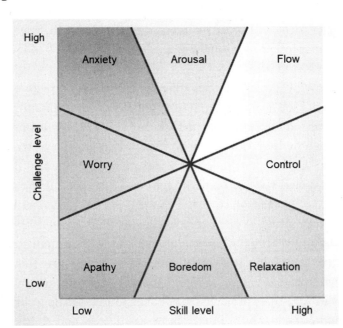

Source: Mihaly Csikszentmihalyi, Flow. *The Classic Work on How to Achieve Happiness*

Csikszentmihalyi found that across both super-achievers and regular people, 'Flow' occurs when the person's skills were fully involved in overcoming a challenge or accomplishing a task that was just about within reach. The magical 'Flow' experience, the bright cone on the top right-hand corner in the diagram, involves just the right balance between one's ability to act (skills) and the available opportunities for action (challenges). When the challenges are too high, one will inevitably get frustrated and worried and, if this situation continues, end up in a state of high anxiety. If the challenges are too low for one's abilities and skills, the state of relaxation one feels initially will slide into boredom, and thereafter apathy, sooner rather than later. But when the 'right' high challenges are matched with high skills, a deeper focus and sense of engagement occurs, which sets the experience of Flow moments apart from the more mundane experiences of life.[26]

'Flow' experiences can certainly act as a magnet for motivated self-learning on a sustained basis. But ordinarily, one does not remain in a state of Flow for very long. Is it possible to somehow induce a return to Flow? This is where Arousal, the zone directly to the left of Flow, gains prominence. Being in this state keeps one mentally alert and focused, but not quite cheerful or in control, since the challenges one is faced with are just a little ahead of one's abilities. Depending on one's level of curiosity and thirst for knowledge, this can then naturally create the urge to develop or sharpen one's skills. Translating this into the workplace scenario, if a professional possesses an appetite for learning, then projects that challenge the person's abilities or tend to be just out of reach in terms of skills and ability, but never overwhelmingly so, can keep that person placed much of the time between the Arousal and Flow zones.

Our natural aptitude for learning depends on what has come to be known as the 'growth mindset'. According to Professor Carol Dweck, who has spearheaded research on this front, possessing a growth mindset has a lot to do with the way one views hurdles, delays and setbacks. Is failure in any given instance an opportunity to grow, or does it mark a firm boundary around one's capabilities? The answer to this deceptively simple question makes all the difference. The callouts in the diagram below illustrate some of the attitudinal differences between a growth mindset and a fixed mindset.

Key to the growth mindset is belief in the principle of 'Yet'. Imagine you were up for promotion, and had been working hard to achieve this milestone. Yet, when the announcements are made, you find that you have not made it. At this juncture, disappointing as the result doubtless is, do you view it with a depressed finality, as a sort of sentence passed on your abilities? Or do you say to yourself, even if the boss or HR representative doesn't, 'I'm not there Yet'? Research has found that adopting this latter point of view, even in the face of a setback, leads to a more confident and positive outlook, wherein the milestone one may have just missed remains a possibility in the future.[27]

Figure 4.6: Growth and Fixed Mindsets

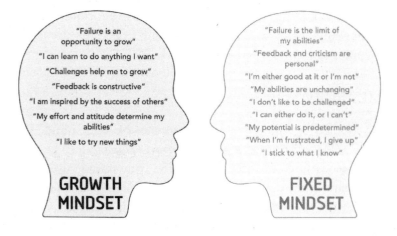

"Failure is an opportunity to grow"

"I can learn to do anything I want"

"Challenges help me to grow"

"Feedback is constructive"

"I am inspired by the success of others"

"My effort and attitude determine my abilities"

"I like to try new things"

GROWTH MINDSET

"Failure is the limit of my abilities"

"Feedback and criticism are personal"

"I'm either good at it or I'm not"

"My abilities are unchanging"

"I don't like to be challenged"

"I can either do it, or I can't"

"My potential is predetermined"

"When I'm frustrated, I give up"

"I stick to what I know"

FIXED MINDSET

Source: Mindset: The New Psychology of Success, Carol S. Dweck, Phd

It is interesting to note that the growth mindset framework strongly urges teachers, supervisors and managers to avoid labelling those in their charge or working in their teams, in particular as 'stupid' or 'smart'. The first label is obvious—it's insensitive and demeaning to call someone stupid. In fact, this could well be a symptom of a deeper underlying issue—one of bullying or harassment. The second—calling someone smart—is a bit more complicated. Ordinarily, praise would be considered something highly desirable. Professor Dweck, however, advises us to praise wisely, applaud not the talent, intelligence or end result, but the process, the approach followed, the journey that led to the achievement. It should also be noted that the growth mindset is not an absolute. Instead, it usually operates over a range or spectrum across different areas of life. For example, a high-performing product developer in a technology domain may exhibit a high growth mindset when it comes to response to setbacks and delays in research, viewing them as valuable opportunities to learn and improve. Yet, that same person may possess less of a growth mindset when it comes to acclimatizing to other cultures in the context of a global workplace, or display a fixed mindset when it comes to attire and cuisine.[28]

MEASURE FOR MEASURE

Psychometrics—literally, measurement of the mind—has been around for over a century now. The earliest form of such evaluations was used by the US Army during and in the aftermath of the devastating First World War, in an attempt to predict which soldiers would suffer from 'shell shock' or post-traumatic stress disorder. From those tenuous steps towards a new science to the present day, psychometric testing has grown to become a full-fledged global industry worth more than $500 million, with current annual growth estimated at 15 per cent. The pandemic, in casting a spotlight on behavioural competencies and mental health, has to accelerate the growth of this industry. Of course, psychological analysis continues to be part of the norm for candidates seeking to join the armed forces across the world. But now, in the corporate sphere, psychometrics has found applicability across a range of functions—from recruitment, leadership and competency development and career progression, to evaluating individuals and teams around stress and resilience, anxiety and depression, alignment to the organizational culture, and biases around diversity, equity and inclusion.

The industry has seen a proliferation of product companies and an army of psychologists, coaches and business advisers to interpret the results of those assessments for their clients. Some, such as the Five Factor Model or OCEAN, Myers Briggs, Hogan, Thomas, Korn Ferry, Caliper, to name only a few, have entrenched themselves in workplace functions. In certain cases—e.g., Myers Briggs—they have come in for their own share of controversy and scandal. In more recent times, Plum, Traitify, Predictive Index, Pymetrics and Mercer-Mettl are creating assessments powered by advanced technologies, such as NLP and AI-enabled chatbots, integrating assessments into business processes and workflows to glean insights into a professional's behavioural competencies. The research underpinning psychometric assessments has also undergone a shift, from traditional psychological and psychiatric frameworks to studies in personality, cognitive psychology, neuroscience and positive psychology. Gallup's Clifton Strengths, Alex Linley's Capp and NUVAH, all offer curated assessments based on the research and advances in positive psychology.[29]

Traditional psychometric measures typically follow the 'disease model' of medical practice. Anywhere in the world, when one walks into a doctor's consulting room, the same question is asked universally: 'What's wrong?' Traditional psychometric models work in much the same way. The objective is primarily to seek out 'what's wrong', diagnose the problem accurately and address it. Questionnaires are framed accordingly and, as a consequence, the responses also reflect the same original goal—to find and fix a problem. This approach neglects some crucial questions. What's right? What's working well with an individual? What are one's true strengths and passions, and how can they be best utilized within the work sphere, and beyond?

This is where 'Positive Psychology' makes a difference. It challenges the key preoccupation of traditional psychology— the 'disease model'—supplanting it with the mission of improving human well-being and the conditions of life. Over the last three decades, spearheaded by Dr Martin Seligman, the positive psychology movement has blossomed, with Mihaly Csikszentmihalyi, Christopher Peterson, Angela Duckworth and others making significant contributions. The fundamentals of the inclusive, empathetic approach of positive psychology are encapsulated in Martin Seligman's PERMA schema:[30]

1. **Positive emotion** – This means feeling good about oneself, one's work and others at the workplace. But it can involve acceptance of the past, including mistakes, and anticipating in a positive frame of mind what the future may hold.
2. **Engagement** – This refers to something an individual can get engrossed or absorbed in, an experience we have already seen in 'Flow'.
3. **Relationships** – This entails empathy, the need for interactions, rapport and camaraderie. It entails going beyond the transactional to establish rapport, trust and longer-term working relationships with clients, business associates, peers, juniors and supervisors.
4. **Meaning** – This involves seeking a deeper sense of purpose, value and fulfilment in one's work. Such introspection may result not only in a rediscovery of one's true potential, but also in redirection in one's career and exploration of avenues one may not have earlier considered.
5. **Accomplishments** – These are a function of self-motivation, perseverance and the passion to attain goals. Flourishing

results when accomplishment is linked to striving towards things from internal motivation rather than merely for the sake of the pursuit and improvement.

Transposing this ethos on to the workplace effects a definite transformation in mindset. Instead of plugging gaps around stress, absenteeism and low morale, the focus of the stakeholders shifts towards well-being. There are multiple constructs of what this means, in the work as well as personal sphere. Gallup, for instance, views it as comprising five key elements, which also form the kernel of the book *Wellbeing: The Five Essential Elements*, by Jim Harter and Tom Rath:[31]

- **Career well-being:** How you occupy your time or simply enjoy what you do every day
- **Social well-being:** Having strong relationships and love in your life
- **Financial well-being:** Effectively managing your economic life
- **Physical well-being:** Having good health and enough energy to get things done on a daily basis
- **Community well-being:** The sense of engagement you have with the area where you live

As with all behavioural elements, the first step in any successful initiative is the measurement of well-being. Jim Harter, chief scientist of Workplace Management and Well-being at Gallup, explains:

We need to first understand what dimensions we can measure, and whether we can act on them to increase the likelihood that we're thriving in our overall lives, having more good days and less of those negative emotions. We have to get ahead of it by helping people measure what matters the most and give them some insights into how they can improve their overall lives. That's one side. The other part is to make it personalized.[32]

Psychometric assessments need certain statistical conditions to be met. The first is validity. We may be attempting to assess an individual on motivation, but are we inadvertently asking questions around job satisfaction? Reliability or robustness, developed over time and multiple populations, is a close second. An assessment may prove to be quite effective for recruitment in the Indian ecosystem, but would the same test work as well for UK and US workplaces? Constant compilation of data, validation and re-standardization means that the business of designing, testing, refining and updating psychometric scales is a time-consuming and expensive one, and only large corporate houses can afford to commission purely customized psychometric assessments.

An alternative approach is the use of surveys, which has come under fire in the past. Surveys in the workplace have often been criticized as being self-serving, inaccurate, prone to bias, and too diffuse to be able to inform focused decision-making. However, there are some steps that can be taken to address these aspects. Conducting anonymous, online self-reporting removes inherent biases that can creep into an in-person interview, where the interviewee tries to project a particular image of herself. Similarly, surveys woven into the rubric of processes can ensure a high response rate, and structuring questions in a focused manner obviates the need to conduct an extensive principal control analysis (PCA). Interestingly, even in self-reporting surveys, the chance of bias may be higher when the focus or purpose of the survey is announced, compared to scenarios where this is not the case.[33] Designing an impactful survey comes down to the fundamental premise: *Are we asking the right question, and are we asking it in the right way?*

CHOOSING THE 'RIGHT' SKILLS

In Chapter Three, we explored the ongoing shifts in demand in the workplace, globally and in India, across three related dimensions—domains, sectors and skills, which in turn impact job roles. Earlier in this chapter, we explored the behavioural competencies most likely to be in demand, going forward, why they will need to be developed and how organizations will benefit from them. Developing new skills begins at the level of the individual. However, with the overflow of information and the range of skills being advocated by various experts, it may become difficult, if not overwhelming, to choose the 'right' skills for oneself. In this section, we combine the learnings across the two chapters into a simple schema, to gauge the specific skills you might need to develop in the near future and make a plan for it.

Figure 4.7: Approach for Identifying Skills to be Developed

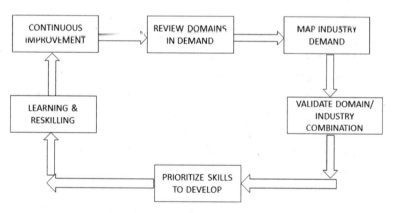

Source: This framework has been developed by the authors.

- **Review domains in demand:** The starting point can be a somewhat knotty problem. Should one begin with the industry, domain, skills, job roles, or some combination of these? Our recommendation is that you begin by considering the domain, e.g., sales, marketing, finance, for multiple reasons. Domains are more closely linked to skills than industries. Job roles, designations and associated tasks/deliverables are increasingly dynamic in our present times. One may opt for a change in domain as well—for this, refer to our discussion in Chapter Three and choose a new domain that is likely to be in high demand over the next few years.

- **Map industry demand:** Once you have selected the domain you wish to focus on, you can turn your attention to the industry you wish to work in. Refer to the discussion on emergent and declining industry sectors. For instance, you may be naturally strong in your domain, but your current industry might be in a state of stagnation. In such a scenario, it might be useful to choose from the industries which are likely to be in higher demand in the future. In case you are making a change in the domain itself, it may be advisable, at least for the immediate future, to stick to the industry where you already have relevant experience.

- **Validate domain/industry combination:** You have now arrived at the combination of domain, e.g., marketing, and industry, e.g., FMCG. At this point, it will be useful for you to validate this choice before moving forward. Although it may have taken a fair amount of deliberation to get to this point, the next steps in the process are more time-consuming. Therefore, it is useful to review your choice. If any calibration or course correction is required, this is the juncture at which to undertake it.

- **Prioritize the skills to develop:** Validating the domain/industry combination for the near term also enables you to arrive at a finite set of behavioural skills and competencies.

The task for you now is to prioritize the specific skills within that set that you would need to develop first. This may seem like a small step in the overall journey but it's a very important one. This is because most of us have an inherent bias for action, and so, presented with a bouquet of skills, our natural tendency would be to choose and start working on all of them at once. Such an approach may in fact reap great synergies, where the skills are interrelated or where there is a causal relationship between them, e.g., nurturing positive emotions and building resilience, as we have seen earlier in the chapter. However, if this isn't the case, it is advisable to choose no more than a couple of competencies to focus on, in terms of self-development.

- **Learning & reskilling:** This step in the journey is a process in itself, involving training oneself in the new skills and competencies. This may entail learning on the job, coursework or instruction-based training, assessments and certification, the breaking of old habits and the forming of new ones, with all the attendant changes in routine and rewiring, from the neurological standpoint. Much of this takes time; for instance, a new habit can easily take between sixty and ninety days to take root in your personality. Similarly, it may be difficult to shed methodologies and techniques that have outlived their utility, if you find yourself attached to them as the boundary walls of your comfort zone. While this may often seem like a big step, Jon Parry, head of research in Skills for Justice and Health (whose team supports employers, large and small, and across the UK, to develop workforce, leadership and research strategies to improve and retain skilled staff), points out that this may be less daunting than one may think. When we enter the workforce, we often possess multiple general competencies which we may have partially lost when focusing on a specialism, but remembering, refining and relearning some of these, albeit in a somewhat changed environment, may not be as onerous as it sounds.

- **Continuous improvement:** This is a checkpoint for you. Given the pace of change in the demand for specific skills and job roles, it stands to reason that the process outlined above would need to be repeated multiple times, to a greater or lesser degree, over a full career span. This becomes all-important in a milieu where there's a distinct shift towards gig work, and consequently no pre determined retirement age. The periodicity of your internal review obviously depends on a number of factors, such as your domain, industry, level of expertise and the direction and quantum of market shifts. One of the key determinants in this whole journey is the level of advances and flexibility that has developed in the education and training system, the extent to which it has been impacted by the pandemic, the spate of technological disruptions that began before it, and the extent to which a sector embraces innovation in response to market shifts. This is the subject of our discussion in the next chapter.

CHAPTER 5

Education, Innovation and Productivity

Even though we live in a world that's increasingly globalized and 'flat',[1] there remain significant differences in the living standards and quality of life of people across nations. This question of why some nations are rich while others are poor has always been a key problem for economists and policymakers. The subject matter of Adam Smith's famous book, *An Inquiry into the Nature and Causes of the Wealth of Nations*, is self-explanatory from its title.[2] Our own focus in this chapter is the classic inquiry: what is the variance in productivity and innovation across nations and to what extent does a gulf in educational attainment explain any divide that exists? We are also interested in productivity being translated into income. This is not to say that non-income attributes, such as well-being, are not important, but understanding income inequality and its causes is, in itself, an important exercise. There is also the issue of how income is distributed, as countries with similar overall levels of income may have divergent concentrations of income and wealth. We take up this important issue in Chapter Seven.

There is no doubt that there are significant disparities in wealth across and within nations.[3] At first glance, this might seem surprising, as one would expect the effects of increasing prosperity, led by globalization, to trickle down to all nations. Indeed, classical economic theory suggests that capital should flow from richer countries to poorer countries. The rationale behind this is that rich countries have more capital and poor countries have little. Therefore, if there are diminishing returns on capital in the rich and developed counties, the returns earned on capital should be higher in poorer countries, leading to an inflow from the richer economies. This will, in turn, fuel growth in the poorer countries. However, in the 1990s, Robert Lucas (who won the Nobel Prize in economics) pointed out that very little capital did in fact flow from rich to poor nations.[4] Several reasons have been proposed to explain this lack of flow of capital—which has since come to be known as the Lucas Paradox.

The two principal theories are as follows. First, it has been posited that the quality of labour in poor countries is lower than in the wealthy ones. A back-of-the-envelope calculation suggested that a US worker was nearly sixty times as productive as an Indian worker! Consequently, this unskilled labour would negate any gains made from higher returns on capital. The second theory is that the politically risky poorer countries may not pay back the capital they get from the rich countries in terms of goods produced. While capital flows and the pace of development have improved in some countries since the 1990s as we will show presently, significant disparities remain. Thus, an understanding of the Lucas Paradox remains relevant. The first of the explanations has been proposed (i.e., in terms of differences in labour quality or skills) in terms of 'human capital'. This implies that there is a significant impetus for poorer nations to upskill their labour and that, broadly speaking, education has a major role to play. The specific form of education that is needed to enhance human capital, and whether that is being implemented, is discussed in the section on STEM and its 'discontents'. The issue of political risk remains critical, such as with the conflict in Ukraine, which was raging while this chapter was being revised. We, however, take a conscious decision not to delve into the subject of political risk, but to limit our discussions to the problem of improving human capital and what that means in the context of the emergent workplace.

We begin with a snapshot of the global differences in productivity, innovation and educational attainments, and India's position in these globally. We then go on to discuss how these may be interlinked and provide thoughts on the different ways productivity and innovation have been conceptualized and what an educational curriculum for the next-generation worker should consider, with particular reference to India.

PRODUCTIVITY, INNOVATION AND EDUCATION

We open this section with a query that might seem obvious. With all the advancements in technology and access to massive amounts of information, is the quality of thinking and research in our times much better than that in earlier eras? Not necessarily, according to American researcher-writer Nicholas Carr. In his celebrated 2011 book *The Shallows: What the Internet Is Doing to Our Brains*, Carr shows that there's a price to pay for the benefits accorded by technology. One worry is that humans are giving up many of their inherent skills for a system, where users need to adapt to their computers rather than the other way around. In the Internet Age, the quiet, deep-thinking capacity of humans is replaced with the task of processing an overwhelming amount of information.

But our brains are not equipped to navigate constant distractions and data overflow while creating deep and meaningful new elements of knowledge. More alarming is Carr's assertion that the incessant and programmatic use of technology rewires our brains in undesirable and disturbing ways. When it comes specifically to research, the evidence presented is shattering. Using official studies, statistics, and an analysis of citations in peer-reviewed publications, Carr shows that greater access to scholarly databases notwithstanding, the number of citations in many published articles has gone down compared to several decades ago. Further, the depth and productivity of the research has also diminished, since scholars take recourse to piecemeal reading from results yielded by keyword-searches, instead of close reading followed by deep, time-consuming analysis.[5]

With this cautionary background, let us briefly look at productivity and innovation figures across the globe. The table below[6] shows GDP (PPP) per hour across the top ten most productive economies in 2022. Even within these ten nations, the productivity differences are stark, close to $25 per hour. While the average Norwegian worker, ranked #1 in the world, has a productivity equal to $75 per hour, for Danish workers (ranked #10) it is just $56 per hour. In comparison, for the typical Indian worker productivity per hour is just over $3. While less astonishing than the sixty times differential that Lucas had estimated, the twenty-five-times differential (between Norwegian and Indian workers) remains too wide to ignore.

Table 5.1: Productivity of Workers per Hour (in US Dollars)

Country	Hourly productivity (in $)
Norway	75.08
Luxembourg	73.22
United States	67.32
Belgium	60.98
Netherlands	60.06
France	59.24
Germany	57.36
Ireland	56.05
Australia	55.87
Denmark	55.75

Source: World population review: Most productive countries (2022)

Admittedly, this is but one snapshot in time. Further, productivity measures are usually in terms of wages, which may present a slightly misleading picture, especially if the relation between wages and productivity varies across countries. For example, the bargaining power of workers may vary, depending on whether they are unionized and the extent to which they can be substituted by capital/machines/automation. Many underdeveloped countries only have a small unionized sector but a large unorganized sector. Consequently, the low wages of the typical Indian worker may in part be due to his poor bargaining power, and not necessarily (or fully) due to low productivity.

Second, worker productivity changes over time.[7] A major factor here is innovation via improved or new products that have higher market value or improvements in processes, which allow more to be produced for the same effort. Across companies, innovation is often gauged from the expenditure made on research and development (R&D). At a macroeconomic level too, differences in R&D can lead to changes in productivity. So, the snapshot we presented can change over time if some nations spend relatively more on innovation.

Besides conventional R&D for new products, innovation also includes training or process improvement. Governments often spend considerable amounts to boost labour productivity, and this has led to the emergence of a bunch of high-performing Asian economies. This has often been referred to as the 'East Asian Miracle'—the high rate of growth that a league of Asian countries achieved. They were Japan and the so-called 'Four Tigers': Hong Kong, Singapore, Taiwan and South Korea; and the three newly industrializing economies of Southeast Asia: Thailand, Indonesia and Malaysia. Their success was at least partly attributed to strong government interventions, including investments in improving the skills of the workforce.[8] The impact of these interventions relative to market-friendly policies, such as export promotion, is a matter of debate.

Though there is no single way of measuring innovation, the Global Innovation Index has fairly wide acceptance. This uses several indicators associated with innovation and provides annual rankings by country in terms of their capacity for, and success in, innovation. The method of creating this index, though, is not without controversy. Some of its indicators have been criticized, (e.g., by Nick Skillicorn, founder of Improvides Consulting[9]) as being too far removed from 'innovation' as one ordinarily understands the term. For example, in measuring innovation outputs, under the 'creative outputs' section, the following feature: 7.2.2 – National Feature films/mm pop 15-69; 7.2.4 – Printing & publishing manufacturers, %; 7.3.3 – Wikipedia monthly edits/mm pop 15-69; 7.3.4 – Video uploads on YouTube/pop 15-69. Not only are these indices removed from the concept of innovation, but as Skillicorn points out, in the case of printing and publishing are actually measuring an index for an industry which is in decline thanks to innovation in digital.

Some of the innovation inputs can also be problematic, describing indicators that are more linked to general economic indicators or ease of doing business. These weaknesses are partly a data issue, innovation being hard to measure directly. Further, it is well known that a high percentage of all product innovation fails. There is a notion that the failure rate is as high as 95 per cent, though empirical studies suggest a much lower rate.[10] Across nations, there are naturally differences in the rate of innovation, because poorer nations cannot afford to invest in innovation. Table 5.2 looks at the Global Innovation Index 2021 rankings (based on eighty-one different indicators) of the top ten innovative countries across the world.

Table 5.2: Excerpt from Global Innovation Index 2021

Country	Global Innovation Score
Switzerland	65.5
Sweden	63.1
United States of America	61.3
United Kingdom	59.8
Republic of Korea	59.3
Netherlands	58.6
Finland	58.4
Singapore	57.8
Denmark	57.3
Germany	57.3

As with productivity, the difference between the leaders and laggards is high. Thus, top-ranked Switzerland has an innovation score[11] of 66.5, while Angola, ranked 132, registered a score of 15. The latest report also warns of the possibility of innovation divides being accentuated in the next few years as many emerging economies have become fragile.

Tracking the Global Innovation Index over time shows some movement in the rankings. India's absolute rank at 46 is low, but among the lower-income groups it has improved and has entered the top fifty for the first time. Globally, The Republic of Korea and Singapore are the only two countries outside Europe to feature in the top ten, and China (at 12) and Japan (at 13) are just outside it.

There are also differences in the rankings between productivity and innovation. Nonetheless, both Korea and Singapore are still dominated by the richer countries as the latter can afford to spend more on innovation, in turn indicating that the gap between rich and poor nations may not close so easily. However, R&D spending by itself is not the only factor driving innovation. Countries that cannot spend on R&D in the way that the developed nations can may nonetheless innovate using frugal techniques and flexible management. We examine this possibility in our section on 'Jugaad' innovation later in the chapter. Moreover, there are often differences within a country in terms of productivity. Innovation can lead to significant wage differences between workers performing analytic tasks and those performing more routine tasks, as the former can often adapt better to new technologies,[12] leading to sectoral differences within a country. Interestingly, there is strong evidence that this asymmetric impact of innovation, particularly when it comes to innovations that are technological in nature, on the labour market, also leads to geographic differences.[13] In particular, there is a higher concentration of firms that require more analytic tasks in urban areas. This accentuates the urban wage premium.

Is there a common input that can explain global rankings as well as differences within a country on the innovation front? One possible factor is the difference in what is called human capital—i.e., the skills possessed by labour, contributing to its productivity, differ dramatically across countries. Given the key role that human capital is supposed to play, one obvious candidate is education.

The evidence that education and productivity increase via human capital accumulation is well-established, though education is not the only way to accumulate human capital. Nor is the relationship between the two free from criticism. Some have argued that education does not significantly increase productivity but may simply be a signal of productivity.[14] This suggests that the returns from education are high because employers believe that educated workers are more productive. If the educational curriculum is designed in a way that makes it easier for high-productivity workers to acquire it, then it can be possible that education is correlated with productivity, even if it does not add to productivity, and hence employers correctly pay educated workers more.

A growing volume of evidence over the years suggests that education is indeed one of the major components that enhances productivity and human capital.[15] However, whether these productivity changes always translate into wage changes remains a matter of debate.[16] If wages and productivity are not perfectly linked, then comparisons of productivity across firms, and even more across nations, using wage differentials, is bound to be flawed. As we showed earlier, wages do not necessarily reflect productivity in all circumstances. Indeed, many have argued that wages are as much affected by collective action or power as by productivity.[17] Hence, unless we control for factors other than productivity, wage differentials do not capture productivity differences, and this caveat should be kept in mind when considering transnational comparisons of productivity.

Yet others note that the human capital theory itself is flawed because, rather than productivity, income differentials are often better explained by hierarchy, which is also related to power within an organization.[18] This is an important question that we shall split into two parts. We will discuss the issue of wage inequality next, and the more general implications for societal inequality separately, in Chapter Seven. For now, we note that while education has a role, other factors can also augment human capital, in particular experience or 'learning by doing' (i.e., on-the-job training) as well as acquired skills. How much education versus 'learning by doing' plays a role in enhancing productivity is an important debate, as it will determine how much policymakers should invest in education as opposed to investing more in 'on-the-job experience'.

A related, but less studied, effect is the impact of firm-provided training on worker productivity and wages. The results of the studies in this area also have interesting implications for the wage-productivity gap we mentioned earlier. For instance, if the impact on wages is lower than that on productivity, it provides evidence that increases in productivity do not necessarily translate into an equivalent shift in wages, lending empirical support to the caveats about measuring productivity differences by looking at wage differences. We do not attempt to conduct a survey of the evidence around the impact of firm-provided training on worker productivity. Instead, we consider a couple of studies to provide a flavour of the findings as well as the challenges in estimating this relationship.

A study by Konings and Vanormelingen[19] used firm-level panel data from Belgian companies of on-the-job training to estimate its impact on productivity and wages. A standard problem in understanding whether the associated increases are in fact due to company training is because it does not take into account firm characteristics that affect both training opportunities and productivity, as well as any selection effect i.e., workers who choose to be trained may have different innate characteristics from workers who do not. This poses a problem in inferring any causal impact. The study's approach for estimating production functions, however, allows the researchers to correct for such issues. They found that the productivity premium for a trained worker is substantially higher compared to the wage premium. In particular, they found that the productivity premium for a trained worker was estimated at 23 per cent, but that this did not translate into an equivalent wage increase (the wage premium of training being found to be 12 per cent).

These results demonstrate the productivity-wage gap, whereby productivity changes do not translate into equivalent wage changes. This is consistent with recent theories that explain work-related training because of imperfect competition in the labour market. This imperfection implies that workers who improve their productivity through on-the-job training cannot perfectly signal their market worth to outside employers, and thus will stay on even when paid less than what they are worth. Thus, firms can and do offer generalized training to workers, knowing they will profit from it as they can pay workers less than the productivity gain that results from training.

The link between education and innovation is less well studied, but nonetheless a recent review[20] established some of the main channels this occurred through. An important ingredient appeared to be the content of education. Barbara Biasi and Song Ma explored the education-innovation question in a novel and imaginative way. Their approach centred on a new measure, the 'education-innovation gap', defined as the textual distance between syllabi of courses taught in colleges and universities and frontier knowledge published in academic journals. The idea behind this was to understand how far university curricula are behind in terms of teaching 'state-of-the-art' knowledge (as measured by the latest articles in the area). The gap was gauged using a novel measure, based on textual analysis techniques, using information consisting of the text of 3 million university syllabi taught across nearly three decades and 20 million academic publications. While trying to proxy innovation merely by the content of 'frontier' academic knowledge may be debatable, the results, which we summarize below, do indicate some interesting findings.

The results led to a set of new findings on frontier knowledge delivered across US higher education institutions. First, significant variation in frontier knowledge was found to exist across university courses, both across and within institutions, the largest part of which is accounted for by the quality or skills of instructors. Second, more selective schools (i.e., those serving students from wealthier backgrounds), and schools serving a smaller proportion of minority students, offered courses with smaller gaps in their syllabus vs. frontier knowledge. Third, instructors played a large role in shaping the content they taught, and more research-active instructors were more likely to teach courses with smaller gaps. Fourth, the gap is correlated with student outcomes, such as graduation rates, their income levels ten years after graduation, production of more patents (a proxy for innovation) by them as well as intergenerational mobility. And the correlation is particularly pronounced for schools serving more disadvantaged students. Overall, the study suggests that the education-innovation gap is important in studying how human capital is produced in higher education.[21]

Psychology and sentiment—as perceptions among students and entrepreneurs—can also play a role. A 2019 study focusing on 269 student-entrepreneurs in China investigated this question. Their findings showed that (1) there is a positive relationship between perceptions of entrepreneurship education and perceptions of innovation, (2) political skills and entrepreneurial opportunity recognition individually play a mediating role between perceived entrepreneurship education and innovation, and (3) political skills and entrepreneurial opportunity recognition play a chain mediating effect between perceived entrepreneurship education and innovation.[22]

Let us now take up that most fundamental ingredient of education—literacy.

BACK TO BASICS: LITERACY

The importance of basic literacy for workplace productivity is not in doubt. In recent years, this has become critical as technology adoption has spread globally and a growing number of occupations use technologies that require a threshold level of education. Indeed, without this level, all but the very lowest-skilled jobs will be closed to the unemployed. Having to rely on low earnings may mean workers not being able to train either themselves or provide adequate mentoring of new entrants to a company. A low-literacy, low-education ecosystem thus creates a vicious circle that perpetuates low productivity.

While the association between education and productivity is well-established, empirical estimates of how much additional years of schooling add to productivity can be challenging to determine. As the famous labour economist David Card summarized it,[23] '... it is very difficult to know whether the higher earnings observed for better educated workers are *caused* by their higher education or whether individuals with greater earnings capacity have chosen to acquire more schooling'. Nonetheless, even after controlling for such selection effects, he finds a consistently positive effect across numerous well-controlled studies of around 10–16 per cent wage increases for every additional year of education. While some later analyses have found smaller effects, there is more recent research that once again shows the large impact of education on productivity.[24] The returns are particularly high among disadvantaged groups who have had low education outcomes, suggesting that closing the literacy gap may help in improving productivity.

Even with high global literacy, there are significant differences between the most and least developed countries. The most developed countries have literacy rates of over 95 per cent, while in less developed countries over a third of people are not literate.[25] According to the National Survey of India,[26] the literacy rate in India in 2021 was 77.7 per cent, up from 73 per cent in 2011. As per UNESCO, India will achieve universal literacy in the year 2060. Globally, there are also significant gender differences. It has been estimated that nearly two-thirds of the 800 million adults worldwide who cannot read or write are female. This gender disparity is more pronounced in less developed countries, where women are often expected to adopt traditional roles (e.g., stay at home and look after the house and children) while the menfolk go to work. That the gender literacy gap needs to be closed goes without saying. An educated mother not only improves her own life but also has a better chance of raising educated children who, in turn, can become more productive workers of the future.

While the male literacy rate in India is 84.7 per cent (which is not far short of the global average), for females it is only 70.3 per cent. This is a significant gender gap that needs to be bridged. Often, girls drop out of school because of economic difficulties. But, with the launch of many female literacy campaigns in India, it is hoped that the gender gap will narrow in the future. Already, there is some evidence of success. For example, though the state of Bihar remains one of the least

literate states, with current female literacy at 70 per cent, it is
a distinct improvement from 47 per cent in the 2001 census
and just under 64 per cent in the 2011 census. Bihar is also no
longer the least literate state, the dubious distinction for which
has transferred to Andhra Pradesh. Bihar's female literacy rate,
too, is no longer the lowest—Rajasthan now has the lowest
female literacy rate, according to the 2021 census. The rural–
urban differences are also significant, with urban literacy of
nearly 88 per cent and rural literacy at just under 74 per cent in
the country.

While literacy contributes to productivity, the causality is
not entirely clear. Kerala outshines all other states in literacy
and yet is not the richest state in terms of income per capita—
presenting a puzzle for some. In the past, the state had
performed commendably on human development indices,
such as high literacy and life expectancy, low infant mortality
as well as birth rates, but remained a relatively poor state in
a poor country.[27] While that doesn't hold any more—Kerala
ranked ninth in India in terms of GDP per capita in 2020–21,[28]
it is still not among the top performing states. This suggests
that the association between literacy/education and income is
imperfect. Further, Kerala's high literacy has not translated into
a high female labour-force participation.[29]

Overall, India's female labour-force participation has
always been relatively low, by global standards. But it has fallen
still further in the aftermath of the COVID-19 pandemic,
continuing a downward trend from nearly 32 per cent in 2005
to less than 19 per cent in 2020.[30] This is low even by the
standards of its neighbours, with Bangladesh at 35 per cent[31]
and Sri Lanka at 31 per cent.[32] There may be several reasons
for India's performance on this front, including the fact that
if some of the female labour-force participation is need-based,
higher family income may actually lower women's willingness

to work when the need to work is not acute. Nonetheless, this goes against the evidence in most parts of the world with regards to the factors associated with female literacy.[33]

The somewhat ambiguous relationship between literacy and growth may be masking individual differences in literacy and numeracy skills, with neither necessarily translating into ability to be productive or to solve problems faced in the actual workplace. In other words, literacy numbers may not indicate much about the skills acquired by an individual in the workplace. When looking at worldwide data, there is a wage premium and better employment opportunities for those with better literacy or numeracy skills,[34] which can be considered a proxy for productivity. Thus, it's not just the spread of education that's important but the quality of it too. Being literate may not translate into being productive in the workplace; the content of education matters when it comes to the imparting of skills needed in the workplace. Progress reports based purely on literacy figures do not capture the nuance of quality. This has an important implication for policymakers, as this indicates that programmes aiming to enhance human capital through education need to focus on the depth and quality of the education being imparted and not on merely the number of people covered under such programmes.

Apart from higher education, vocational education also has an important role to play in addressing the market demand for specific skills and for creating job opportunities for the youth. In this context, the role of Vocational Training Centres and ITIs assumes greater importance.

Examination of the efficacy of education in improving human capital opens up two basic questions. First, what specific skills and competencies are sought to be developed through the education being imparted? Second, what subjects are being taught? Chapter Three addressed the first of these questions in some detail. We now take up the second question.

STEM AND ITS DISCONTENTS[35]

We have seen in Chapter Three that there has recently been greater demand for higher-order cognitive and behavioural skills in the workplace, a need further accelerated by the pandemic. Why is it, then, that the vast majority of curricula for higher education in India still centres on STEM instead of being more well-rounded and multidisciplinary? A big part of the answer lies in the fact that, over the past three decades, we have witnessed a revolution whereby increasingly sophisticated technologies have formed a ubiquitous part of our lives. From mechanization to automation, from robotics to artificial intelligence, from miniaturization to nanotechnology, from software to embedded systems, from the internet to the internet of things—technologies are not just transient but advancing by leaps and bounds. Not surprisingly, this has led to a greater focus on subjects that help in building careers in these fields—in other words, a curriculum based on STEM.

The acronym 'STEM', coined by the US National Science Foundation, was proposed as a new focused approach to education in response to a market problem faced in the mid- and late 1990s. Those were the heydays of the technology revolution, when demand for engineering, science and IT skills in the US economy surpassed the number of graduates in these disciplines. It was widely believed that a sustained shortage of these niche competencies would see the US fall behind its economic competitors. This reinforced the need for a STEM-based educational system. As the technology revolution spread across the globe, particularly to countries such as India, where it played a major part in fuelling economic prosperity, STEM-based education also began to take root there. For a long time, this system of emphasis on technical or 'hard skills' continued in many parts of the world, with relatively less focus on behavioural competencies.

However, thirty years on, the picture in the US has changed. The notion of a long-term, secure 'STEM job' has been debunked as a myth. Multinational giants were compelled to reverse their earlier, no-retrenchment policies, especially during the pandemic period. Further, over time, the mass outsourcing of IT and allied jobs resulted in largely stagnant wage levels in the US. As jobs and associated skills have become increasingly commoditized, the individual has been rendered more dispensable, and employer loyalty has diminished.[36]

Demographer Michael S. Teitelbaum, who has studied the data on STEM graduates and the corresponding statistics for employment for their skills, argues that there's scant evidence of the claimed widespread shortages in the US science and engineering workforce. His work reveals that unemployment rates among scientists and engineers have actually remained higher than in other professions (e.g., physicians, dentists, lawyers and registered nurses). His conclusion is telling: 'Far from offering expanding attractive career opportunities, it seems that many, but not all, science and engineering careers are headed in the opposite direction: unstable careers, slow-growing wages, and high risk of jobs moving offshore or being filled by temporary workers from abroad.'[37]

Now, turn the lens to India. From the standpoint of the US and other economies that have outsourced jobs over the years, India has been one of the principal beneficiaries. But, viewed from an internal standpoint, within India a different picture emerges:

- Being a globalized economy, India isn't insulated from uncertainties in other parts of the world. Consequently, recessions in the US and other economies can and do have a downside impact on the Indian market, including the prospect of retrenchment on a large scale.
- The schemes centred on skills development, as well as programmes such as Start-Up India (urgently advocated by the government), attest to the fact that state-run enterprises and corporates aren't able to absorb the numbers graduating from colleges across the country. There is, therefore, a need for expertise building, self-reliance and employment creation at the individual, micro-level, in order to sustain economic growth.
- Among Indian engineering graduates, there is still a rush for technology or consulting jobs, where wages are relatively high and careers are perceived to be glamorous, at the expense of careers in other sectors (e.g., scientific research).[38]

As we have seen in Chapter Three, the complex mosaic of skills and competencies needed in the emergent workplace points towards one conclusion: STEM by itself is no longer the full answer. Expanding one's cognitive abilities does not prepare one emotionally to adapt to an increasing pace of change, nor endow one with the abilities to continuously unlearn, relearn and acquire new skills to influence and motivate oneself and others, and to continuously deliver value in a workplace requiring higher-order thinking. Any framework claiming to be holistic and comprehensive can no longer ignore the dimension of emotional enablement.

Given the gap between the availability of STEM-skilled resources on the one hand and the market demand for those skills on the other, two key questions present themselves. If not STEM, what disciplines in this changing order of things should education embrace? While it is accepted that, going forward, economic growth will be largely driven by continuous innovation, how would the skills of creativity and innovation be institutionalized and standardized? There has been an ongoing debate between proponents of STEM and its critics. The champions argue that the principles of STEM can be found in virtually every discipline, not just limited to the subjects of science, engineering, technology or mathematics. Rather, they say, technical knowledge and the scientific mindset of inquiry go hand in hand with creativity, leading to innovative ideas across disciplines.[39] The critics of STEM contend that exposure to the wider sphere of the arts equips a person for better decision-making, creativity and innovation. In their view, it's not deep scholarship but practical application of the arts that sets one up for success. Thus, alternative frameworks such as STEAM (i.e., STEM plus arts) and STEMMA (STEM plus medicine and arts) have entered the discourse.[40]

This also links in with the push to create a more diverse and inclusive workforce that many firms and governments have adopted, both to lower barriers to entry for traditionally under-represented groups and because a diverse workforce also brings ideas and skills that improve workforce productivity.[41] Moving from recruiting people from purely STEM backgrounds to hiring people from other disciplines also leads, naturally, to acquisition of a more diverse workforce. As Professor Jo Duberley, (deputy pro vice-chancellor, equality, diversity and inclusion (EDI) at the University of Birmingham) points out, EDI is not just an admirable principle: '. . . research on board diversity suggests more diverse boards are more effective'. Professor Duberley feels that even when leadership is serious about EDI, '. . . barriers that certain groups face and work hard to reduce/remove' often take time to overcome. Being open to recruiting people with more than a particular type of education will make it easier to create a more diverse workforce, which brings in diverse skills and life stories, making for a more empathetic workplace.

Our own position is that there's a need for holistic education programmes that advance empathy, understanding and creativity, alongside technological savvy. STEM undoubtedly equips students with analytical and problem-solving skills, but some of the raging problems of today's world—poverty, intolerance and political conflict—require capacity for ethical decision-making, compassion and creativity as well. These capabilities must also grow in tandem with our ability to operate sophisticated technology and gadgets, warranting expansion of the STEM system. This can be supported by a framework such as ESTEEM, 'EE' standing for 'emotional enablement'— the process or journey by which inculcation of behavioural competencies, such as emotional intelligence, becomes second nature. Several aspects distinguish ESTEEM from other frameworks:

- With STEM, the four constituent elements provide sharp clarity to the subjects being taught. But they also end up limiting the scope of the education imparted under this model. By contrast, in ESTEEM, the focus on emotional enablement opens up a range of subjects in the arts and humanities, broadening the educational scope and, by corollary, the canvas of human development.
- Therefore, ESTEEM does not champion or prescribe any particular discipline; instead, it underscores the need to explore what disciplines would best work to provide a comprehensive, holistic education to today's youth. Thus, a grounding in the humanities may end up being a worthy addition in the ESTEEM curricula, as may the disciplines of positive psychology or neuroscience.

- STEM, STEAM and other alternatives are all educational models that concentrate on fitment for today's job market, but there is very little discussion on continued self-development once one enters the workforce. In the ESTEEM framework, this initial preparatory phase is merely the starting point of a continuous, long-term journey to become emotionally enabled.
- ESTEEM offers a model for longer-term success and well-being. Our gauge is that the study of a given discipline under an ESTEEM-based model may in fact make a person more employable. We believe that emotional enablement allows a person to cope better with the vagaries of an increasingly uncertain job market.
- Emotional enablement helps set up an individual for professional accomplishments over a longer time frame. Routine and repetitive tasks across industries are increasingly getting automated, and many of the jobs previously operated manually are dying out. ESTEEM provides a broader framework for success in the jobs of the future.

It is interesting to note that the new National Education Policy (NEP), published by the Indian government in 2020, advocates a more holistic and multidisciplinary approach to education. This would involve inclusion of arts and humanities subjects for science and engineering students, and vice versa. The policy also calls for establishment of multidisciplinary education and research universities (MERUs) across the country, offering a quality of education at par with the premier institutes in the country, such as IITs (India Institutes of Technology, India's premier institutions in the field of technology) and IIMs (Indian Institutes of Management, India's premier set of business schools).[42]

INNOVATION AS IMPROVISATION: JUGAAD AND ITS DISCONTENTS

We saw earlier that rankings in the Global Innovation Index are dominated by the developed countries who can afford to spend more on R&D. However, many contend that such indices, by using conventional metrics, miss other types of innovation at which developing countries, perhaps by necessity, have trialled. We now turn to one such: the concept and practice of 'Jugaad' which, in the Indian context, has often been equated to innovation. The Hindi word 'Jugaad' translates roughly into 'ingenious and clever improvisation', and has in the last decade been elevated to a business philosophy of frugal innovation, something that giant, top-heavy corporations can borrow a leaf from. The big proponents of Jugaad have been Navi Radjou, Simone Ahuja and Jaideep Prabhu, whose 2012 bestselling book, *Jugaad Innovation: Think Frugal, Be Flexible, Generate Breakthrough Growth*,[43] triggered wide-scale debate, discussion and recommendations around innovation and problem-solving in the workplace. Their basic premise is clear: the mammoth hierarchical corporations of (but not limited to) the West have developed intricate methods and processes that have stood them in good stead through much of their history. However, many are struggling or have lost their footing more recently because they failed to adapt to the needs of a rapidly changing world. They have failed to be flexible, nimble-footed, swift and frugal. The traditional Western practice of innovation, which is time-consuming and expensive, can lose out on opportunities. According to the authors, this is where the practice of Jugaad can make a huge difference.

Radjou, Ahuja and Prabhu make the case that Jugaad doesn't imply a haphazard, piecemeal approach to problem-solving. Instead, it lends itself to a set of specific ideas and practices to help companies challenge entrenched notions about doing business, enabling them to achieve more with less. One idea is that outdated R&D methods and top-down approaches, as seen in many Western firms, hinder innovation. An example of this, in their view, is the 'Six Sigma' approach (involving a set of techniques and tools for process improvement) for production, adopted by many Fortune 500 firms over the years. However, while Six Sigma is highly effective in reducing errors in production—ensuring that 99.99966 per cent of products will be manufactured defect-free—it does not allow much room for innovative thinking and changing the way we think of and run businesses. In short, Radjou, Ahuja and Prabhu argue that creative, unconventional methods can solve complex business problems that traditional, structured methods might struggle with.

Another key idea is that Jugaad views constraints not as obstacles but as opportunities. A case in point is the journey of Tulsi Tanti, a small-scale textile manufacturer, who felt hampered by expensive and unreliable energy supplies. After some experimentation, he found wind turbines to be an alternative that was dependable, sustainable and affordable. But in the process he also realized it wasn't just his own textile mill that could benefit from affordable alternative energy, but that there was a tremendous demand for it worldwide. His ambition soared in this direction, leading him to found the company Suzlon Energy. Set up in 1995, the company is now the world's fifth-largest wind energy supplier, with operations in over thirty countries across six continents and employing over 13,000 personnel. In this instance, the Jugaad mindset not only solved Tanti's immediate problem but also led to mass-scale operationalization of his solution in a new and growing market. This leads directly to the third big idea about Jugaad innovators: they don't just think outside the box—they can create boxes (markets) that are altogether new.

According to the authors, the downfall of many large Western firms lies in their inflexibility and complacency about established business processes that have worked in the past, and in their hierarchical models of management. Consider the case of Dr V. Mohan, a globally renowned diabetes expert who runs a mobile telemedicine clinic in India that services some of the country's most remote villages. The traditional notion of medical consultation is that patients visit their doctors. Challenging this fundamental notion, Dr Mohan devised a process of consultation that involved a van and 'commuting', remotely, through video-feed. In this new model, physicians help their patients from their own offices, using video monitors, while direct care is provided by a network of primarily urban doctors who travel in a van equipped with telemedicine technologies that allow for diagnostic tests as a last-mile service to patients.

The fourth critical idea in Jugaad is to go beyond mainstream demographics to include the margins in one's focus. Many global multinationals cater to the educated, upwardly mobile section of society and their increasingly evolved consumption needs. For them, ventures for the marginalized sections of the population are tantamount to corporate social responsibility (CSR) and not new profitable businesses. But across Africa, India and Latin America, hundreds of millions of underprivileged people represent a major customer base in their own right. Dr Rana Kapoor was a visionary innovator who recognized this. In 2004, he set up an inclusive bank that aimed to serve the financial needs of a broad range of consumers, including economically weaker sections of the population. His purpose was to serve the 600 million Indians who, at that point in time, had no access to a bank. YES BANK, the financial institution he founded, was able to give back to the community on an economy-wide scale, and without compromising on profit margins.

Jugaad proponents feel that its methods can complement existing Western practices. They don't advocate the throwing out of all Western thinking and practices, but believe in striking a balance. This usually involves identifying situations where Jugaad is more likely to be successful than traditional methods of production, logistics, sales and overall management. Jugaad is especially effective in highly disruptive scenarios, where product life cycles are short, customer trends are shifting, competition is on the rise, and/or government regulations are unpredictable. Jugaad methods also excel in settings where industries are hungry for resources, and in sectors in their early stages of development. With industry benchmarks yet to be established, innovators are able to create more out of less, spot opportunities within adversity and embrace marginalized consumers.

For all its glamour and appeal, Jugaad has not been without its detractors. Of the critiques, perhaps the most compelling is the one by journalist-author Manu Joseph.[44] Besides making the charge of forcible intellectualization of a practice of improvisation, Joseph makes several other observations. First, while the application of the term Jugaad might have come into vogue recently, its practice goes back centuries, if not millennia, without the need for fancy business jargon to describe it. For instance, the practice of using clay pots to cool food and beverages has been around since ancient times, and it does not have to be rediscovered as a new business idea, as a substitute for the fridge. The fundamental recommendation of Jugaad practices to large companies has also come under attack. As 'frugal innovation', Jugaad implies resource constraints, mainly—but not limited to—funds. The question raised is why giant corporations with massive profits need to be frugal about research, development and innovation. A poor Indian vendor struggling to make ends meet has every reason to be frugal, but why must a giant corporation follow suit?

Jugaad's implications for ethics and legality can be problematic too. It implies taking creative shortcuts and improvising swift solutions as opposed to following conventional and more time-consuming processes. The sense of adventure and experimentation suggested by Jugaad can be exciting. But its critics worry that the street-smartness it calls for can easily stray into cutting of corners and law breaking. What the proponents of Jugaad always gloss over are, as Joseph points out, the fact that Jugaad is not merely the smartness of an individual, more so the ability to 'think outside of the box'.

In following the interests of expediency and creating more from less, Jugaad may naturally lead to practices and shortcuts that are illegal and unethical. The image of the neighbourhood milkman who adds a dash of water to his produce has become a bit of an archetype in its own right. Sometimes, the effects can be severe and far-reaching, as with developers who use inferior but more cost-effective materials in an infrastructure project or a drug manufacturer that cuts corners in its clinical trials in order to take its drugs to market faster. Joseph's final verdict on Jugaad is damning: the existence of Jugaad is merely evidence that the circumstances of a society are so bad that its smart people are doing what smart people in other civilizations do not have to do.

PRODUCTIVITY AND INNOVATION VIA EDUCATION: THE CASE FOR INDIA

Historically, India post-Independence has been a relatively slow-growth economy. While in the 1950s, India's levels of income were comparable to South Korea's and Taiwan's, the performance of those two countries really took off since that time. In comparison, India's growth per capita remained low, around the 1.3 per cent mark, until India's economic reforms commenced in earnest in 1991 under the finance minister of the time, Dr Manmohan Singh. The programme of economic liberalization unshackled the bureaucratic 'License Raj' and implemented a series of market-friendly reforms.

Successive governments have differed in their methods of pursuing the liberalization agenda, but the days of the insular, protectionist 'License Raj' are irrevocably over. Whether the spurt in growth was entirely caused by liberalization is disputed,[45] but growth undoubtedly improved after that, and over the years India began to be seen as an emerging economic power. However, by world standards, India's growth has not translated into increased labour productivity, and even today the level of innovation remains low. Part of this can be attributed to the fact that educational standards did not accelerate at the same time as the economy and much needs to be improved in the depth of pedagogy and outreach of education across the country.

The evidence we have presented in this chapter shows that, although not uni-causal, education clearly does play a role in improving productivity and enabling innovation. We mentioned in our section STEM and Its Discontents that there is an urgent need for students to get a more rounded education and not remain stuck in disciplinary silos. In that respect, the 2020 NEP makes recommendations in the right direction: 'Education thus, must move towards less content, and more towards learning about how to think critically and solve problems, how to be creative and multidisciplinary, and how to innovate, adapt, and absorb new material in novel and changing fields.'

The NEP includes suggestions on fostering deeper engagement between private and public institutions. For example, it says,

. . . twinning/pairing of one public school with one private school will be adopted across the country, so that such paired schools may meet/interact with each other, learn from each other, and also share resources, if possible. Best practices of private schools will be documented, shared, and institutionalized in public schools, and vice versa, where possible.[46]

There is also an emphasis on the need for private institutions with public-spirited commitment to high-quality equitable education.

The NEP objectives have been lauded by many. Others envisage that a greater degree of privatization in education will lead to yet more inequality. There is also concern around whether the divide among the elite and the non-elite will be further exacerbated by the use of one's native language as the mode of instruction in the first five years of education.[47] While these are plausible concerns, the precise impact of greater privatization of higher education is far from clear, as it depends on multiple factors, such as the nature of competition and the effectiveness of the regulatory regime in the economy. Indeed, with additional oversight of and subsidies for the economically disadvantaged, an increased entry of private players into the sector may improve reach, access and quality. Its success or otherwise must be measured by what we feel must be the three pillars of an educational framework for India: access, quality and affordability.

Rudra Sensarma, professor of economics at IIM-Kozhikode, advises both speed and focused action if the objectives of the NEP are to be realized: 'There must be incentives and consultations to implement NEP in schools. Otherwise, it will end up as a box-checking exercise. School councils must come out with model syllabi and pedagogies for effective implementation of NEP. Teachers need to be trained to be able to implement NEP in the right manner and spirit.'

While not dismissing any criticisms raised about the NEP, for us the big question is how the praiseworthy aspirations in that policy are to be implemented, since it would need radical changes in how education is currently delivered in India. As Professor Sanghamitra Bandyopadhyay, director of the Indian Statistical Institute, points out: 'The current education system still encourages non-participative linear learning, where a person is tested on how much the person remembers what has been taught. The testing pedagogy needs an overhaul, where the testing should not only be on how much a person has understood the concepts taught, but also on how much a person is able to innovate based on what has been taught as well as when faced with new problems.'

Professor Bandyopadhyay also has practical ideas on how to implement the NEP vision of a more broad-based form of education that goes beyond STEM. They are in line with our discussions on ESTEEM education. She says, 'The main approach for implementing a broad-based comprehensive form of education, going beyond STEM, is to first have a comprehensive curriculum review of all courses. A choice-based credit system appears to be the way forward.' She advocates a less rigid degree curriculum, moving towards the flexibility that US universities offer and many UK universities are considering. In her view, 'The combinations of major and minor subjects should be left completely to the student, who should be allowed full flexibility in this choice. It has become very important for academic programmes to be flexible, interoperable and holistic, so that they equip the learner with the knowledge and technical skills to earn a livelihood, turn out a creative individual who can find an identity and prepare the mind and body so the student becomes a global citizen mindful and respectful of local culture and values.'

But to be innovation-ready one needs to start earlier. Indeed, Professor Bandyopadhyay says, 'We have been thinking that by driving HEIs to look at various aspects of innovation, we can create the innovative ecosystem in India. I think the correct place to address the problem is at the school level, in the school education system. Unless the quality of state-delivered primary education improves, education will continue to divide society. Of course, education is not the only driver of productivity and we need to be cognizant of the role played by, e.g., social entrepreneurship, to help improve human capital among the disadvantaged sections of society. There are excellent initiatives in India. For example, Luis Miranda, banking leader, educationist and social entrepreneur, says that he has noticed first-hand in his work at the Centre for Civil Society how markets can work for the poor—be it micro-entrepreneurs, tribals or marginal farmers. Both organizations have made me realize the importance of the individual in deciding their future and not top-down approaches from a centralized ivory tower.'

For Professor Rudra Sensarma, 'Being ranked 46 on the Global Innovation index is not a bad score for a country that is ranked 131 on the Human Development Index and 160 in per capita income. India has made rapid progress in start-ups and now has the third largest start-up ecosystem in the world. However, the country needs to increase spending on R&D. As a share of GDP, spending on R&D by both government and private sector is very low. Private sector can be given fiscal incentives to spend on R&D, e.g., by letting it be reported as CSR spend. The government can encourage rural start-ups by setting up rural business incubators in villages. Government schools and colleges need a combination of right leadership, light-touch regulation and incentives. The government can increase financial support for research in both public and private universities, and must also encourage colleges and universities to work with industry on live projects to solve real problems.'

This view looks at the state as an enabler rather than as one which unilaterally drives innovation and productivity changes through a detailed blueprint. The substantial presence of the informal sector in India is no coincidence. Paul Abraham, former chief operating officer (COO) of IndusInd Bank and president of the Hinduja Foundation, has this to say on the subject: 'The gig economy is big and the unorganized sector is huge and the labour market was thrown into disarray post the pandemic. Technology solutions should help in getting the labour market formally organized. This enables labour to access large pools of demand and over a period of time create track records of behavioural indicators and also credit histories. This gives them vast benefits of access and reach into services which they would never have been able to buy into, including key services like finance, insurance, health and job security.'

FIELD NOTES: START-UPS, PATENTS AND EDUCATION INITIATIVES[48]

In this concluding section, we take a look at some on-the-ground data for start-ups, patents as an index for innovation, and statistics on education.

Start-ups in India have seen a remarkable spike in recent years. During 2021, over 14,000 new start-ups were registered, against a mere 733 during 2016–17. Overall, more than 61,400 Indian start-ups have come into operation as of 10 January 2022. Between April 2019 and December 2021, Delhi, with over new 5000 start-ups, replaced Bengaluru, with 4514, as the start-up capital of India. Among the states, with a total of 11,308 start-ups, Maharashtra has the highest number of recognized start-ups. In 2021, India saw a record forty-four new start-ups reach unicorn status, overtaking the UK to have the third highest number of unicorns globally, after the US and China, who had 487 and 301 unicorns, respectively. As of 14 January 2022, India had eighty-three unicorns with a total valuation of US$ 277.77 billion. While these are glowing statistics, they need to be mapped against the sustainability and scaling-up of the start-ups. Thus, the metrics for the number of start-ups that continue to be in operation after three or five years, as well as the number of ventures that have scaled up revenue by a multiple of five, may be calculated as a percentage of new start-ups that emerged during the same period.

At the time this chapter was being finalized in July 2022, the prognosis for the Indian start-up ecosystem was anything but rosy. After record investments in 2021, the sector saw a relative drying up in 2022. For instance, Indian start-ups raised only $1.6 billion in April 2022, only around half the capital raised in April 2021. With a greater focus on profitability and longer-term survival, many start-ups have resorted to layoffs as a cost-cutting measure. According to a report by IBM[49], of the 60,000 start-ups in the country, 90 per cent could fail. Between January and June 2022, over 12,000 professionals were laid off in the start-up sector. Financial worries apart, the excitement one usually associates with the start-up sector has also been marred by ugly public spats between founders and investors, as well as by acrimonious social media wars between rival ventures.[50]

While start-ups in the technology and product development space are associated with innovation, as regards patents their performance falls far short of expectations. India's ranking in the Global Innovation Index has climbed from 81 in 2015–16 to 46 in 2021. However, the number of patents granted in India is still a fraction of those in other economies. According to the World Intellectual Property Organization (WIPO), the number of patents granted in China, the USA and Japan in 2020 were 5,30,000, 3,52,00, and 1,79,000, respectively. The corresponding figure for India was 28,391. A big reason for this is India's relatively low expenditure on R&D, e.g., a mere 0.7 per cent of its GDP in 2020, as opposed to Sweden's 3.5 per cent in the same year. The complexity and delays inherent in the process are also a major source of concern. The average pendency in formalizing patents in India was forty-two months in 2020, multiple times higher than the twenty-one, twenty and fifteen months, respectively, in the US, China and Japan.

Part of this can be traced back to the low number of patent examiners in India—615 of them in 2020, as opposed to 13,704 in China, 8132 in the US and 1666 in Japan. A further issue is that there is no time limit prescribed in the statute for the controller to conduct a hearing to determine the validity of responses to any outstanding objections which may have been raised. This process in itself usually takes about six to nine months. Finally, the decision after the opposition hearing by the controller, which ought to be completed in one month, typically takes as long as three to four months. At the institutional level, creating conditions for propelling patent-based innovation will need a multipronged approach: more specifically, a streamlined and less time-consuming process, a much larger pool of qualified certifiers, and reassurance that compliance will be within the timelines stipulated.

Finally, let us take a brief look at education. Official government figures were available only for the years up to 2019–20, and so the Annual Status of Education Report (ASER) report for 2021 has been considered for more recent data. ASER found that despite the pandemic, the number of children not enrolled in education in the age cohort of fifteen to sixteen years declined from 12.1 per cent in 2018 to 6.6 per cent in 2021. However, in the rural sector, among children aged six to fourteen, the number 'not currently enrolled in schools' increased from 2.5 per cent in 2018 to 4.6 per cent in 2021. More worrying was the finding that the existing digital divide further exacerbated access to education. Availability of smartphones increased from 36.5 per cent in 2018 to 67.6 per cent in 2021, but students in the lower grades found it difficult to do online activities compared to higher-grade students. Non-availability of smartphones and internet networks, or connectivity issues, were the challenges faced by children.

To address these challenges, the Central government undertook various initiatives for school education during the pandemic, as listed below:

- PM e-VIDYA: Launched in May 2020, PM e-Vidya unifies efforts around digital/online/on-air school education under one initiative. Its components are: One Nation, One Digital Education (DIKSHA) Platform; One Class, One TV channel through Swayam Prabha TV Channels; extensive use of radio, community radio and podcasts; and, for the differently abled, One DTH channel, dedicated to hearing-impaired students in sign language. Over 3000 audiobook chapters, 602 videos and 490 textbook-based videos have been uploaded on DIKSHA.

- National Digital Education Architecture (NDEAR): The blueprint of NDEAR was launched on 29 July 2021. Its digital architecture is expected to support teaching and learning activities as well as educational planning, governance administrative activities of the Centre, states and union territories, in a manner that ensures autonomy of the states and union territories.

- Vidyanjali: Launched on 7 September 2021, to connect government and government-aided schools through a community/volunteer management programme. The

Vidyanjali portal enables volunteers to interact and connect directly with schools of their choice to share their knowledge and skills and contribute assets/materials/equipment.

- The Samagra Shiksha Scheme will be continued until 2025–26. The major interventions for all levels of school education proposed under the scheme are: (i) universal access, including infrastructure development and retention, (ii) foundational literacy and numeracy, (iii) gender and equity, (iv) inclusive education, (v) quality and innovation, (vi) financial support for teacher salaries, (vii) digital initiatives, (viii) RTE entitlements, including uniforms and textbooks, (ix) support for early childhood care and education (ECCE), (x) vocational education, (xi) sports and physical Education, (xii) strengthening of teacher education and training, (xiii) monitoring, (xiv) programme management, and (xv) focus on Regional Balance, particularly in special focus districts and educationally backward areas.

- NIPUN Bharat Mission: On 5 July 2021, the government launched a National Mission on Foundational Literacy and Numeracy. The National Mission lays down priorities and actionable agenda for states/UTs to achieve the goal of proficiency in foundational literacy and numeracy for every child up to the age of nine.

- Pradhan Mantri Poshan Shakti Nirman (PM POSHAN) Scheme: The scheme, earlier known as 'National Programme for Mid-Day Meal in Schools', covers all schoolchildren studying in Balvatika (a level just below Class I) and in Classes I–VIII in government and government-aided schools. During 2020–21, about 11.8 crore children studying in 11.2 lakh institutions benefited under the scheme. The PM POSHAN Scheme for schools has been approved for implementation from

2021–22 to 2025–26 with financial outlays from the Central and state governments.

Besides school education, some programmes have also been undertaken for higher education through the first two years of the pandemic:

- The National Apprenticeship Training Scheme (NATS) has been extended for another five years to make 9 lakh students employable through apprenticeship. NATS now offers apprenticeship to students from the humanities, commerce and science streams, apart from the engineering stream.
- The Academic Bank of Credit was launched on 29 July 2021 with the aim of digitally storing academic credits earned by students from various HEIs to make them fungible across institutes for awarding of degrees.
- e-PGPathshala: 154 universities have come on board to conduct Massive Online Open Courses (MOOCs). The e-PGPathshala has been offered as an online gateway of post graduate courses; 778 papers with 23,000 e-modules in sixty-seven subjects have been developed. The pandemic period saw extensive use of the e-PGPathshala website across universities.
- The Unnat Bharat Abhiyan has been launched to engage reputed HEIs, both central and state, public and private, to focus on the rural sector. As of mid-2022, 2897 institutions were participating in the programme, adopting around 14,500 villages.
- Scholarship schemes for weaker sections, such as the Central Sector Scheme of Scholarship for College and University Students, have impacted over 1,50,000 students in 2021–22.

In this chapter, we have explored the nuances of innovation globally as well as in India; and formal patent-based innovation as well as the Jugaad variety. We examined the relationship between education, innovation and productivity, with special reference to the Indian economy. The relation between the three is complex, but in particular, looking at the content of education (rather than at just literacy rates) is crucial to ensuring that we prepare the worker of the future with the right skill sets to be productive and to innovate in the workplace. We took a hard look not only at the disruptions in education caused by the pandemic, but also across at the start-up ecosystem. In the case of the latter, we noted how, in the wake of the pandemic, fears of global recession, continued geopolitical strife and problems specific to India have cast a veil of gloom over otherwise buoyant projections. Challenging as these issues are, they still tend to remain within the boundaries of business resilience. However, as we shall see in the next chapter, the pandemic has had a debilitating effect on the emotional and psychological well-being of people, on a scale that is nothing short of a global mental health pandemic.

CHAPTER 6

Mental Health: The Other Pandemic

> *. . . Canst thou not minister to a mind diseased,*
> *Pluck from the memory a rooted sorrow,*
> *Raze out the written troubles of the brain*
> *And with some sweet oblivious antidote*
> *Cleanse the stuffed bosom of that perilous stuff*
> *Which weights upon the heart?*

—William Shakespeare, *Macbeth*, Act V, Scene III

As with Macbeth's plea to the doctor, millions of people today wonder if there is an antidote to the problem of 'a mind diseased', something that in our times has become ubiquitous. Now, 'mental health condition' is an umbrella term used to subsume a range of conditions differing in severity and causes, including anxiety, depression, psychoses, bipolar disorder, schizophrenia, dementia and developmental disorders such as autism, all of which affect an individual's cognitive, emotional and social abilities. According to the Institute of Health Metrics & Evaluation (IHME), mental health conditions are estimated to affect a billion people globally.[1]

The number is even more frightening when we realize that this particular estimate predates the COVID crisis, which has been associated with damaging mental health and well-being. Indeed, as waves of the pandemic wax and wane, many experts worry whether the mental health burden on the population will not exceed the direct health impact from the disease. In other words, the mental health pandemic, following insidiously on the heels of successive waves of lockdowns and new variants of the coronavirus, may likely be even worse than the original COVID-19 crisis.

There are several reasons why COVID-19 has exacerbated mental health issues across the world. For many, this stemmed from personal trauma, grief and bereavement—having lost family members or friends to the disease, often without being able to say goodbye to them. Tens of millions of people, including the authors here, have faced illness, having been infected by the virus. There are also the debilitating symptoms of what has come to be known as 'long COVID', with estimates suggesting that anywhere between 20 million and 40 million people globally may have been impacted by it.[2] For an even larger section of society across geographies, even for people not directly infected by the virus, anxiety and depression have resulted from the social isolation, alienation and loneliness caused by lockdowns or other forms of restrictions on social interaction. As if these weren't bad enough, the challenges have been aggravated by economic uncertainty. For example, at one point, 70 per cent of businesses in the UK were reporting higher uncertainty due to COVID.[3] Those employed in sectors such as travel, hospitality, tourism and entertainment have been particularly hard-hit, with many facing the prospect of a long layoff. Such spells of unemployment are not just bad news for one's economic health, they also have a particularly scarring effect on one's psychological well-being.

A cross-Europe study[4] conducted prior to the pandemic found that even a six-month spell of unemployment could lead to a reduced quality of life and life satisfaction in people over the age of fifty. This is in line with evidence from the US and other countries, with the main point of contention across these studies being how persistent the reduction in wages and unemployment are.[5] This effect is doubly debilitating, as poorer well-being can in turn lead to reduced earnings and employment. While there are no comparable studies in India on the long-term emotional and psychological impact of unemployment, given the absence of unemployment insurance or social safety net in the country, the impact is likely to be higher here. Recent surveys in India during the time of COVID[6] painted a grim picture. Unemployment reached a thirty-year high of 24 per cent in April 2020, with online reports of suicidal behaviour increasing by 68 per cent during the first national lockdown.

In this chapter, we explore the state of mental health across large cohorts of people, and also how they are impacted by mass-scale measures such as lockdowns. We do this by examining various population surveys across geographies. We look at some of the coping mechanisms people adopted, and their efficacy, during the period when the healthcare system was overwhelmed with COVID cases and medical professionals worked in an atmosphere of incessant stress and risk, many getting infected by the virus too. WFH and, stemming from it, various modes of hybrid working, have emerged as the dominant forms of business operations as a direct result of the COVID experience. While these offer economic benefits to companies in terms of cost savings, we also look at the emotional and psychological challenges that WFH brings.

In the workplace, COVID has shifted the levers of onus, accountability and empowerment, with the spotlight placed firmly on HR to lead organizations and people out of the deep crisis.[7] We look at some of the implications of WFH from an HR perspective, as well as the key opportunities that the crisis has opened up for the HR domain and its practitioners across sectors. At the same time, we also note the challenges that have cropped up for HR. We then delve into the dark and disturbing phenomena of self-harm and suicide as extreme consequences of mental health conditions, and explore how the incidence of suicide has been impacted globally by the pandemic. Next, we take up the mental health situation in India, in the workplace and beyond. In the absence of large-scale published studies, we attempt to gauge the full scale of the crisis by gleaning insights from anecdotal evidence, reports and surveys, from the predicament relating to mental health insurance, and from commentaries by mental health experts.

In the final sections of the chapter, we aim to provide a ray of hope. While the scale and surge of the pandemic, and the disruptions wrought by it, have certainly overtaken us multiple times, it should be borne in mind that each time, experts and analysts, private and government think tanks, and specialists of all stripes have come together to debate, align on, and announce how to deal with the crisis and how to move ahead with some semblance of future-mindedness. We conclude the chapter by providing insights, guidelines and recommendations for measuring and managing mental health in the workplace. In particular, we consider the best practices adopted in workplaces around stress management, development of resilience, and enhancement of emotional and psychological well-being. The absence of economy-wide regulations on mental health in the Indian workplace presents a considerable challenge. To overcome it, we consider the norms that Indian organizations could adopt, and propose a specific framework that companies could follow in order to design, execute, implement, audit and refine policies around psychosocial risks and mental health at work.

THROUGH A LOOKING GLASS, DARKLY

Organizations across the world regularly survey their respective target customer populations across a range of parameters and behaviours. This practice increased during the COVID pandemic, so much so that there is now a legitimate worry that survey fatigue may skew both the responses from people who participate in them, as well as the quality of responses. Thus, we need to be careful about how we interpret such surveys. This is particularly important as we may be systematically missing out on particular socioeconomic demographic groups. To take an example, in the 2016 US presidential election, Hillary Clinton found that there was a large number of so-called 'shy Trump voters'. As has been pointed out,[8] this was not really because they were too shy to admit to voting for Trump. Rather, Trump voters formed a disproportionately large section of the group that did not respond to surveys, and this led to every poll prediction being inaccurate.

Many of those who do not answer surveys are distrustful of government and may have deep-rooted paranoia about the state or less trust in society or institutions.[9] This is not limited to surveys on polling matters but cuts across the entire spectrum of surveys, including those that aim to gauge health and well-being. Conventional surveys will offer little insight into the mental health of the section of the population that feels the globalized world has left them behind. Understanding their attitudes is vitally important, something that analysts need to consider when designing policy for those specific sections of the population. First, though, we will try and look at the mainstream, which does participate in surveys. Having sifted through numerous surveys of varying degrees of quality across a range of countries, we focus on those that offer clear insights into what is driving mental health conditions, limiting ourselves to some broad findings.

As is to be expected, lockdowns around the world have had a negative impact on mental health. In the UK, multiple studies report[10] fluctuations in mental health and well-being, with deteriorations and improvements broadly corresponding with lockdowns. For example, levels of resilience were found to be stable during periods when lockdown restrictions were relaxed or lifted, with approximately two-thirds of the population being considered mentally stable. However, lockdowns are associated with poor mental health outcomes. The UK Household Longitudinal Study data suggests that two-fifths of the population experienced elevated levels of distress. Furthermore, suffering was not equal across the different groups—for instance, younger people, women and those who were single experienced higher levels of distress.

Further insights can be gleaned from surveys by the UK charity, Mind, which provided one of the most comprehensive surveys on mental health in England and Wales during the first lockdown. This survey is particularly insightful as it did not just ask about mental health but queried respondents on coping strategies as well as access issues, and was obtained from the vignettes of a varied group of people sharing their experiences and what worked for them in getting through the pandemic. It also looked at the small minority of people whose mental health actually improved during the pandemic and the reasons behind it. One caveat of the survey was that it looked at the experiences of those with mental health problems rather than assessing how the general population's overall mental health changed across the pandemic.

Mind carried out two surveys: among young people aged thirteen to twenty-four, and among adults aged twenty-four and above, both of these gauging the state of mental health of people in England and Wales. The sample included 10,023 adults and 1756 young people. A vast majority of both adults

(85 per cent) and young people (91 per cent) had experienced mental health distress, with 26 per cent and 18 per cent, respectively, experiencing distress for the first time. Also, 65 per cent of adults and 68 per cent of young people reported that their mental health got much worse and continued to deteriorate after the first national lockdown. The numbers are also high for those whose economic conditions were poor. For example, over half of the people (58 per cent) living in households that received state benefits had poor or very poor mental health. According to the findings, 72 per cent of these people felt much worse after the initial lockdown in March 2020, against 63 per cent of those who did not receive any benefits. Further, 19 per cent of the young people and 16 per cent of the adults surveyed accessed mental health services for the first time in their lives.

Among the mental health stressors, 88 per cent of young people experienced loneliness, and 53 per cent had concerns about family, jobs or financial issues, against 37 per cent of adults. Self-harming as a coping mechanism was found to be worse among young people (32 per cent) than among adults (14 per cent). While ethnic minorities are usually thought to be disproportionately affected by any crisis, this particular survey did not find a big difference. Ethnic minority groups were slightly more likely to be affected by restrictions on outdoor movements than their white counterparts: 75 per cent of ethnic minority adults against 66 per cent of adults from both white and BAME (black, Asian and minority ethnic) communities. However, as the survey acknowledges, BAME were under-represented in the survey.

Many people reported connecting with friends and families online, which was a healthy way of coping. However, there were certain coping strategies adopted by the affected people that were worrisome. For example, some people reported overeating, which may have implications for their physical health. Most worrisome were the coping strategies that relied on use of drugs and alcohol, and for young people this was particularly prevalent, with one-third using this as a coping strategy. Even more concerning is that a third of young people with existing mental health problems were self-harming as a way of coping.

While only 12 per cent of the people surveyed said their mental health had improved during the lockdown, understanding who they are and why this was the case is instructive. Those who spoke about the positive effects of the restrictions saw the pandemic as providing them a break from their daily life or as a chance to consider a new career or focus on health and fitness. Some people with social anxiety felt better not to have to make the effort to mingle. As one participant put it, she 'used to dread having to attend a pub quiz every Thursday and would spend days rehearsing potential conversations'. But she herself realizes that this is a mixed blessing, reported the survey, 'as staying inside all the time and not confronting her fears may set her recovery back, and she may struggle with resuming social contact and reaching the goals she set herself at her local Mind, once lockdown is over'. Thus, apart from a select few who used the pandemic time to 'reset' their lives, even the relief that some people with social anxiety experienced might be short-lived, and the pandemic was indeed impeding their progress towards their longer-term goals.

According to a Gallup survey published in 2022, fewer than one in four US employees—less than 25 per cent—feel strongly that their organization cares about their well-being, the lowest percentage in nearly a decade. This finding has significant implications, because in light of the pandemic experience, work and life have become more blended than ever before. Consequently, employee well-being matters—

or at least ought to—for the employees themselves, and for the resilience of the organizations they work in. The finding came from a random sample of 15,001 full- and part-time US employees who were surveyed in February 2022. Prior to COVID-19, in 2014, around the same percentage (25 per cent) of employees strongly agreed that their employer cared about their overall well-being. Then, at the onset of the pandemic in 2020, employers responded quickly with plans and communicated what many employees believed was genuine concern for them, their work and their lives. The percentage who felt cared about nearly doubled, reaching a high of 49 per cent in May 2022. Since that point, however, this perception has progressively decreased, plummeting to the previous low levels.[11]

The findings from other surveys mirror those from Mind. For example, a recent US survey carried out by the National Center for Health Statistics (NCHS) in collaboration with the Census Bureau on the Household Pulse survey. They collected data during different time periods of the pandemic, with a specific focus on anxiety and depression disorder symptoms. Their results show that a greater percentage of younger people suffered from these symptoms compared to older people. NCHS pointed out that mental health estimates from the 2019 National Health Interview Survey could be used as a benchmark for comparison. The 2019 NHIS survey shows that in general, 8 per cent of adults showed symptoms of anxiety, 7 per cent for depressive disorders and 11 per cent symptoms of both types of disorders. These figures have more than doubled across the pandemic period.

As is clear in countries with heterogeneous populations, such as India, focused and region-specific surveys give different answers, depending on where the surveys are conducted. For example, a survey conducted in India's capital, New Delhi, to assess the impact of the lockdown on the residents after a week of its imposition,[12] had a large sample (n = 992 residents aged twenty-one years and above), but only those who had at least a graduate degree were asked to complete the survey, which was administered in English and so does not represent all communities. The survey found the lockdown affected the income and work of 63 per cent, mostly aged between thirty-six and fifty, followed by those aged between fifty-one and sixty-five. Seven per cent had feelings of anxiety and restlessness, 12 per cent felt helpless and depressed and could not do anything about it.

These levels are considerably lower than figures captured in other worldwide studies, reflecting the relatively optimistic view of the educated urbanite during the early phase of the pandemic in India. This is further corroborated by the fact that 79 per cent of the respondents were optimistic and believed the disease could be contained. Nonetheless, some of the answers as to what their habits were provide clues that their mental health was affected more than their direct responses indicated. Over half (55 per cent) had trouble sleeping and 26 per cent had started to smoke and drink alcohol as a direct result of lockdown. This underscores the fact that those same worrisome coping strategies found in the Mind survey were also being adopted across other parts of the world. In economic matters, the survey was evenly split in terms of concern around sufficient funds to manage the household during the lockdown, with half saying they had enough funds to tide over the crisis, and the other half being uncertain or not having sufficient funds.

Larger surveys in India present an even gloomier picture. During the initial phase of the pandemic, an online survey of over 1800 people was conducted by the Indian Psychiatry Society,[13] which found that over 40 per cent of the people surveyed had either anxiety or depression, or both; nearly 75 per cent of respondents reported moderate levels of stress, and over 70 per cent reported poor well-being. The silver lining was an improvement in interpersonal relationships at home, with almost half the respondents reporting a marked improvement in their relationships with their spouse/partner (47 per cent), children (44 per cent) and parents (47 per cent) after the start of the lockdown period. Social relations appeared to improve, with 60 per cent reporting a marked improvement in their relationship with their neighbours (62 per cent) and office colleagues (60 per cent) during the lockdown period. However, such findings should be interpreted with caution, reflecting a temporary reconnecting with people during the first lockdown. While some have used the pandemic to spend more time with their families and connect with colleagues, there was a rise in the incidence of domestic violence, as we shall see in the next section.

That survey results can be biased is acknowledged widely, but until recently there were few tools that could do more than make somewhat ad hoc corrections to account for the 'missing population' in them. But advances in data analysis—for example, machine learning—allow for more sophisticated ways of weighting underrepresented groups. Further, there are other tools to analyse unstructured data, such as spontaneous interaction on social media, allowing analysts to feel the pulse of the population in real time. Such sentiment analysis is a powerful way to complement survey findings. For example, a sentiment analysis in India during the first lockdown recorded some negative sentiments, including fear and distrust, but the dominant sentiment was positive.[14] This is likely to have been a reflection of the high levels of trust in and agreement with the government's decision to implement a total lockdown. It should be borne in mind that this was in that initial period of solidarity witnessed, when the lockdown was first imposed, the common motto being that 'we are all in it together', geared towards a common goal—i.e., to 'flatten the curve'.

Several cycles of the pandemic later, this may have eroded, with resilience falling sharply as it became increasingly apparent that COVID would not disappear any time soon, and as new waves of the virus brought more uncertainty, hardship and suffering. Indeed, a sentiment analysis was conducted of 11,807 COVID-related Reddit posts from 1 February 2020, from when the number of cases started to rise in north America, to 14 January 2021. Using machine learning, messages were classified as positive, neutral or negative; and it was found that negative posts exceeded the positive ones.

In summary, there were serious issues of mental health, burnout and economic anxiety during the time of the pandemic. The effect was not uniform, with women and younger people being affected more. While people did exhibit resilience and connected better with their families, some of the coping strategies that were adopted raise cause for concern.

WHEN HOME IS WORK: IMPLICATIONS, CHALLENGES AND OPPORTUNITIES

One feature of our pandemic-era workforce has been its increasing ability to work remotely. The twin advancements of globalization and technology that we discussed in Chapter One have meant that for a growing number of professions and job roles, the worker is no longer tied to a physical workplace and, for the gig worker, even to any particular employer. This has led to the rise of models of teleworking or telecommuting; for many, this equates to WFH. What many of us tend to overlook is that even before the pandemic struck, there was already a move towards a hybrid model for certain types of work.

The COVID pandemic accelerated this trend out of compulsion and sheer survival needs. In sectors such as education, the MOOCs mode had to swiftly find a way to deliver education remotely and for a mass audience. There have been contradictory findings on whether teleworking is good for the worker, and this ambiguity comes from the opposing forces that impact the teleworker.[15] Analysing the opposing factors that affect well-being at work allows us to understand both the positives and negatives.[16] Freeing up commute time reduces exhaustion and positively affects worker well-being. Remote workers, in many cases, can also have more flexibility around their work schedules. Against these advantages, they inevitably miss out on the informal networks at the workplace and subsequently experience feelings of isolation or of being disconnected from their colleagues. It is also more difficult to switch off work at home, especially in the absence of a dedicated workspace in the home which others will keep away from.

Another impact of WFH has been the perceived threat to jobs. While professionals working in IT, BPO and KPO have been used to variants of WFH even before the pandemic, for people in other sectors this is a new mode of working, and so it is important that we find ways to measure well-being among the WFH workforce. While there are established measures for conventional full-time employees, less is known on what measures can work when it comes to people working in the hybrid model or as gig professionals and freelancers. There are newly developed scales, such as the EWL (eWork Life Scale),[17] recently tested to help us understand the different dimensions of a remote worker's work life, including well-being.

The pandemic disrupted what could have been a phased move towards this hybrid model. Suddenly, everyone was either WFH or a front-line 'warrior', and both groups faced stress and burnout. For the WFH single worker, losing the social connections at work increased feelings of isolation and loneliness. Tensions within the family rose. Reports of domestic violence and child abuse shot up, though the very nature of these incidents or crimes makes it hard to precisely estimate prevalence. Consequently, analysts rely on proxies, such as calls to domestic and child abuse helplines and increased google searches on helplines for domestic violence, to infer whether there has been a significant increase in such incidents. In particular, a strong correlation has been noted between incidence of domestic violence and cases of mental health conditions.[18] Similarly, child maltreatment has been associated with development of mental ill health in later life.[19]

However, WFH as a conscious choice may be a boon for workers, particularly if it is part of a temporary or hybrid arrangement, lessening their commute time while not cutting them off from their informal work networks. The precise balance may need fine-tuning; for instance, how many days should one come to the office, should it depend on whether one is new or a seasoned hand, etc. Regardless, WFH and hybrid working will certainly continue to be the norm for many firms, post the pandemic. The 2021 Work Trend Index found nearly 70 per cent of workers demand it, and more and more employers are willing to implement these models. For the latter, WFH and hybrid models with a greater reliance on remote work have come as an unequivocal financial boon. For organizations, overheads include a number of items, from office lease and use of utilities to paying for commutes, carpools and the coffee in the pantry. A measure designed for risk mitigation and immediate survival of operations soon became the norm.

Companies opting for WFH—in some instances, permanently for non-customer-facing departments—and shifting to smaller, less expensive office premises has meant a sizeable cut in the overheads. Company stakeholders argue that this approach has allowed them to remain afloat and retain personnel they'd otherwise be compelled to let go. The positive impact of the hybrid model is seen in a survey in India, by Atlassian and conducted by Australian research agency PaperGiant,[20] done during the early part of the pandemic, though recent surveys find experiences of hybrid working more evenly divided.[21] Indeed, a survey in 2021 by LinkedIn (Future of Work Perception study) of Indian workers reinforced the message that workers want a hybrid model, with 86 per cent thinking it helps them maintain work-life balance.[22] The same study also highlighted the remote workers' feeling of being disconnected from their boss and fellow workers, emphasizing that firms need to work through what mix works best and for whom. The conscious choice that people were making to work remotely, or more commonly adopt a hybrid model, was a mixed blessing, and there are clearly concerns and open questions about its net impact.

The American Psychiatric Association's May 2021 survey of US adults[23] found a majority have experienced a negative mental health impact, including feelings of loneliness and isolation, because of the pandemic. Nearly two-thirds of people working from home feel isolated or lonely at least sometimes, and 17 per cent do all the time. While 54 per cent said their employer had become more accommodating of their mental health needs since the pandemic, only 20 per cent said they were offered more support, down from 35 per cent in 2020.

More worrying, four in ten feared retaliation if they sought mental healthcare or took time off because of their mental health condition. This was more pronounced among younger workers, with 59 per cent of employees in the eighteen-to-twenty-nine age group and 54 per cent of employees between thirty and forty-four in age being 'somewhat or very concerned' about retaliation or about being fired if they took time off for mental health needs. This compares to 39 per cent for the forty-five-to-sixty-four age group. The impact of such stress morphs into a vicious cycle, which, unchecked, can be catastrophic. Unhappy people make unhappy life choices, and this increases the likelihood of self-harm and suicide.

MENTAL HEALTH, INSURANCE AND SUICIDES IN INDIA

First, a few words about the healthcare sector itself. It would remiss of us not to note how the pandemic has thrust healthcare professionals into the role of front-line COVID warriors. Unrelenting stress and prolonged hours of service in critical situations have taken their toll on the mental health and well-being of healthcare workers. Dr Simmardeep Gill, a medical practitioner by training, is the former COO at CK Birla Hospitals, overseeing over 1000 hospital beds across four facilities in India. He says: 'The COVID-19 pandemic has taken a toll on the psychological well-being of healthcare workers, with rapidly rising issues of anxiety, fear, panic attacks, depression, post-traumatic stress, etc. It is in these trying times of distress that human empathy takes a leap forward. The doctors, nurses, clinicians, have been overworked, and treated patients while themselves being exhausted, with maybe forty winks a day. My standing ovation to them all! Here, I would like to say that we have taken every possible step to assuage the trauma of these brave hearts, by involving them in varying stress-relieving activities in our hospital.' But thousands of medical practitioners elsewhere across the country have not been so fortunate.'

People with mental health conditions face difficulties in everyday life, be it in the workplace, relationships or social activities. This has different manifestations, depending on the type of condition involved. For example, depression may be characterized by feelings of sadness, loss of interest or pleasure, feelings of guilt or low self-worth, disturbed sleep or appetite, tiredness and poor concentration.[24] This, of course, affects the well-being of the individual, but also negatively affects friends and family. While distress cannot be adequately quantified, global estimates of how much it costs are staggering: lost productivity and poor health were estimated to cost the world economy $2.5 trillion dollars in 2010, and the figure is expected to rise to $6 trillion in 2030.[25] Treatments that are cost-effective do exist for many mental health conditions. However, as a recent paper in *Lancet Global Health* notes,[26] care is patchy. The WHO Mental Health Atlas 2017 asks countries how mental healthcare costs are funded. It has found that in many countries (27 per cent of 169 countries), care and treatment for severe mental disorders is not included in national health insurance or reimbursement schemes. Care for less severe mental illness can be even harder to access and fund.

Given the worldwide prevalence of mental ill health, we would expect India with its 1.4 billion population to be home to a considerable number of such people. While often under-counted, a comprehensive study in 2017[27] suggests that the number is around 200 million. Yet, it was only in 2014 that India launched its first National Mental Health Policy and a revised Mental Healthcare Act in 2017 to provide equitable, affordable and universal access to mental healthcare. In principle, this is a good start, but how does this translate into actual provision and payment for the care of those with mental ill health?

Insurance is explicitly covered in Section 21 (4) of the Act, which states, '. . . every insurer shall make provision for medical insurance for treatment of mental illness on the same basis as is available for treatment of physical illness'. However, the Insurance Regulatory and Development Authority of India did not act to ensure that insurance companies did indeed cover mental health. Finally, it needed the involvement of courts as well as the increased mental illness following COVID[28] for the regulatory body to get its act together. Gradually, some forms of mental illness are being covered; however, rejection of claims remains high, and many do not make claims, fearing rejection.[29] This, coupled with the stigma associated with mental ill health, leaves many untreated. Together with the precarity of people's economic existence, as well as the burden of expectation, the consequences can be devastating—and for some, end in suicide.

Now, this may come as a surprise to some of our readers, but India reports the highest number of deaths by suicide in the world.[30] While these numbers are partly a reflection of its mammoth population, the trends are indeed worrying. Between 1990 and 2019, the proportion of suicides in India as a percentage of the global numbers has increased. This is particularly pronounced for women and girls, for whom it rose from 27 per cent in 1990 to 37 per cent in 2019, with a smaller but nevertheless worrying rise, from 17 per cent to 21 per cent, during the same period for men and boys. Ever since the 1970s, farmer suicides in India have been making headlines in most years, actuated by economic debt, but the problem is much larger. Suicide remains the largest cause of death in younger people (aged fifteen to thirty-nine) in the country.

While self-harm and suicide can be an extreme consequence of unrelated mental health issues, there is much cause for concern about the longer-term adverse impact of the pandemic on the mental health of professionals in the emergent workplace. Dr Vinay Mishra, a professor of psychology at the Bhopal School of Social Sciences, a psychological counsellor, author, speaker and company adviser, says: 'Strategies like quarantine, necessary to minimize viral spread, can have a negative psychological impact, such as causing post-traumatic stress symptoms, depression and insomnia. Job loss and financial struggles during a global economic downturn have been associated with a long-lasting decline in mental health.

'Historically, the adverse mental health effects of disasters impact more people and last much longer than the physical health effects. If history is any predictor, we should expect a significant 'tail' of mental health needs that continue long after the infectious outbreak resolves. As far as which mental health issues connected to the COVID-19 pandemic are most likely to last in the longer term, psychologists believe obsessive-compulsive disorder (OCD) could be one of the main candidates. Alongside OCD, which is a manifestation of anxiety, general anxiety is also a very important mental health issue to watch out for. There are many people who suffer from anxiety already in our modern society, but because of the pandemic, people who tend to feel anxious more easily may find their condition worsens. Even when the COVID pandemic ends, some people might be over-anxious because of the threat of a variant strain.'

Mental health expert Dr Jai Ranjan Ram, senior psychiatrist at Apollo Hospitals, cofounder of the Mental Health Foundation and columnist, says: 'Access to mental health services across industry is a concern that can only be improved if there is a greater recognition at all levels that adverse mental health affects productivity. So, if your workforce is happy, they will be able to deliver their work far better than if a proportion of the workforce is psychologically unwell. The key is awareness: once there is increased awareness, there would be a reduction in stigma, and people would be more willing to accept help. The second thing is—the majority of the mental health services in India are poorly resourced, so again there has to be greater investments, maybe between private and public initiatives, to invest more money in mental health so that it is more accessible. The need for taking care of one's psychological health is not going to decrease. On the contrary, the COVID pandemic has made us more aware about the need to take care of one's mental health.'

With regard to the adverse impact of a long-term, remote, WFH mode of working, the concerns run equally deep. As Dr Ram puts it: 'One of the problems of working from home is that many people miss the camaraderie which is present in the office and physical workspace; they find this mode more tiresome, and this in turn can lead to quicker burnout. Another problem is that for most of the workforce—homes were never meant to have workstations and so forth—there will be intrusions. Especially for working women. They have to be "working for home" in addition to "working from home"—this becomes a very difficult challenge. This is one of the major burdens of a model that encourages a complete shift to WFH. Obviously, there are advantages. But the disadvantages also must be taken note of, by the senior management at companies promoting work from home. The other aspect is, if you are expected to work from home, unfortunately there are no boundaries. Many of the employees working in such a scenario say that the intrusion into their family time is too much. Somehow there's a belief that if you are working from home, then it's a grand gesture on the part of the company, so they can intrude on your personal time. There are nations where there's a regulation where one cannot call up employees beyond a particular time—and I think all companies should adhere to that, otherwise the intrusion of work and colleagues into personal time can be very demoralizing.'

Employee burnout has emerged as one of the biggest fallouts of all this in the global workplace. In fact, surveys conducted by Gallup in 2020 and 2021 found that managers reported more stress and burnout and worse physical well-being and work-life balance than the juniors they manage.

Multiple factors account for this. Stress and anxiety levels have remained high for managers, even as they declined for others, in 2021. Diagnosed depression increased for managers in 2021 but was relatively unchanged for individual contributors and project managers, and actually declined for leaders. Only one in four managers surveyed in 2021 strongly agreed they were able to maintain a healthy balance between work and personal commitments. Continuing stressors could also be a function of unfair treatment at work, unmanageable workload, lack of role clarity, lack of communication and support from one's manager, and unreasonable time pressures. Gallup suggests a combination of effective top-down communication from leaders and skilful upward management by the managers themselves, to address these issues.[31]

Gallup's recent study involving the meta-analysis of employee engagement and performance outcomes, too, offers little solace. The research, involving more than 1,00,000 teams across 122 countries, found ties between their engagement and eleven performance outcomes, and then arrived at indices for positive and negative emotions. The numbers involved have been substantial—Gallup conducted 3500 interviews in China, 3000 in India and 2000 in the Russian Federation. And the results are unambiguous. There is a global rise in unhappiness. The Positive Experiences Index showed a decline, even from the 2020 levels, which were alarming in themselves. 'Enjoyment', 'smiling' and 'feeling well-rested' seemed to have almost vanished. On the other hand, the Negative Experience Index continues to record a rise, with sadness, stress and worry reaching record levels.[32]

The findings of the Deloitte Mental Health Survey published in September 2022 are particularly damning from a global perspective, but especially for India. The survey relied on the top stressors, from the employee perspective, to arrive at an estimate of the yearly economic cost to Indian companies arising from poor employee mental health.

The critical findings are:[33]

- Poor mental health among employees costs Indian employers around US$14 billion each year, due to absenteeism, attrition and presenteeism—the last of these being defined as the phenomenon of attending work while under mental stress, and hence performing at low productivity.
- 80 per cent of the Indian workforce has reported mental health issues during the past one year.
- 47 per cent of professionals surveyed consider workplace-related stress as the biggest factor affecting their mental health, followed by financial and COVID-specific challenges.
- Societal stigma prevents around 39 per cent of the affected respondents from taking steps to manage their symptoms.
- 33 per cent of all respondents continued to work, despite poor mental health, while 29 per cent took time off and 20 per cent resigned, in order to better manage their mental health.

DEEPENING THE 'HUMAN' IN HUMAN RESOURCES

As we have seen through the various sections of this chapter, the COVID-19 crisis has impacted every domain and discipline in the workplace. But, as regards the departments in an organization, none has been as affected—and many a times, overwhelmed—HR.[34] The international financial crisis in 2008 understandably put the spotlight firmly on finance and accounts. In comparison, the extended stretch of the pandemic has been a deeply human crisis that seeped into every domain of life and the workplace. Not surprisingly, therefore, the onus of leading organizations and people through and in the aftermath of the crisis has fallen on HR departments. But two consecutive years of the pandemic have shown how HR departments in organizations, globally and across sectors and industries, have struggled to address the repeated and unpredictable waves of disruption. In India, if anything, the challenges have been more pronounced than in other economies. There are several reasons for this.

First, unlike many organizations, especially in the Western world, large companies in India employ tens of thousands of people, overseen by an HR team that is numerically too small to handle a sudden disruption that affects everyone in the organization, let alone a crisis of the scale and time frame as that of the COVID-19 pandemic. Likewise, in the pre-pandemic scenario, funds, budgets and resources for HR tended to be limited, particularly in comparison with customer-facing departments. The pandemic experience has sensitized employers to the sufferings and anxieties of their internal customers—i.e., employees. However, such a sense of greater awareness is still far from endemic, and is limited only to large companies and Indian operations of multinational organizations.

Another challenge stemmed from the myriad unpredictable ways in which successive waves of the virus changed modes of working back and forth, often affording people no time to acclimatize to any given method. While designing and executing employee polices, compliance norms and handbooks of various kinds have been under the purview of HR, these have largely been one-time turnkey assignments and remained stable and static over time, often over a period of decades. Multiple erratic cycles of overhauling of procedures have been quite overwhelming for a department used to longer shelf lives of its policies and procedures.

Moreover, for HR professionals—by way of their education, their continued learning and daily work experience—aren't equipped to handle issues that are, strictly speaking, the reserve of professional counsellors and psychologists. HR professionals across the world—and this is certainly true of India—do not have working knowledge of counselling or of the latest advances and applications of organizational and industrial psychology. This is something that we have noted in Chapter Five, when discussing the challenges in the current system of education. As a result, the HR community has been doubly overwhelmed, not only with regard to its lack of readiness but in being challenged by way of not possessing the right skills and training for dealing with psychological crises.

We should note that, amid all these challenges, there have also been a few silver linings for HR in light of the pandemic. In many organizations, for the first time in their history, HR has been asked not only to lead from the front, but is also being supported, funded and empowered by top management. Consequently, HR has more options to deal with the crisis, in the form of greater engagement of coaches, business advisers, industry experts and, increasingly, psychologists.

A second major advantage for HR is technology. Traditionally, technology in the context of HR has meant a well-developed software, a human resources management system (HRMS) that is integrated with payroll and other functionalities in finance. But the pandemic experience has warranted that technology be used in a more broad-based way, through automated processes and increased use of AI, to engage with employees and answer queries. In particular, conversational AI for HR enables organizations to deploy digital HR assistants—intelligent bots that handle a wide range of queries in real time, accurately and cost-effectively. These bots can be set up to offer a walk-through of the common processes around benefits, provide updates around employee policies and enterprise-level decisions, and so forth. A standard argument against their extensive adoption, especially in a highly labour-intensive economy such as India, is that it would naturally slash jobs for HR practitioners. Our position is that this doesn't necessarily have to be the case. Typically, a substantial proportion of the time and effort of HR professionals is spent in routine, repetitive tasks and communication. Adopting technology for these tasks means that the HR team can dedicate their time to the more sensitive and difficult tasks of counselling, coaching and creating cultures and work practices that are more inclusive, empathetic and positive.[35]

The third opportunity is through employee assistance programmes (EAPs), which, when designed and executed well, can be effective in alleviating employee trauma. The pandemic experience has increased bereavement, isolation, loss of income and fear, triggering mental health conditions or exacerbating existing ones. Many people are facing increased levels of alcohol and drug abuse, insomnia and anxiety. The aftereffects of COVID-19 themselves can lead to neurological and mental complications, such as delirium, agitation and stroke. People with pre-existing mental, neurological or substance-use disorders are also more vulnerable as they may stand a higher risk of severe outcomes and even death.

Professor Vinay Mishra, who advises companies and working professionals, feels that there is a set of good practices that can protect and promote mental health in the workplace, by way of EAPs. These include the following:

- Implementation and enforcement of health and safety policies and practices, including identification of distress, harmful use of psychoactive substances and illness, and providing resources to manage them.

- Informing everyone in the company that anonymous mental health support is available.
- Involving employees in decision-making, bringing in them a feeling of control and participation; organizational practices that support a healthy work-life balance.
- Career-development programmes for employees, recognizing and rewarding the contribution of employees, increasing the involvement of mental health providers.
- Examining state insurance to ensure that mental health parity or equal treatment of mental health and substance-use disorders is enforced.
- Bolstering tele-health infrastructures, enacting plans to help children and families of employees access mental health resources.
- Mental health interventions should be delivered as part of an integrated health and well-being strategy that covers prevention, early identification of problems, support and rehabilitation.

In India, employers have tended to take the view that work and the workplace are not etiological factors in mental health problems. Although effective mental health services are multidimensional, the workplace is an appropriate environment in which to educate individuals about and raise their awareness of mental health problems. It is possible for the workplace to promote good mental health practices and provide tools for recognition and early identification of mental health problems, and it can establish links with local mental health services for referral, treatment and rehabilitation.

The key issues are social stigma and misunderstanding of the recovery process. For people with mental health problems, finding work or returning to work and retaining a job post-treatment are often a challenge. However, as Prof Mishra points out, this too can be overcome by means of the following:

- Examining the importance of mental health problems in the workplace.
- Considering the role of the workplace in promoting good mental health practices.
- Examining the importance of work for persons with mental health problems.
- Discussing the different vocational strategies and programmes for persons with mental health problems.
- Providing examples of good practices, such as good mental health-promoting practices in the workplace, appropriate handling of an employee who is struggling with a mental health problem, and vocational rehabilitation models/programmes for persons with long-term mental health problems.

All this is important learning that has arisen for HR from the pandemic experience. There is now greater scope and opportunity to engage psychologists in HR work initiatives and for HR to learn from them in the process, as part of the assignment or through formal training, and therefore be better prepared for exigencies in the workplace that have a psychological impact.

This section has principally focused on the organized sector. But what of the MSME sector, which employs the larger proportion of the urban workforce? With minimal or zero access to mental healthcare, what can be done to address the issue at a broader, more macroeconomic level? These are some of the questions we posed to Prem Seshadri, adviser to the board and chief mentor at 1to1help.net, one of India's largest emotional wellness companies.

He said: 'The inflection point is just round the corner. The EAP industry is maturing; however, the total consumption of emotional wellness programmes is limited to about 2,000 enterprises in the country. The marketplace that exists is close to another 20,000 business enterprises and thousands of educational institutions. Emotional strengthening at the college level as a 'soft skill' requirement is the direction we shall go as a country. We have touched only the tip of the iceberg, in terms of the depth of EAP, the opportunities here again are both in the context of depth and breadth.' Many experts feel that the building of MSME infrastructure for emotional health needs to be a state-sponsored programme. As Seshadri puts it: 'Pradhan Mantri Manasik Swaasth Vyvastha (PMMSV) is an imperative.'

RECOMMENDATIONS AND INITIATIVES

In the early part of Chapter Four, we noted the definite trend towards specialism in the workplace along two dimensions: a) technical and domain skills; and b) behavioural skills and competencies. We also saw how the preeminent think tanks and analysts in the world had advocated specific behavioural skills, with a broad consensus around them. In this section, similarly, we present two sets of insights. We shall outline how seven leading global companies across sectors—Google, Microsoft, Intel, Apple, Aetna, Nike and Goldman Sachs—are addressing stress management, mindfulness and resilience for their teams and people, through mental well-being initiatives. But first, we take a quick look at what some of these same think tanks have stated as the pandemic's impact on mental health and the workplace practices they advocate to address those issues.[36]

Table 6.1: Agencies' Views on Mental Health Impact of Pandemic, and Recommendations

Serial No.	Agency	Impact on Mental Health	Recommendations
1	McKinsey	• Behavioural health problems were widespread pre-pandemic. The pandemic made things worse. E.g., 90 per cent of 1000 employers said COVID-19 affected the behavioural health and productivity of workers • Both mental and substance-use disorders have been exacerbated for people who faced care disruption and there were new cases of disorders[37] • Issues with job losses or economic crises adding additional pressure and psychological distress	• Measure behavioural health and make it a transparent priority • Hold leaders accountable for making progress on employee mental health • Consider onsite mental health services • Work closely with health-benefits administrators to ensure adequate coverage • Explore a range of new services, including online interventions
2	Gartner	Employees experience mental health through five dimensions: • Financial security (job loss, burnout) • Living situation (blended work-life, loneliness) • Physical health (quarantine, being a caregiver)	• Consider the various ways in which workers experience stress • Communicate well-being issues to employees

Serial No.	Agency	Impact on Mental Health	Recommendations
		• Work setting (working onsite, prolonged remote work) • Life-stage demands (being new to the workforce, graduating in a recession)	
3	Forrester	• 50 per cent of people are afraid to go to work • The pandemic is causing stress, anxiety, anger, overwhelm and sadness, and this could have some long-term impacts on mental health if not addressed • Mental health disorder diagnoses have doubled from their pre-pandemic levels • Those with existing conditions are faced with new challenges	• Encourage open conversations about how workers are dealing with stress • Resources should be made available and awareness should be raised regarding where to find assistance • Help workers understand the costs and options available to them • Assist employees to get connected to services that are HAS/FSA-eligible • Reach out to insurers to help support employees
4	Harvard Business Review	• A survey[38] indicated that out of the 30 per cent of employees who felt comfortable discussing their mental health, half have experienced negative effects on their mental health	Strategies to help with mental health issues: • Understand company policies on mental health • Avoid pressuring employees to speak about their mental health • Check in with team • Lead by example • Listen with empathy

Serial No.	Agency	Impact on Mental Health	Recommendations
5	Deloitte	Conducted a global survey involving nearly 23,000 Gen-Zs and millennials. Some of the findings are: • Job prospects are a leading stressor; higher for women than men due to the disproportionate care responsibilities and job losses they face • 26 per cent and 31 per cent of millennials and Gen-Zs, respectively, say their own mental health and that of close family and friends contribute a lot to their anxiety levels • 33 per cent and 35 per cent of millennials and Gen-Zs, respectively, mention that their own physical health contributes a lot to anxiety levels	• Better workplace support needed as only one in five of both generations say their employers are performing well • Promote work-life balance • Avoid discriminating against people for their mental health
6	Pricewaterhouse Coopers	• Front-line workers tend to be affected the most • Canadian study shows mental health issues are prevalent in more than 40 per cent of front-liners	• Organizations should report on well-being equally as they do on sustainability and equality • Create a friendly workplace environment where people can flourish

Serial No.	Agency	Impact on Mental Health	Recommendations
			• Create a sense of belonging, inclusion and support connections • Create a network of people whose aim will be to champion mental health in the organization • Leaders must create a legacy for others to inherit • Provide access to employee assistance programmes
7	Egon Zehnder	• WFH leads to employees struggling through stress, loneliness and isolation • An estimated 40 per cent of the workforce will experience mental health disorder • Adults in the US were eight times more likely to experience serious mental issues, compared to the previous in-person work mode • High anxiety levels in four out of ten people in the UK	Companies should not overlook resilience, which is a powerful tool for positive mental health. As such, employers should support the five levers of resilience which include: • Self-care • Support • Meaning • Strengths • Perspective Firms that show care about workers' life experience see a 23 per cent surge in workers' mental health and 21 per cent of them are high performers

Serial No.	Agency	Impact on Mental Health	Recommendations
8	Entrepreneur. com	• More than 50 per cent of WFH workers have reported a mental health disorder because of increased anxiety levels, reduced face-to-face contacts, leading to loneliness	Employers should create a psychologically safe work environment where employees can express concerns about work pressures, stress and mental health. Effective ways to create such an environment: • Strong HR strategies • Taking the transition slowly • Offering well-being workshops • Ergonomic care • Prioritizing those still working from home
9	Korn Ferry	• Those who work from home suffer from loneliness, anxiety and depression, leading to reduced output • The likelihood of Gen-Zs and Millennials suffering mental ill health is significant when they work from home, as even while working in the office, 75 per cent of them face the risk of loneliness	• Do not separate mental health from the overall wellness conversation. For instance, by linking exercise routines or nutrition to a meditation class • Reduce workloads and long working hours • Create awareness of specialist help services provided • Employ more outside specialists like psychologists or other professional organizations that deal in mental health • Leaders should use technology to promote a workplace-like community for employees

Serial No.	Agency	Impact on Mental Health	Recommendations
10	Russell Reynolds	• Survey of HR leaders across industries, found mental health issues have affected 85 per cent of workers • Globally, 75 per cent of young people (Gen-Zs and Millennials) have left their jobs because of mental health issues	• Appoint well-being leaders • Invest in culture • Transform leaders into allies • Get employees educated
11	United Nations	People may resort to alcohol,[39] tobacco, drugs and addictive behaviours like online gaming due to COVID-19 stressors, such as: • Fear of infection and death of loved ones • Widespread misinformation about virus/ prevention measures • Loss of livelihood • Isolation from loved ones • Stay-at-home orders • Domestic violence against women/ children	• Apply a whole-society approach to promote, protect and care for mental health • Ensure there is widespread availability of emergency mental health and psychological support • Support recovery by building mental health services for the future

Serial No.	Agency	Impact on Mental Health	Recommendations
		National surveys in 2020 show 35 per cent, 60 per cent and 45 per cent distress prevalence in China, Iran and the US, respectively And a 33 per cent prevalence rate of distress symptoms in the Amraha regional state in Ethiopia[40]	

The table below lists the main mental well-being initiatives undertaken by companies across sectors, internationally. All of them being culture-agnostic, companies in India can borrow a leaf from them and introduce initiatives for their own teams.

Table 6.2: Mental Health Initiatives by Leading Companies

Organization	Mental Well-being Initiative
Google[41]	Led by resilience expert Lauren Whitt, the company has set up a cadence of pit stops and activities for its employees, regardless of whether they are working remotely or in the office, to help them develop resilience over time. These include regular morning and sleep routines, taking mental breaks throughout the day, planning ahead, and infusing one's activities with meaning. Its mindfulness course, 'Search Inside Yourself', leverages elements of mindfulness-based stress reduction (MBSR). Employees also regularly watch short digital video clips, called 'Meet the Moment', focusing on topics such as sleep, avoiding anxiety and parenting.

Organization	Mental Well-being Initiative
Microsoft[42]	Inspired by the work of Carol Dweck, Microsoft stakeholders identified the growth mindset to become the foundation of Microsoft's desired culture. A range of initiatives has since been taken to drive efforts for long-term change, e.g., engaging senior leaders to talk about and role-model the growth mindset, employee-awareness campaigns to drive adoption, and ongoing measurement of how employees experience the growth mindset in the company. Growth mindset principles have been embedded in the fabric of business operations—across learning, team development and performance management processes, talent review and succession planning practices.
Intel[43]	The company believes that its ability to maintain proven capabilities and develop new ones amid rapid changes in the market stem from the tenets of its culture: customer orientation, risk-taking, discipline, being a great place to work, and quality and results orientation. In 2014, Intel had invested $75,000 in its mindfulness training programme, Awake@Intel, with ninety-minute weekly sessions of meditation, breathing and journalling. After a nine-week programme, participants reported improved interaction with peers and direct reports, increased focus, decreased stress, ability to solve problems more quickly, a two-point increase in new ideas, insights, mental clarity, creativity, focus, quality of relationships and engagement at work, leading to overall improvement in team performance.
Apple[44]	For years at the vanguard of inclusive employee engagement initiatives, the company rose to the challenge of the pandemic, offering well-being solutions to its users. The 'Breathe' app had been an integral part of the Apple Watch; a new app, 'Mindfulness', was introduced in watchOS 8, using an innovative feature that prompted users to be more reflective. Around the same time, however, in August 2021, Apple was reported to be scaling back an ambitious healthcare project, HealthHabit. For a significant period of time, around fifty of its employees had been working on an application for Apple employees to track their fitness goals, talk to clinicians and manage hypertension. It was envisioned that the application could also be offered commercially to the end-customers.

Organization	Mental Well-being Initiative
Aetna[45]	Aetna has been one of the early adaptors of mindfulness and meditation training, setting up a Mindfulness Center at its headquarters in Hartford. In 2012, it saw a 7 per cent reduction in medical claims, translating to $9 million in savings and an increased sixty-two minutes of productivity/week/worker which translates to around $3000/worker/year. In 2018, the company was able to measure the success of its mindfulness initiatives through the Mindfulness Challenge programme, with attendees reporting 18 per cent stress reduction after completing the challenge. A key benefit of such programmes is that employees have been able to use these skills in the workplace and beyond.
Nike[46]	Nike was another global giant that bought into mindfulness and well-being well ahead of the pandemic. In 2018, it partnered with guided meditation and mindfulness app Headspace to offer programmes to athletes and NikePlus users. The aim was to strengthen motivation, increase focus, improve resilience, enhance form, optimize recovery and get users immersed in an enjoyable and fulfilling training session. During the pandemic, the company was also highly responsive to concerns among employees. Following a period of unrest and anxiety, Nike closed all of its offices worldwide in the third week of August 2021 to give its people additional time off to recover and rest. This formed part of the company's plan to institute a return to office-based work in the autumn in 2021.
Goldman Sachs[47]	At Goldman Sachs, training programmes have been introduced in the framework of psychological resilience, the approach aimed at managing stress in a way that allows one to avoid burnout and 'stay in the game'. In August 2019, during the mental health awareness month, the company's wellness team conducted a 'Global Resilience Series' in its offices around the world. This offered employees programmes and activities to help them manage work and life priorities, strengthen relationships and improve their overall well-being. Over 4000 employees across the Americas, Europe, the Asia Pacific region and India participated in the series.

Admittedly, many of the initiatives involve longer-term comprehensive programmes, engaging coaches, psychologists, industry experts and business advisers, and at a substantial budget. But there are also simple practices that come at no cost, which companies and professionals can deploy right away. One of these is the T.E.A. break observed at Google. The company recognizes that resilience is a skill that can be built, practised and cultivated through our attitudes and behaviours. It devised a T.E.A. (Thoughts. Energy. Attention.) check-in for individuals and teams, as a way for them to reflect on the daily and momentary habits and routines affecting their well-being. This guide can be used for personal reflection or as a structure for a group conversation. This activity can be done daily or even multiple times throughout the day, as a self-check-in to remain focused on what is helpful and useful at any given time.

THOUGHTS

Purpose: Learning to differentiate between helpful and unproductive thinking patterns, as our thoughts influence our actions and attitudes. Drawing awareness to our internal self-talk and its impact on us.

Today my mind is . . .

To refocus, I need to . . .

Reflection & Discussion Questions:

- What trends do you notice when your thoughts are helpful and useful?
- Are there people, places or things that help you refocus and recentre your thoughts?
- What's one routine you can use to focus on helpful and useful thoughts?

ENERGY

Purpose: Observing how we are feeling in the moment, and intentionally investing in activities or people that fuel positive enthusiasm and motivation. Creating awareness of when we need to take on new challenges and when we need to invest in our own recovery to extend and renew our energy.

Today my energy is . . .

To change or maintain, I need to . . .

Reflection & Discussion Questions:

- When do you have the most energy during the day, and what gives you energy?
- How can you align your most important work (whatever that is) with this time of day?
- What (or who) drains your energy and how can you manage or minimize the impact of this?

ATTENTION

Purpose: Intentionally choosing where to place our focus and concentration, while being flexible to adapt priorities in the moment as needed.

To be my best today, I will focus on doing or being . . .

Reflection & Discussion Questions:

- What are the three things that deserve most of your attention today?
- What steals your attention, and what can you eliminate?
- What routines, places or things help you focus your attention?

ENHANCING MENTAL HEALTH IN THE INDIAN WORKPLACE

In the previous section, we have seen how there's a concerted focus on mental health and psychological safety in the workplace. We also looked at some instances of how some of the most forward-looking organizations have set up initiatives around stress management and developing better mindfulness, resilience, and overall mental health among their workforce. Anecdotally, a good deal of what has been discussed can be leveraged by organizations in India.

At governmental levels, while mental health and well-being are talked about in official documents and publications, there is no published document that specifically seeks to alleviate the emotional and mental trauma of bereavement, economic hardship and loss of livelihoods in the wake of the pandemic outbreak. At the individual level, things remain almost equally bleak. Insurers have been tardy in reacting to the mental health pandemic and, even today, there are relatively few whose policies cover mental illnesses. Even in cases when they do, the insurance policies cover inpatient and not outpatient costs related to mental illnesses. This means a person so severely (mentally) unwell that he absolutely must be hospitalized, might, if he is lucky to have signed up in advance with the right insurer, hope to have his hospital expenses covered. However, a manager who has experienced bereavement, a wage cut, and the possibility of retrenchment, and undergoing treatment for anxiety—and, in our estimate, representing the large majority of people suffering from mental distress—has no insurance cover. Another handicap that puts organizations at a disadvantage is the absence of a normative framework that addresses the issue of mental health in the Indian workplace.

This is where the guidelines formulated by the International Organization for Standardization (ISO) can play a crucial role.[48] The agency had published detailed guidelines around Occupational Health and Safety, ISO45001. In August 2021, amid the severe disruptions wrought by the continued pandemic, a new set of guidelines, ISO45003, was published. This document provides norms for management of psychosocial risk within an occupational health and safety (OH&S) framework, based on the earlier ISO45001. It enables organizations to prevent work-related injuries and ill health among their workers and other interested parties, and to promote well-being at work. It is applicable to organizations of all sizes and in all sectors for development, implementation, maintenance, and continual improvement in the health and safety of workplaces. We argue that in the absence of mental well-being norms institutionalized either by governmental or industry bodies, ISO45003 can serve as a useful point of reference for companies in India to formulate and execute policies on mental health.

ISO45003 comes on the back of research on psychosocial risks and how they affect the workplace. But it builds on a cognizance of the wider implications. For instance, it recognizes that the impact of psychosocial risks for a company includes increased costs due to absence from work, attrition, reduced product or service quality, higher recruitment and training costs, as well as workplace investigations, the possibility of litigation, and damage to the organization's reputation. Likewise, it also recognizes that timely and effective management of psychosocial risks can lead to benefits such as improved worker engagement, enhanced productivity, increased innovation and organizational sustainability.

According to the ISO guidelines, hazards of a psychosocial nature span three aspects: a) how work is organized; b) social factors at work; and c) work environment, equipment and hazardous tasks. This last category, which includes workplace conditions such as space, lighting, noise and temperature levels, tools and equipment, and the physical safety of the work environment, have been traditionally applicable, especially in assembly-line situations. The pandemic has universalized their applicability, from addressing the question of masks, sanitizers, mechanisms for fumigation, locking down and reopening of premises for organizations in all sectors, to PPE kits for those working in critical healthcare. But, in the context of longer working hours, remote and hybrid work models, blurring of professional and personal spheres of life, the first two aspects— how work is organized, and social factors at work—have assumed a fresh urgency.

The ISO45003 guidelines can serve as an important starting point for organizations to become cognizant of the various psychosocial risk factors, their warning signs, symptoms and manifestations, as well as some measures for preempting or addressing them. But they also open up another question. What should be the sequence of steps, procedures, checks and balances involved in the design, implementation and refining of the policy itself? Fortunately, ISO45003 does offer some ideas on this front too.[49]

Culling details from the ISO guidelines, we present a practicable framework, which can be adopted by organizations and teams across sectors and domains.

Figure 6.1: NUVAH Framework to Enhance Mental Health in the Indian Workplace

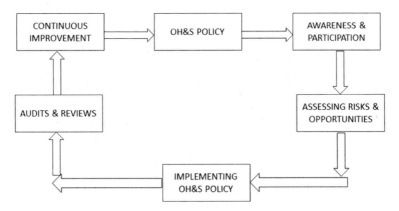

- **OH&S policy:** The process starts with creation of a comprehensive OH&S. Company stakeholders should ensure that commitments to prevent ill health and injuries and promoting well-being at work are included, determine if there is a need for a separate policy for managing psychosocial risk; and consider how other policies, e.g., HR and CSR, support the OH&S policy to achieve the common objectives. The OH&S policy should be communicated to all personnel so that they are aware of their rights and responsibilities.

- **Awareness and participation:** One of the main reasons why well-intentioned organization-wide policies fail to make an impact on the ground is lack of awareness. In a matter as sensitive as psychosocial risks in the workplace, it is essential that the top management sustains a clear and transparent line of communication with its people, through periodic updates, road shows, in-person or virtual townhall meetings, as well as newsletter bulletins. Top management can thus graduate from a mode of communication to one of genuine involvement and participation. In the process, stakeholders encourage reporting of psychosocial hazards, reduce fear of reprisals associated with reporting, and promote trust in their OH&S management system.

- **Assessing risks & opportunities:** Before deploying the policy, company stakeholders need to assess the risks and opportunities involved. Such an assessment would be twofold, the first involving either behavioural surveys or in-depth psychometric evaluation (see Chapter Five), and the second an evaluation of business readiness for implementing its OH&S policy. The assessment should a) provide information about the potential harm from psychosocial hazards; b) compare groups differing in exposure to psychosocial hazards; c) consider the interaction of psychosocial risks with those from other identified hazards; d) prioritize hazards, based on the level of risk; e) consider the diversity and specific needs within the organization; and f) provide information on control measures and opportunities for improvement.

- **Implementing the OH&S policy:** When managing psychosocial risks, a combination of the following levels of intervention can be used: a) primary: organizational-level controls to prevent or reduce harmful effects and promote well-being at work; b) secondary: increasing resources that assist workers to deal with psychosocial risks by raising awareness and understanding through effective training and other appropriate measures; c) tertiary: reducing the harmful effects of exposure to psychosocial hazards by implementing rehabilitation programmes and taking other corrective and supportive actions. It is important for company stakeholders to appreciate that a number of factors, such as economic downturns, pandemics and ecological crises, mergers and acquisitions, changes in work processes or in mode of operations, including remote or hybrid work for extended periods of time, will have an impact on psychosocial risks within the organization.

- **Audits and reviews:** The organization should conduct internal audits at periodic intervals and use the findings to assess the effectiveness of identification and management of psychosocial risks, identify gaps in performance as well as opportunities to improve their management. Apart from such audits, a top-management review ensures its continued focus on psychosocial risk performance, and a greater awareness of the extent to which the organization has met its objectives on this front. Inputs to management reviews include audit findings and data on incident investigations and corrective actions taken to prevent psychosocial risks to workers.

- **Continuous improvement:** The results from the audits, management reviews and behavioural assessments provide the basis for analysing the organization's effectiveness in managing psychosocial risk. Companies should focus on opportunities for overall improvement of their management, fulfilment of their legal and other requirements, and achievement of their OH&S objectives. Companies should proactively take steps to implement changes, prioritizing those that have the greatest potential for improving psychological health, safety and well-being in the workplace. Finally, the learnings, insights and recommendations for improvement are incorporated back into the OH&S policy.

MEASURING PSYCHOLOGICAL SAFETY

As we have noted in Chapter Four, all behavioural frameworks need one crucial aspect to make them successful on the ground: a robust mechanism to measure their constituent attributes.

When it comes to psychological safety, in academic circles as well as in application of research at the workplace, much of what is currently in vogue stems from the work of Professor Amy Edmondson and her associates at Harvard University. Psychological safety, in Professor Edmondson's view, describes people's perceptions of the consequences of taking interpersonal risks in a particular context such as a workplace. Since the late 1990s, her social psychological analysis has explored themes of trust and collective learning in teams. She has examined interpersonal risks that can inhibit collective learning, distinguished psychological safety from trust, and explained why psychological safety mitigates interpersonal risks and facilitates a structured learning process in teams.

Edmondson's research, used in field studies in several organizational settings as well as in wellness initiatives in leading companies such as Google, has been used to support her theoretical model, to show how leaders can help their teams manage the risks of learning.[50] Edmondson offers three simple things individuals can do to foster team psychological safety: a) Frame the work as a learning problem, not as an execution problem; b) Acknowledge your own fallibility; and c) Model curiosity and ask lots of questions.

From the very start, Edmondson had been interested in a set of clear, tangible questions that can be asked of people in the workplace, to gauge the level of psychological safety that they are experiencing. Her initial formulation of seven key questions has become so influential that most applications by leading companies have made use of her questionnaire or a variant thereof. At the same time, every serious measure of psychological safety to emerge since her work first appeared has referenced the questions.

Here are the seven items in Edmondson's survey:
If you make a mistake on this team, it is often held against you.

Members of this team are able to bring up problems and tough
issues.
People on this team sometimes reject others for being different.
It is safe to take a risk on this team.
It is difficult to ask other members of this team for help.
No one on this team would deliberately act in a way that
undermines my efforts.
Working with members of this team, my unique skills and
talents are valued and utilized.

Perhaps the most well-publicized example of arriving at the need
for enhancing psychological safety at work is the Aristotle project
conducted at Google. Of the five key dynamics of effective teams
that the Google researchers identified, psychological safety was
by far the most important. The other characteristics of enhanced
teams were dependability, structure and clarity, meaning and
impact. Google found that individuals on teams with higher
psychological safety were less likely to leave the company; they
were more likely to harness the power of diverse ideas from their
teammates; they would bring in more revenue; and they would
be rated as effective twice as often by executives.[51]

More recent measures have expanded on the previous
research, creating sector-specific assessments. For instance,
in 2020, Róisín O'Donovan, Desirée Van Dun and Eilish
McAuliffe studied the critical matter of psychological safety
in the healthcare sector. They arrived at a final composite
measure, consisting of two parts: a team-meeting observation
measure and an adapted survey measure, tailored for use in
healthcare teams. The observation measure has thirty-one
observable behaviours fitting seven categories: voice, defensive
voice, silence behaviours, supportive, unsupportive, learning or
improvement-oriented and familiarity-type behaviours. The
survey consists of nineteen items in three sub-dimensions: the

team leader, other team members and the team as a whole. Three additional items capture the perceived representativeness of the observed team meeting compared to other similar meetings. Final adaptations were made in order to integrate the observation and survey measures.[52]

In India, too, there is now increasing awareness of the importance of psychological safety at work, along with suggestions on measures that could evaluate them effectively. As Prem Seshadri says: 'Psychological safety would emerge as the biggest focus area of HR benefits, as the two dimensions of psychological safety, viz., emotional risk at the individual employee level, and organizational cultural contours that stifle openness/learning and inclusiveness. The two key indices that one should focus upon are Employee Emotional Risk Index (EMP-ERI) and the Employee Fearlessness Index (EMP-FI). Together, they make the culture vibrant and agile.'

For our own part, we have aimed to study psychological safety in a comprehensive manner. At NUVAH, the firm that Avik Chanda leads, we have worked with psychologists, leveraging the work of Edmondson and her associates, the ISO guidelines on psychosocial risks, as well as advances and applications in the workplace made in more recent times, in order to arrive at our own psychological safety survey for professionals. The key factors in our framework for evaluating psychological safety at work, are: i) Supportive leadership practices; ii) Supportive organizational practices; iii) Team characteristics; iv) Relationship networks; and v) Individual differences.[53]

In this chapter, we have discussed a range of aspects, from the impact of the pandemic on mental health in the workplace, the deepening of the crisis on this front, to guidelines on norms to ensure psychological safety and well-being in the workplace, as well as the measures to identify and address psychosocial risks in the emergent workplace. We have collated much here, by way of insights, good practices, guidelines and recommendations. It's sobering, therefore, to note that even if all these were to be implemented, it would still benefit only a small proportion of the workforce in India, i.e., only those in large corporations with access to mental health professionals, business coaches and advisers, industry bodies, publications, and most importantly, funds.

The majority of the Indian workforce employed in the MSME and unorganized sectors have minimal or no access to any support. Their condition is made all the more precarious by unprecedented economic and technological disruptions and the urgent need for change across education, innovation, greater opportunities for employment, and increased access to digital media and technology, wrought by the pandemic. In the language of social scientists, there is a term for this weakest, poorest and most marginalized stratum of the economic pyramid—'subalterns', a term that comes from a historical context, referring to marginalized, dispossessed people. And they are our focus in the next chapter

7

Inequality in the Post-COVID World

'A rising tide lifts all boats.'

—John F. Kennedy, 1963[1]

This quote, possibly an inspired line from one of one of Kennedy's script-doctors, is symbolic in multiple ways. It captured the zeitgeist of the economic miracle (at least in the Western world) that would last all though the 1960s. This also encapsulated the optimistic vision that an improved economy would benefit everyone within it. It was also unconsciously the dogma of a school of thought, supply-side economics,[2] that growth is best achieved through deregulation, lower taxes and free trade. The proponents of supply-side economics zealously maintain that this is the magic troika that will lead to sustained growth and prosperity. They make a further claim that tax revenues would actually increase as taxes are cut because of the higher economic growth that would result. The criticism this fetched from most mainstream economists notwithstanding, this was the rationale for the tax-cutting and deregulation agenda in the USA under President Ronald Reagan, well into the 1980s. As the years passed, a new dimension came to be added to the troika—globalization. And there a broad consensus prevailed among economists (with a few dissenting voices from the Left), that globalization would indeed lead to unprecedented growth, and hence prosperity for all, ironically buying into the implicit supply-side argument that most of them had criticized.

Today, however, the tax cut-growth link seems even less compelling. A meta-study published in April 2022 concludes that there is no impact of tax cuts favouring the rich on growth, and that it causes increases in inequality.[3] Another study on corporate tax cuts finds no significant effect of it on growth either.[4] The income tax cut-revenue link appears to be just as dubious. While very high tax rates can lower investments as well as encourage tax evasion, few economists have been convinced that the rates which the USA promulgated during the Reagan, Bush or Trump tax cuts would actually bring more revenue. In a 2012 survey of economists, not a single expert agreed with the view that cuts in the US federal income tax rates would result in increased annual tax revenue within five years.[5] However, their conviction in the benefits of globalization still held firm.

Perhaps the belief was that the overall quantum of gain from globalization would be so high that it would naturally lead to a downward cascading of prosperity. It may also have stemmed from the hope that the gains from innovation would spread to everyone in a world without barriers. In the event, globalization, while raising standards of living in some parts of the world, brought a fresh set of concerns around growing inequality in developing nations. More recently, signs of rising inequality have emerged in developed economies too, with a study by Philipp Heimberger in 2020 finding 'an average inequality-increasing impact of globalization in both advanced and developing countries'.[6] Noted sceptics of globalization, such as the Nobel laureate Joseph Stiglitz, had long argued that its benefits had been exaggerated.[7] The promise of deeper adoption of globalization leading to benefits for all has turned out to be somewhat illusory. Inequality, especially in the wake of the COVID-19 experience, has reared its Gorgon head again, and cannot be dismissed.

Historically, the big challenge with inequality has been that policymakers have never cared much about it. Indeed, many analysts in the past used to view an initial rise in inequality as a natural and inevitable consequence of growth. They argued that with the process of development, inequality first increases and then decreases. As an illustration, the Industrial Revolution in England undoubtedly led to a long-term increase in the standards of living. However, at least initially, some saw this as a dark period, with workers living in crowded unsanitary conditions in what the poet William Blake called the 'dark, satanic mills'.[8] While the ultimate role of the Industrial Revolution in raising living standards is well accepted, the fact that there was an initial fall in living standards is today fairly undisputed. Certainly, there was rising inequality, with the capitalists gaining enormously and the workers very little, if at all.[9]

In the mid-1950s, a hypothesis advanced by the economist Simon Kuznets,[10] arguing that in the process of development, inequality first increases and then decreases, provided a formalization of an idea that was already in favour among experts. While Kuznets himself was very cautious in his conclusions, noting that his data was pertinent only for the time frame that he had analysed, policymakers embraced it wholesale and used that as a reason not to bother about inequality. Very soon, it took the form of a law, becoming a staple in the teaching of development economics for decades until, finally, the growing evidence of rising inequality in developing countries became too enormous to ignore any further. As Thomas Piketty has pointed out in his highly influential book *Capital in the Twenty-*

first Century, inequality has in fact grown and this has not been transitory. The level of income inequality in the twenty-first century in fact has exceeded that of the early decades of the twentieth century.[11]

The principal free-market policies favoured by international bodies, such as the International Monetary Fund and the World Bank, were formulated in what came to be known as the so-called Washington Consensus.[12] This manifesto indicated that development required the unleashing of market forces, with the government's job being mainly to deregulate the economy, lower and simplify tax rates, and privatize many state enterprises, while protecting property rights. The originator of the term, the economist John Williamson, was himself far more nuanced and careful in his articulation. For example, his ten-point agenda included redirection of public spending from subsidies, 'especially indiscriminate subsidies', towards broad-based provision of key pro-growth, pro-poor services like primary education, primary healthcare and infrastructure investment. Acolytes and enthusiastic policymakers, however, came to view the term as a move towards unbridled free-market policies, regardless of the consequences for inequality.[13] And, since any rise in inequality that did occur was believed to be transitory, policymakers paid little attention to it. Such a methodology led not just to an exacerbation of the problem but also to an increase in poverty through highly painful periods that were often not transitory. Such was the case in almost every Latin American economy adopting this approach.

Yet, such painful growth is far from necessary. As we have seen earlier in the book, the progress that occurred as part of the East Asian Miracle was actually accompanied by a decrease in poverty and a corresponding rise in several 'quality of life' indicators. This was possible because there was active state management of the transition process, with market-friendly processes, particularly that of trade openness, accompanied by redistributive measures such as land reforms, high wages and universal education.[14] Hence, tapping of the potential for market reforms was also accompanied by state intervention in key areas that resulted in the benefits of growth trickling down to the weaker segments of the population.

Our focus in this chapter is not on the growth-versus-inequality debate, but on inequality itself. We begin by outlining the concepts and frameworks of inequality in modern economics, tracing the multidisciplinary influences on their development, and the measures and recommendations for public policy that emerged in the process. We examine how inequality has fared across the world, as well as in India, in tandem with economic growth. We then debunk the myth that in matters of inequality, COVID-19 has been a great equalizer. On the contrary, we show how the pandemic experience has sharpened the divide between the privileged and the marginalized, both across and within geographies. We note the possibilities for social entrepreneurship and share some perspectives about its role in tackling inequality across societal segments, as well as the role that can be played by the government. Finally, we cast the spotlight on CSR, and provide a set of high-level guidelines on how corporates can play a leading role in using CSR to effectively combat inequality and enhance social capital, while also enriching the human capital within their own organizations. We explore, in this last regard, how the creation of 'CSR verticals' in large companies can offer a partial or temporary buffer against technological unemployment.

INEQUALITY REVISTED

The world has always been an unequal place. However, as we have noted, inequality has had less prominence in discussions around growth and development in countries until recently. A combination of detailed and compelling data, such as that from the World Inequality Report, and growing evidence of a rise in inequality in the globalized world and a backlash against it, have caused a rethink and have forced inequality back on to the agenda of mainstream discussions. Of major concern is how individual workers are being affected, as well as the implications of a global unrest against globalization. In this section, we outline some seminal conceptual issues which shed light on the many dimensions of inequality. We trace the work of Amartya Sen,[15] John Rawls[16] and Martha Nussbaum,[17] who have made passionate arguments about why society should take inequality seriously, and have proposed measures and frameworks by way of solutions.

Fundamental to the ethos of this parallel development of research and intellectual thought are the choice and ability of the workers to participate fully in the workplace in a *way they wish to*. This idea of autonomy, or participation in the way one wishes to, is important in and of itself, especially in an ecosystem where unequally distributed resources may prevent those at the lower end of the distribution spectrum from being able to function or lead the kind of life they value. For example, if their income prevents them from getting the kind of education they need to participate in the benefits of globalization, their income inequality translates into inequality of opportunity in the workplace. This is why Rawls, in his *Theory of Justice*, focuses on the 'primary goods' that every member in society ought to have, including rights, liberties and opportunities for earning income and wealth.

This means that a minimal level of these primary goods is needed, and Rawls lists a number of dimensions where every member should have a threshold level. However, as Sen points out, even while acknowledging the multidimensional nature of inequality, most discussions about inequality on the economic dimension inevitably look at inequality of income. This has some practical implications. For example, two people with the same income may be able to achieve vastly different things in life with it. Sen suggests a number of reasons for this variation in what one can achieve in terms of functioning in life (i.e., being able to do things that we value in life) with the same income.

The first is personal heterogeneity. People who are ill, of an advanced age, or of a specific gender may need different incomes to achieve the same functioning as others. The second stems from environmental disparities—for example, drought or floods may affect what a person is able to get out of a given income. The third has to do with the social environment—i.e., variations in public investments in health and education, or the level of crime in a society, will again affect what well-being one can derive from a certain level of income. The fourth relates to a difference in what Sen calls relational perspectives—e.g., a relatively poor person in a rich society may find it hard to take part in the life of the community compared to someone of the same income in a poorer community. This, in particular, suggests that simply looking at absolute levels of poverty even in the income dimension, without looking at the distribution of income as a whole, does not capture how one is able to function in a society. Finally, distribution of income within a family is also of consequence—i.e., rules of how family income is spent with respect to, say, gender or age, will affect what individual members can achieve.

This focus on well-being rather than income is part of a tradition that can be traced to Aristotle's understanding of human flourishing.[18] Sen suggests that we should focus on what sort of functioning in life we can achieve and what sort of freedom we have to choose across various options, or capabilities. The Human Development Index[19] formulated jointly by Sen and Mahbub ul Haq considers longevity, literacy (years of schooling), and gross national income per capita, which are weighted equally. Thus, even for analysing economic inequality, one needs to consider inequality of health or education or environmental conditions, as they translate into very different levels of well-being for people with similar incomes.

Sen also rejects the sole use of people's own happiness to measure equality in functioning, arguing that people may become accustomed to their disability, for instance, and so reconciled to their lot, but they represent objective differences in functioning.[20] Looking purely at economic inequality may not be enough to understand how well a person is able to function in life. Nussbaum, who at one point collaborated with Sen on this subject, has approached this from the perspective of a just society. She cites a number of capabilities, including the ability to be able to engage in critical reasoning and reflection as well as the ability to develop emotionally. Nussbaum's list is, of course, much more exhaustive than what we have outlined here. We mention these as only a few of the critical capabilities that every worker needs to develop, to flourish in the emergent workplace.

In 2011, a review by Oded Galor[21] suggested that while inequality may have played a part in the development of societies in the past, that need not be so in modern times:

> . . . the modern approach has demonstrated that in the presence of credit market imperfections, income distribution has a long-lasting effect on investment in human capital, entrepreneurial activity, aggregate income, and economic development. Moreover, in contrast to the Classical viewpoint, which underscored the beneficial effects of

inequality for the growth process, the modern perspective advanced the hypothesis that inequality may be detrimental for human capital formation and economic development.

This provides an understanding of how inequality in modern societies impedes workers from realizing their potential, delays human capital development and, by corollary, stunts innovation in the workplace. Thus, the normative concerns around inequality have indeed been shown to be empirically relevant.

A couple of points may be made at this stage. First, the substantial research we have alluded to does not, however, determine the threshold level of inequality at which a person could begin to function. Figures for this would likely vary, depending on the level of development of a society, among several other factors. Second, in this chapter, we continue to focus on income inequality, with only excursions around elements such as wealth and carbon footprints. The main reason for this is the wide availability of data on the distribution of income inequality in comparison to other factors. Further, income inequalities over time often create wealth inequalities and certainly lead to differences in outcomes in education and health. In principle, the impact of income or wealth differentials can be mitigated via equality in opportunity in basic public goods, viz., free and universal access to healthcare as well as education. This, in turn, would enhance capabilities and indeed can do so in societies where there is already an egalitarian provision of public good.

It is no accident that Europe, which is the least unequal region in an unequal world, does provide near universal access to health and education. But even in Europe, income is correlated with health and educational outcomes of the family.[22] This correlation with income is seen even in political voice (i.e., influence in the political sphere) where money can have an undue effect on political outcomes and impact the size of the welfare state.[23] Our focus on looking at differences in income and wealth, while not providing the whole picture, provides strong clues on other dimensions of inequality that exist within and across countries. Reducing these gaps is vital to ensuring that the worker of the future at least has the opportunity to take advantage of the rising tides that technology and globalization can offer.

This briefest of reviews nevertheless sensitizes us to the fact that inequality is a highly complex, multidimensional concept. Therefore, given the heterogeneity of the needs and environment of each individual, looking at income inequality is inadequate and even misleading. Approaches such as Sen's, which focus on the understanding these different heterogeneities and thus, on *what one can achieve through that income*, provide a more comprehensive evaluation of differences in well-being. This approach also helps us understand how inequalities in opportunity in terms of education, health and other inputs may constrain the worker of the future from achieving his or her full potential.

INEQUALITY IN EVIDENCE

Over the past two decades of the twenty-first century, there has been a growing, albeit grudging, acceptance of a couple of facts around inequality. First, it is far from a transitional phase in an economy's growth journey that can be sorted out in due course by market forces. And second, that there has been a recorded rise in inequality across geographies, as well as within nations. For the analysis that follows in this section, we shall be referencing data primarily from the World Inequality Report published in 2022.[24] It is worth mentioning the emphasis that the report has placed on the role of the state and its policies in addressing issues of inequality. In writing the foreword to the report,

Nobel Laureates Abhijit Banerjee and Esther Dufflo observed that in the immediate post-pandemic scenario, India was one of the most unequal countries in the world. They ascribe this to a loosening of state control and the allowing of unabashed accumulation of private wealth. Policies, they stated, had kept inequality in check, and policy changes had let it run amok.[25]

It has been observed that globalization has seen rising wages in many sectors across developing countries, with the income of labour increasing.[26] However, wages for unskilled workers may have concurrently fallen in those countries that face high competition. For example, a paper that examines the impact of competition from China on the US local labour market concludes that 'rising imports cause higher unemployment, lower labour-force participation, and reduced wages in local labour markets'.[27]

Viewed through a countrywide lens, things seldom seem as stark as this, though. For one, lower prices at least partly offset wage declines, and firms facing competition also have the chance to diversify their business, and/or reorganize production methods.[28] Therefore, the wage declines do not present a complete picture of how labour has been affected. However, even in cases where the net impact on labour is beneficial, there are likely to be significant distributional consequences, and assuming that the market will somehow correct for this seems misplaced. There are bound to be winners and losers. Let us take a deeper look.

The World Inequality Report finds that inequality has increased globally since the 1980s. The figure below gives a snapshot of income distribution across different regions in the world. As we can see, inequality exists across all geographical clusters globally—but some regions definitely have more inequality than others. Whereas in Europe, the top 10 per cent of earners accounts for 36 per cent of income, in the Middle East and North Africa (MENA), this is much higher, an alarming 58 per cent.

Figure 7.1: Income Distribution across Geographies

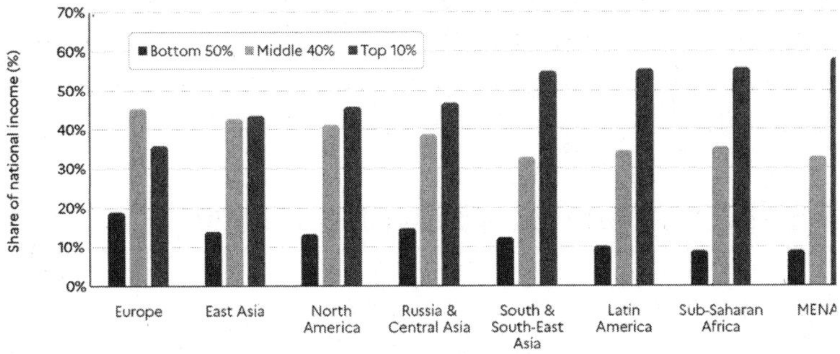

Interpretation: *In Latin America, the top 10% captures 55% of national income, compared to 36% in Europe. Income is n̄ after pension and unemployment contributions and benefits paid and received by individuals but before income taxes ai transfers.* **Sources and series:** *www.wir2022.wid.world/methodology.*

This, of course, is a snapshot in time. The immediate question is: How has inequality changed over time? The report has analysed both income and wealth inequality to arrive at its finding that global inequalities have been on the rise since the 1980s. This process of change is not uniform, so that some countries, such as Russia, the USA and India, have seen spectacular increases, while others, including several European countries and China, have not. This suggests that inequality is not inevitable and that the policies undertaken by the respective governments have had some part to play in leading to the differences. But there is an even more distinctive and surprising finding: over the last two decades, within countries, inequality has increased, while inequality across countries has actually decreased.

Let us turn to the next figure, below. It shows the average income of the richest 10 per cent of countries as a multiple of the average income of the poorest 50 per cent of countries over 200 years (1820–2020). In 1820, the average income of the top 10 per cent was eighteen times the average income of the bottom 50 per cent. Since that time, this has kept increasing, with the ratio more than doubling in 1910, to forty-one times. There have been some peaks and troughs along the way, but the ratio reached a high in 1980 at 53, falling thereafter, to 30 in 2020. While the gap is still substantial, it nonetheless shows a decrease.

Figure 7.2: Global Income Inequality, 1820-2020

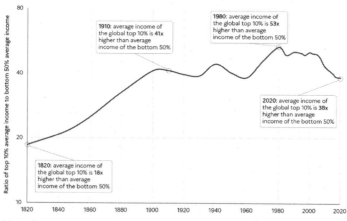

Interpretation: *Global inequality, as measured by the ratio T10/B50 between the average income of the top 10% and the average income of the bottom 50%, more than doubled between 1820 and 1910, from less than 20 to about 40, and stabilized around 40 between 1910 and 2020. It is too early to say whether the decline in global inequality observed since 2008 will continue. Income is measured per capita after pension and unemployment insurance transfers and before income and wealth taxes.* **Sources and series:** *wir2022.wid. world/methodology and Chancel and Piketty (2021).*

By contrast, within countries the level of inequality has gone up, with the Inequality Report finding that 'the gap between the average incomes of the top 10% and the bottom 50% of individuals within countries has almost doubled, from 8.5x to 15x'. This is seen even more starkly in the figure below. Inequality across nations represented only 32 per cent of total global inequality in 2020, whereas inequality within economies accounted for an astonishing 68 per cent. Things were quite the opposite in 1980, when inter-economy inequality accounted for as much as 57 per cent of global inequality. This dramatic shift in such a short period of time indicates that inequality is not a transitory phenomenon and will not reduce on its own.

Besides income, wealth is another important indicator of inequality. On this parameter, the report notes the disproportionate rate at which the rich have been accumulating wealth. In particular it says: 'Global multimillionaires have captured a disproportionate share of global wealth growth over the past several decades: the top 1% took 38% of all additional wealth accumulated since the mid-1990s, whereas the bottom 50% captured just 2% of it.' These inequalities are reflected in yet another inequality—the rich contribute overwhelmingly to carbon emissions, with the top 10 per cent of emitters responsible for close to 50 per cent of all emissions, while the bottom 50 per cent produce 12 per cent of the total. Within income inequality, gender differences remain stark, with women's share of income being only 35 per cent of total world income and showing only a small upward trend from the 1990s. This is true not only of the MENA countries, but also of most of the Asian economies, excluding China.

Figure 7.3: Global Income Inequality, Between and Within Countries.

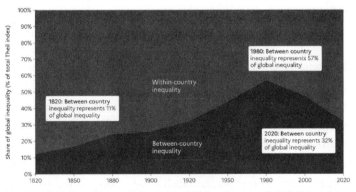

Interpretation: *The importance of between-country inequality in overall global inequality, as measured by the Theil index, rose between 1820 and 1980 and strongly declined since then. In 2020, between-country inequality makes-up about a third of global inequality between countries. The rest is due to inequality within countries. Income is measured per capita after pension and unemployement insurance transfers and before income and wealth taxes.* **Sources and series:** *wir2022.wid.world/methodology and Chancel and Piketty (2021).*

The findings here show that the world is growing at a very uneven pace, with the super-rich accumulating wealth faster than the others. One possible reason for this rising inequality, as we have mentioned before, is the lingering belief that a free market is the best, if not only, path to development. That has led to globalization being blamed, though other factors, notably technology, have played a part too, and so it is hard to separate out what has had the most influence on rising inequalities. Indeed, globalization may lead to changes in the skill premium which cause skilled workers' wages to rise more, relative to wages of unskilled workers.[29]

This accords well with the issues long raised by Stiglitz. While the initial discontent with globalization was in poorer countries, over the years there has been a rising anti-globalization feeling across the developed world too, as they have felt the squeeze in wages. This is most pronounced in countries such as the US, where inequality has risen sharply. This has inevitably led to both the rise of nationalist policies as well as a move by many national leaders towards protectionism. And, while technology may have played as big a role in eliminating jobs in the developed world, it is harder to organize against technology—hence most of the ire has been directed against globalization.

What other factors may have contributed to inequality? One of them has been analysed at length by Thomas Piketty in his celebrated book, *Capital in the Twenty-First Century*.[30] Piketty argues that if the returns on capital exceed the growth rate, there will be a concentration of wealth. Therefore, inequality in the distribution of wealth will increase. One can view this as a particularly important factor that explains wealth inequality in the era before World War I, and which might also contribute to our understanding of rising global inequality as late as in the 1980s. Piketty himself is swift in pointing out that this factor may not be the main driver of inequality in the twenty-first century.[31] For instance, he has this to say about the rising inequality over the 1980–2010 period in the US:

> . . . is due for the most part to rising inequality of labor earnings, which can itself be explained by a mixture of two groups of factors: rising inequality in access to skills and to higher education over this time period in the United States, an evolution which might have been exacerbated by rising tuition fees and insufficient public investment; and exploding top managerial compensation, itself probably stimulated by changing incentives and norms, and by large cuts in top tax rates.

The inference is unambiguous. Unchecked market forces will not, on their own, lessen the gap between the rich and the poor. On the contrary, they may well widen the divide. An all-pervasive programme of investment in education is therefore needed, for people to avail of opportunities offered by the market. Another worry expressed in the Inequality Report is around dwindling state wealth in the developed nations, which implies a diminished capacity of the state to address the problem of inequality. The implications for rising inequality are serious cause for concern. In the absence of the required level and scale of investment in education, there will be a small elite, equipped and eager to take full advantage of all that technology and globalization have to offer. But the large majority will struggle to earn a decent living, or worse, slide into unemployment, with few job prospects in sight. And this is no longer a 'developing country' issue. In the US, a middle-class life, as characterized by a decent job with some security and the ability to send one's children to college, are getting out of reach for an increasing number of people. Yes, there are new vistas of opportunity— but in an unequal terrain. The stress of 'falling off the ladder of opportunity' has health consequences, and American life expectancy, as recorded in 2016, was actually in decline.

A word to the wise. Protectionist posturing and speech-making can be very popular among one's electorate in the short term. But this same rhetoric, once implemented via official governmental policy, can swiftly disrupt global supply chains, contort the supply and price of essential commodities, trigger trade wars, and worse. At the very least, the repercussions are adverse, as we have witnessed both during the Trump regime in the US and in post-Brexit UK. They have caused severe uncertainties across the economy, while not enhancing either well-being or growth and income opportunities for the supposed beneficiaries of these policies—the local workers.

NOT ALL IN THE SAME BOAT

At different points throughout the pandemic, a diverse set of people, all the way from bloggers and self-styled pundits to seasoned journalists, academics, policy advisers and senior politicians, have gravitated towards a certain common viewpoint—that across social, economic and class divides, COVID-19 has been the Great Equalizer. At first read, the view does seem to be quite true.

If, towards the end of August 2022, when this chapter was being completed, one looked back at the trajectory of the pandemic since its earliest days, many things would be undeniable. First, that it wasn't just the poor and marginalized who were infected, but monarchs, heads of state of some of the world's most powerful nations, cabinet ministers, high-ranking officials, industry tycoons, film stars and sports personalities, fashion designers, and academics—in short, members of the elite. Second, in many of these cases where the privileged members of society contracted the disease, the individuals infected weren't from the poorest nations, but from the richest—e.g., the late Queen Elizabeth II and the British premier at that time, Boris Johnson, and Donald Trump, then president of the US. Third, governments were providing vaccines to large sections of their populace at hugely subsidized rates, or even free of cost. None of this is in dispute, so surely there is some merit in the view of COVID-19 being an equalizer?

Except that countering these facts are other equally undeniable ones. The fact that anybody could contract the virus did not make it an equal burden for everyone. From the very start of the pandemic, the likelihood of getting COVID, being hospitalized for it and dying from it has varied across population groups. Research in Western countries has shown a disproportionate mortality rate for certain ethnic groups. In particular, a study for England and Wales in the first wave of COVID-19 found that both deprivation and the proportion of minority community members were important factors affecting deaths occurring from COVID-19. Areas where both these factors were higher than the average showed significantly higher COVID 19 mortality.[32] Further, the overall global picture has hardly been one of uniform cooperation. The World Health Organization (WHO) has had to send out formal requests on multiple occasions to the healthier nations not to hoard vaccines. In most instances, such pleas went unheeded, at least in the immediate term.[33]

Why, then, did highly astute and well-intentioned experts get it wrong? Our sense is that the simplest explanation is in this case also the likeliest one. The thinkers and analysts, out of great genuine concern, and at times perhaps desperation, have spoken in haste. Consequently, in many cases the pronouncements, analyses and predictions were made during what we now know to be only the first few months of the pandemic as it was unfolding then. To take a prominent example, the popular philosopher and cultural theorist Slavoj Zizek brought out his book, *PANDEMIC! COVID-19 Shakes the World*, in June 2020, when the first deadly outbreak had not even completed its first six-month period. This also means the author could not possibly have had more than a few weeks to put his thoughts (and prognosis) together.[34]

The very first chapter of Zizek's book is captioned 'We're All in the Same Boat Now'. This is how the chapter ends:

> *Reacting to the threat posed by the coronavirus outbreak, Israeli prime minister Benjamin Netanyahu immediately offered help and coordination to the Palestinian authority—not out of goodness and human consideration, but for the simple fact that it is impossible to separate Jews and Palestinians there—if one group is affected, the other will inevitably also suffer. This is the reality which we should translate into politics—now is the time to drop the 'America (or whoever else) First' motto. As Martin Luther King put it more than half a century ago: 'We may have all come on different ships, but we're in the same boat now.'*[35]

With the benefit of hindsight, we can say that the facts that emerged over the several months subsequent to the book's publication strongly indicated otherwise. In January 2021, precisely a year post the outbreak of the global pandemic, Human Rights Watch was still making appeals to the Israeli government to provide vaccines to the 45 million Palestinians in the occupied West Bank and Gaza Strip.[36]

Zizek uses no data in his slim volume. However, there are other instances where important publications have used data, the trends for which have since changed course. This is true of the National Bureau of Economic Research (NBER) paper[37] by the Nobel laureate Angus Deaton, revised in February 2021. Deaton, relying on IMF inequality forecasts in October 2019 and October 2020, posited that global inequality had decreased. However, a more recent World Bank paper,[38] published in January 2022, found that COVID-19 had increased inequality both within and across countries, noting that such inequalities might in fact increase even more over time. There is no saying that the results believed to be true at the time of writing this chapter will not once again be overturned at a future date, as further evidence and new data come to light. However, based on the data available as of August 2022, the present position is one of a rise in inequality.

The results of the 2022 World Bank report leave us with much cause for concern. Drawing on novel data from its high-frequency phone surveys (HFPS), along with simulations, the World Bank paper provides detailed estimates of the distributional impacts of COVID-19. The data is not confined to earnings but includes the following key indicators: (i) job losses; (ii) income losses; (iii) food insecurity; and (iv) learning losses.

Some of the key findings are:

- Even assuming no change in income distribution within countries, the projections are of higher global inequality due to COVID-19, which would have led to a rise in inequality from 2019 to 2021. This is driven not so much by the initial impact of the crisis but more due to incomes of the poorest 40 per cent not recovering in 2021, unlike the incomes of the top 60 per cent which did, and the largest improvements seen for the top 20 per cent. They find that, by 2021, average income of the top 40 per cent would have almost returned to the pre-COVID level. In contrast, the average income of the bottom 40 per cent would be around 2 per cent less than what it was pre-pandemic. These are likely underestimates as income distribution within every country is held unchanged in the simulations. Hence, these estimated distributional impacts are entirely due to differences in growth in (per capita) GDP across countries. Taking account of the increases in income inequality within each country would show even bigger increases in global inequality.

- This is not the only way in which inequality has increased. In addition to the widening gaps in well-being across countries, within-country inequality has also increased, which contributed to the widening global inequality. One mechanism is through the short-term impact of the pandemic on within-country inequality in developing countries. To understand the distribution of economic impacts within countries in the first three months of the pandemic, the paper presented evidence of the distribution of job and income losses, food insecurity and continued learning, based on harmonized HFPS data from fifty-two developing countries and up to 47,000 respondents.

- It has been seen that the impact on employment was not distributed equally. For job losses, the rate of inequality in the first three months of the pandemic (April–June 2020) was much higher for women, younger workers and workers with lower levels of education. They found that women were 8 percentage points more likely than men to stop working in the initial phase of the crisis, and gender disparities were larger compared to gaps by age, education and location (urban versus rural). The figures for self-reported job losses show a similar picture of women, less educated workers, and workers with school-aged children likely to be reporting loss of family income.

- Food insecurity increased in lower-income countries during and in the painful, lingering aftermath of the COVID-19 crisis. More than 30 per cent of households in some countries in sub-Saharan Africa reported having to go without food for at least one full day in the last one month (of the surveys) because of lack of resources.

- Regarding education, the existing digital divide led to unequal access to education, which was mainly delivered remotely. An average of 66 per cent of households with children in school prior to the pandemic reported their children engaging in learning activity when schools were closed. As expected, the share of children who did engage in any learning was higher for countries with higher levels of (pre-pandemic) per capita income and human capital development, as measured by the Human Capital Index.[39]

Particularly with regard to education, the timing of reopening of schools has had an important role to play in reducing the digital divide. This was all the more important for an economy such as India, where only around 25 per cent of Indian households were estimated to have broadband connections fully suitable for online classes. In November 2020, when sectors of the economy were transitioning to an 'unlock mode', Nobel laureate Abhijit Banerjee argued that India was nevertheless slower than other countries in opening up schools again, further exacerbating inequalities across the country.[40]

These sobering results suggest that existing inequalities were exacerbated in light of the COVID-19 crisis, with government response also less adequate in poorer countries. This also explains why inequalities are projected to remain up to the medium term, if not rise further.

THE INDIAN EXPERIENCE

As we have seen earlier, in the period post-liberalization, India moved from being a low-growth economy to one with much higher growth. Per capita GDP accelerated from a mere 1.3 per cent in the three decades after Independence to 7.5 per cent on average, until just before COVID.[41] In those infrastructure sectors which have been opened to competition, such as telecom and civil aviation, the private sector has proven to be extremely effective, and growth has been phenomenal.[42] While questions were raised around inequality, in line with what has been witnessed in other economies, such concerns took a backseat in light of the unprecedented, almost miraculous, growth that began to be experienced on the ground. Incomes grew across the board, albeit at an uneven rate. The overall level of poverty also saw a decline, amid continuing concerns about the lack of investment in health and education. Then, in 2020, when COVID-19 struck, the challenges of an already unequal economy began to unravel rapidly.

The World Inequality Report 2022 presents some astonishing findings around the rise in inequality in India. It discovers that India under the British Raj certainly had high income inequality, with the top 10 per cent enjoying an income share of 50 per cent. However, the report says this about the post-Independence situation:

> . . . socialist-inspired five-year plans contributed to reducing this share to 35-40%. Since the mid-1980s, deregulation and liberalization policies have led to one of the most extreme increases in income and wealth inequality observed in the world . . . While the top 1% has largely benefited from economic reforms, growth among low-and-middle income groups has been relatively slow and poverty persists.

This has led to the top 10 per cent earning 57 per cent of income—a staggering picture of inequality.

The basic thesis of unequal distribution of income is borne out by other data sources as well, although the magnitude of the problem is seen to be lower. The latest (as of August 2022) Annual Report of the Periodic Labour Force Survey (PLFS) indicated that the wage share of the top 10 per cent had been between 30 per cent and 35 per cent over the previous three years.[43] We hasten to add that this average figure represents anything but a uniform picture for the country, since there is tremendous intra-state variation. While the figure ranges between 50 per cent and 55 per cent in high-income states, such as Maharashtra, Gujarat and Karnataka, in low-income states, such as Chhattisgarh, it hits a much higher 65 per cent. This indicates a need for women to work for sustenance, consistent with the so-called 'U-shaped hypothesis' about female labour-force participation and income.[44]

Perhaps just as worrying is the assertion in the World Inequality Report that 'over the past three years, the quality of inequality data released by the government has seriously deteriorated, making it particularly difficult to assess recent inequality changes'. This caveat notwithstanding, the trends in inequality post-1951, a few years after Independence, and until 2019, are shown below. The data for the post-liberalization period, starting a few years prior to the 1991 reforms, is contained in the subsequent graph. Wealth inequality is seen to be worse, with the bottom 50 per cent owning very little, just 6 per cent of all wealth in the economy, the top 10 per cent owning 65 per cent (suggesting a relatively wealth-poor middle class), and the top 1 per cent a staggering 33 per cent of all wealth in the economy.

India's gender inequality, as measured by the female labour-force participation, also remains low, at 18 per cent. This figure is low even against the average for Asian economies as a whole, post-1990, excluding China, which has a much higher female labour-force participation. Note, once again the picture is different when viewed through the prism of the PLFS data, which shows an increase in the previous three years, with the latest data showing female labour-force participation of 30 per cent.

Finally, coming to carbon inequality, India remains a low emitter—'a person in the bottom 50% of the population in India is responsible for, on average, five times fewer emissions than the average person in the bottom 50% in the European Union and 10 times fewer than the average person in the bottom 50% in the US'.

Figure 7.4: Income Inequality in India, 1951–2019

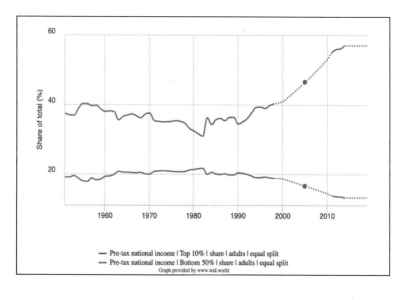

Pre-tax national income I Top 10% I share I adults I equal split
Pre-tax national income I Bottom 50% I share I adults I equal split
Graph provided by www.wid.world

Figure 7.5: Income Inequality in India, 1988–2019

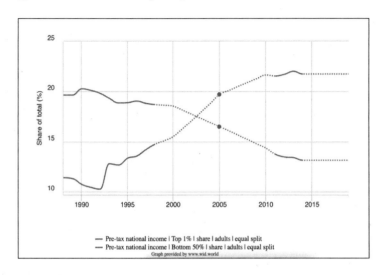

Figure 7.6: Income Inequality in India, 1820–2020

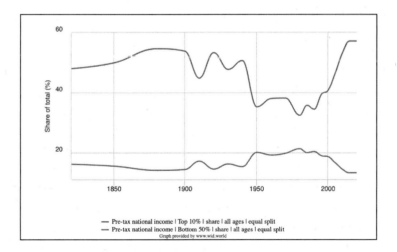

Figure 7.7: Evolution of Average Income in India, 1922–2021

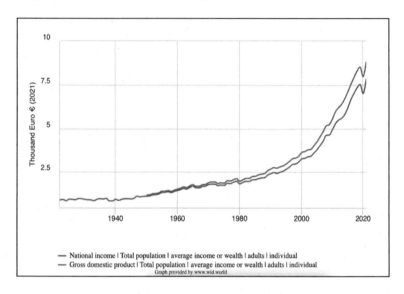

In an article provocatively headlined 'Poor Country with Affluent Elite, India is Going Nowhere',[45] Jayati Ghosh, a professor of economics at Jawaharlal Nehru University, used the findings from this report to claim: 'Globally and within India, inequality is not just killing people but destroying the planet.' Having reviewed the same report ourselves, we cannot say that we infer such a doomsday scenario from the data. Inequality by itself does not kill, nor does the inequality in the carbon footprint of the rich over the poor prove that the planet is being destroyed. In fact, if reduction in inequality is achieved by an increase in the carbon footprint of the middle class and the poor, the health of our planet will be further jeopardized. In some ways, this reflects the conundrum around inequality, especially when combined with other burning issues, such as climate change. By itself, decreasing inequality is a desirable normative goal. However, if income inequality were to be lessened by making everyone worse off than before, and/or carbon footprint inequality decreases because the middle class increases its carbon footprint, that would indeed make a bad problem worse.

Interestingly, the feeling of being worse off is not only in relation to others, but can also occur with relation to oneself, over time. The psychological and emotional impact of climate change disruptions is a case in point. For instance, Gallup's study on climate change and wellbeing found that globally, people faced thrice as many 'high-temperature days' in 2020 than in 2008, and rising temperatures have decreased well-being by 6.5 per cent. The same report found that the impact of rising temperatures on the quality of life was felt more pronouncedly by the older generations across geographies and by people across demographic groups in poorer and developing economies with large populations. Given the climate projections, high-temperature days could decrease global well-being by an estimated 17 per cent by 2030, which would by itself decrease well-being substantially.[46]

Before we conclude this section, it is also useful to summarize the findings of 'The State of Inequality in India Report' prepared by the Institute for Competitiveness (IFC), commissioned by the Economic Advisory Council to the prime minister (EAC-PM) and published in April 2022. The State of Inequality Report has tried to present a holistic understanding of the depth, structure and nature of inequality in India. Its coverage includes economic variables like income distribution, labour profiles, and socioeconomic variables like health, education and household characteristics, that attempt to give a comprehensive diagnosis of the developmental lacunae. The stock-taking carried out is thus of both inclusion and exclusion.[47]

The following are the report's key assertions and recommendations:

- Measuring poverty in a multidimensional context requires mapping of the mobility in and out of poverty. Therefore, it is recommended to establish airtight slabs that make class-based distinctions clear to trace movement within a class and in and out of the class. Additionally, this would help define the middle-class income share and target beneficiaries of social protection schemes that constitute the lower-middle class, lower class, and those below the poverty line.

- Raising minimum income and introducing universal basic income are two critical initiatives advocated to reduce the income gap and equalize distribution of earnings in the labour market.

- Taking into view the difference between the labour-force participation rates in the rural and urban areas, the report concludes that the urban equivalent of schemes like MGNREGS that are demand-based and offer guaranteed employment should be introduced so that the surplus labour is rehabilitated.

- The report urges the Central government to allocate a higher percentage of its expenditure towards social services and the social sector to make the most vulnerable population resilient to sudden shocks and to stop their descent into poverty.

- The report asserts that equitable access to education and creation of more jobs with long-term growth prospects are vital for triggering upward mobility among the poor.

- The report also urges the government to encourage regular exercises like the Foundational Learning and Numeracy Index and Ease of living Index, for the purpose of stock-taking the extent of vulnerability among households and to gain a better understanding of how to promote their overall well-being.

Finally, let us now look at a few alternative measures of poverty in India that provide us with a little glimmer of hope. The National Sample Survey (NSS), considered the most definitive data for India, is carried out once every ten years. Therefore, when we look at trends, we use extrapolations, including the inequality trends that we have seen throughout this chapter, or we use surveys from the private sector, such as the Consumer Household Pyramid Survey. A 2022 IMF working paper by economists Bhalla, Bhasin and Virmani[48] found that extreme poverty (defined as $1.9/person/day, at purchasing power parity of the 2011 dollar) was at a low of 0.8 pre-pandemic (2019) and remained at this low level, despite the pandemic. This estimate takes cognizance of the impact of food subsidy in lowering poverty levels. Not surprisingly, this conclusion has been contested, not least because of the indirect way in which consumption has been measured, which in turn may cause an overestimation.[49] A subsequent report by Sinha Roy and Van der Weide, also published in 2022, corroborates that poverty has indeed declined, though not by as much as Bhalla et al. had estimated.[50] According to this new report, inequality (as measured by the standard Gini coefficient, which measures income or wealth inequality within a country, taking values between 1, highest possible inequality or concentration of income/wealth, and 0, representing no inequality) has reduced and is close to its lowest level ever. They estimate inequality in 2020–21 at 0.292, close to the lowest recorded Gini of 0.284 in 1993–94.

Regardless of the precise magnitude of the reduction that one considers, it emerges clearly that interventions, whether food subsidy or cash transfers (and more generally, the country's tax and transfers) need to be considered while measuring both poverty and inequality. Hence, pre-tax measures may overestimate, or underestimate, inequality and income inequality and may not translate into the same level of consumption inequality. Hence, while eye-grabbing, the impact of India's high (and rising) inequality may be mitigated through schemes to help people on low incomes. In rural areas, this includes the MGNREGS programme, which provides 100 days of guaranteed employment to the poor. The scheme has been credited with poverty reduction[51] in rural areas as well as with other positive outcomes, such as improved female labour participation rate.

PUBLIC POLICY AND SOCIAL ENTREPRENEURSHIP—SOME PERSPECTIVES

We have seen how, in the years following liberalization in 1991, India underwent a definite shift from a centrally planned economy to a more globalized, market-friendly regime. In this new order of things, deregulation and free-market practices, for all the protests and disruptions they led to, replaced the earlier ecosystem of bureaucratic licensing, one where Central planning played a key role. However, the previous sections as well as our discussions in Chapter Five show that in the spheres of providing quality and accessible education for all and making social protection schemes available for the weakest sections of society, central planning and a governmental mandate can make a tangible difference on the ground. In all initiatives that have societal and normative goals, the role of the government warrants a revisitation.[52]

This does not in any way imply that we're advocating a reversal of economic liberalization in favour of a return to centralized planning. However, there is a pressing need to find mechanisms for economic growth to benefit a wider section of people across society, especially in the middle and lower-income categories. Inequality assumes ominous proportions when not accompanied by redistribution of wealth, leading to stagnant or falling wages and loss of employment in many sectors. And there are no inbuilt market incentives or state actions to remedy this. When there is extreme concentration of wealth, people also worry that the super-rich can influence the government of the day to calibrate its policies in ways that are advantageous to the lobbyists. Faced with such a prospect, it becomes all the more important for the government and other agencies to conduct themselves objectively and work with commitment towards a common goal.

In this section, we shall offer no framework of our own, but instead share the perspectives of experts we spoke to on this subject. Preeminent among them is Bibek Debroy, chairman of the influential EAC-PM, thought leader and economist, and a prolific author, translator and columnist. Debroy says: 'When we are in the midst of a pandemic, it is often possible to give undue importance to the transient and the temporary. The disruption and dislocation passes. It leaves a longer-term imprint, nevertheless. For instance, I can think of the following: (a) Digitization; (b) Formalization. (c) India becoming integrated into global supply chains in manufacturing; (d) Substitution of labour by technology. These were part of secular trends. The pandemic has accelerated the process.'

However, he advises caution about adducing all manner of disruptions as well as accelerations in market trends to the effect of the pandemic: 'I think one should be careful about making assertions about the digital divide. A digital divide has existed. This proposition is true. "Covid has increased it"—I don't think that proposition is true. Witness the sharp increase in smartphone penetration in the middle of the pandemic. I am inclined to argue that the pandemic has triggered a reduction of the divide, in G2C, C2B, B2C and even G2G transactions.'

Regarding the performance of the different regions and states across the country with regard to inequality as well as other parameters, Debroy says: 'For economists, productivity is computed as a residual, after the factor inputs of land, labour and capital. Different states are in different stages of development and will tap different sources of productivity and growth—but essentially, efficient land, labour and capital markets, with technology as an enabler.'

Luis Miranda, chairman of the Centre for Civil Society and CORO India, founder-director of the Indian School of Public Policy, Manipal Cigna, senior adviser at Morgan Stanley and an alumnus of the University of Chicago Booth School of Business, looks at inequality quite differently: 'Inequality as a derivative of entrepreneurship, creativity and hard work is not morally wrong. What is, however, morally wrong is to see the extreme poverty around us. What I'm really worried about is the number of people who have slipped back into poverty in India during the pandemic. India had done a fabulous job of taking people out of poverty—United Nations Development Programme (UNDP) reported that India had taken 271 million out of extreme poverty from 2005–06 till 2015–16. However, the past two years would have seen a huge reversal in that trend. This is something that *sarkaar*, *samaaj* and *bazaar*[53] have to come together to fix, on a war footing. Helping micro-entrepreneurs in all sectors, including the social sector, is extremely important, therefore. Government schemes like Pradhan Mantri Mudra Yojna and ATAL Innovation Mission are two examples. And there are other initiatives like Global Alliance for Mass Entrepreneurship (GAME), which have a key role to play. The Centre for Civil Society continues to highlight the challenges to "ease of doing business" for micro-entrepreneurs.'

Miranda has personally learnt a great deal from his experience at CORO India, which runs a grassroots leadership development programme in Maharashtra and Rajasthan, and where 70 per cent of the fellows over the past twelve years have come from disadvantaged communities. Miranda said: 'We strongly believe that unlocking their "power within" helps them contextualize their experiences of discrimination to help develop relevant and participatory solutions. "Imported" interventions have more often failed to create sustainable impact. At the same time, I have seen at the Centre for Civil Society how markets can work for the poor—be it micro-entrepreneurs, tribals or marginal farmers. Both organizations have made me realize the importance of the individual in deciding their future and not top-down approaches from a centralized ivory tower.'

We also spoke to Paul Abraham, former COO of IndusInd Bank and currently president of the Hinduja Foundation. He said: 'The belief that start-ups can only serve the aspirational and privileged sections is outdated. Also, we have to stop believing that to bring people out of poverty we have to deliver services in free/charity mode. People are willing to pay but we have to find new ways of making services available for a "new price", or new structures that receive compensation, as affordability increases. This demands new constructs in product development, delivery mechanisms and pricing structures. There are many who are delivering creatively in social entrepreneurship, that create impact while being sustainable. Corporates need to support and partner with government and the start-up ecosystem, to deliver services that include the bottom of the pyramid, not only in accessing but in bringing them up the curve in reducing inequality and exclusion.'

A financial sector leader, besides being a social entrepreneur, Abraham is quick to spot the problems that may erupt if adequate attention isn't paid to financial literacy as well as safeguards: 'Access to services in this new world is increasingly digital, and learning to navigate that without the basics of financial literacy means being excluded. With increasing formalization of our economy, commerce and financial access, the advantages of being financially literate to access the banking channels and the world of digital commerce is manifold. I feel that schools, NGOs and government agencies must work through on-ground and online channels to educate not only the children, but the elders too, who run the risk of being left behind. Adult literacy is key to the betterment of communities, especially in accessing government programmes and being financially included.'

Prerna Mukharya, Chevening Fellow at Oxford University, Fortune 40 under-forty awardee and founder of Outline India, has this to say: 'As a result of the pandemic, the divide between the haves and the have-nots has become more apparent. On the one hand, we do need our AI/ML/networking/space tech start-ups, but on the other hand, we have so rightly realized the need for social entrepreneurs who cater to those who are not as educated and are not as well-connected, perhaps, and are not in the best of health or are missing out on opportunities owing to their poor socioeconomic status. Take the case of India; about 65 per cent of India lives in its villages, and a big chunk of its population, 60–70 per cent, is disconnected. A majority of these are women and kids, and their needs and wants never get factored into our debates. They are not online, and there is only one way and one way alone of reaching them, i.e., by having a face-to-face conversation with them. Hence, solutions should be developed that work within the ambit of their financial constraints and location. The investment ecosystem is evolving, but the pandemic has made it apparent that we need our PE firms and philanthropists to take risks on start-ups that may not generate returns that are similar to our commercial tech start-ups. Social entrepreneurship can be in the form of agritech or even non-tech-driven investments. The returns are perhaps smaller, and the germination period is longer. But this is about changing the world at one level and about working with volumes at the other.'

For Mukharya, a dual focus on health and education is paramount for success, where, she feels, our investments, as a percentage of GDP, have to be substantially higher than what they are currently.

INEQUALITY IN THE WORKPLACE: DIVERSITY, EQUITY & INCLUSION

In this section, we shift the lens to another perspective of looking at inequality and unfairness at work—through the prism of diversity, equity and inclusion (DEI). While interest in DEI has deepened, debates around it remain contentious, and the emerging research, case studies, workplace applications and efficacy of such initiatives are collectively too vast to be reviewed here. Instead, we offer a very broad sketch of the global DEI market and some of the challenges, and then focus on the problem of gauging perceptions, behaviours and mindsets with regard to DEI.

It is interesting to note that DEI has not only been projected by employees as a masthead under which to raise their voice of outrage at nepotism and unfairness in the workplace, but employers are also increasingly using DEI to suit their own imperatives. The global DEI market is estimated to have touched $7.5 billion in 2020, with projections of this figure doubling by 2026. This overt market-centricity has meant a shift in the mindset of many company leaders when they think of DEI—from it being a position about fairness and values to it being a new means of improving profits or the bottom line, through enhanced teamwork and productivity. This swiftly takes the form of a circular commercial logic. If DEI is beneficial for business, a higher budget is required for it, which, in turn, ought to translate into greater profits for the company. Many organizations have in fact taken to linking DEI to profitability, openly, in their statements and website content. Such practices, more often than not, threaten to be counter-productive, putting unreasonable expectations of financial outcome from DEI initiatives, while not necessarily improving the well-being of those sections for whom DEI is designed in the first place.

The most obvious problem of linking diversity to corporate profits may be a turnoff for the underrepresented individuals the organizations are trying to attract. In fact, use of the business case to justify diversity can result in underrepresented groups anticipating less belongingness in organizations, since they feel undervalued. This in turn makes them less likely to wish to join the company, or to remain with it over any substantial tenure. Research conducted by Oriane Georgeac, professor at Yale School of Management, and Aneeta Rattan, professor at London Business School, found that as many as 404 of the Fortune 500 companies indicated on their corporate website that diversity was important because it would contribute to their profits in some way. However, when women professionals, college students and individuals from the LGBTQ+ community read these statements, the large consensus was that they would be stereotyped in such organizations and would therefore be less willing to join a company that used such a business case, as compared to one which provided no justification at all for its DEI imperatives.[54]

The second issue is one that muddies the water in terms of how the three principal agents—the employees, managers and employers—view DEI and initiatives around it. Joanne Duberley, professor of organizational studies and deputy pro-vice-chancellor (Equality, Diversity and Inclusion) at the University of Birmingham, explains why this is so: 'The challenge as a manager is to create real attitude/behaviour change, and that takes time. It is easy to develop policies/frameworks, but getting those embedded in people's everyday behaviour is much harder. For employees it is often frustrating as they don't see real change and think management is not committed. We need diversity in outlook—otherwise we risk making very bad decisions and also losing out on the huge pool of talent that is present in traditionally underrepresented groups.'

She also emphasizes the importance of mechanisms that enable the effective translation from framework to employee experience on the ground: 'This is the key question that EDI practitioners need to solve. How to embed change within the organization. I think there needs to be a consistent message about the importance of EDI as a strategic priority from top management. That's not enough on its own though—EDI concerns need to be integrated in all policies and there needs to be active consideration of the EDI implications of decisions at all levels in the organization—and it needs to be prioritized. Too often, it's seen as a nice-to-have that can be dropped if it costs too much or forces the leadership team to make difficult decisions. Only when people see clear action and consideration of EDI will they trust that leadership is serious about this.'

Our own sense is that, as in the case of behavioural skills or mental health in the workplace, the fundamental premise for DEI initiatives has to be a deeper understanding and awareness of perceptions and positions within the organization. For DEI, there are two different dimensions to this understanding. The first is at the stakeholder level. It is imperative that leaders revisit the DEI question not with respect to budgets and projected profits, but with a deeper awareness of their own psychological perceptions with regard to DEI, their own biases, and with a better understanding of the motivations and drive of their peers, and of the organizational readiness for DEI, as a whole.

The second is with regard to the sentiments and perceptions of the employees in the organization. Aiming to reap multi-layered behavioural analytics from the employees, this centres on the knowledge that the components of diversity, equity and inclusion are single, monolithic aspects, but in turn entail multiple elements, as indicated in the table below.

NUVAH, the company that Avik has founded, has developed survey-based solutions for both these dimensions of understanding.

Category	Diversity	Equity	Inclusion
Components	Diversity of Hiring Diversity of Culture	Equity-Belongingness Equity-Culture Equity-Career Development Equity-Learning & Development	Inclusion-Culture Inclusion-Identity Inclusion-Discrimination
	Policies and Procedures		

Source: NUVAH framework for gauging DEI

There are, of course, several ways in which company stakeholders can approach their DEI initiatives. Here is the three-pronged approach advocated by Gallup:[55]

1. Identify DEI priorities based on a rigorous assessment of the organization's current state. Obtain accurate quantitative and qualitative data to gauge employee perception and sentiment. Respect, strengths and trust could be the key factors in such an evaluation, as could engagement, innovation, agility and belonginess. This is essential in order to set realistic and impactful DEI goals, along with time frames.
2. Select a dedicated team to steer, execute and champion a strategy that's tailored to the plan. DEI teams are found to be more effective when they have: a structured

charter with the purpose of the work, processes, goals and a shared understanding of what success looks like; executive sponsorship, financial and non-financial resources to support related activities; access to leadership; communication that fuels organization-wide awareness; metrics that assess and report on progress on a regular basis; and mechanisms to gather employee feedback across all levels of the organization.

3. Finally, plan to sustain momentum. Clear expectations support ongoing individual and collective dedication. Accountability embeds DEI in an organization's strategy. And both of these require leadership commitment, which conveys the company's values, sets an example for employees and helps sustain momentum. In this context, it's particularly important that leaders practise what they preach.

While our collective understanding of the nuances of DEI will continue to deepen, in light of new research findings or evidence of the efficacy of initiatives in organizations, one thing seems clear. The effective addressing of DEI imperatives will have to take an empathetic, highly nuanced and multidisciplinary approach.

CORPORATE SOCIAL RESPONSIBILITY— UNTAPPED POTENTIAL AND OPPORTUNITIES

So far in this chapter, we have noted the role of two principal agencies that can be effective in addressing inequality. First, the government, with social protection schemes on the one hand and skill-building as well as employment-generation opportunities on the other. The others are what are typically bundled as 'NGOs', social entrepreneurs, firms and consortiums of individuals, often working on a not-for-profit basis. Both sets of agents take up projects to enhance education, skills, earning opportunities or well-being among the marginalized sections of society. In this final section, we explore how profit-focused organizations, especially large corporates, can make a significant dent in inequality, through effective engagement in CSR. Beyond its relevance to addressing inequality in society, we shall also see how CSR also connects back meaningfully to important aspects of building emergent skills and sustaining employability, which we have discussed earlier in the book.

In simple terms, CSR can be understood as the mandate within a company to raise greater public awareness of socioeconomic, ethical and ecological issues, and to act upon a vision to change things for the better. The remit of CSR covers all manner of projects undertaken by a company towards the fulfilment of these goals. The whole idea is for the firm to demonstrate its commitment to improve the health and well-being of society in a sustainable way. The global CSR software market was valued at US$673.8 million in 2020 and was predicted to reach US$1308.5 million by 2027, growing at a CAGR (compound annual growth rate) of 8.34 per cent from 2021 to 2027.[56] The prospects for CSR in India are particularly heartening. In 2014–15, the ministry of corporate affairs made it mandatory for companies to spend 2 per cent of their annual profits on CSR projects. A CRISIL report released in 2021 stated that Indian companies had spent over one trillion rupees on CSR projects since it came into law. Even during the fiscal year 2021, with the economy still being ravaged by unpredictable waves of new variants of the COVID-19 virus, the overall CSR spend in India is estimated to have crossed Rs 22,000 crore.[57]

We present below a set of guidelines that can serve as a basic framework for firms embarking on their CSR journey or revisiting their CSR strategy, focus and past performance.

- **Establish a CSR practice:** For many stakeholders, CSR may be a spend, a cost item. But for its efforts to make a real impact on the ground, the company stakeholders have to commit to it and demonstrate their conviction through execution. The CSR practice should be set up as a separate vertical or department, with the same seriousness, enthusiasm and expectancy that goes into establishing a new research lab or digital marketing wing. Within the organization, even if resources brought in are part-time, management should ensure that these are personnel who're genuinely excited about working on CSR projects, and for whom a 'high' performance rating in CSR is at par with a high rating on a billable client project, vendor negotiation, quality assurance assignment, production or shipment delivery.

- **Develop a focused vision:** With regard to CSR initiatives, it's important to address both empowerment and accountability at the outset. One good way of doing this is to appoint a leader with tenure in the company and in-depth knowledge of its strengths, values and culture to head the CSR vertical. The CSR lead researches the burning issue(s) of the day and maps them to the company's imperatives as well as to government or privately run initiatives on the same issues. If there are synergies, conversations with such agencies can provide valuable insights for forming the company's CSR strategy. This is also an important point at which to engage with CSR experts and consultants who can advise on strategy. In the end, though, it is the CSR lead who must own and lead the company's strategy and vision.

- **Build in-house CSR skills:** An important question relates to the extent to which a company's employees are to be involved vis-à-vis external CSR consultants. One end of the decision spectrum is to outsource the entire CSR project(s) to an external agency, limiting the company's role to reviews and budgetary approvals. Such an approach would obviously negate the need for a separate CSR function within the organization. But importantly, it would negate the possibility of exploring some very important questions. What are the core, intrinsic values of the organization, for example? Which of the current employees have skills and mindsets that are already attuned to the company's philosophy? What additional skills would some of those personnel need to be more successful in their roles as CSR champions or team members? How would such skills and competencies be identified, benchmarked, and then mapped to the current proficiency levels of the employees who've been selected for the CSR initiatives? Would certain others make a better fit?

- **Sustain employability:** The questions above lead us directly into those that we encountered in Chapter Four, investigating the emergent skills of the future workplace. The same question presents itself to the company stakeholders in the specific context of CSR. And, using the framework outlined in Chapter Four and with the help of behavioural measures to gauge employee skills, it is possible to arrive at the desired skills basket for CSR and identification of employees who might be naturally attuned to undertaking and leading such initiatives. Besides creating a more palpable sense of the impact of CSR through in-house resources and enhancing human capital, developing CSR capabilities within the organization has another enormous potential benefit. In light of the danger that current jobs in any company may be eliminated either due to technology or market uncertainties, the relative stability of a CSR practice would allow management to build and sustain a 'buffer zone of employability'.

Traditionally, the very idea of meaningful engagement in social entrepreneurship has always been considered as beyond the grasp of corporate enterprise, in terms of the required sensibilities, aptitude and also appetite. Effective practice of CSR has the full potential to effect a healthy reversal of that notion. With a newer-generation workforce, the ubiquitous adoption of social media for expressing both appreciation and criticism in real time, and an expectation from management for the company to be serious about societal, ethical and ecological concerns, companies are compelled to think beyond profit maximization. The introduction of legal CSR mandates in India and several other economies has ensured the carving out of a corpus of investment for fruitful initiatives. And a judicious combination of competence building, the motive of sustaining employability and the will to make a genuine impact on the ground, together hold out the promise of achieving outcomes for the greater good.

CHAPTER 8

Emergent Technologies and Probable Futures

'The final destination of Time is very subtle.'

—The Mahabharata, 15.46 (as translated by Wendy Doniger)

Readers who've read up to this point have certainly noticed that what we've aimed to do through the course of the book is to build a picture of the current ecosystem, comprising work, worker and workplace, keeping in mind the continuous change taking place on all three fronts. We began by looking at the broad trends around technological advancement across sectors globally, and across sectors, predictions on unemployment, and the actual situation on the ground. We studied the emergent sectors, job roles and the new dualism of evolved skills for success in the future. Next, we took a deeper look at the behavioural competencies required, at work and beyond, and examined the underlying opportunities and challenges in developing them swiftly at the nation–state level, especially for an economy like India. We explored the relationship between education, research, innovation, productivity and growth. We then gained an understanding of the current state of mental health across the entire ecosystem, as well as the economic circumstances and well-being of the weakest sections of society, both in light of the continuing pandemic situation.

Now, we come to focus on the exciting, controversial phenomenon of the Metaverse and its underlying technologies: blockchain, bitcoins and Non-Fungible Tokens (NFTs). There are some fundamental challenges in attempting a comprehensive—let alone exhaustive—discussion of the subject. Unlike AI, machine learning and automation, where there's already a great deal of application and impact on the ground, the broad consensus is that the Metaverse, in terms of delivering its full promise, is still several years away. At the same time, when it comes to innovation and research that find application in the Metaverse, ideas, prototypes, pilots and new ventures are all taking place at such a stunning pace that doing justice to them would take up a large volume by itself—a volume that would also be largely academic, since by the time such a book is published, all the details contained in it would be dated.

Instead, this is what we aim to do in this final chapter of our book. First, we lay out the foundation of the Metaverse and its associated technologies, all of which depend on one fundamental element for their sustenance: data. We then offer a brief, simple and non-technical outline of the Metaverse, its origin and progress so far, as well as the technologies that support it, listing some advantages and challenges in their usage. As with previous chapters, the Metaverse projects discussed here and the insights for future progress that emerge from them are anecdotal and should not be read as a comprehensive review. We then discuss what honesty, ethics and integrity mean in the emergent workplace. And, to conclude, we provide glimpses—

captioned notes on some key themes—by way of a rough sketch of what the workplace of the near future might look like.

WORK, WORKER, WORKPLACE—AND DATAISM

Since the earliest days when the concept and practice of 'work' came into force across civilizations, to the first Industrial Revolution in the late eighteenth century and right through most of the time period that we have regarded as Work 2.0— work, worker and workplace have been tied together in a clear relationship. The worker has performed his or her work at the workplace. The skills and qualifications of the worker have certainly undergone a transformation through the ages, as has the corresponding range of vocations and occupations that have kept humans gainfully employed. The physical sphere that we have come to understand as the workplace has likewise expanded manifold: from sweltering fields to assembly plants, to air-conditioned halls and offices. But the underlying relationship between the three elements, by and large, has sustained—until now.

With Work 3.0, there is a definite break from the past. To begin with, the nature of work has changed substantially and will continue to do so at a rapid pace. Work, in the traditional sense of an occupation, has involved a fixed set of skills, meant for executing a fixed and limited set of tasks, to deliver a pre-defined output. In the emergent paradigm, professionals change career tracks multiple times over a lifetime and also undertake a range of different tasks concurrently, which requires diverse skills. In fact, as we have seen earlier in the book, a successful Career 3.0 requires a professional to be highly competent at multiple combinations of tasks at the same time. Thus, a start-up entrepreneur who is superb at creating products also needs to learn how to look after, manage and motivate his people. A salesman has to swiftly become an effective user of technology, enthusiastic about AI-driven forecasts, sales apps and customer relationship management (CRM) databases. And the reclusive writer of old too would be well-advised to be an eloquent marketer of his own work, in his Work 3.0 avatar.

Next, consider the position of the worker. Traditionally, this term has meant a full-time employee, attached to a single organization for the duration of his employment. However, there is a growing trend towards gig or freelance work, accelerated by the pandemic, mainly for economic reasons. The contract market, fairly mature in Western economies, is now finding takers across other geographies, including India. We have seen previously how gig work is being perpetuated across the economy in two distinct and markedly different ways. The first is the highly skilled white-collar worker, who, for reasons of personal choice and independence, prefers to work as a freelancer and not be 'tied down' as a full-time salaried employee of an organization. The second is the vastly greater number of blue- and grey-collar workers who are retained as contract workers, in many cases exploitatively, without the perks and safeguards of full-time employment. But in both these practices, the net effect is to increase the overall proportion of gig workers in the economy.

Finally, let us look at the workplace, where the break with the past is perhaps the most prominent. The emerging mode of operation is 'work from anywhere' (WFA), involving a hybrid of home and office. In many firms, however, entire departments are being reorganized to continue working remotely on a long-term basis, even as the pandemic situation eases into a new business-as-usual scenario. Remote working or WFH is not an entirely new phenomenon. As the information technology revolution that began in the 1990s took firmer root, computer programmers were encouraged to work from home. As consultants, they would often be required to operate from the client's premises. Consequently, their office attendance was more piecemeal or periodic, and on these occasions, they operated from temporary workstations or 'hot desks'. Such practices are now being extended across many major sectors of the global economy. This clearly means that going forward, the need for a clearly designated, immovable space called the 'workplace' will swiftly diminish.

Translated into practice, it involves the systematic production, analysis, interpretation and consumption of information, mainly for the purpose of decision-making, at individual, team and organization levels. Interconnectedness—across individuals, organizations, machines and systems—is key for 'dataism' to be successful in the workplace. It is in many ways the logical—if originally unintended—conclusion of the IT revolution that began almost two and a half decades ago, the promise of the internet of things (IOT) delivered on a platter of state-of-the-art integrated circuits.

In tracing back its roots, Harari says:

> Dataism is most firmly entrenched in its two mother disciplines: computer science and biology. Of the two, biology is the more important. It was the biological embracement of Dataism that turned a limited breakthrough in computer science into a world-shattering cataclysm that may completely transform the very nature of life. You may not agree with the idea that organisms are algorithms, and that giraffes, tomatoes and human beings are just different methods for processing data. But you should know that this is current scientific dogma, and that it is changing our world beyond recognition. Not only individual organisms are seen today as data-processing

systems, but also entire societies such as beehives, bacteria colonies, forests and human cities.[2]

Three key observations can be made at this point.

First, while Dataism may sound relatively novel, as a formulation the widespread application of its principles has been taking place for several decades. Among the earliest adopters of Dataism were material requirements planning (MRP) systems built in the 1960s, by J.I. Case, a manufacturer of tractors and construction machinery, in collaboration with IBM. By the 1990s, the scope of such computer systems had expanded from inventory and production tracking to finance and controlling, sales and purchases, and most important, establishing robust integration across them all. Gartner had a nice new name for these sophisticated software systems that SAP, Oracle and others were developing: enterprise resource planning (ERP). According to Gartner, ERP is defined as 'the ability to deliver an integrated suite of business applications. ERP tools share a common process and data model, covering broad and deep operational end-to-end processes, such as those found in finance, HR, distribution, manufacturing, service and the supply chain'.[3]

Second, as Harari points out, Dataism is neither liberal nor humanist. There is no natural empathetic streak in it that will make its programes and algorithms lean towards creating safeguards for the poorest sections of the economy, mandating safety nets of blue-collar workers with no job security, increasing access to technology to those made worse off, at least in the near term, by a growing Digital Divide. It is propagated by corporates and data analysts, largely for use by the market forces. Therefore, its usage for the benefit of a larger section of society, beyond boardroom executives, shareholders and stockbrokers, depends on the way we find means to channelize its use.

Nevertheless, there can be definite social benefits to Dataism. One could be the creation of skills databases in organizations, collating the proficiency of behavioural skills and competencies of their people and updating them periodically, say, once a year. Here, the proviso should be that, while companies may use the matrix for decision-making such as training and calibration of job roles, the ultimate custodians of the data at the individual level are the professionals themselves. Another could be the practice of maintaining the emotional and mental health of the people, and for the authorities to be able to create a heat map of issues, in the same way as is currently conducted for the incidence of COVID-19 cases and vaccination reach. However, this should be displayed without the accompanying personally identifiable information, to guard against any discrimination at an individual level.

Third, in the passage from Harari quoted above, he says that Dataism has two mother disciplines: computer science and biology, the latter being more important. This implies a duality, and consequently tension, competition, and possibly even a question of choice, by the practitioners of Dataism, of one over the other. But the reach of computer science is ubiquitous. The daily practice of modern biology, whether in X-ray scans and blood test reports, or in creating the database of COVID infections, vaccinations, recovery and death figures at global, country and local levels, cannot function without it. Likewise, this is true of an increasing proportion of research being conducted in the social sciences and humanities. As Harari puts it: 'Data science provides analytical leverage on long-standing questions such as what factors determine economic development and well-being? What leads to well-functioning societies and democracy? Why are some societies plagued by violence, repression, and conflict?'[4] Under the regime of global Dataism, the discipline of computer science, in particular data science (and by corollary, the practice of technology and data analytics), has emerged as the single largest one, with a tangible impact cutting across almost all other disciplines and practices. There is no 'Other'.

THE METAVERSE AND ALTERNATIVE FUTURES

The term 'Metaverse' was first coined by science fiction author Neal Stephenson in his 1992 novel *Snow Crash*. In it, Stephenson visualized it as a three-dimensional digital world, a shared virtual reality experience that enabled its users to escape from a real physical world that had become unappealing. Thirty years on, the Metaverse has achieved cult standing. A growing number of futurists, technologists, product companies and investors view it as the Next Big Thing which will transform our lives in the future. Its creative arms of virtual reality (VR) and augmented reality (AR) have seen a combined global spending of $12 billion on AR/VR headsets in the midst of the pandemic. The overall AR and VR markets have been projected to grow at an astounding CAGR of 46 per cent from 2020 to 2025, or by $162.71 billion in absolute terms. In fact, global tech industry leaders are optimistic that the Metaverse market will achieve the $800 billion mark by 2024 and reach 1 billion people by 2030.

On 28 October 2020, Mark Zuckerberg made the landmark announcement that Facebook would change its name to 'Meta', from the Greek root word meaning 'beyond' or 'outside of', underscoring the technology's potential to replace the mobile internet. The US business mogul asserted that the company's purpose would now be entirely devoted to transitioning its users to the Metaverse. A month later, Microsoft announced Mesh, which is envisaged to be the natural successor of Teams. Since then, firms such as Google, Sony and Apple have followed suit by announcing their respective agenda on Metaverse projects to the wider media and user community. It is now undebatable that some of the largest technology product manufacturers and service providers are investing heavily to create new, multipurpose virtual worlds that offer immersive experience to users on par with the real world, and enable ways of interacting with the real world at the same time. But beyond its legion of champions, there are those who are highly sceptical of the Metaverse's ubiquitous usage and the possible dangers that this presents.

But before delving further into these, let us briefly distinguish the Metaverse from a couple of other terms that are sometimes used interchangeably. The first is Web3, which, simply put, is the internet in its most unencumbered, democratized and decentralized form, developed on distributed technologies such as blockchain. No single entity will have the authority to control and manipulate the network, even if it owns the entire hardware that it is operating on. Web3 is so named since it's widely anticipated to be the third big evolution of the internet after the worldwide web (Web1) and the user-generated web (Web2, or social media). The Metaverse, on the other hand, is a term used to describe evolving, state-of-the-art virtual worlds, where users can interact with each other and engage with apps and services, and also bridge to the real world in an immersive way. It refers to all online spaces that strive to create immersive environments, from games to retail stores, real estate properties and the workplace. There is an important crossover between the two. The technology used for Web3, blockchain and cryptocurrencies has huge implications for the way in which we will use the Metaverse for work, socializing and learning.[5]

The second term is the similar-sounding Multiverse. While the Metaverse lays the groundwork for a connected virtual world, the Multiverse provides the potential for multiple digital ecosystems. The former, in many conceptualizations, such as Mark Zuckerberg's, is a unified, centralized virtual universe. The Multiverse, by comparison, is necessary for integrating multiple decentralized Metaverse projects into a unified experience. In a way, therefore, the Multiverse can be said to be the creation of decentralized Metaverse projects, combining to create a unified Metaverse experience. There is a specific order to the flow of information in the Metaverse, but no such particular order in the Multiverse. Digital assets and experiences can be owned by users in the Metaverse, whereas in the Multiverse, users cannot own assets in separate virtual worlds. Metaverse participants are inclusive of AI, robots, human avatars and digital avatars. By contrast, virtual worlds are the only entities that constitute the Multiverse.[6]

The Metaverse is a promise, not only of a fully immersive experience in a virtual world, but the fusion of that virtual world with the real world we live in. In terms of engaging and immersing an audience through a virtual medium, this is hardly a new phenomenon. The TV is not quite the 'idiot box' it was once dubbed to be. In fact, all of us have at some point been moved to high emotion, laughter or tears by what we have seen on the screen. But, at the same time, the experience of two years of the pandemic has proved beyond doubt that 'Zoom fatigue' is a very real issue. According to a poll conducted by the Lumina Foundation and Gallup, 32 per cent of students enrolled in a bachelor's degree considered withdrawing from their programme for a semester or more in the past six months, while 76 per cent reported experiencing great emotional stress. The quick-fix solution of online classes was seen to be unimaginative and stressful.[7]

In other words, extended hours in front of a computer screen is distracting, tiring and ultimately demotivating, even though we may be constantly be in the virtual presence of other people. This is because the fundamental constituents of the body—the pulse rate, neurons, hormones—are not activated in an online meeting in the same way they would be if the interaction were taking place in person. How will such a problem be resolved in the Metaverse?

Let's start with the real feeling of being in a particular place. Metaverse, through AR and VR, can cause exactly such an experience in a person, by activating the hippocampal cells through one's headset—the exact same 'GPS neurons' that inform the brain in the real world that one is in such-and-such a physical place. Next, consider the experience of inhabiting your own body in the Metaverse through your digital clone. This could be achieved through a combination of VR and AR by directly using body swapping or rubber-hand illusions on devices or digital accessories worn by the user, as well as indirectly, using the Proteus effect (i.e., changing one's appearance in the digital space). Further, in the Metaverse, VR and AR can activate the same brain-to-brain attunement between individuals that occurs during interactions in the real world, affecting empathy and recognition of intentions. Likewise, in a Metaverse group meeting of multiple individuals, VR and AR can also activate the same brain-to-brain synchrony in neural oscillations which take place in group interactions in the real world, affecting collective performance and creativity. And in the course of all these interactions, specific emotions and responses can be induced in users, and even the ability to regulate them.[8]

Equipped with this basic understanding, let us now briefly sketch the implications of the Metaverse for India and the global economy in the near future, the impact on sectors, the nature of jobs, new markets, as well as the challenges in its implementation. The indications are that in the initial days of development, the industry euphoria about the Metaverse isn't met by consumer demand and excitement. According to a large-scale study carried out by Forrester across the US and UK in December 2021, only 34 per cent of US and 28 per cent of UK online adults are really enthusiastic about what the Metaverse will offer them. In sharp contrast, the same study found that 76 per cent of US business-to-consumer (B2C) marketing executives had planned to invest in Metaverse-related activities in 2022. It has been suggested that the Metaverse has better chance of wide-scale adoption in the workplace through implementations of hybrid virtual offices and digital avatars.[9] However, even industry leaders envisage the current market to be limited largely to highly tech-savvy male online users who are millennials or Gen-Zers. In the immediate term, there is thus a clear need for Metaverse creators to engage more deeply with the customer base and also establish a greater value exchange.[10]

Undeterred by the current challenges, some of the largest companies in the world are forging ahead with their Metaverse plans, investing billions of dollars into bringing their vision of the future to life. Meta (formerly Facebook), Microsoft, Apple, Unity Software, Nvidia, Roblox and Epic Games have emerged as the influential players globally in the initial phase of developing the Metaverse. Interestingly, Neal Stephenson, the originator of the term Metaverse, launched his own blockchain project in 2022 under the aegis of his company, Lamina.[11] Indian players too are rising to the opportunity. According to a report by DappRadar, India is ranked 50 in the world in terms of its interest in Metaverse projects, behind the US, Indonesia, Japan and the Philippines. It has the third largest start-up ecosystem globally, and mature domestic markets— factors that could be instrumental in making it a test ground for new projects. Finally, India boasts that its young and STEM-educated talent pool of programmers, designers, data analysts and entrepreneurs is almost inexhaustible.[12]

The massive technological, economic and sociological challenges in the way of mass-scale rollout of the Metaverse notwithstanding, companies across Delhi, Pune, Bengaluru, Ahmedabad and Mumbai have made Metaverse a key priority in their business goals. TopSoftwareCompanies.co has published a list of the top ten Metaverse development companies in India in 2022. The companies are Hyperlink Infosystem, HCL Technologies, Infosys, Capgemini India Pvt. Ltd, Zensar Technologies, Tech Mahindra, Wipro, TCS, Accenture and HData Systems.[13] Across the board, globally and in India, there is vibrant intellectual debate as to the most effective and impactful ways of creating the Metaverse.[14] Top-ten lists have also been published, featuring the most exciting Metaverse projects to look out for in 2022.[15]

Let us look at a few examples.

Reliance made its foray into the Metaverse in February 2022 by buying a 25 per cent stake (worth $15 million) in Two Platforms, a Silicon Valley-based deep-tech start-up founded by Indian-born scientist Pranav Mistry.[16] In June 2022, Airtel introduced the first multiplex in the Metaverse in India. This is part of the Airtel Xstream Premium offering, introduced in collaboration with Partynite, a blockchain-powered digital parallel universe. The Airtel Xstream Multiplex consists of twenty screens and allows viewers a multiplex experience across multiple over-the-top (OTT) platforms (e.g., Eros Now, Lionsgate Play, Hoi Choi and Hungama Play).[17] Jewellery brand Tanishq launched its wedding collection, 'Romance of Polki', offering the audience views of the jewellery pieces in 3D and allowing them to try on the items by scanning a QR code. IT market leader Infosys launched the 'Infosys Metaverse Foundry', bringing together AI, data analytics and simulations for a Metaverse experience. Tata Consultancy Services (TCS), for its part, helped the Pune Municipal Corporation build a 'digital twin' to improve its COVID management. TCS believes its digital twin tech will drive Metaverse adoption in several sectors.

Tyre manufacturer Ceat Limited has created its own Ceat Shoppe, integrated with its e-commerce platform. Buyers and customers will be able to view products in 3D and book orders simultaneously. The company will also offer buyers the option of tyre delivery and fitment at home. A pick-up facility from the physical stores will also be available. Mahindra & Mahindra has experimented with NFT marketing by auctioning four Thar-themed NFTs, each costing Rs 26 lakh. Winners of the auction got the chance to enjoy an off-road experience of driving the Thar. Travel company MakeMyTrip launched virtual vacation NFTs, themed on India's best travel destinations. Each NFT was valued at Rs 14,999. MG Motor India announced its plans to launch a total of 1110 NFTs starting at Rs 500. These NFTs will have four themes, namely, collaborative art, community and diversity, car-as-a-platform and collectibles, by means of which MG fans can own a piece of the company.[18]

Internationally, major investments, mergers and acquisitions have been announced in the gaming space, believed by many to be spearheading the Metaverse revolution. In January 2022, Microsoft announced plans to acquire World of Warcraft and Candy Crush maker Activision Blizzard in its largest all-cash acquisition ever at $69 billion, hoping that bestseller games will help attract sceptics to the Metaverse. This news came in shortly after the maker of Grand Theft Auto, Take-Two, announced it would buy Farmville creator, Zynga, for $13 billion. Post-2021, there has been a record $117 billion worth of acquisitions in the gaming sector. Microchip manufacturers, too, need to make the requisite investments if they are to realize their potential of powering the Metaverse. Around this same time, Intel also announced it would spend $20 billion on two plants in Ohio, with the proviso that this investment could shoot up to $100 billion across eight manufacturing plants if things go according to plan.[19]

Across the world, creators of the Metaverse are in agreement that when it comes to the overarching ethos of the Metaverse, it must ultimately be created for the benefit of people, and that it ought to be humane and deeply human-centric.[20] In principle, this is a noble, inclusive position. But its implementation raises several legal, ethical, security-related and societal questions. How will the inclusive agenda of creators play out against the motive of immediate-term profit maximization, which is bound to arise once full-fledged implementation commences? What checks and balances will be present in the system to avoid unethical scenarios, such as what occurred with Cambridge Analytica? What legal stipulations and processes will be in place to preempt, detect and punish cybercrimes, which may be widely prevalent in the Metaverse? How will general data protection regulation (GDPR) guidelines work in the virtual world to safeguard against discrimination on grounds of race, ethnicity, political opinions, religious or philosophical beliefs? How will the privacy of sensitive and confidential data be preserved? Governments have so far largely distanced themselves from the Metaverse discourse. If this trend continues, what implications does it have for virtual world scenarios that can create cross-border tension? What could be the risks in matters such as national security, maintenance of law and order, and how can they be mitigated in the Metaverse?[21]

These problems will be compounded in an economy such as India, with its Digital Divide, high levels of inequality and economic disparity, and widely heterogeneous population in terms of community, creed and caste. Data security, privacy and lack of capital and infrastructure are usually cited as the impediments in the path of an accelerated rollout of the Metaverse in India. But these overlook a far more fundamental problem. In Chapter Seven, we have gauged how colossal this issue is. Overlooking it will result in a Metaverse that is exclusively of, by and for the privileged, digitally savvy, elite. Any dream of creating an inclusive Metaverse that is as accessible and affordable for the general populace as, say, a basic, functioning cell phone, must take into account the needs, aspirations, challenges and consumption patterns of the economically and educationally weaker sections of society.

THE METAVERSE AND THE FUTURE OF WORK

In this section, we cast a glance at some key aspects where the Metaverse makes a definite impact on the future of work in the more tech-savvy, organized sector globally. Let's start with its effect on the workplace itself. Two years of the pandemic have brought to light the pros and cons of extended periods of remote work. Commute time is undoubtedly saved, and companies make material savings on their overheads, but the sense of belongingness, teamwork, collaboration and, ultimately, motivation and productivity, are all affected in the long run. A hybrid mode of work is now preferred by many companies, where employees work to a roster, working from the office and home on alternate days. With the Metaverse, 'hybrid' attains a new meaning. While occasional visits to a new, smaller workplace might be necessitated, much of the in-person interaction for office work can be replicated through virtual offices.

IT global tech giant Accenture has created a virtual location, called 'Nth floor', under the aegis of the Metaverse Continuum Group, enabling employees to socialize and participate in immersive work and learning experiences. In April 2022, the company announced 1,50,000 new hires, all of whom would work from the Metaverse, using VR headsets starting from the first day. To this end, 60,000 such headsets were deployed in the company's offices across multiple countries. Group chief executive and chief technology officer Paul Daugherty, a Metaverse champion, had himself conducted multiple meetings on Nth Floor.[22]

Such facilities are no longer the preserve of Fortune 500 companies. For instance, India-based company NextMeet offers an immersive platform where digital avatars move between virtual offices, help desks and meeting rooms in real time, deliver live presentations, socialize with colleagues in a virtual lounge, and find seats at a conference centre. Employees access the virtual environment via their desktop computer or mobile device, curate their avatar and use keyboard buttons to navigate the virtual workspace.[23] Virtual offices, digital avatars and colleagues enable ideation and collaboration to remain as effective and accessible as before, in the work-from-office scenario. This allows greater interoperability and is successful in smoothing out many of the issues arising from the mode of remote work witnessed during the first two years of the pandemic.[24]

In this context, avatars—of both real employees and 'digital colleagues'—have a key role to play.

Increasingly, the workplace of the future is likely to include this second category of workers—a range of 'digital colleagues'—which are highly realistic, AI-powered, human-like bots. These will replace the more onerous chatbots, providing a far better user experience for employees and end customers for administrative queries, technical trouble-shooting, real-time assistance on applications, onboarding of new recruits and various other tasks. The underlying algorithm can understand text, voice conversations, converse in natural language, sense and interpret context, show emotions, make human-like gestures, and make decisions. An example is UneeQ, a technology platform that focuses on creating 'digital humans'. The company's creation, Nola, is a digital shopping assistant or concierge for the Noel Leeming stores in New Zealand. SoulMachines, another New-Zealand-based technology start-up, has created lifelike, emotionally responsive digital humans, taking on roles such as those of skincare consultant, COVID health adviser, real-estate agent and educational coach for college applicants.

Learning, development and training is a major area that would be completely transformed by the Metaverse. Digital coaches would be at hand to assist in employee training and providing career advice. In the Metaverse, every object—a training manual, machine or product, for example—could be interactive, providing 3D displays and step-by-step 'how to' guides. Virtual reality role-play exercises and simulations will become common, enabling worker avatars to learn in highly realistic, 'game play' scenarios that can be 'the high-pressure sales presentation', 'the difficult client', or 'a challenging employee conversation'. VR technologies are already being used in many sectors to accelerate skills development.

Surgical technology company Medivis is using Microsoft's HoloLens technology to train medical students through interaction with 3D anatomy models. Embodied Labs has used 360-degree videos to help medical workers experience the effects of Alzheimer's disease and age-related audiovisual impairments to assist in making diagnoses. Bosch and the Ford Motor Company have pioneered a VR training tool using the Oculus Quest headset to train technicians on electric vehicle maintenance. UK-based company Metaverse Learning worked with the UK Skills Partnership to create a series of nine augmented reality training models for front-line nurses in the UK, using 3D animation and AR to test learners' skills in specific scenarios and to reinforce best practices in nursing care. MGM Resorts teamed up with Strivr to give potential employees a chance to try out their jobs in VR before accepting an offer. If someone realizes the job isn't for them, MGM saves time and money by not having to recruit, onboard and train them, only to have them leave the company after a short stint.[25]

Marketing is another important area for the Metaverse. Product manufacturers and service providers can interact with their customer base in a more immersive and visceral way than is currently possible via social media platforms.[26] As technology progresses and the seamlessness of user experience improves, the role of digital humans graduates from concierge to adviser. This may take the form of new subject matter experts (SMEs), endowed with the knowledge of real-life advisers, and with the capacity to process, analyse and interpret masses of information, at a pace and with accuracy surpassing that of humans. In a global, multicultural work environment, API-enabled services, such as Google Translate, may be embedded in digital colleagues who translate speech and text real-time into multiple languages as a meeting progresses. This reduces miscommunication and the chances of things getting 'lost in translation', which often happens in multicultural discussions in the real world.[27]

Digital human technology can be deployed in multiple locations at once. Digital assistants can be deployed to more repetitive, dull or dangerous work in the Metaverse. This purportedly frees up human employees from much of the tedious and repetitive work, engaging them in more creative, value-added work. However, as we have seen in the previous chapters, mass-scale deployment of digital humans also brings with it certain risks, such as increased automation and displacement of human work for lower-skilled workers, who generally have fewer opportunities to move to alternative roles. There is also the possibility of erosion of cultural and behavioural norms. For example, if humans become more disinhibited in their interactions with digital humans, that behaviour could then seep into their interactions and relationships with other people in their real-world lives.

We shall not go into any detailed discussion on specific sectoral impacts of the Metaverse. In many sectors, while the future is full of promise, development on the ground is incipient. On other fronts, things are advancing at such an astonishing pace that any predictions posited now will merely appear to be historical data points, or wide off the mark. It is fair to assume that gaming, e-commerce and trading, technology and product development, education, workplace solutions, communications and customer service, are all industries that may see large-scale application of elements of the Metaverse in the very near future. On the other hand, with the proliferation of virtual real estate properties, travel, tours and entertainment, all replete with virtual-world selfies, mementos and a good dose of the emotions that had accompanied pre-Metaverse vacations and outings, there may well be a dampening of demand for tourism and exotic vacations in the real world. The silver lining is that, with the reduced demand, real-world experiences may once again start to become more affordable for people.

BLOCKCHAIN, CRYPTOCURRENCIES AND NFT

The Metaverse is run on the blockchain technology. Readers would have no doubt noticed several references to blockchain, and to a lesser extent, to cryptocurrencies, in this chapter so far. The nuances involved in these emergent modes and currencies of transaction are highly technical and complex. A detailed discussion of the technological constructs is beyond the purview of this chapter. It would involve, at the least, some projections about their relative volatility or stability in the future, their varied adoption across different sections of demographic groups, society and industry, the potential regulatory requirements that may be mandated in future, the power of governments to ban them (as China has done) and the socioeconomic impacts resulting from their use. Instead, what we'll aim to do in this section is to provide a brief, simple, non-technical outline of blockchain, cryptocurrencies, NFTs and other associated technologies. We will list some advantages as well as challenges in working with these technologies, and offer some anecdotal evidence of how they are impacting the workplace.

Simply phrased, blockchain is a distributed digital ledger or database that stores data of any kind. A blockchain can record information about assets, persons, teams, organizations, as well as financial transactions, such as sales and expenses, using cryptocurrency. Each unique data cluster is a 'block', and linking multiple blocks together makes up the chain. Whenever fresh data is added, a new block is formed and linked to the chain. The key to blockchain is the fact that it works in a decentralized, distributed fashion. Unlike a centralized database (e.g., as used in banks), several identical copies of a blockchain database are held on multiple computers across a vast network, each computer known as a 'node'. Transaction processing is secured using cryptography, involving highly sophisticated mathematical equations. The check in place is that a majority of nodes must validate and approve the new data for it to be added to the ledger. Blocks are securely linked together, forming a digital chain from the beginning of the ledger to the present. In a public blockchain, anyone in the network can view or write the data, with no single authority controlling the nodes. A private blockchain, by contrast, is controlled by an organization or group which decides viewing and editing access.

There are several distinct advantages when it comes to working with blockchain technology. As each transaction needs to be verified by multiple nodes, this reduces the likelihood of error. Also, since every asset is individually tracked on the blockchain ledger, there's no possibility of double-spending it, as in a bank overdrawing. Through the 'smart contract' mechanism in blockchain, two parties, whose identities remain private, can confirm and complete a financial transaction directly, without working through an intermediary (e.g., a bank), resulting in savings of time and charges. The rigorous process of validation, approval and proof-of-work transaction verification methods in cryptocurrency makes it exceptionally difficult, though perhaps not totally impossible, to make fraudulent transactions. Further, the blockchain technologically operates incessantly, on a 24/7 mode. This allows users to make efficient financial and asset transfers, especially internationally, without any lead time for banks, government agencies or other intermediaries to manually confirm the details.

As with any system, there are certain inherent disadvantages as well. By its very process, blockchain relies on a larger network to approve transactions, compared to earlier technological systems. Consequently, there's a limit to the speed with which it can transact. For example, Bitcoin, which we shall discuss presently, can only process 4.6 transactions per second, as opposed to 1500 or more on established banking platforms. A larger load of transactions may lead to network speed issues, impeding scalability. Another challenge with blockchain is its high carbon footprint. Transactions consume significantly more electricity than a single database or spreadsheet. This also results in blockchain transactions being more expensive. In certain cases, digital assets are secured via a cryptographic key. If one loses it, recovery may not be possible, meaning that access to the asset may be gone permanently. Since the system is decentralized, one can't contact a central authority, such as a bank help desk, for assistance to regain access. Moreover, while decentralization accords greater privacy and confidentiality to users, it is likely to attract cyber criminals.[28]

Next, we briefly discuss cryptocurrencies. A cryptocurrency is a peer-to-peer payment system that processes financial transactions digitally, using encryption, with entries being saved in an online blockchain public ledger. The aim of encryption is to provide security and safety. Units of cryptocurrency are created through a process called mining, which involves using computer power to solve complicated mathematical problems that generate coins. Users can also buy the currencies from brokers, then store and spend them using cryptographic wallets. Unlike paper currency or assets in the real world, units of cryptocurrency do not represent any tangible asset. Founded in 2009, Bitcoin was the first cryptocurrency and is still the most widely traded, followed by Ethereum, created in 2015. Litecoin and Ripple are two other cryptocurrencies, also in contention for the burgeoning market. Units of cryptocurrency can be bought with a credit card on mainstream platforms such as PayPal.[29]

Let's first briefly view the advantages of working with cryptocurrency, in what is relatively still an adolescent stage in its evolution. To begin with, the risks for users and investors seem to be adequately compensated by the returns. Prices are determined by the relative supply of coins from miners against purchaser demand. The price of Ethereum, to cite just one example, roughly doubled between July 2021 and December 2021. As mentioned earlier in this section, the underlying technology of blockchain that cryptocurrency uses is essentially secure because of the intricate checks and balances in place.

An entry once made in the blockchain cannot be erased and, owing to its distributed, decentralized structure, no hacker can access the entire chain all at once. Third, compared to the banking system, which has already witnessed major crises and scandals in the last twenty years, the blockchain-cryptocurrency combination offers a more transparent alternative. Fourth, unlike any of the major stock exchanges around the world, with their fixed work times, cryptocurrency works round the clock, on a 24/7 basis. Finally, by design, the total supply of each cryptocurrency is capped. Bitcoin has an overall cap, while for Ethereum it's an annual one. In both cases, the system avoids the inflation that results from artificial increase in supply, as is the case with printing of paper money by governments.

Now, on to the challenges. The most obvious one is the difficulty of mastering its nuances. Unless one is a digital native with an interest or background in finance, the sheer level of the complexities involved can be overwhelming. Second, given the incredibly high returns quoted above, cryptocurrencies are by the nature of their processes highly volatile, making them a less suitable option for investors looking for stable returns. This volatility has severe tax implications as well. Taxes are applicable on the value at the time of the transaction, rather than at the time of tax filing. For example, imagine that a transaction has resulted in earnings amounting to $1,00,000 in cryptocurrency but, due to volatility, the value decreases to $60,000 over a few months. At the time of tax returns, the tax incidence will still be on the original transaction value of $1,00,000. Moreover, unlike the stock markets or age-old tokens of value, such as gold, with their long history of operations, cryptocurrencies have been operational for just a little over a decade, and are yet to prove themselves. Fourth, the intrinsic capacity limitation with blockchain that we noted earlier means that this has a direct dampening effect on the speed and scalability of cryptocurrency transactions. Fifth, working with cryptocurrencies is fraught with its own share of security risks, from losing one's private key to hacking, phishing, and being lured on to apparently bona fide digital currency trading sites designed to defraud the unsuspecting user.[30]

To round off this part of our discussion, let us also look at NFTs or non-fungible tokens. An NFT is a digital asset that represents real-world objects, such as a painting, a sculpture, videos or a piece of antique furniture. Like art, music, in-game items and videos, they are bought and sold online, frequently using cryptocurrency, with the same encryptions and security in place. However, unlike cryptocurrency or paper money, which are fungible, NFTs can't be exchanged for one another. NFTs 'minted' from digital objects, such as art, GIFs and videos, are subsequently held and transacted on a blockchain. An art investor, instead of acquiring an original oil painting, becomes the sole and exclusive owner of a digital painting. Powered by blockchain technology, NFTs empower artists and content creators with a unique opportunity to monetize their wares. They no longer need to rely on galleries to sell their art, and can sell their work directly to the consumer. This eliminates the gallery's intermediary charges and allows the artists to enjoy a greater share of the profits. Artists can also programme in royalties so that they receive a percentage of sales each time their work is sold to a new owner. There is an increasing number of NFT marketplaces, the largest among them being OpenSea.io, Rarible and Foundation.[31]

Some of the key advantages of NFTs, such as wide accessibility and a high level of security, are inherited from blockchain and cryptocurrency. But there are also some others, such as fostering of greater marketplace efficiency. They can streamline processes, eliminate intermediaries, enhance supply chains and bolster trading security. NFTs have certainly created a new market for artists around the world. They provide investors a means of diversifying their portfolios, with the feel-good factor of owning something of unique value. As with other investment classes, there is significant potential for growth in value. Another advantage with NFTs is that they can be used to fractionalize ownership of physical assets. In the real world, dividing assets such as a piece of real estate among multiple stakeholders is a complicated task. Through NFTs, it is relatively easier to divide digitized versions of a building among the owners. Proponents of NFTs envisage their application going far beyond the usual marketplace scenarios. For instance, they could prove to be a secure and efficient means of storing, managing and controlling sensitive records, such as passport details, or organization-specific information, for individuals.

Among the disadvantages, those inherent in blockchain technology and cryptocurrency are carried over to NFTs. These include high energy consumption for transaction processing, which can harm the environment. In fact, at the current rate, it is possible that the carbon emissions from mining cryptocurrencies and NFTs will exceed those associated with the entire city of London. The long-term viability of NFTs, like that of cryptocurrencies, remains to be proven, and NFTs too can be misused by criminals to defraud users in the network. But there are other issues. NFTs, while being volatile, are illiquid and difficult to trade, unlike digital currency. Unlike traditional assets, such as dividend-paying stocks, interest-bearing bonds and rent-generating real estate, NFTs don't generate any income in and of themselves. Like antiques and original paintings, their price depends on their perceived value in the market, and that can be volatile or dampened, especially during economic slowdowns and recessions. All the great expectations around NFTs notwithstanding, the fact remains that they do not constitute an asset class and are essentially a sophisticated technological means of establishing ownership.[32]

To conclude this section, we now outline, under some broad categories, how these new technologies can be applied in the workplace of the future.

Financial transformation

Cryptocurrency offers options that aren't possible with paper money. For instance, programmable money can enable real-time and accurate revenue-sharing while enhancing transparency to facilitate back-office reconciliation. Digital currency enables the enhancement of traditional treasury activities, such as real-time and secure money transfers, strengthening control over the capital of an enterprise, managing the risks and opportunities of engaging in digital investments. The blockchain functionality of self-executing agreements or 'smart contracts' can prove to be a breakthrough move for businesses mired in manual contractual deliberations that lead to delays. Smart contracts are enacted automatically between parties, once their pre-defined conditions are met. For instance, a payment for a good might be released instantly once the buyer and seller have met all specified parameters for a deal. Payees would no longer depend on intermediaries, such as banks, to process their payments. Digital currencies offer an alternative investible, balancing asset to cash, which loses value owing to inflation.[33]

Optimizing production

Bitcoin and other financial applications of blockchain may grab headlines, but companies in the industrial manufacturing sector are also developing innovative commercial solutions based on the emergent technology. And here's the interesting fact: while the forced restrictions of the pandemic may have hastened advancement on this front, this is a trend that had begun earlier. A PricewaterhouseCoopers survey from 2018 shows that 12 per cent of companies in the industrial products and manufacturing sector stated that they had involvement in, or live projects associated with, blockchain technology. Unlike the flamboyant, news-making fashion in which blockchain applications are highlighted in the financial services sector, it may turn out to be a quiet adoption in the case of manufacturing. Besides supply chain monitoring, blockchain is effective when it comes to materials management, assets tracking, identity tracking and engineering design, as well as quality assurance, all of which are relevant to the production of ready-to-ship finished goods.[34]

Supply Chain Monitoring

For a large number of companies, the supply chain poses the biggest challenge in their business, calling for processing of massive amounts of information, and keeping track, not only of movements across state and national boundaries, but also calculating, processing and storing information on tax incidence, together with incidental damages wherever they occur along the way. While with traditional data storage, it is difficult to maintain a real-time audit trail of the movement of goods and the quality of goods at the level of individual shipments, this is possible through blockchain, by involving track-and-trace accelerators to enable monitoring of the supply chain every step of the way, down to the level of individual containers in their respective carriers. With real-time visibility of the status of shipments, the onward delivery process can be planned more efficiently. Moreover, the chances of fraud arising from mileage tampering or tax evasion are also severely curtailed, thanks to the up-to-the-minute transaction audit afforded by blockchain technology.[35]

Empowering Human Resources

According to The State of Talent Acquisition Report 2021, 81 per cent of companies chose virtual platforms to hire talent during the pandemic. Nearly 50 per cent of respondents said they invested in technology and shifted to a virtual, remote hiring system. In the sphere of HR, blockchain can eliminate fraudulent applications with its robust background and employment-history checks. The only thing the recruiters need is a single digital identity. This will also resolve the problem of fake qualifications mentioned in résumés. Owing to the decentralized data stored on the blockchain, there's no place left for hackers to access and corrupt data. The process will save time, by removing the mediators, such as placement agencies, and by accessing, processing and long-listing candidates. Furthermore, smart contracts for employees, as well as for gig workers, can be executed through blockchain, automatically releasing payments from escrow as soon as the professionals complete their assigned tasks.[36] Going forward, a growing number of companies may offer salaries or part of the compensation to their employees in the form of cryptocurrency.[37]

One of the most fascinating ways in which blockchain and associated technologies can transform the way we view work is through the relationship between work and compensation. Imagine that you are a technical architect, expert in product development, as well as in research that can possibly lead to patents for your company. In a world where everything is tracked on blockchain, each line of code that you write, each product specification document you design, each note you develop to support the filing for a patent, can all be viewed and monitored by stakeholders with their relevant access. Now, instead of paying you a salary, it may be possible to compensate you based on the number of times your code or other artefacts are used, as a proportion of the revenue being generated from each such usage. Moreover, blockchain, in combination with NFT-type means of compensation, could allow you to negotiate for 'royalties' for your work. This would mean that instead of receiving a one-time payment for a piece of code, you could be entitled to earning a royalty or commission in perpetuity.

Of course, not all sectors or industries have job roles that are conducive to as granular an identification of tasks and deliverables as software development. However, this example gives us a good idea of the possibilities of reordering the entire relationship between work, worth and compensation in the workplace of the future.[38]

ETHICS AND INTEGRITY IN THE NEW WORKPLACE[39]

The protracted COVID-19 experience has compelled a pace of nimbleness with regard to behavioural unlearning and learning, as well as a revisiting of policies and procedures in response to shifting and unpredictable external situations. Many aspects unheard of in the pre-pandemic ecosystem have become normalized. For instance, the combining of outdoor COVID restrictions with technologically robust workplaces at home, the ability of firms to transition from WFH to Return to Office (RTO) to Hybrid along the slide-rule of working modes, with continuous updates to safety protocols, crisis management SOPs and employee policies.

There is, however, the continued risk involving matters of honesty, ethics and integrity in the emergent workplace. These three constructs collectively denote an intrinsically motivated need to follow set rules, codes of conduct and ethical principles that organizations and their employees take a firm stand to adhere by, irrespective of external circumstances. A case in point is the mandate of providing equal opportunity to all employees, regardless of caste, creed, socioeconomic background, age, gender and/or sexual orientation. The intention behind this is to create a culture of candour and transparency, enabling individual teammates to share feedback with each other or to escalate grievances to the management without fear of retribution or judgement.

Forced remote working and the increasing use of technology in the wake of the pandemic have led to wide-scale digitization of the workplace and its processes and, with it, undoubtedly, greater transparency. For instance, in many organizations, online meetings are recorded. With this approach, compared to the pre-pandemic in-person meetings, all participants, especially managers, are far more aware of the tone, messaging and non-verbal aspects of their own communication at such meetings.

This enhanced transparency notwithstanding, the cumulative result hasn't eradicated the age-old problems of nepotism, bullying, harassment and discrimination. Under certain conditions, a proliferation of these traits can be witnessed. This is because the COVID-19 pandemic not only gave us successive waves of mutations of the virus, but also mutations of workplaces themselves. And, much like the virus, the old issues around honesty, ethics and integrity have also undergone mutations in the new paradigm and therefore have succeeded in slipping under the radar.[40] How, then, does one detect instances of bullying, harassment, discrimination or exclusion? The following are some of the key warning signs (that someone is suffering bullying, harassment or discrimination) that leaders can sensitize themselves towards:

1. Increased absenteeism.
2. Increased criticism in meetings or other group settings.
3. Being singled out, over others, for shortcomings.
4. Being passed over for upcoming projects or roles, without any rational explanation.
5. Being put down in front of the team, by means of derogatory or sarcastic comments.
6. Being heavily micromanaged.
7. Consistent underperformance, quite possibly as a direct outcome of stress.
8. Recurring instances of depression and other mental health issues.

It's important to highlight that sensitization to these factors doesn't necessarily make their identification much easier. If anything, accurate detection and root cause analysis in a remote or online work scenario can be even more of a challenge, compared to what it was in the pre-COVID workplace.

First, the pandemic has brought in tremendous amounts of uncertainty and social disconnect among people. Enforced remote work, social distancing and isolation, wage cuts and job insecurity have exacerbated loneliness, stress and depression. It becomes difficult in many cases to ascertain whether the stress experienced by an employee, even when correctly identified, is due to bullying and discrimination by the manager as opposed to, say, alienation arising from a semi-permanent WFH situation. Second—and this is ironic—the very same technology-reliant new modes of working that have led to greater digitization and transparency can actually inhibit clear means of detection of issues such as discrimination or bullying. Let's illustrate this by considering two items from the list above.

In a pre-pandemic, on-premises scenario, the practice of a clock-in, clock-out system and specific work timings at an employee level, though reminiscent of an assembly-line work ethic, could ensure easy detection of absenteeism. But progressively, with online and WFH models of working becoming the norm, the hours of the day are interspersed with professional and personal tasks, and so the time-specific clock-in, clock-out mechanism no longer works. Further, in situations where several team members participate in meetings, in an 'off camera, mute' mode, even when some people are physically present, the absence of non-verbal cues or even the basic level of energy displayed makes it impossible or difficult to ascertain whether an individual is genuinely engaged in the discussion.

Next, consider mental health in the workplace. Even in an on-premises scenario, identification of something being amiss is exceedingly difficult. The vast majority of HR professionals in organizations, let alone line managers, aren't equipped with the nuances of psychological counselling, therapy or the ability to detect signs of mental ill health in people. However, even to the untrained eye, a sudden dip in someone's performance or energy levels, or their appearing apathetic or sad, is noticeable when interacting with the individual daily, in person. Such an opportunity is lost in an online work scenario. Most companies are still to institutionalize effective EAPs. Even in cases where employees make use of EAP services, there are meagre prospects of in-depth examination of mental health issues leading from the root cause of workplace discrimination or harassment.

The following are measures that may help a company navigate some of these new challenges:

1. Revisit existing company policies and SOPs, especially in the HR domain, and create content to incorporate online behaviours.
2. Chart out online work etiquette.

3. Conduct regular meets and workshops around online workplace bullying, discrimination, harassment, etc., to raise awareness.

4. Conduct regular courses on online ethical work practices, diversity, equity and inclusion, as mandatory training for all employees.

5. Engage psychologists to conduct training for the HR team, to create a greater awareness of mental health issues in the workplace.

6. Manage micro-aggression by discussing its subtle signs, and by encouraging employees to speak up (e.g., through enterprise-wide surveys or on an online platform), so people can communicate their concerns and find solutions together.

7. Provide mental health services to employees, where they can safely and anonymously address their concerns; this can be through EAPs and curated group and individual counselling programmes.

8. Establish a regular cadence of feedback from employees about workplace culture, backed up by a demonstrated commitment to act on serious concerns.

A new code of good online work practices is essential if companies are to create a psychologically safe, inclusive and empathetic work environment in the new paradigm. But this also requires a new mindset among leaders and new frames of reference through which to view the post-COVID workplace.

The discussion above has largely focused on on-premises, remote or hybrid modes of working, all in the real world. With the workplace moving into the Metaverse, the challenge of detecting, preempting and resolving issues of bullying and harassment takes on a new level of complexity. Similar to Accenture's Nth Floor, Microsoft too had acquired and scaled up a virtual location, AltSpace VR, to foster greater and more immersive socialization. However, in February 2022, the company was compelled to enforce security restrictions and monitoring norms, setting up safety bubbles and shutting down certain virtual public hubs in response to complaints of harassment in the virtual world of AltSpace VR.[41] These lessons from early experiments in the Metaverse show that norms and processes for psychological safety, in particular, supportive leadership and organizational practice, are essential for a Metaverse-driven workplace to thrive.

PATTERNS, PRACTICES AND LEGISLATION

Reams have already been written on the way employers, employees and analysts have viewed the impact of continuous disruptions on the emergent workplace. Instead of attempting a fully comprehensive review, we will leave the reader with some captioned notes on some key themes and trends in the workplace.

The 'Great Burning Out'

The Gallup study, State of the Global Workplace 2022 Report, alerts us to some inescapably worrying insights with regard to employee well-being. The global survey-based study found that although the development and delivery of effective vaccines offered hope that the worst of the pandemic was behind us, 1.6 million more people died of COVID-19 in 2021, in addition to the 1.9 million who lost their lives in 2020. Some regions across the world saw signs of partial recovery, but others were significantly worse off than they were in 2020. While 33 per cent of the employees surveyed seemed to be thriving in their overall well-being—one key silver lining—only 21 per cent of the respondents reported that they were engaged at work. The findings or the well-being metrices at the daily level are far more alarming. Forty per cent reported Daily Worry, 44 per cent Daily Stress, 21 per cent Daily Anger, and another 23 per cent stated that they experienced Sadness on a daily basis. We call this state of being of the global employee *The Great Burning Out*.[42]

The Leadership Inaction Trap

In September 2021, PwC led a global survey of around 4000 executives and HR-focused leaders globally. The survey, covering twenty-six countries across twenty-eight sectors, included 210 leaders from India, 51 per cent of whom were business leaders and 49 per cent HR-focused leaders. One of the key findings was that 54 per cent of leaders in India, compared to 33 per cent globally, realize the importance of identifying the skills needed to keep pace with the changing times. They were, however, reluctant to take action for fear of potential consequences. On other fronts, such as anticipating and planning for the future, building trust and optimizing workforce productivity and performance, different reasons are cited for the Indian leaders' inaction, such as costs, digital and infrastructure constraints, culture, and so forth. But, the outcome in all cases is largely the same—lack of immediate and decisive action by leaders. Such inaction will only impede Indian firms and their employees as they attempt to successfully navigate the rapid structural and technological disruptions of the emergent workplace.[43]

End of the Five-Day Work Week?

On 1 July 2022, the Indian government implemented a set of new labour codes, effecting changes in Provident Fund contributions, in-hand salary, leave entitlements as well as weekly working days and hours, the last of these being of immediate interest to us. Under the new rules, companies have the option to change their mode of business operations to a four-day week, but are still required to adhere to the forty-eight working hours per week mandated by law. In such a scenario, employees would need to work for twelve hours on each of the four working days of the week.[44] While time will tell how successful this part of the labour code is, prima facie we see problems with it. Effort and hours put in at work should not be conflated with outcome and quality—this is a cultural change that is needed in the Indian work ethos. Second, diminishing returns to a factor of production has long been accepted as an economic truism. And this particularly applies to work involving critical thinking, analysis and decision-making, requiring higher-order behavioural and cognitive capabilities, when it comes to diminishing returns.

Instead, it would be useful to take a leaf from initiatives in the UK and other economies. For example, Iceland, Spain and New Zealand have all experimented with the four-day work week, reducing working hours from forty to thirty-five or thirty-six hours in a week, with positive changes in productivity. In mid-2022, the UK spearheaded the world's largest forty-hour work scheme, with the universities of Cambridge, Oxford and Boston collaborating with seventy companies, to bring this in to effect. The indications—at the time this chapter was being written—are that this move brings about progressive change in the workplace and improvement in people's mental health and well-being.[45]

Remote/Hybrid Work is Here to Stay

In 2021, Prudential's Pulse of the American Worker survey showed that one in three American workers would not want to work for an employer that required them to be on-site full-time.[46] A Gartner survey in the US conducted the same year reflected a broad consensus among employers on this new mode of operations. Their report found that 82 per cent of employers were willing to allow some proportion of the work to continue remotely, 47 per cent would allow employees to continue working remotely full-time, while 36 per cent were willing to recruit employees who were 100 per cent remote, living anywhere in the US or even internationally.[47] While there are costs in terms of remote working, as we have noted before, on the whole employers have gravitated unequivocally towards the economic benefits of a fully virtual, work-from-anywhere mode of operations, making huge savings in overheads.[48] Interestingly, the inevitability of remote work is accepted even by firms like Gensler, whose core business revolves around the creation of engaging workspaces.[49] There are nuances in the way different organizations and professionals understand hybrid, but a trend towards it in the near future seems to be definite. According to the findings of a 2022 survey by Gallup, nearly 60 per cent of respondents said hybrid is their preferred arrangement, nearly twice the 32 per cent who say they'd like to work remotely all the time.[50]

Goodbye, Middle Manager

In 2019, at a time when no one could have imagined the pandemic, Gartner, looking ahead to 2028, had boldly envisaged the end of the road for the traditional middle manager. It predicted that by then the sheer scale and complexity of businesses would warrant the widespread use of digital avatars, language software, conversational interfaces and real-time dialect translation. A new work philosophy would emerge: 'We Working'. This would encourage companies to create small, autonomous and high-performing teams that form, converge, act and dismantle as the nature and expectations across assignments changed. Leaders would invest in HR-specific algorithms, identifying worker skills and competencies, and optimizing worker-work portfolios. Through enhanced autonomy and trust among colleagues, coupled with behaviourally accurate tools, 'We Working' would significantly reduce the need for the human manager of old, to monitor performance.[51]

The Great Shift

We noted earlier that a trend towards a dual specialism meant there would be a need to learn new skills. As new jobs and occupations come up and many traditional, repetitive jobs give way to automation, this would naturally result in professionals changing their jobs. A McKinsey publication, 'The Future of Work After COVID-19 Report', shows us just how large this shift might be. In its pre-pandemic estimate, only 6 per cent of workers were expected to find jobs in higher-wage occupations. In the post-COVID-19 paradigm, not only would a larger share of workers need to transition out of the lowest wage brackets but roughly 50 per cent of them would require new, advanced skills in order to move to these higher-paid jobs. Overall, as much as 25 per cent more workers might need to switch occupations than before the pandemic. The skill mix required for the shift has also changed. For instance, in India, the share of total work hours expended using physical and manual skills will decline by 2.2 percentage points, while time devoted to technological skills will rise 3.3 percentage points.[52]

The Social Sector in Focus

In 2019, the World Bank published a report, The Changing Nature of Work. Among its recommendations was strengthening of social protection through assistance, inclusion and regulation, creation of a new social contract and financing of social inclusion.[53] As we have seen, rising inequality, widening polarization and declining social mobility have been some of the effects of the global COVID-9 pandemic in the short term. The need for a social contract is now sharper than ever before. In May 2022, a World Economic Forum white paper urged investments in the social sector as a key strategy for economic recovery, post the pandemic. According to this document, investments in three foundational social institutions—education, healthcare and care—can restart the engine of social mobility across economies. Taking the example of the US, every dollar of investment would deliver a multiplier effect of 2.3 times. Most jobs created as a result would be in teaching (4.2 million), followed by personal care and service (1.8 million workers), and healthcare (0.9 million professionals), with a corresponding increase in real wages at the same time.[54]

The New CXOs

The trend of dual specialism—technical and domain skills on the one hand, human-centric skills on the other—has seen a new set of designations, roles and job opportunities coming up for leaders. We'll mention one at each end of the spectrum. In an increasingly technology-driven workplace, the office of the chief security information officer (CISO) will only gain in importance as time passes. Typically, the CISO is tasked with establishing cybersecurity as a value enabler, building relationships of trust with other functions in the organization, evaluating the effectiveness of the cybersecurity function and updating the cybersecurity capabilities of the firm.[55] At the other, human-focused end of the spectrum is the chief philosophy officer. Employee engagement, compensation and compliance falls to the traditional lot of HR, but it needs a completely different orientation to reimagine possibilities for the firm's vision, mission, culture and the values that it wants to be known for—hence the need for a chief philosophy officer.[56]

Diversity, Equity and Inclusion (DEI)

As we have seen earlier, while the peaks of the Great Resignation may plateau out, employees/candidates with the right skills will continue to have the upper hand over employers, compelling them to create policies and processes that are more transparent and empathetic, and demanding a fresh focus on critical aspects. In the wake of the pandemic, DEI has emerged as being one of the biggest such areas. However, acknowledgement is not the same thing as action. As a 2021 Society for Human Resource Management (SHRM) report shows, 86 per cent of US employers wished to recommit to corporate culture and values in the coming year, and 82 per cent stated they would practise inclusive hiring and promotion. However, only half to two-thirds, depending on country, had actually taken concrete steps on the ground, such as increasing leadership diversity, calibrating benefits to foster inclusion, or organizing an inclusion event.[57] In India too, as the PwC 2021 'Hopes and Fears Survey' shows, CEOs believe that diversity and inclusion are important for an organization's success in the future, but employee experiences tell a different story, with 72 per cent of the respondents saying that they had experienced discrimination at their workplaces and had lost out on opportunities for career progression.[58]

Now, as we near the end of the book, it is worthwhile to take a step back from all the reports, trends, projections and data, and focus on a critical question. Who or what is—or ought to be—the final beneficiary of all the technological and methodological advancements, all the insights and findings?

This takes us right back to Harari's statement, which we critiqued at the beginning of the chapter: 'Dataism is most firmly entrenched in its two mother disciplines: computer science and biology. Of the two, biology is the more important.' If the answer, as we worryingly stated earlier, is 'computer science', then clearly the beneficiaries are the consumers and users of increasingly complex sets of information, a highly evolved, super-intelligent, digitally powered working cohort that is a tiny fraction of the employable global population, serving the needs of corporations. If, however, there is truly to be a choice in the matter for all of us, the answer needs to be the 'biological'—in other words, the human.

In the final analysis, no matter how fast Work and the Workplace continue to self-disrupt or reinvent themselves, they ought to be anchored to the Worker, the human. Bringing the human dimension back to the centre of the equation will, sooner rather than later, effect a change in the way that leading companies and their small, elite workforce think about business and its benefits. The economic efficiency arising due to automation would then be balanced against the anxieties and hardships of people likely to be displaced by such automation. Employers instructing whole sections of their workforce to shift to permanent remote working might stop to ponder the human costs of their decision—loneliness, disconnectedness, lack of belongingness. And the shapers of the imminent Metaverse might think of safeguards that protect users emotionally and psychologically—not simply against fraud—as prerequisites for deploying their platforms.

The future may indeed be infused with possibilities and benefits beyond our present imagination. But it would need to be a human-centric future.[59]

Conclusion

'Things fall apart; the centre cannot hold'

—W.B. Yeats, *The Second Coming*

Yeats wrote these disturbing words in 1919, when the world, burdened with a sense of utter devastation after the end of the First World War, was struggling to find new meaning. A hundred years on, technology, healthcare, education, and the basic amenities of life have all advanced in immense measure. However, in the wake of the global pandemic crisis, and faced with new challenges, including geopolitical conflicts, economic uncertainties, and fears of a fresh global recession—at a personal, human level, we find ourselves in an eerily similar situation. Much of what we knew, the way we thought of going about our lives, of working and interacting with others, have all changed irrevocably. There is no fixed centre, no formulaic set of answers or magic method to hold on to as we grapple with our daily uncertainties.

We have covered much ground in our book, and the anecdotes, tables, figures that we've presented have yielded a variety of findings and recommendations. Across all these, though, there's a common theme emerging—the story of relentless change. As we have seen, there are three levers of this change. First, the speed of disruption and the unpredictability of the pace of change itself. Second, the all-pervasive breadth and depth of change—impacting the economy, businesses, society and people. And, leading from the second, the transformative effect of change on systems—political, economic and social. These three levers of change, which collectively characterize the Fourth Industrial Revolution or Industry 4.0, have been driven to a state of high acceleration by the pandemic experience. What we shall see in the next section is that they are likely to work in directions that are anti-human-centric, if the levers of change are left entirely to themselves.

THE TROUBLE WITH INDUSTRY 4.0

To pursue this line of inquiry, let us go over the broad themes, in the sequence that we have presented them in our book. First, consider technological advancement and its impact on employment, which we examined in Chapter Two. Such an advancement, we have learnt, can be through multiple modes—AI, automation, robotics, or even some sophisticated combination of these modes. Now, it is undeniable that in many cases across sectors, the application of robotics and automation has been beneficial and not just to companies in terms of lower operational costs. For instance, the use of robotics in packing, lifting and transportation/delivery of goods has been invaluable in reducing the risk of infection in a pandemic scenario. Robotics cleaning a hospital ward, in lieu of human cleaners, would likewise substantially reduce risk of infection. However, the issue is that if these practices become the longer-term norm post the pandemic, their impact on employment prospects for low-skilled human workers is likely to be highly adverse, especially in the absence of any inbuilt mechanisms to reskill those displaced by automation and robotics.

Next, consider the emergent jobs in the workplace, which we examined in Chapter Three. If we take the WEF report as a benchmark, with the sole exception of a job role relating to business development, the other nine of the top ten emerging jobs are all technology-centric. In conjunction with this, all the major job roles that are declining in demand are either human-centric (managers) or labour-intensive (clerks) in nature. The net effect of these dual forces, the waxing and waning of demand for certain job roles, is likely to converge into a situation where certain pockets of specialized job openings that are unfulfilled coexist with large cohorts of the workforce whose skills are growing less relevant in the workplace. This, in turn, indicates a fundamental mismatch of skills in emerging job roles, sectors and domains, on a macroeconomic scale. There is nothing inherent in the market forces, or in the way the levers of change have been observed to function, that naturally aids the reskilling of low-skilled workers or those whose work experience and capabilities have become, or may soon be, rendered obsolete.

So, let us turn to the skills of the future workplace, which we explored in Chapter Four. What emerged clearly from it is that there is a growing need for a new dual specialism of skills—those related to technology/technical/domain-specific knowledge, and also a second cluster of skills that is quintessentially human-centric. In mapping this dual specialism back to the emergent job roles, you may have come across an apparent disconnect. From data analysts to cybersecurity specialists and programmers, there is a rapid spurt of technical jobs emerging in the market. However, there is no significant influx of purely behavioural or human-centric jobs. After all, there is no imminent flurry of emotional regulators or mindfulness specialists in the workplace. Newly minted designations (e.g., chief ethics officer, happiness officer, and chief philosophy officer) are outliers—too few and far between to be numerically significant. The same is true of creative leadership tags that start-ups invent all the time, and subsequently, are all too often forgotten. This begs the basic question: if the very large majority of all emergent jobs are likely to be technical in nature, why would there be a growing need for behavioural skills at all, alongside the emergent technical skills?

A normative answer would be that skills, such as emotional intelligence, mindfulness and optimism, enhance well-being and are therefore important in their own right, regardless of any gains in productivity they might yield. A second, more business-focused response is that they are critical for leadership, to design and execute their various employee-centric initiatives. There's also a third answer. In light of the dual specialism of skills, while opportunities in new sectors (e.g., the green economy) open up, others are phased out. This often creates a situation where a very high, almost overwhelming, level of expectations is set upon professionals. Take the IT sector as an illustration. Two or three decades ago, there were three groups of people—those that wrote code (programmers), those that devised or reviewed it (architects), and those that managed all the people (managers). However, as the role of the generic (or generalist) manager gets phased out over time, the job of managing the programmers falls upon the architect. If the technical architect is not equipped, either by formal education or the nature of his prior experience, to handle complex human-centric problems, the gap in behavioural skills will be felt all the more acutely. Such a sequence of events isn't human-centric: it benefits neither the overwhelmed technical architect nor the increasingly dissatisfied programmers in his team.

Let us move on to research, innovation, education, and their relationship with productivity—the main subject of our investigation in Chapter Five. In terms of their vision, many initiatives across the world, especially with regards to education, can be said to be human-centric. In the West, the change in thinking to broaden education beyond STEM and include the arts and humanities as part of curricula is a welcome step. Likewise, the programme of the National Education Policy 2020 in India, to develop multidisciplinary curricula and a new set of universities that champion such curricula, as well as to foster greater engagement between public and private schools, is praiseworthy. However, the implementation of such initiatives has been dealt a devastating blow by the pandemic. Protracted periods of lockdown and restrictions on mobility have accelerated the use of technology and online platforms in education. At the same time, it has also brought to sharp light a widening Digital Divide and the challenges in disseminating education across different socioeconomic segments of students. Inadvertent as this may have been, the combination of internet connectivity, digital devices, infrastructure and technological skills as a prerequisite for obtaining education in an online mode has regrettably turned education itself into being more elitist and non-inclusive.

Now, let us turn to the matter of mental health, which we examined in Chapter Six. On this front, the effect of the levers of change have been shattering. Of course, no one could have predicted the pandemic, or the pace of its outbreak across the world when it first came to light in January 2020. But, over the next two years, extended lockdowns and enforced restrictions on mobility, institutionalized WFH regimes, fears and misinformation about the vaccines, and new, unpredictable variants of the COVID-19 virus, combined to unleash upon the world a mental health pandemic it was totally unequipped to handle. In the personal sphere, as well as in the workplace, it brought mental health conditions into the open. For the first time, globally, the issue of mental health has come to be recognized as something that can no longer be brushed under the carpet or dealt with by denying its magnitude or by living in denial of it altogether. In the workplace, mental health and psychological safety have finally entered the boardroom. The ubiquity of mental health issues and the pressing need to enhance resources around counselling, treatment and care have come to the fore. However, all this has come at the cost of unimaginable anguish and suffering. And, even today, in spite of widescale awareness, not nearly enough is being done to address the mental ill health phenomenon, be it at the workplace or beyond.

In Chapter Seven, we attempted to take a hard, unflinching look at the current state of inequality across the world. We have seen the dramatic and unambiguously adverse effect of the pandemic on the level of inequality, as well as the extent of the divide between the affluent and the marginalized. Far from the pandemic being the equalizer that placed us all in the same boat, we saw how unequal the pandemic experience had been for different sections along the socioeconomic spectrum, from vaccine awareness, to availability, administration, treatment and patient care. In academia, there has been a tradition going back decades that focuses on ecological balance, equitable distribution of wealth and poverty alleviation, as opposed to unbridled growth. However, this has always been sidelined in the face of the dominant mode of economic thought, which is obsessed with sustained growth. Rising inequality across the globe and within economies has continued to be condoned, as long as it delivered the requisite growth numbers. This, of course, is an anti-human-centric practice, but one that has enjoyed wide patronage among economists, policymakers and legislators.

Finally, in Chapter Eight, we outlined the Metaverse which, according to many market experts, industry leaders and even philosophers, defines the way we will lead much of our lives, at work and otherwise, in the future. We traced the truly remarkable array of technologies, supporting and buoying each other, to imagine new possibilities for us. However, here too, we have noticed that there is nothing intrinsic in the ethos or algorithm of the Metaverse that mandates processes that safeguard the privacy, financial security or psychological safety of users. Already, the evidence is clear. Unless specifically regulated, or a suitable system of checks and balances put in place, fraud, identity hacking or theft, bullying, harassment, discrimination (and more) will continue in the Metaverse, albeit in an altered form from what it is in the real world. In the final section of the chapter, we listed some of the key trends of the workplace, among them the leadership inaction trap, the phasing out of the middle manager, and the great shift of professionals as they transition out of their current jobs and occupations. Such shifts are fraught with anxiety, tension and unpleasantness for the agents undergoing them. But there is nothing in the process that warrants alleviation of the insecurity or discomfort of all these people. There is no cause for the system to be human-centric, by design.

Social scientists, in particular economists, are said to be obsessed with causality. What we are concerned about here, though, is the net effect of the forces of change that underpin Industry 4.0. We are not about to suggest that there is some sinister global conspiracy at work, resolved to remove the human worker from the workplace, skew jobs continuously towards automation and robotics, or destroy the marginalized and impoverished. However, across all of the different themes that we have explored, what comes across unambiguously is that, unless acted upon or regulated, the levers of change will naturally drive market forces and the ecosystem of work, worker and workplace, in a direction that is disadvantageous to the human worker (i.e., in ways that are anti-human-centric). And, as we have seen throughout our discussions, there are three principal agents that can engage with the levers of change: institutions (primarily government bodies), firms, and individuals themselves. At various points in the book, we have pointed out the initiatives made by leading government agencies as well as individual companies, aimed at enhancing well-being. However, our big thrust has been to focus on the responsibility of the individual to be more acutely aware of the changing ecosystem and begin to take charge of her own career and well-being.

THE FIRST INNER REVOLUTION

As regards the question of how the individual should cope with violent shifts in circumstances, external conditions as well as emotional and psychological pressures, our position is very definite. The current disruptions across the world are of a scale, pace and quantum that are quite unprecedented in human history, and this rate of change is very likely to continue in the foreseeable future. Governments and organizations, both grappling with the sheer pressure of these changes, have begun to formulate, and even undertake, transformative measures, more in some economies and sectors than in others. But, even if all these well-intentioned initiatives were to be perfectly executed, they would still be inadequate in insulating the individual against the shifting challenges that disruptions will continue to bring up. It is, therefore, incumbent upon every individual to take up the challenge and find means of transitioning from a state of constant coping to that of successfully navigating change. The transformation that we are advocating is needed is mass-scale, swift, drastic and urgent. We shall call it the First Inner Revolution—or IR 1.0.

This coinage is not arbitrary. From the time of the drastic changes brought about as a direct result of the First Industrial Revolution, humans have been dealing and coping with transformative change brought about by technological disruptions, and economic as well as geopolitical upheavals. Yet, this is the first time when so many around the world are impacted in the same way by the force, velocity and direction of the relentless onslaught of changes. A conscious decision on the part of a large mass of people globally to take a deeper look at the experience of their lives, working conditions, aspirations and fears, and resolving to take concrete steps to improve their own well-being, will necessarily be a first of its kind. Much of the work involved in the transformation process is deeply emotional, psychological, and all of it deeply personal—hence, inner. From a psychological standpoint, 'locus of control', a term we encountered while discussing emergent behavioural skills in Chapter Four, becomes paramount. In particular, the internal locus of control—the belief that the individual can determine her own life and work environments and events, sustained by deep conviction and a sense of purpose in life, emerges as a key tool in IR 1.0.

For each individual, the transformative experience will be a revolution in the true sense of the term. It is decisive and it marks a distinct break with the past, in terms of attitudes, mindsets and beliefs about the world around us and about ourselves. Another critical element in any successful revolution is speed. With changes in the external world occurring at such a frenetic speed, there is little luxury for charting out a multi-year plan that would prepare you for a future that's already knocking at the door. The work for IR 1.0 has to be executed as swiftly as possible. The power of a successful revolution is the collective force of the mass of people involved in it, gathering in town squares, marching through the streets in solidarity or storming the bastions of oppressive regimes. In IR1.0, too, the force of the collective can be harnessed, not in individual towns but globally, and using technology and communication. Learning from the experiences of others, sharing tips, coaching others, and being coached by those further down the path, the ability to achieve all of this is possible—through digital platforms, progress bulletins, discussion forums and groups, set up for the purpose of sharing and encouraging one another.

There is an array of behavioural capabilities, covered in Chapter Four, most of which, sooner rather than later, would prove useful in IR 1.0. However, a few of them are of immediate need. The first of these is to develop a Sense of Stillness. In the face of daily information overflow, we try to up the ante by consuming more information, on the go, commuting to work, or during a quick dinner, or as a ritual first thing in the morning. We fill our waking hours with increasing activity and longer checklists, at times to breaking point. The ambitious and affluent among us plan for that special vacation, when we shall go completely 'off the hook', being solely with ourselves in the midst of pristine natural surroundings. A vacation, when it occurs, passes all too swiftly, leaving one anxious and wistful. This is what we must realize. The one still point in this turning world is to be found within each one of us—to be sought again and renewed each time we lose sight of it. Developing the Sense of Stillness is indispensable for allowing ourselves that crucial time for rejuvenation.

The second attribute is Overcoming Fear. We use the term not as denoting the grip of emotion in a sudden and terrible life-changing moment, but in a broad sense, to include tensions and anxieties, as well as our reactions in situations of crises. The constant sense of tension is palpable in the many things that we do under pressure, often to our own detriment. In an economic downturn, we panic and sell stocks at a loss, fearing further declines instead of waiting out the rough patch. We fear we might lose our jobs, and the incessant stress may make us behave in certain ways that may end up damaging our position in the firm. We fear that our work-related skills are fast becoming obsolete, so we enrol ourselves concurrently in a bunch of courses, and then struggle to keep up with the workload. This sense of fear stunts free, critical thinking and drives us into immediate action in ways that we may later regret. On the other hand, being able to overcome one's fears opens one's mind to possibilities in life which wouldn't have been apparent otherwise.

The third is Future-Mindedness. Here too, we are using this term in the broad and inclusive sense, to subsume hope, optimism, open-mindedness and a sense of curiosity and openness about the world. Overcoming despair, dejection, a sense of failure and unworthiness is absolutely necessary if one wishes to move ahead in life. However, removal of sadness transitions the individual from a state of intense negativity to at best an emotional ground zero. But it does not provide the psychological or emotional impetus to look forward to the future with a sense of positive expectation, while at the same time preparing oneself for the many challenges that may lie ahead. Future-Mindedness is not some passive belief that things will work out for the best. It is active expectation of the best outcomes in the future, and about the renewing of that belief time and again. It is the conviction that one's preferred outcomes can truly be brought about in reality and, in tandem, one can take concrete steps in order to achieve them.

The fourth is Resilience. This has been covered in some detail in our discussion in Chapter Four, so what we shall do here is to go over the salient points again. To begin with, we must appreciate that resilience, even in the psychological sense of the term, is not just applicable at a purely personal level, but also at the team, department or organizational level. As a leader, manager or team member, it is important to understand and develop the components of personal resilience before focusing on workplace resilience. With regard to the latter, remember that it is not a single, monolithic skill but the combined effect of a range of skills and attributes. And that, subsequently, different skills can be called upon at will, based on the situation at hand. For instance, faced with a sudden crisis at work, stress management becomes immediately critical. However, in a scenario where business is growing, demonstrating workplace resilience still continues to be helpful—for instance, in interacting cooperatively with colleagues and collaborators, nurturing relationships with stakeholders and key customers, and focusing on living more authentically. Resilience is not to be rummaged out of the behavioural cupboard only in times of dire crisis. It is a set of skills for all seasons. Finally, resilience can be nurtured within the workplace, not only through training and coaching interventions but also organically, by creating a congenial atmosphere and a culture of positive emotions.

The fifth critical attribute comprises Letting Go and Renewal. Difficult as the other attributes doubtless are, developing and demonstrating this specific duo of capabilities can be quite a challenge. Leaving an organization where you've made friends can certainly pull at the heartstrings, but 'moving on' isn't 'letting go'. On the other hand, imagine building a team, department or company, up from scratch and making it successful. To create a new design, system or process you had immersed yourself in and then having to let go of it would be difficult. It is never easy to let go of a project or venture where one has met with setbacks, delays or failure. In certain cases, it could be harder still to let go where one has been particularly successful, because it is strongly attached to our ego, self-esteem and sense of achievement. We get emotionally attached to them and feel proprietorial. And yet, to sustain success in the Inner Revolution, letting go is precisely what may be required, time and again, as this will set the stage for renewal, for imagining new and greater roles, projects, ventures and possibilities. In certain instances, this may take the more forceful form of creative destruction, which we have discussed early in the book.

The attributes outlined above do not come in binary states of 'achieved' and 'not achieved', but rather as notches along a long slide rule of development. There is no absolute state, upon attaining which no further attention is required to that attribute. As we have already noted, developing a behavioural skill is a process that warrants time, energy and emotion, and there are no shortcuts to success. It's just that we urge the process to commence *now*.

What would be the workings of the Inner Revolution, and what would be some of the benefits for an individual? We have provided a flavour of this in Chapter Four, where we discussed a method by which each individual can converge to the combination of sector/domain/job-role/skills that one should focus on in the near future. Developing the necessary behavioural attributes gives you greater focus, clear-sightedness and poise. Consequently, it is likely that the specific skills basket that you arrive at, and the decisions you take, will be more authentic and beneficial than if you were undertaking the exercise in haste, in a state of great stress. For practitioners of the Inner Revolution, the possibilities that open up for them at a personal level can be immense.

THE SENSE OF AN ENDING

There are very few definite, cast-iron answers in a project such as ours. For each of the key themes, we have presented data and anecdotes, and have suggested specific frameworks, methods or leading practices that may be followed. All these recommendations themselves are indicative, and should be revisited, questioned and calibrated, depending on the specific situation you find yourself in. Markets will continue to change and, with this, associated skills, jobs, sectors and domains will all self-disrupt. In the same way, the specific stressors, challenges, anxieties and opportunities that one encounters will keep changing with great swiftness. The answers cannot remain immutable. What will, we hope, continue to be helpful, is the process by which we have arrived at those answers. So, a specific framework for enhancing psychological safety may not be a perfect fit in a system where almost all of the work and interactions are taking place in the Metaverse. However, our method for devising such a framework remains pertinent and can be used to formulate new frameworks. What we have offered are *ways of looking* at emergent problems related to the workplace.

This tells us a few important things, not only about the recommendations and suggestions that we have offered, but also about the scope and effectiveness of work-focused solutions in general, going forward. First, that there will be no quick and easy solutions to the big questions that the ecosystem may face in the future. Likewise, that it would be nearly impossible, if not totally futile, to attempt to design a mother-of-all system, model or handbook that aims to resolve all major categories of problems in the emergent workplace. And third, that today's solutions to even a very specific workplace problem will not necessarily hold in the future. In fact, there are not likely to be lasting or permanent solutions of any kind, with regard to the work, worker and workplace of the future. Leaders, supervisors and junior personnel have to reconcile themselves to a new reality where they will be required to design, implement and adhere to new solutions and processes with increasing frequency. As this becomes the norm, it may lead to a sense of incompleteness, of unfinished business, pervading most aspects of our lived experiences. In fact, you may be feeling so already.

If experiencing such feelings is expected to be a regular part of our lives, how are we to cope? What leading practices should we follow? The first question takes us to the attributes required for the Inner Revolution that we outlined in the previous section, in particular Letting Go and Renewal. As for the second question, we could, as advisers and economists are rather fond of doing, attempt to formulate a new framework, made to measure. Instead, we will leave you with a little story that may be just as illuminating.

In Kolkata, formerly Calcutta, where both of us authors are originally from, there is a great tradition of intricately crafting clay idols of gods and goddesses. In terms of faith and festivities, none is greater than the Goddess Durga. In the old and dingy by lanes of *Kumortuli*—literally, Potter's Lane—across 450 workshops is where the magic happens. At first, a mixture of bamboo sticks and straw is used to make the basic frame on which the idol will be modelled. Next, the framework is coated with layers of soft clay. Two different forms of clay, *entel mati* (sticky black clay) and *Ganga mati* (soft white clay from the riverbed) combine to form that supple material with which the idol is shaped. Dried under the sun, the idol assumes its final contours, and then layers of paint are applied. Hair, robes, ornaments, weapons and decorations are added to her person. Finally, the eyes are painted in.

Then the festival begins. Four days and nights of uninterrupted lights, prayer, laughter, song and merriment. The *kumor*, stepping out of obscurity into the blinding stage lights, is felicitated, celebrated, featured in the media and nominated for competitions where handsome cash prizes are handed out. More than 10 million people, dressed in their finest, pour out on to the streets and into the pandals where the Goddess smiles her benediction upon her devotees. Then, on the fifth day, with grand pageantry, the idols are borne to the riverside. There, to the blowing of conch shells and chants, the idols are respectfully, lovingly, immersed in the holy Ganga. The devotees return home, distribute sweetmeats and embrace, marking the conclusion of the festival. The smile of the Goddess melts away into the waters. The *kumor* prepares for fresh inspiration for the coming year.

Letting Go and Renewal. Living in Creation. This is the most meaningful and constructive advice that we could hope to offer. The findings, methods, tools and practices we have presented—the bamboo and straw—are already at your disposal. As are the bright colours with which you can craft your future. And that magic clay is wet and ready.

Acknowledgements

Although the writing of the book commenced well into the pandemic in 2020, it was originally commissioned in 2018. We would like to thank former Penguin Random House editor Lohit Jagwani, as well as our literary agent Priya Doraswamoy, both now friends, for helping shape the original conception of the book, and especially Milee Ashwarya, for believing in this project from the very start.

While this was a considerable undertaking, we have had the advantage of an excellent team of researchers and associates. Pre-eminent amongst these has been Samiratu Wahab, who provided invaluable research notes across the manuscript, in particular for Chapter 3. Amy Burrell and Jo Baker read the entire manuscript and sense-checked chapters, but also picked up several inconsistencies and typos. Shikha Kakkar assisted with the references to various business publications and case studies. Tamoghna Bose helped with cross-checking references and compilation of endnotes. Manish Kumar, who edited our book, has been a constant source of support and encouragement. Shreya Mukherjee provided excellent copy-editing and made the text read sharper. Yash Daiv, along with associates in the marketing team, shaped the book into a state of completion. Leah Fitzsimmons provided a fountain of ideas which we hope will bring the book's insights to a wider audience. The authors take responsibility for any errors or omissions that remain.

Books such as *Work 3.0*, which dare to gaze into the future, can benefit immensely from the review of experts—and in this, we have been extremely fortunate. A host of very eminent and exceptionally busy people spent time to read the manuscript, offer comments and endorse the book. We are grateful for their help. In (alphabetical order) they are:

- Adrian Tan, podcast host at Channel NewsAsia
- Anuradha Kedia, co-founder of The Better India
- Aubrey Blanche, senior director of Equitable Design, Product & People, Culture Amp and founder-CEO of The Mathpath
- Bhaskar Chakravorti, dean of Global Business, The Fletcher School of Law & Diplomacy, Tufts University; chairman of Digital Planet and former partner at McKinsey and Company
- Bibek Debroy, chairman at Economic Advisory Council to the Prime Minister
- Catherine Cassell, professor and executive dean of Durham Business School
- Clara Mattei, The New School, author of *The Capital Order: How Economists Invented Austerity and Paved the Way to Fascism*
- Daniel Nath, Google, *Forbes* 30 Under 30 Asia; Global Shaper, World Economic Forum; former founder of Cybersecurity SaaS venture
- David Lloyd, police and crime commissioner for Hertfordshire
- Dipesh Chakrabarty, Lawrence A. Kimpton Distinguished Service professor of history, South Asian languages and civilizations, and the College, University of Chicago; winner of the Arnold Toynbee Prize

- Dr Maha Hosain Aziz, NYU MA IR professor and author of *Future World Order* (2020) and sequel *Global Spring: Predictions for a Post-Pandemic World* (2022)
- Eddie Kane, professor and director of Centre for Health and Justice, Nottingham University
- Gurcharan Das, author and former CEO, Procter & Gamble India
- Hisham Mehanna, professor of head and neck surgery, deputy pro-vice chancellor (interdisciplinary research), director of The Institute for Global Innovation (I.G.I.) & the Institute for Advanced Studies (I.A.S), University of Birmingham
- Jim Harter, chief scientist of Workplace Management and Wellbeing at Gallup
- Joanne Duberly, professor of organisational studies, deputy pro-vice chancellor (equality, diversity and inclusion), University of Birmingham
- Joey Uppal, director of Global Faculty Network at EMERITUS Executive Education
- Jon Parry, head of research, Skills for Justice Research
- Kate Field, global head of health, safety and well-being at British Standards Institution
- Khursheed N. Khurody, chairman of Shivia Livelihoods Foundation; managing committee member of Seva Sadan Society
- Krishnan Srinivasan, former foreign secretary of India
- Krusha Sahjwani Malkani, director of Sociabble; co-founder of The Pink Thread; LinkedIn 2022 Top Voice
- Luis Miranda, chairman of Indian School of Public Policy, Centre for Civil Society, CORO India, and senior adviser, Morgan Stanley
- Mohan S. Gundeti, professor of paediatric urology (surgery) and MFM (Ob/Gyn) and paediatrics, The University

of Chicago Medicine & Biological Sciences; director
Paediatric Urology, Comer Children's Hospital
- Ng Hooi, author, president of Malaysian Association of
Certified Coaches
- Paul Abraham, president of Hinduja Foundation; board
member, former COO of IndusInd Bank
- Prerna Mukharya, founder of Outline India; Fortune 40
under 40; Chevening fellow
- Prof. Jonathan Passmore, Henley Business School, and
SVP Coaching, CoachHub, the digital coaching platform
- Pushpak Kypuram, co-founder and director at NextMeet®,
India's First Metaverse for Meetups
- Raghavendra Hunasgi, Global Shaper, World Economic
Forum, chief adviser at UN, TED speaker, bestselling
author and branding leader
- Ram Gopal, chief executive officer at Barclays Bank India
- Rick Smith, professor and vice dean of education &
partnerships at Carey Business School, Johns Hopkins
University; former partner and managing director,
Accenture Singapore
- Rudra Sensarma, professor of economics and former
dean, research, innovation and internationalization at IIM
Kozhikode
- Sachin Lulla, EY Principal and Americas Consulting
Sector leader
- Sanghamitra Bandopadhyay, director of Indian Statistical
Institute and Padma Shree Awardee
- Sankarshan Basu, dean of Ahmedabad University and
former professor at IIM-Bangalore
- Sarah Nadav, behavioural economist; senior strategist at
World Economic Forum Expert Network and LinkedIn
Top Voice
- Shantanu Rooj, founder of TeamLease Edtech

- Soumitra Dutta, Peter Moores Dean and professor of management at Saïd Business School, University of Oxford
- Steve Cadigan, LinkedIn's First CHRO; PeopleHum Top 200 Global Thought Leader; Future of Work Keynote speaker, author
- Subir Verma, head HR at T&D Companies, Tata Power and author of the bestselling book *Job Search Secrets*
- Sudipto Banerjee, professor and chair of the Department of Biostatistics, UCLA and 2022 president of the International Society for Bayesian Analysis
- S.V. Nathan, chief people officer at Deloitte India, and national president of the National HRD Network
- Tanmay Bandyopadhyay, senior vice president of technology and digital at AmerisourceBergen (US Fortune 10 Healthcare Delivery Corporation)
- Tirthankar Roy, professor of economic history, London School of Economics
- Vikash Dash, ET 40 under 40; Fortune 40 under 40; Britannica 20 under 40; World Financial Review's Top 10 Financial Inclusion Heroes Globally and World Economic Forum Global Shaper.

Many of those listed above have also provided their views and recommendations as part of the interviews that we conducted. Besides them, there are others who have also enriched the quantum of knowledge that the book contains: Dr Jai Ranjan Ram, psychiatrist, columnist and founder of the Mental Health Foundation; Dr Vinay Mishra, psychologist, author and professor at the Bhopal School of Social Sciences; and Premkumar Seshadri, business leader, investor and healthcare growth strategist. We thank them wholeheartedly for their insights.

Finally, we would like to express our personal thanks to our families and friends.

For Avik, the extended stretches of social restriction throughout the pandemic were reinforced by a second layer of self-imposed seclusion, as work on the book got under way. He would often disappear into his room for several days of non-conversation, his phone off the hook, resurface, light-footed, as one does after a long illness, and on being asked about his reticence, say something to the effect of 'I've been trying to think about work.' Avik would like to thank his parents, Barun and Manjusree Chanda, as well as Shikha Kakkar and all his close friends who bore this temperament with good humour, patience and encouragement.

Sid would like to thank his parents Banshi Bandopadhyaya (who sadly did not live to see the book completed; his immense curiosity about the world and constant probing led Sid to think more deeply and move beyond his comfort zone) and Chandana Bandopadhyaya for their constant encouragement in his life journey and for their interest in the book. Among friends whose helped shape the book through informal chats, he is especially grateful to Rob Lees (who also commented on an early draft of some of the chapters), and Sandip Kar. Colleagues at the University of Birmingham were inevitably enthusiastic about the venture and provided much needed confidence during periods of writer's block.

And finally, to all our teachers, to whom *Work 3.0* is dedicated, who have helped shape our intellectual curiosity and worldview, we owe a cumulative debt.

Notes

DIALOGUE

1. Bhowmick, Nilanjana, 2021, https://www.nationalgeographic.com/science/article/how-indias-second-wave-became-the-worst-covid-19-surge-in-the-world

INTRODUCTION:

1. For more on this, see https://hbr.org/2014/01/what-vuca-really-means-for-you
2. J. Cribb, (2019), *Intergenerational Differences in Income and Wealth: Evidence from Britain*, Fiscal Studies, 40: pp 275–299, https://doi.org/10.1111/1475-5890 12202; For the US instance, see Ben S. Bernanke and Peter Olson, Are Americans Better Off than They Were a Decade or Two Ago?, Brookings, 19 October, 2016, https://www.brookings.edu/blog/ben-bernanke/2016/10/19/are-americans-better-off-than-they-were-a-decade-or-two-ago/
3. An economic recovery plan drawn up by the World Economic Forum (WEF) in response to the COVID-19 pandemic, see https://www.weforum.org/great-reset/
4. Klaus Schwab and Thierry Malleret, *COVID-19: The Great Reset.* Taking stock of the COVID-19 situation in July 2020, and its impact across the world, the book lays out a possible overview of the future landscape at the macroeconomic, microeconomic and individual levels.
5. Covid Impact: 40% of Indian Start-Ups Hit, but Recovery Is Strong, Says Report, The Hindu Business Line, 14 October, 2020

6. 6.https://www.business-standard.com/article/current-affairs/after-uganda-india-saw-longest-school-closures-due-to-covid-says-govt-122031401233_1.html

7. For some, see International Labour Organization; Global Commission on the Future of Work, Work for a Better Future, 22 January 2019. https://www.ilo.org/global/publications/books/WCMS_662410/lang--en/index.htm; International Labour Organization; ILO Research Paper Series: Working Time and the Future of Work, 07 November 2018, https://www.ilo.org/wcmsp5/groups/public/---dgreports/---cabinet/documents/publication/wcms_649907.pdf; International Labour Organization, Research Department Working Paper no. 29, The Future of Work: A Literature Review, 17 April 2018, https://www.ilo.org/global/research/publications/working-papers/WCMS_625866/lang--en/index.htm; International Labour Organization, The Future of Work We Want: A Global Dialogue, 7 April 2017, https://www.ilo.org/wcmsp5/groups/public/---dgreports/---cabinet/documents/publication/wcms_570282.pdf; International Labour Organization. UNDP. Employment, Lives and Social Protection Guide for Recovery Implementation 2021; International Monetary Fund, Automation, Skills and the Future of Work: What do Workers Think? 20 December, 2019, https://www.imf.org/en/Publications/WP/Issues/2019/12/20/Automation-Skills-and-the-Future-of-Work-What-do-Workers-Think-48791; International Monetary Fund, Group of Twenty: Future of Work: Measurement and Policy Changes, 18 July, 2018, https://www.imf.org/external/np/g20/pdf/2018/071818a.pdf; International Monetary Fund, Rethinking the World of Work, 2 December, 2020, https://www.imf.org/external/pubs/ft/fandd/2020/12/pdf/rethinking-the-world-of-work-dewan.pdf; International Monetary Fund. Technology and the Future of Work, 18 July 2018, https://www.imf.org/external/np/g20/pdf/2018/041118.pdf

8. Alvin Toffler, *Future Shock*, Introduction.

9. Karl Polyani, *The Great Transformation*. The arbitrariness of labelling epochs is very apparent in Hobsbawm's books: *Age of Revolution* (1789–1848), *The Age of Capital* (1848–1875), *The Age of Empire* (1875–914) and *The Age of Extremes* (1914–1994), the last in the

series marking what he called *The Short Twentieth Century*. Unlike the neat demarcations here, major historical movements rarely exist in siloed compartments, one ending just as the other commences—there are overlaps and highly complex interplays between the constituent forces.
10. Clayton Christensen, *The Innovator's Dilemma*, Harvard Business School Press, 1997.

CHAPTER 1:

1. Joseph Schumpeter, *Capitalism, Socialism, and Democracy* (third edition), Harper Perennial Modern Thought (paperback), 4 November 2008, this version was first published in 1950.
2. See https://www.history.com/news/who-were-the-luddites
3. Rahul Tandon, 'India's Street Typists Heading for a Final Full-stop', BBC News, Kolkata, 16 January 2014, https://www.bbc.com/news/business-25620755
4. Klaus Schwab, 'The Fourth Industrial Revolution', World Economic Forum, 2016.
5. Interview with Yuval Noah Harari, 'The Age of Cyborgs has Begun—and the Consequences Cannot Be Known', *The Guardian*, 5 July, 2015, https://www.theguardian.com/culture/2015/jul/05/yuval-harari-sapiens-interview-age-of-cyborgs, See also Dr Rob F. Walker, *Artificial Intelligence in Business: Balancing Risk and Reward*, A PEGA Whitepaper; Van Harmelen, Frank, Vladimir Lifschitz and Bruce Porter (Eds), *Handbook of Knowledge Representation. Foundations of Artificial Intelligence*.
6. Brynjolfsson and McAfee, The Second Machine Age, page 11.
7. Danny T. Quah, 'The Weightless Developing Economy', United Nations University, UNI-WIDER, 2000, https://www.wider.unu.edu/publication/weightless-developing-economy
8. See for example, https://techcrunch.com/2022/05/10/the-age-of-the-centaur-100m-arr-is-the-new-cloud-valuation-milestone/
9. Team Inc42, 'Here are the 42 Startups that Entered the Unicorn Club in 2021', Inc 42, 29 December 2021, https://inc42.com/buzz/indian-startups-that-entered-the-unicorn-club-in-2021-in-india/

10. Joseph Stigltiz, *Globalization and its Discontents*, Penguin India, 30 July 2012.

11. ILO Website, 'World Employment and Social Outloo—Trends 2021', https://www.ilo.org/global/research/global-reports/weso/trends2021/lang--en/index.htm

12. Kim Karbrough, 'These Are the Sectors Where Green Jobs Are Growing in Demand', World Economic Forum, 23 September 2021, https://www.weforum.org/agenda/2021/09/sectors-where-green-jobs-are-growing-in-demand/

13. Table 1.1 and the figures quoted in the subsequent paragraphs are from multiple reports by the World Economic Forum (WEF) and McKinsey Global Institute (MGI). While WEF's projections are principally for 2022 and 2025, MGI's estimations, globally and for India, are for 2030. Between 2018 to 2022, the WEF projected certain jobs that will be in high demand. For India these include, managing directors and chief executives, sales and marketing professionals, sales representatives, wholesale and manufacturing, technical and scientific products, software applications developers and analysts, general and operations managers, data analysts and scientists, assembly and factory workers, human resources specialists, financial analysts, and financial and investment advisers. The WEF projections were based on the fifteen industries and twenty-six economies used in the WEF (2020) report.

14. Mark Winterbotham, Genna Kik, Sam Selner and Sam Whittaker, 'UK Employer Skills Survey 2019: Summary Report', November 2020, https://assets.publishing.service.gov.uk/government/uploads/system/uploads/attachment_data/file/936488/ESS_2019_Summary_Report_Nov2020.pdf

15. Stuart Gentle, 'UK Hiring Plans Up, While Skill Shortages Greater than Ever Before, Says Monster Report', Onrec Website, 22 April 2022, https://www.onrec.com/news/statistics/uk-hiring-plans-while-skill-shortages-greater-than-ever-says-new-monster-report

16. Winter 2022 Fortune/Deloitte CEO Survey, 'CEOs Eye 2022 with Optimism and a Dash of Uncertainty'; See also Heather Conklin, 'The Skills Shortage is 2022's Biggest Threat: Here's how to navigate Through', Fortune, 8 April, 2022, https://fortune.com/2022/04/08/online-learning-workforce-training-digital-skills-gap/

17. 'A Look at Skill Gaps in the USA in 2022', TC Global Website, https://tcglobal.com/a-look-at-skill-gaps-in-the-usa-in-2022/

18. 'How Covid-19 has Pushed Companies Over the Technology Tipping Point—and Transformed Business Forever: Survey', 5 October 2020, McKinsey website. https://www.mckinsey.com/business-functions/strategy-and-corporate-finance/our-insights/how-covid-19-has-pushed-companies-over-the-technology-tipping-point-and-transformed-business-forever; See also From Street to Screen Economy: How has Covid-19 Accelerated Digital Transformation, 28 July 2021, https://timesofindia.indiatimes.com/business/india-business/from-street-to-screen-economy-how-has-covid-19-accelerated-digital-transformation/articleshow/84815847.cms

19. 'Bhavya Dore, 'In India's COVID-19 Crisis, the Internet Is Both a Lifeline and a Barrier', The New Humanitarian, 25 May 2021, https://www.thenewhumanitarian.org/news/2021/5/25/india-COVID-19-digital-divide-hampers-vaccine-and-healthcare-access

20. Dr Amanda Gilbertson, Joyeeta Dey, Dr Andrew Deuchar and Professor Nathan Grills, 'India's COVID-19 Divide in Digital Learning', University of Melbourne, https://pursuit.unimelb.edu.au/articles/india-s-covid-19-divide-in-digital-learning

21. NCSDE—Skill Gap in India, https://www.ncsde.in/skill-gap-in-india/

22. See https://www.pib.gov.in/PressReleasePage.aspx?PRID=1741942

23. Kaivan Munshi and Mark Rosenzweig, 'Networks and Misallocation: Insurance, Migration, and the Rural-Urban Wage Gap', *American Economic Review 2016*, 6, 106(1): 46–98; https://www.repository.cam.ac.uk/bitstream/handle/1810/254304/Munshi%20&%20Rosenzweig%202015%20American%20Economic%20Review.pdf?sequence=1

24. The Mahatma Gandhi National Rural Employment Guarantee Act, 2005 is a programme providing guaranteed 'right to work' in rural areas, via at least 100 days of wage employment in a financial year to at least one member of every household whose adult members volunteer to do unskilled manual work.

25. Sindhu Hariharan, 'Online Festive Shopping Attracts Cybercrime, McAfee India Survey Finds', 17 November 2021, Times of India,

https://timesofindia.indiatimes.com/business/india-business/
online-festive-shopping-attracts-cybercrime-mcafee-india-survey-
finds/articleshow/79260351.cms

26. Kartikeya Tripathi, Sarah Robertson and Claudia Cooper, 'A Brief
Report on Older People's Experience of Cybercrime Victimisation
in Mumbai', India, *Journal of Elder Abuse & Neglect*, Volume 31,
2019, Issue 4-5 https://discovery.ucl.ac.uk/id/eprint/10084093/1/
Cooper%20AAM%20Brief%20report.pdf

27. Savvy Soumya Misra and Tejas Patel, 'The Inequality Virus—
India Supplement 2021', 22 January 2021, Oxfam India, https://
www.oxfamindia.org/press-release/inequality-virus-india-
supplement-2021

28. FirstPost Staff, 'Despite Low Female Participation in the Workforce,
Why More Women Are Facing Unemployment in the Pandemic,
Explained', FirstPost, 21 July, 2021, https://www.firstpost.com/
india/despite-low-female-participation-in-the-workforce-why-
more-women-are-facing-unemployment-in-the-pandemic-
explained-9825261.html

29. For a short overview of CSR, see https://www.investopedia.com/
terms/c/corp-social-responsibility.asp

30. See https://labour.gov.in/sites/default/files/SS_Code_Gazette.pdf

31. Cathy O'Neil, *Weapons of Math Destruction: How Big Data Increases
Inequality and Threatens Democracy*, New York, Crown, 2016.

32. This section draws to an extent on Bandyopadhyay, Banerjee and
Das (2021)

33. World Bank Group, 'World Development Report 2021, Data for
Better Lives', Washington, DC: 2021, https://www.worldbank.
org/en/publication/wdr2021; See also Photopoulos, Julianna,
Fighting Algorithmic Bias in Artificial Intelligence, Physicsworld.
https://physicsworld.com/a/fighting-algorithmic-bias-in-artificial-
intelligence/

34. Anja Prummer, 'Micro-targeting and Polarization', *Journal of Public
Economics*, Volume 188, August 2020, 104210

35. Thomas H. Davenport, 'The AI Advantage: How to Put the
Artificial Intelligence Revolution to Work'; EY, Intelligent
Automation, https://www.ey.com/en_in/intelligent-automation;
Fulcher, John, *Computational Intelligence and its Applications Series:*

Advances in Applied Artificial Intelligence; Ben Goertzel and Cassio Pennachin (Eds.), *Artificial General Intelligence*; R.J. Anderson and W.W. Sharrock, *Ethical Algorithms: A brief comment on an extensive muddle*, Tony Boobier, *Advanced Analytics and AI Impact, Implementation and the Future of Work*; Matt Carter, *Minds and Computers: An Introduction to the Philosophy of Artificial Intelligence*; Hattori, Hiromitsu, Takahiro Kawamura, Tsuyoshi Ide, Makoto Yokoo, and Yohei Murakami (Eds.), New Frontiers in Artificial Intelligence; John Haugeland (Ed.), *Mind Design II. Philosophy Psychology Artificial Intelligence*; Harry Henderson, *Milestones in Discovery and Invention, Artificial Intelligence: Mirrors for the Mind*; Lawrence Hunter (Ed.), *Artificial Intelligence and Molecular Biology*; IndiaAI, 'AI Is Being Used by the UP Police to Catch Criminals', 16 August, 2019, https://indiaai.gov.in/case-study/ai-is-being-used-by-the-up-police-to-catch-criminals; IndiaAI, 'IIT-D Launches New Lab on AI for Judiciary', 16 July, 2021, https://indiaai.gov.in/news/iit-d-launches-new-lab-on-ai-for-judiciary; IndiaAI, 'Indian Researchers Use ML to Create Mortality Prediction Model for COVID-19 Patients', 12 May, 2021, https://indiaai.gov.in/case-study/indian-researchers-use-ml-to-create-mortality-prediction-model-for-covid-19-patients; IndiaAI, 'This AI-powered Backpack Helps the Visually Impaired Navigate World', 30 April, 2021, https://indiaai.gov.in/case-study/this-ai-powered-backpack-helps-the-visually-impaired-navigate-world; Infosys; Leadership in the Age of AI: Adapting, Investing and Reskilling to Work Alongside AI, Infosys, 2018.

CHAPTER 2:

1. For a history of the Luddite movement in England and its impact, see Alessandro Nuvolari, *The "Machine-Breakers" and the Industrial Revolution*. See also Kevin O'Rourke, Ahmed S. Rahman and Alan M. Taylor, *Luddites, the Industrial Revolution, and the Demographic Transition*.

2. A pamphlet written in 1848 by German philosophers Karl Marx and Friedrich Engels, which summarizes their theories concerning the nature of society and politics

3. Karl Marx, *Grundrisse: Foundations of the Critique of Political Economy (Rough Draft)*.

4. Herbert Marcuse, *One-Dimensional Man: Studies in the Ideology of Advanced Industrial Society*, p.33; See also Allan R. Wilson, One-Dimensional Society Revisited: An Analysis of Herbert Marcuse's One-Dimensional Man, 34 Years Later, thesis submitted for master of education.

5. Otto Eckstein, *Perspectives on Employment under Technical Change*, chapter 6, pp. 96–98; Jack Stieber (ed.), *Employment Problems of Automation and Advanced Technology: An International Perspective*,

6. Jeremy Rifkin, *The End of Work: The Decline of the Global Labor Force and the Dawn of the Post-Market Era*, p. 143.

7. Martin Ford, *The Lights in the Tunnel: Automation, Accelerating Technology and the Economy of the Future*, 2009; See also his subsequent book, *Rise of the Robots: Technology and the Threat of a Jobless Future*, 2015.

8. Ray Kurzweil, *The Singularity is Near: When Humans Transcend Biology*.

9. Michio Kaku, *Physics of the Future: How Science Will Shape Human Destiny and Our Daily Lives by the Year 2100*.

10. Peter Diamandis and Steven Kotler, *Abundance: The Future is Better than you Think*.

11. Steven Kotler, *Tomorrowland: Our Journey from Science Fiction to Science Fact*.

12. Open Culture, '*Jules Verne Accurately Predicts What the 20th Century Will Look Like in His Lost Novel, Paris in the Twentieth Century, 1863*'.

13. Adam Smith, *An Inquiry into the Nature and Causes of the Wealth of Nations*, Indianapolis, Indiana, Liberty Classics/Oxford University Press, 1979; See also Jean-Baptiste Say, *A Treatise on Political Economy; Or The Production, Distribution and Consumption of Wealth*.

14. Carl Benedikt Frey and Michael Osborne, *The Future of Employment: How Susceptible Are Jobs to Computerisation?* Oxford Martin Programme on Technology and Employment, 17 September 2013.

15. McKinsey Global Institute (MGI), 'Jobs lost; Jobs gained: Workforce Transitions in a time of Automation 2017'.

16. HFS, 'Automation to Impact 750,000 Low Skilled Indian Jobs, but Create 300,000 Mid-High Skilled Jobs by 2022'; See also Ernst

& Young, 'Future of Jobs in India: A 2022 Perspective', Ernst & Young LLP, India, 2017; For more recent perspectives, see 'Building Workplaces and Workforces for The Future: The View From India', pwc.in, 2021; Deloitte, 'From Survive to Thrive: The Future of Work in a Post-Pandemic World', Deloitte Paper, 2021; Forrester, European Edition, 'Predictions 2021; Accelerate out of the Crisis', Forrester Research Inc., 2020, https://go.forrester.com/wp-content/uploads/2020/10/Forrester-Predictions-2021-EMEA-1.pdf; International Federation of Robotics, World Robotics Report 2020, https://ifr.org/ifr-press-releases/news/record-2.7-million-robots-work-in-factories-around-the-globe; Press release at IFR Press Conference, Frankfurt, 24 September 2020, https://ifr.org/downloads/press2018/Presentation_WR_2020.pdf

17. 'Factory Workers Need to Worry About Automation More than Techies', *Economic Times*.

18. 'India's Unemployment in 2020 at Worst Level in 29 Years', Shows Study, BusinessToday.In

19. Kalpana Pathak, 'Freshers in India Have Better Opportunities: Team Lease EdTech'.

20. Anecdotal evidence has come to light at some points. For projections of job loss in the IT sector, see Srishti Pandey, TCS, Infosys, Wipro, Cognizant, HCL, Tech Mahindra, Other IT Firms to Lay Off 30 Lakh Employees by 2022!, Daily Blog, 17 June 2021, https://dailyblogday.online/tcs-infosys-wipro-cognizant-hcl-tech-mahindra-other-it-firms-to-lay-off-30-lakh-employees/

21. Abhijit Bhaduri, 'What will Career 3.0 and Jobs 3.0 Be Like?'; See also Esther Perel, 'How the Growing Identity Economy Is Reshaping the Future of Work'.

22. The data used in this section has been taken mainly from chapter 10, 'Social Infrastructure and Employment', pages 365–374, of the Economic Survey of India 2021-22, published by the Government of India, Ministry of Finance Department of Economic Affairs Economic Division, January 2022; Also see the Quarterly Bulletin of the Periodic Labour Force Survey (PFLS), January–March 2021, Government of India, Ministry of Statistic and Programme Implementation, National Statistical Office, 30 November 2021; see also, 'Impact on Jobs Across Emerging Technologies During the

Current Pandemic Crisis', *Analytics India Magazine*, 4 August 2020, https://analyticsindiamag.com/impact-on-jobs-across-emerging-technologies-during-the-current-pandemic-crisis-by-aim-jigsaw-academy/

23. Max Tegmark, *Life 3.0. Being Human in the Age of Artificial Intelligence.*

24. PricewaterhouseCoopers India, 'Artificial Intelligence in India— Hype or Reality, Impact of Artificial Intelligence Across Industries and User Groups'.
    For perspectives on digitalization and the increasing role of technology in the future of work, see World Economic Forum, 'Digital Culture: The Driving Force of Digital Transformation'; World Economic Forum, 'Disrupting Unemployment'; World Bank Group: Siddhartha Raja, Luc Christiaensen, 'The Future of Work Requires More, Not Less Technology in Developing Countries'; World Bank Group, 'Framing the Future of Work'; Daniel M. West, *The Future of Work. Robots, AI and Automation;* See also Jay Tuck, *Evolution Without Us.*

25. Jujjavarapu Geethanjali, Elonnai Hickock, Amber Sinha, 'AI and the Manufacturing and Services Industry in India'; Cem Dilmegani, 'Top 12 AI Applications in Manufacturing in 2021'; 'Five Successful AI and ML Use Cases in Manufacturing', Hackernoon Website; Swasti Mitter (ed.), *Computer-aided Manufacturing and Women's Employment: The Clothing Industry in Four EC Countries*; Dattaraj Rao, 'Role of Artificial Intelligence in the Indian Manufacturing environment'; 'Machine Learning and AI in Manufacturing: A Quick Guide to the Fundamentals', Seebo Website.

26. 'How Surgical Robot Assistants Are Becoming a Reality in Indian Hospitals and Healthcare Sector', *Analytics India Magazine*; 'AI In Healthcare Is Challenging: What Can India Do?' *Analytics India Magazine;* 'Top 20 Start-ups in India Revolutionizing Health-Care Industry with Artificial Intelligence', Analytics Jobs; Tarun Bhardwaj, *'Technology-led Innovations Will Be the Mainstay of Future Healthcare in India';* Amit Chadha, 'India's Healthcare Has a New Best Friend: Robots', *Fortune India;* 'Artificial Intelligence for Healthcare: Insights from India, Chatham House', 30 July 2020; 'India's Top Artificial Intelligence Organizations in Healthcare', *InnoHealth Magazine;*

Dwarikanath Mahapatra, 'Overview of AI in Indian Healthcare'; PricewaterhouseCoopers India and Bengal Chamber of Commerce and Industry (BCCI), 'Reimagining the Possible in the Indian Healthcare Ecosystem with Emerging Technologies'; Analytics India Magazine, 'AI In Healthcare Is Challenging: What Can India Do?' '10 February 2021, https://protecteu.mimecast.com/s/ KfoHCGvRrSjV6EMUKFPMC?domain=analyticsindiamag. com/' https://analyticsindiamag.com/ai-in-healthcare-is-challenging-what-can-india-do/; See also Trisha Medhi, 'These Made-in-India Robots are Helping Health Workers Fight COVID-19', YourStory, 5 August 2020, https://yourstory.com/2020/08/made-in-india-robots-coronavirus-aatmanirbhar-bharat/amp

27. Meha Agarwal, 'How Artificial Intelligence Algorithms Are Changing India's Banking Industry?' Inc42; Vivek Kumar, 'Banking of Tomorrow: Top Indian Banks Using Artificial Intelligence'; Mike Thomas, '11 Robotics Applications in Banking and Finance'; Chris Wilds, 'Robotics in Banking with 4 RPA Use Case Examples + 3 Bank Bot Use Case Videos'; Dr C. Vijai, 'Artificial Intelligence in Indian Banking Sector: Challenges and Opportunities'; for robotics in banking, see Krishnaprasad S. Nair, 'Impact of Robots in the Financial Sector', *IOSR Journal of Business and Management* (IOSR-JBM) e-ISSN: 2278-487X, p-ISSN: 2319-7668, pp. 72–76, ADMIFMS International Management Research Conference 2018, http://www.iosrjournals.org/iosr-jbm/ papers/Conf.ADMIFMS1808-2018/Volume-1/11.%2072-76.pdf; Ayushman Baruah, AI Applications in the Top 4 Indian Banks, Emerj, 27 February 2020, https://emerj.com/ai-sector-overviews/ ai-applications-in-the-top-4-indian-banks/

28. Calum Chace, 'The Impact of Artificial Intelligence on Professional Services'; Deloitte, 'Machines with Purpose: From Theory to Practice, Artificial intelligence in Professional Services'; Alex Kelly, '3 Ways AI Is Revolutionizing Professional Services'; 'How AI and ML Will Revolutionize Professional Services', Laurie McCabe's Blog; Avik Chanda and Gautham Tummala, 'How "Conversational AI" Will Shape Future Workplace Interactions'; 'Three Steps to Hyperautomation', Gartner; Raza, Muhammad Raza, 'IT Automation Trends to Watch in 2021'; 'Overview of IT

Automation', IBM; See also Aayush Rathi and Elonnai Hickok, *Future of Work in India's IT/IT-eS Sector,* 'Center for Internet and Society, and Future of Skills Report 2019', LinkedIn, https://business.linkedin.com/talent-solutions/recruiting-tips/future-of-skills-for-asia-pacific-2019

29. Change2Crowd, *'Automation in the Tourism Industry'*; Justin Pierce, eHotelier Website, 'Insights, *How COVID-19 Has Sped Up Hospitality technology'*; HotelTechReport, *'How to Think About Automation's Impact on Hospitality'*; ReviewPro, *'Why Hotel Automation is the Next Big Thing in Hospitality'*; Aviral Gupta, *'Reshaping the Hospitality Industry: New Technologies that Can Be Used to Enhance Services in the Post-COVID era'*; Gravity Flow, *'How Automated Workflow Tools Can Help the Travel Industry with Bookings'*; Sandeep Verma, *'Advanced Guide to Marketing Automation for Travel Industry'*; A.J. Singh, *'Impact of COVID-19 on the Hospitality Industry and Implication for Operations and Asset Management'*; Sanskriti University, *'Machine Learning, AI & Big Data Analytics in Travel & Hospitality Industry'*; Silway, Rebecca, *'AI in Travel and Hospitality Market Industry Analysis 2021–2031'*; Infosys, *'Role of AI in Travel and Hospitality Industry,* published by Infosys, 2018'.

30. 'Succeeding in the AI supply-chain Revolution', McKinsey & Company; 'AI is Reshaping the Supply Chain', IBM; Tina Jacobs, 'Artificial Intelligence in Supply Chain & Logistics'; Adam Robinson, 'The Top 5 Impacts of Artificial Intelligence (AI) in Logistics'.

31. See also Avik Chanda, *'Kindness and Empathy Will Be Skills of the Future in India's Media and Publishing Industry',* *Quartz*, 15 June 2020, https://qz.com/india/1868170/how-indian-media-and-publishing-firms-can-survive-covid-19-slump/

32. For applications in agriculture, see 'AI to Play a Key Role in India's Growth in Agriculture: Nasscom EY Report', *Mint*, 25 March 2021, https://www.livemint.com/technology/tech-news/ai-to-play-a-key-role-in-india-s-growth-in-agriculture-nasscom-ey-report-11616681716106.html. Also see Samiksha Mehra, 'Conversations: How IIT-H is Decoding the AI Black Box with Research on XAI', IndiaAI, 15 July 2021,: https://indiaai.gov.in/article/how-iit-h-is-decoding-the-ai-black-box-with-research-on-xai

33. See also Report: 'State of Artificial Intelligence in India—2020', *Analytics India Magazine*, 8 September 2020, https://analyticsindiamag.com/report-state-of-artificial-intelligence-in-india-2020/; Chetan Kumar, India Doubles Number of Industrial Robots in 5 Years, *Times of India*, 30 September 2020, https://timesofindia.indiatimes.com/india/india-doubles-number-of-industrial-robots-in-5-years/articleshow/78407600.cms; Monomita Chakraborty, 'Top 10 Affordable Personal Robots to Buy in India This Year'; See also, 'Top 5 Robotic Start-Ups Pushing Boundaries in India', *The Hindu Business Line*, Mumbai, 1 June 2020, https://www.thehindubusinessline.com/info-tech/other-gadgets/top-5-robotic-start-ups-pushing-boundaries-in-india/article31720944.ece.; Smriti Srivastava, 'Top Robotics Companies Redefining Indian Automation Industry', 23 May 2020, https://www.analyticsinsight.net/top-robotics-companies-redefining-indian-automation-industry/; Ashish Pratap Singh, 'Artificial Intelligence in India 2021 (Strategy of AI in India)', TechGecs, 19 January 2021, https://www.techgecs.in/2020/08/artificial-intelligence-in-india.html?m=1; Bernhard Schaffrik, The Forrester Wave™: *Robotic Process Automation, Q1 2021'; 'The 14 Providers that Matter Most and How They Stack Up'*, Forrester; '"Daksh" Bomb Disposal Robot Will Roll Out Soon for the Indian Army', Asian Defence, http://theasiandefence.blogspot.com/2009/08/bomb-disposal-robot-daksh-for-indian.html; 'Industrial Robots & Cobots to 2025: Can Domestic Manufacturers Compete with Foreign Robots and Impact India's New Automation Market?' Asian Robotics, https://asianroboticsreview.com/home337-html; 'Top Robotics Companies to Look Forward to in 2021', *Analytics India Magazine*, 2 January 2021, https://analyticsindiamag.com/top-robotics-companies-to-look-forward-to-in-2021/; 'Robotics in India', Journals of India, 28 February 2020, https://journalsofindia.com/robotics-in-india/; Leslie D'Monte, 'Robots Are Coming for India's Shop Floors', *Mint*, 10 September 2019, https://www.livemint.com/technology/tech-news/robots-are-coming-for-india-s-shop-floors-1568135022807.html; Isabel Gerretson, 'Robots Are Joining the Fight Against Coronavirus in India', CNN Business,

https://edition.cnn.com/2020/11/11/tech/robots-india-covid-spc-intl/index.html

34. Yasunari Kawabata, *The Master of Go*, New York, Penguin Random House, 1996.
35. 'AlphaGo: Computer Defeat "Painful" for Chinese Go Prodigy', BBC News
36. Stephan Schwanauer and David A. Levitt (eds.), *Machine Models of Music*; See also Charles Patrick Martin, Kai Olav Ellefsen, and Jim Torresen, Deep Predictive Models in Interactive Music.
37. Selmer Bringsjord, 'Artificial Intelligence and Literary Creativity: Inside the Mind of BRUTUS, a Storytelling Machine'.
38. 'Can the Great Master be Brought Back to Create One More Painting?', NextRembrandt.

CHAPTER 3

1. MGI, 2017.
2. MGI (2021) pp. 71–74.
3. '8 Trends Including Automation, Aging Populations, Increased Technology Use, Marketization of Unpaid Work, Rising Incomes, Rising Educational Levels, Infrastructure Investment and Climate Change', MGI, 2021.
4. All pre-covid trends including accelerated automation and e-commerce, reduced business travel and increased remote work.
5. More details on pages 69 to 74 with advanced country(s) comparison.
6. MGI (2017), p. 97.
7. Net employment is the estimated labour demand when all effects of modelled trends are applied, MGI, 2021.
8. MGI (2021); column 1, p. 73, column 2, p. 114.
9. MGI (2021) p. 15.
10. MGI (2021) p 114.
11. Per 1,00,000 jobs.
12. International Renewable Energy Agency (IRENA).
13. IRENA (2021), pp. 304–306 and ILO (2021), pp. 54–57.
14. Here, I computed based on the differences with the 1.5°C given in the report.
15. WEF (2020), pp. 30, 81.

16. Emerging jobs will grow from 7.8 per cent to 13.5 per cent of the total employee base of companies surveyed.

    See also World Economic Forum, Jobs of Tomorrow: Mapping Opportunity in the New Economy; World Economic Forum, Reskilling the Workforce, One Person at a Lifetime; World Economic Forum, Strategies for the New Economy: Skills as the Currency of the Labour Market; McKinsey Global Institute, 'The Future of Work After Covid-19, https://www.mckinsey.com/featured-insights/future-of-work/the-future-of-work-after-covid-19

17. Will decline from 15.4 per cent to 9 per cent of workforce.

18. The strength of redundancy starts from topmost roles downwards. Thus, the roles have been ordered by frequency. For instance, 18 and 19 are projected to be redundant but to a lesser extent compared to the roles from 17 upwards.

19. By proportion of companies likely to adopt.

20. The figures depict the share of respondents (companies surveyed) who assert that they will adopt a said technology by 2025. This was done on a 5-point scale. WEF (2020) does not say much about the projected technologies. Additionally, only 10 of the categories used in the 2018 survey was repeated for the 2020 survey for all countries.

21. WEF (2018, 2020). NB: 2022 and 2025 projections were made in the future of jobs report by WEF (2018) and WEF (2020), respectively.

22. WEF (2020), p. 27. Difference was given with 2022 projection from WEF (2018). I computed this by adding the difference to the previous.

23. WEF (2020), p. 81.

24. WEF (2018), p. 7.

25. WEF (2018), p. 80.

26. Including other forms of AI such as neural networks and NLP.

27. Including other forms of AI such as neural networks and NLP.

28. Including e-commerce.

29. Including e-commerce.

30. Including aerial and underwater robots.

31. WEF (2020), p. 28.

32. WEF (2020), p. 34. The figure shows that 'newer emerging professions such as Data and AI, product development and cloud

computing present more opportunities to break into these frontier fields and that, in fact, such transitions do not require a full skills match between the source and destination occupation'- (p. 31).

33. WEF (2020), p. 33.
34. WEF (2020), p. 33.
35. WEF (2020), p. 33.
36. Topmost skills are increasingly emerging (ordered frequency).
37. WEF (2020), p. 36.
38. WEF (2020), p. 81.
39. WEF (2020) p. 36. Figure shows 'the top skills and skill groups which employers see as rising in prominence in the lead up to 2025'.
40. This change rather represents percentage change in work hours spent on each category due to changes in labour demand (MGI, 2021).
41. This is confusing because almost all countries experience no/negative growth in all except India.
42. India sees an increase relative to other countries due to shifts from agriculture to low-skill and manufacturing jobs (MGI, 2021, p. 94).
43. The list of initiatives and figures used in this section are taken from Chapter 10, 'Social Infrastructure and Employment', pp. 361–365, of the Economic Survey of India, 2021-22, published by the Government of India, Ministry of Finance, Department of Economic Affairs Economic Division, January 2022.
44. Source: https://static.pib.gov.in/WriteReadData/specificdocs/documents/2021/sep/doc202192701.pdf
45. MGI (2021), p. 10.
46. Source: https://thrivemyway.com/gig-economy-stats/
47. Source: https://www.adp.com/-/media/adp/ResourceHub/pdf/ADPRI/ADPRI0102_2018_Engagement_Study_Technical_Report_RELEASE%20READY.ashx (Hayes et. al)
48. Source: https://newsroom.mastercard.com/wp-content/uploads/2019/05/Gig-Economy-White-Paper-May-2019.pdf
49. Hayes et. al
50. 'Unlocking the Potential of the Gig Economy in India', Boston Consulting Group, bcg.com
51. See also Kalpana Pathak, 'Pandemic Pushes Firms to Hire More Temp Staff', *Mint*, 18 June 2021, https://www.livemint.com/

industry/human-resource/pandemic-pushes-firms-to-hire-more-temp-staff-11623955094524.html

52. Source: https://labour.gov.in/sites/default/files/SS_Code_Gazette.pdf
53. Mulcahy, *The Gig Economy: The Complete Guide to Getting Better Work, Taking More Time Off, and Financing the Life You Want,* 2018.
54. Shipra and Minaketan Behera, 'Gig Work and Platforms During the COVID-19 Pandemic in India', *Economic and Political Weekly,* vol. 55, Issue no. 45, 7 November 2020, epw.in
55. Auto News | Latest Automobiles & Auto Industry Information and Updates: ET Auto (indiatimes.com)
56. 56.https://www.paypalobjects.com/digitalassets/c/website/marketing/global/shared/global/media-resources/documents/PayPal_US_Freelancers_Insight_Report_Feb_2018.pdf
57. Column 1- 'likely', column 2- 'equally likely', WEF (2018), p. 81.
58. WEF (2018), p. 82.
59. This is not included in the 2025 categories.
60. See Heger (2007).
61. Browne (2012).
62. Gallup, 'How Millennials Want to Work and Live: The Six Big Changes Leaders Have to Make'.

CHAPTER 4

1. Carmen M. Reinhart and Kenneth S. Rogoff, *This Time is Different: A Panoramic View of Eight Centuries of Financial Crises.*
2. Daniel H. Pink, *A Whole New Mind. Why Right-Brainers Will Rule the Future.*
3. Avik Chanda and Suman Ghose, *From STEM to ESTEEM,* Chapter 5, 'From Command to Empathy: Using EQ in the Age of Disruption'.
4. Ben DeSpain, 'Transforming a Work Culture During a Pandemic', *Forbes,* 11 December 2020, https://www.forbes.com/sites/forbeshumanresourcescouncil/2020/12/11/transforming-a-work-culture-during-a-pandemic/Accessed 04 July 2021
5. World Economic Forum, 'The Future of Jobs Report 2020'.
6. Avik Chanda and Suman Ghose, *From Command to Empathy: Using EQ in the Age of Disruption,* Chapter 6, 'Being Mindful:

Alive and in the Moment'; for details of how companies focus on mindfulness, see 'Why Companies like Intel, Aetna and Google are Investing in Mindfulness Training Programs', Y website; and Henry Stewart, 'Five Big Companies Who Swear by Mindfulness', LinkedIn post; Ema Pateman, 'Mindfulness at Work—Insights from Early Adopters', Shine, 1 December 2019, https://www.shineworkplacewellbeing.com/mindfulness-at-work/

7. Jon Kabat-Zinn, *Full Catastrophe Living: Using the Wisdom of Your Body and Mind to face Stress, Pain, and Illness, Wherever You Go, There You Are*, and *Mindfulness Meditation*

8. Thích Nhất Hạnh, including *Zen Keys*, *The Miracle of Mindfulness*, *Being Peace*, *The Heart of Understanding*, *Living Buddha, Living Christ* and *No Death, No Fear*.

9. Ellen Langer, *Counterclockwise*, *Mindfulness*, *The Power of Mindful Learning*, and *The Art of Noticing*.

10. The Langer Mindfulness Scale is available on the NUVAH platform. For details, see the company website https://nuvah.in/

11. See Continuity Central, *Strengthening Resilience is the Key to Success in 2021: PwC survey*; PricewaterhouseCoopers India, *PwC's Global Crisis Survey 2021: India Insights*; Accenture, *Human Resilience What your people need now. COVID-19: What to Do Now, What to Do Next*; Egon Zehnder, The Future of Great Leadership Lies in Resilience: Parts I, I and III; see also Steven Kotler, *The Habit of Ferocity: Peak Performance Primer*; see also Avik Chanda, Why India Inc Needs to Invest in Resilience, *Economic Times*, 29 March 2020, https://economictimes.indiatimes.com/jobs/why-india-inc-needs-to-invest-in-resilience/articleshow/74874387.cms

12. For a discussion of the findings, see Avik Chanda, 'Resilience in Focus: Individuals, Teams and Processes', PeopleMatters.

13. An assessment corresponding to the factors outlined in this section is available on the NUVAH platform. For details, see the company website https://nuvah.in/

14. For details of how to develop workplace resilience, see Kat Valier, 'HR's Guide to Cultivating Workforce Resilience, HR Factorial website post', 8 October 2021, https://factorialhr.com/blog/workforce-resilience/

Cary L. Cooper, Mustafa Sarkar and Thomas Curran, 'Resilience Training in the Workplace from 2003 to 2014: A Systematic Review'.

15. Jenny J.W. Liu, Natalie Ein, Julia i, Mira Battaion, Maureen Reed and Kristin Vickers, '*Comprehensive Meta-Analysis of Resilience Interventions*', *Clin Psychol Rev.*

16. B.L. Fredrickson, 'The Role of Positive Emotions in Positive Psychology: The Broaden-and-build Theory of Positive Emotions', *American Psychologist*, 2001, 56: pp. 218–226.

17. Avik Chanda, 'From Resilience to Flourish, Through Positivity!', PeopleMatters.

18. Jon Clifton and Jim Harter, *Wellbeing at Work: How to Build Resilient and Thriving Teams;* see also Jon Clifton, *BlindSpot: The Global Rise of Unhappiness and How Leaders Missed It.*

19. 'A Leader's Guide to Developing a Work-From-Home Strategy', Gallup.

20. See also 'Employee Engagement and Performance: Latest Insights from the World's Largest Study', Gallup.

21. Avik Chanda and Suman Ghose, *From Command to Empathy: Using EQ in the Age of Disruption;* see also Travis Bradberry and Jean Greaves, *Emotional Intelligence 2.0*, and Daniel Goleman, *Emotional Intelligence*; Avik Chanda, 'Millennials Will Look for Opportunities Despite Engagement, interview by Rajguru Tandon, BWBusinessWorld', 27 April 2018, http://www.businessworld.in/ article/-Millenials-Will-Look-For-Opportunites-Despite-Engage ment-/27-04-2018-147613/;

22. For more perspectives, see Dan Ariely, *Payoff: The Hidden Logic that Shapes our Motivations*; Daniel H. Pink, *Drive: The Surprising Truth About What Motivates Us.*

23. Belinda Parmar, 'The Most Empathetic Companies', 2016, *Harvard Business Review.*

24. Nathan Christensen, 'Is There ROI In Empathy?', *Forbes.*

25. Theodore Zeldin, *An Intimate History of Humanity.* New York: Harper Perennial, 1996; see also 'The Oxford Muse Conversations: An Invitation to New Ways of Improving Professional, Personal and Intercultural Relations', https://www.oxfordmuse.com/media/ muse-brochure[final].pdf

26. Mihaly Csikszentmihalyi, *Flow: The Classic Work on how to achieve Happiness*; *Good Business: Leadership, Flow and the Making of Meaning*; Mihaly Csikszentmihalyi and Isabella Selega Csikszentmihalyi (eds.), *A Life Worth Living*; and Mihaly Csikszentmihalyi, *Applications of Flow in Human Development and Education*, New York, London: Springer, 2014.

27. For instances of applications in the workplace, see Chris Weller, 'We Talked to 20 Orgs About Growth Mindset—Here Are Our 7 Biggest Findings', Neuroleadership website.

28. Carol Dweck, *Mindset: Changing the Way You think To Fulfil Your Potential*, Constable & Robinson.

29. For Martin E.P. Seligman, see *Authentic Happiness: Using the New Positive Psychology to Realize Your Potential for Lasting Fulfilment*, and *Learned Optimism: How to Change Your Mind and Your Life*.

30. Martin E.P. Seligman, *Flourish: A Visionary New Understanding of Happiness and Well-being*; see also Peterson, Christopher, and Martin E.P. Seligman, *Character Strengths and Virtues: A Handbook and Classification*; and Peterson, Christopher, *Pursuing the Good Life: 100 Reflections on Positive Psychology*; also see Mruk, J. Christopher, *Self Esteem – Research, Theory and Practice: Towards a Positive Psychology of Self-Esteem*;
for an earlier instance of focus away from diseases, see George E. Vaillant, *Adaptation to Life*; Shane Lopez, *Positive Psychology: Exploring the Best in People, Volume 1, Discovering Human Strengths*; Sarah Lewis, *Positive Psychology at Work: How Positive Leadership and Appreciative Inquiry Create Inspiring Organizations*; Robert Biswas-Diener, Robert (Ed.), *Positive Psychology as Social Change*; Marvin Levine, *The Positive Psychology of Buddhism and Yoga. Paths to a Mature Happiness*; Hans Henrik Knoop and Antonella Della Fave (eds.), *Well-Being and Cultures: Perspectives from Positive Psychology, Cross Cultural Advancements in Positive Psychology, Volume 3*; Sreeradha Basu, 'HR Leaders Should Focus on "Wholistic Wellbeing", Use Data and Technology to Enhance Employee Wellbeing: *Report*', https://economictimes.indiatimes.com/news/company/corporate-trends/hr-leaders-should-focus-on-wholistic-wellbeing-use-data-and-technology-to-enhance-employee-wellbeing-report/articleshow/83817697.cms?from=mdr; Diener, Ed, John F. Helliwell

and Daniel Kahneman, 'International Differences in Well-Being', *Positive Psychology Series*; James Garbarino, *The Positive Psychology of Personal Transformation. Leveraging Resilience for Life Change*, New York, Springer, 2011.

31. Tom Rath and Jim Harter, 'The Five Essential Elements of Well-Being', Gallup Website, 4 May 2010, https://www.gallup.com/workplace/237020/five-essential-elements.aspx; see also Rath, Tom and Jim Harter, 'Wellbeing: The Five Essential Elements', Deckle Edge, May 2010.

32. Jim Harter, 'The First Step in Increasing Wellbeing Is Measuring it;, Business and Tech; https://www.futureofbusinessandtech.com/employee-wellbeing/the-first-step-in-increasing-wellbeing-is-measuring-it/#.

33. Philip S. Brenner and John DeLamater, 'Lies, Damned Lies, and Survey Self-Reports? Identity as a Cause of Measurement Bias', *Soc Psychol Q*, 2016 December; 79(4): 333–354. doi:10.1177/0190272516628298.

CHAPTER 5

1. See for example, Thomas L Friedman (2020), *The World is Flat: A Brief History of the Twenty-First Century*, New York, Farrar, Straus and Giroux, 2006.

2. Adam Smith, *An Inquiry into the Nature and Causes of the Wealth of Nations*, the University of Chicago Press, Reprint of Edwin Cannan's 1904 edition.

3. Acemoglu and Dell, AEJ, Macro, 2010

4. See R.E. Lucas Jr., *'Why Doesn't Capital Flow from Rich to Poor Countries'*, American Economic Association, 1990, vol. 80, no. 2, pp. 92–96.

5. Nicholas Carr, *The Shallows: What the Internet is Doing to Our Brains*, New York, London: W.W. Norton & Company, 2010.

6. See Most Productive Countries 2022 (worldpopulationreview.com).

7. In many countries, worker productivity has grown at a slower rate than pay for most (see Mishel and Bivens, 2021 for a US analysis. Source: https://www.epi.org/unequalpower/publications/wage-suppression-inequality/, we do not discuss this here but rather in chapter xx.

8. See page 2016, https://link.springer.com/chapter/10.1057/9781137505385_7

9. See for example, https://www.ideatovalue.com/inno/nickskillicorn/2016/09/problem-global-innovation-index/

10. Source: https://newproductsuccess.org/new-product-failure-rates-2013-jpim-30-pp-976-979/

11. Source: Global Innovation Index 2021 - Executive Summary (wipo.int)

12. Acemoglu and Restrepo, 2018, AER.

13. See Coster and Ogzen, 2021 . . . refer a few earlier studies

14. See Spence, 1973, 1979.

15. See Chevalier et, al, 2004.

16. See S. Kampelmann, F. Rycx, Y. Saks et al, 'Does Education Raise Productivity and Wages Equally? The Moderating Role of Age and Gender', *IZA J Labor Econ* **7**, 1 (2018), https://doi.org/10.1186/s40172-017-0061-4

17. K. Weeden, 'Why Do Some Occupations Pay More Than Others? Social Closure and Earnings Inequality in the United States', *Am J Sociol*, 2002, 108:55–101.

18. Blair Fix, 'The Trouble with Human Capital Theory, Working Papers, 2018, on Capital as Power, No. 2018/07, Forum on Capital as Power—Toward a New Cosmology of Capitalism', s.l.,http://www.capitalaspower.com/?p=2528

19. See Jozef Konings, Stijn Vanormelingen, 'The Impact of Training on Productivity and Wages: Firm-Level Evidence', *The Review of Economics and Statistics, 2015*, 97 (2): pp. 485–497.

20. Barbara Biasi, David J. Deming, and Petra Moser, 'Education and Innovation', NBER Working Paper no. 28544, March 2021.

21. Barbara Biasi and Song Ma, The Education-Innovation Gap, *Journal of Economic Literature*, 29 March 2021.

22. Xingjian Wei, Xiaolang Liu1 and Jian Sha, 'How Does the Entrepreneurship Education Influence the Students' Innovation? Testing on the Multiple Mediation Model', *Frontiers in Psychology*, 10 July 2019.

23. See Card, 1999, *Handbook of Labor Economics.*

24. See Cygam-Rehm 2018, 'Is Additional Schooling'.

25. See Literacy Rate by Country 2022 (worldpopulationreview.com).

26. As reported in Literacy Rate in India 2022 | Kerala & Bihar Literacy Rate – The Global Statistics.

27. Tharmangalam, 'The Perils of Social Development Without Economic Growth: The Development Debacle of Kerala, India', *Bulletin of Concerned Asian Scholars*, 1998, 30:1, 23-34, DOI: 10.1080/14672715.1998.10411031

28. Source: https://m.rbi.org.in/scripts/PublicationsView.aspx?id= 20676

29. Source: https://indianexpress.com/article/gender/high-on-literacy-low-on-workforce-why-are-keralas-women-not-making-it-to-work/

30. Source: https://www.statista.com/statistics/983020/female-labor-force-participation-rate-india/#:~:text=In%202020%2C%20about%2019%20percent,approximately%2030%20percent%20in%201990.

31. Source: https://www.theglobaleconomy.com/Bangladesh/Female_labor_force_participation/

32. Source: https://www.theglobaleconomy.com/Sri-Lanka/Female_labor_force_participation/

33. Source: https://economictimes.indiatimes.com/jobs/despite-policy-support-labour-participation-by-women-still-low/articleshow/90061223.cms

34. Eric A. Hanushek, Guido Schwerdt, Simon Wiederhold, Ludger Woessmann, 'Returns to Skills Around the World: Evidence from PIAAC', *European Economic Review*, 2015, 73, pp. 103–130.

35. This section draws from Avik Chanda and Suman Ghosh's book, *From Command to Empathy: Using EQ in the Age of Disruption*, Harper Business, an imprint of HarperCollins Publishers Limited, 2017, chapter 5, pp 93–102.

36. Robert N. Charette: 'What Ever Happened to STEM Job Security?', *IEEE Spectrum*, 5 September 2013.

37. Michael S. Teitelbaum, 'The Myth of the Science and Engineering Shortage', *The Atlantic*, 19 March 2014.

38. 'India facing shortage of engineers in S&T: DRDO DG', *The Hindu*, 29 January 2013.

39. Vince Bertram, 'STEM or STEAM? We're Missing the Point', The Huffington Point, 26 May 2014.

40. Johan Roos, 'Build STEM Skills, but Don't Neglect the Humanities', *Harvard Business Review*, 24 June 2015.
41. Source: https://nbs.net/how-diversity-increases-productivity/
42. National Education Policy 2020, Ministry of Human Resource Development, Government of India, chapter 11, pp. 36-37.
43. Navi Radjou, Jaideep Prabhu, Simone Ahuja, *Jugaad Innovation: Think Frugal, Be Flexible, Generate Breakthrough Growth*.
44. Manu Joseph, '"Jugaad", India's most overrated idea', *Mint Lounge*, 18 August 2018. Source: https://lifestyle.livemint.com/news/talking-point/jugaad-india-s-most-overrated-idea-111645161837756.html
45. See A. Kotwal, B. Ramaswami & W. Wadhwa, 'Economic Liberalization and Indian Economic Growth: What's the Evidence?', *Journal of Economic Literature, 2011, 49*, 1152–1199.
46. National Education Policy 2022, p. 35.
47. Source: https://feminisminindia.com/2020/08/06/new-education-policy-nep-2020-critical-analysis/
48. Except where referenced through a separate endnote, the figures used in this section are taken from the Economic Survey of India, 2021-22, published by the Government of India, Ministry of Finance, Department of Economic Affairs, Economic Division, January 2022, pp. 336–339 – growth of start-ups in India; pp. 339–342 – the problem of low patents in India, explained; p. 356 – school drop-outs; p. 357 – school enrolment for children, 6-14 years; pp. 358–359 – Government initiatives for students/ school education, during the pandemic; pp. 360–361 – Recent GOI initiatives in higher education.
See also WorldSkills India. 2021. Source: https://worldskillsindia.co.in/worldskill/about.php#section2
49. See https://www.ibm.com/downloads/cas/RG0W6AMB
50. Kritti Bhalla, 'The worst for Indian startups is yet to come — be prepared for layoffs, unicorn slowdown and startup shutdowns in 2022', Business Insider, 20 May 2022. Source: https://www.businessinsider.in/business/startups/news/the-worst-for-indian-startups-is-yet-to-come-be-prepared-for-layoffs-unicorn-slowdown-and-startup-shutdowns-in-2022/articleshow/91681195.cms; Soumyarendra Barik, 'Funding winter sets in for Indian startups, staff out in the cold: Over 12K laid off', *The Indian Express*,6 July

2022. Source: https://indianexpress.com/article/business/indian-startups-funding-winter-lay-offs-8011194/; 'From Public Spats to Feuding Founders: Gloomy 2022 For Indian Startups', Inc42, 12 June 2022. Source: https://inc42.com/features/from-public-spats-to-feuding-founders-gloomy-2022-for-indian-startups/; Vipin Sreekumar, Priya Rachel David, Palash Deb, 'India's startup explosion: more pitfalls than promise?', LSE website, 11 May 2022. Source: https://blogs.lse.ac.uk/businessreview/2022/05/11/indias-startup-explosion-more-pitfalls-than-promise/; Shraddha Goled, 'The tragic twist in the Indian startup saga', *Analytics India Magazine*, 13 June 2022. Source: https://analyticsindiamag.com/the-tragic-twist-in-the-indian-startup-saga/

CHAPTER 6

1. *Institute of Health Metrics & Evaluation (IHME), Global Burden of Disease* study, https://ourworldindata.org/global-mental-health
2. Source: https://institute.global/policy/hidden-pandemic-long-covid
3. Source: https://www.economicsobservatory.com/update-which-firms-and-industries-have-been-most-affected-by-covid-19
4. Mousteri et al, 'The scarring effect of unemployment on psychological well-being across Europe', 2018.
5. Speiser, 2021.
6. Chatterji et al, 2021, https://www.ncbi.nlm.nih.gov/pmc/articles/PMC8395012/
7. Avik Chanda, 'View: New Perspectives on Risk Management, for Covid Times', *Economic Times*, 15 April 2021, https://economictimes.indiatimes.com/news/company/corporate-trends/view-new-perspectives-on-risk-management-for-covid-times/articleshow/82081508.cms
8. Source: https://fivethirtyeight.com/features/trump-supporters-arent-shy-but-polls-could-still-be-missing-some-of-them/
9. Source: https://fivethirtyeight.com/features/why-did-republicans-outperform-the-polls-again-two-theories/
10. Gov.uk. Coronavirus (COVID-19), latest updates and guidance, research and analysis, 2, important findings, updated 18 November

2021, https://www.gov.uk/government/publications/covid-19-mental-health-and-wellbeing-surveillance-report/2-important-findings-so-far

11. Jim Harter, 'Percent Who Feel Employer Cares About Their Wellbeing Plummets', Gallup Website, 18 March 2022, https://www.gallup.com/workplace/390776/percent-feel-employer-cares-wellbeing-plummets.aspx

12. See Kochar et. al, 2020, for a full analysis, 'Lockdown of 1.3 Billion People in India During Covid-19 pandemic: A Survey of its Impact on Mental Health, nih.gov

13. Source: https://www.ncbi.nlm.nih.gov/pmc/articles/PMC7597717/

14. 'Sentiment Analysis of Nationwide Lockdown due to Covid 19 Outbreak: Evidence from India, nih.gov

15. See Sardeshmukh et. al, 'New Technology, Work and Employment', 2012.

16. See Charalampous et. al, 2017, https://www.tandfonline.com/doi/full/10.1080/1359432X.2018.1541886

17. C.A. Grant, L.M. Wallace, P.C. Spurgeon, C. Tramontano and M. Charalampous, 'Construction and Initial Validation of the E-Work Life Scale to Measure Remote e-working', *Employee Relations*, 2019, vol. 41, no. 1, pp. 16–33, https://doi.org/10.1108/ER-09-2017-0229

18. Chandan et al, *Lancet Psychiatry*, 2019.

19. Chandan et al, *B. J. Psychiatry*, 2019.

20. Source: https://economictimes.indiatimes.com/news/company/corporate-trends/66-of-the-indian-employees-want-to-work-completely-from-home-survey/articleshow/79444498.cms

21. Source: https://www.livemint.com/news/india/lockdown-boosted-family-life-but-india-s-young-face-anxiety-wfh-fatigue-11609506992201.html

22. Source: https://www.business-standard.com/article/economy-policy/amid-wfh-burnout-indian-professionals-want-to-return-to-office-survey-121091401055_1.html

23. Source: https://www.psychiatry.org/newsroom/news-releases/as-americans-begin-to-return-to-the-office-views-on-workplace-mental-health-are-mixed

24. Source: https://www.who.int/news-room/fact-sheets/detail/mental-disorders

25. Source: https://www.thelancet.com/journals/langlo/article/PIIS2214-109X(20)30432-0/fulltext

26. Source: https://www.thelancet.com/journals/langlo/article/PIIS2214-109X(20)30432-0/fulltext; see also L. Dadona, 'The Burden of Mental Disorders Across the States of India: The Global Burden of Disease Study 1990–2017', *The Lancet Psychiatry*, 2020, vol. 7, issue 2, pp. 148–161.

27. Source: https://doi.org/10.1016/S2215-0366(19)30475-4

28. See also 'Mental Health Matters', *The Lancet Global Health*, November 2020. DOI: https://doi.org/10.1016/S2214-109X(20)30432-0; and 'The Burden of Mental Disorders Across the States of India: The Global Burden of Disease Study 1990–2017', *The Lancet Psychiatry*, 1 February 2020, articles, vol. 7, issue 2, pp. 148–161;
Shikha Nischal v National Insurance Company Ltd and another, Number W.P.(C)-3190/2021, High Court of Delhi, New Delhi, India, 19 April 2021. There was also a public interest litigation filed by Gaurav Kumar Bansal, an advocate to the Supreme Court on 17 March 2020.

29. Ghosh and Chatterji, *Lancet Psychiatry* correspondence, December 2020.

30. See Institute for Health Metrics and Evaluation, Global Health Data Exchange, 2021. Source: http://ghdx.healthdata.org/gbd-results-tool

31. Jim Harter, 'Manager Burnout Is Only Getting Worse', Gallup website, 18 November 2021. Source: https://www.gallup.com/workplace/357404/manager-burnout-getting-worse.aspx

32. Gallup meta-analysis of employee engagement and performance outcomes.

33. 'Poor Mental Health of Employees Costs Indian Employers $14 Billion Yearly: Deloitte survey', *Economic Times*, 8 September 2022, https://economictimes.indiatimes.com/news/company/corporate-trends/poor-mental-health-of-employees-costs-indian-employers-14-billion-yearly-deloitte-survey/articleshow/94075801.cms;
for a more detailed context and to download the report, 'Mental Health and Well-being in the Workplace', https://www2.deloitte.com/in/en/pages/life-sciences-and-healthcare/articles/mental-health-2022.html?id=in:2os:3or:4in-mental-health:5:6lshc:20220908:dcom_home

34. Avik Chanda, 'How to Manage the "Internal Customer": India Inc Has a Serious Battle Looming', ET Prime, 14 January 2020, https://economictimes.indiatimes.com/jobs/how-to-manage-the-internal-customer-india-inc-has-a-serious-battle-looming/articleshow/73240738.cms; Avik Chanda, 'Why Investment in Human Capital Has Been Such a "Late Starter"', PeopleMatters, 27 December 2020, https://www.peoplematters.in/blog/strategic-hr/why-investment-in-human-capital-has-been-such-a-late-starter-27997; Avik Chanda, 'Why HR Leaders Are Betting High on Behavioural Skills', *Economic Times,* 28 May 2020, https://economictimes.indiatimes.com/jobs/why-hr-leaders-are-betting-high-on-behavioural-skills/articleshow/76058842.cms;   Avik Chanda, 'Sack, Furlough or Reskill? India Inc's Talent Dilemma', *Economic Times,* 13 February 2020, https://economictimes.indiatimes.com/jobs/sack-furlough-or-reskill-india-incs-talent-dilemma/articleshow/74116053.cms

35. Avik Chanda and Gautham Tummala, 'How "Conversational AI" Will Shape Future Workplace Interactions', *Economic Times,* 15 January 2021

36. 'Overcoming Stigma: Three Strategies Toward Better Mental Health in the Workplace', McKinsey Quarterly, 23 July 2021, https://www.mckinsey.com/industries/healthcare-systems-and-services/our-insights/overcoming-stigma-three-strategies-toward-better-mental-health-in-the-workplace?cid=other-eml-alt-mcq-mck&hdpid=15c23ed2-92ab-4e36-9dec-02bc6306a29&hctky=12810559&hlkid=4701bf4f0c034af2974eb850a5914021; see also 'COVID-19 Mental Health and Well-Being Surveillance: Report', Chapter 2, Important Findings, Office for Health Improvement and Disparities (2022); see also Lily Martis, '7 Companies With Epic Wellness Programs', Monster; see also 'National Surveys Reveal Disconnect Between Employees and Employers Around Mental Health Need', McKinsey & Company.

37. MGI podcast in 2020.

38. A survey of 1,000 workers across US industries.

39. Canada statistics show alcohol consumption increase among 20% of people aged 15 to 49 years.

40. A study by Ambaw et al, 2020.

41. For Google, see Laura He, *Google's Secrets of Innovation: Empowering Its Employees*; Christin Parcerisa, *Tips from Google's resilience expert on avoiding burnout*; Jennifer Elias, *Google is tackling mental health challenges among employees through 'resilience training' videos*; and Rita Davidson, *How Google employees cope with stress.*

42. For Microsoft, see Chris Weller and Andrea Derler, *How Microsoft Overhauled Its Approach to Growth Mindset.*

43. For Intel, see Christine Rowland, *Intel's Organizational Culture for Business Resilience (An Analysis).*

44. Brent Dirks, 'How to Use the Apple Watch Mindfulness App in watchOS 8'; BohatALA website, 'Strategic Human Resource Activities at Apple Inc.'; *New York Times*, 'Inside Apple's Internal Training Program'; Chance Miller, 'Apple reportedly scales back ambitious "HealthHabit" project for transforming healthcare'.

45. For Aetna's approach, see the article 'Mindfulness and Meditation: 9 Stress-Management Strategies to Consider in the Workplace', on their website.

46. 'Nike Headspace Partnership Mindfulness Training', Nike News; see also Shoshy Ciment, 'Nike Continues to Emphasize Mental Health by Closing All Global Offices This Week to Give Employees a Break'; Justin Young, 'Nike Inc. Organizational Culture Characteristics: An Analysis'.

47. 'Working Culture. We can't afford to ignore Mental Health', Goldman Sachs CEO Richard Knoddle's blog; See also Eqversity, 'Resilience Programming at Goldman Sachs', the diversity and inclusion section and the article, 'How Goldman Sachs Champions Wellness in the Workplace: A Recap of Our Global Resilience Series', on the Goldman Sachs website.

48. Occupational Health and Safety Management—Psychological Health and Safety at Work—Guidelines for Managing Psychosocial Risks, ISO 45003:2021(en)

49. See also 'Returning to Work: Keys to a Psychologically Safer Workplace', McKinsey & Company, 15 July 2021, https://www.mckinsey.com/industries/healthcare-systems-and-services/our-insights/returning-to-work-keys-to-a-psychologically-safer-workplace?cid=other-eml-alt-mcq-mck&hdpid=15c23ed2-92ab-4e36-9dec-02bc66306a29&hctky=12810559&hlkid=baf5ac2d32044875a970a33f8fa088a0

50. Amy C. Edmondson, 'Managing the Risk of Learning: Psychological Safety in Work Teams', 15 March 2002; MA West, *International Handbook of Organizational Teamwork*, London: Blackwell; See also, Amy C. Edmondson1 and Zhike Lei, 'Psychological Safety: The History, Renaissance, and Future of an Interpersonal Construct', *Annual Review Organizational Psychology*, March 2014, downloaded from www.annualreviews.org.

51. 'Tool: Foster psychological safety', https://rework.withgoogle. com/guides/understanding-team-effectiveness/steps/foster-psychological-safety/; see also, Charles Duhigg, 'What Google Learned From Its Quest to Build the Perfect Team', *Sunday Magazine*, 28 February 2016.

52. Róisín O'Donovan, Desirée Van Dun and Eilish McAuliffe, 'Measuring Psychological Safety in Healthcare Teams: Developing An Observational Measure to Complement Survey Methods', BMC Medical Research Methodology, 2020, 20:203, https://doi. org/10.1186/s12874-020-01066-z

53. To explore NUVAH surveys and how they can benefit your team, visit the website: http://nuvah.in/

CHAPTER 7

1. Source: https://www.presidency.ucsb.edu/documents/remarks-heber-springs-arkansas-the-dedication-greers-ferry-dam

2. See Robert E. Lucas, Jr., 'Supply-Side Economics: An Analytical Review', *Oxford Economic Papers*, vol. 42, issue 2, April 1990, pp. 293–316, https://doi.org/10.1093/oxfordjournals.oep.a041948

3. See David Hope, Julian Limberg, 'The Economic Consequences of Major Tax Cuts for the Rich', *Socioeconomic Review*, vol. 20, issue 2, April 2022, pp. 539–559, https://doi.org/10.1093/ser/mwab061

4. See Sebastian Gechert, Philipp Heimberger, 'Do Corporate Tax Cuts Boost Economic Growth?' *European Economic Review*, 2022, vol. 147, https://doi.org/10.1016/j.euroecorev.2022.104157.

5. Source: https://www.igmchicago.org/surveys/laffer-curve/

6. See Phillipp Heimberger, 'Does Economic Globalisation Affect Income Inequality? A Meta-analysis', *World Economy*, 2020.

7. Stiglitz, *Globalization and its Discontents*, W.W. Norton and Co.

8. William Blake, 'Milton a Poem, Copy B Object 2', *The William Blake Archive*, eds. Morris Eaves, Robert N. Essick, and Joseph Viscomi.

9. For the full historical context of working conditions, rights, employment terms and quality of life of the modern English worker, see E.P. Thomson, *The Making of the English Working Class*, Penguin Modern Classics Paperback, 3 October 2013; for the specific question discussed here, see E.J. Hobsbawm, 'The Standard of Living during the Industrial Revolution: A Discussion', *The Economic History Review*, New Series, vol. 16, no. 1, 1963, pp. 119–134 (16 pages), Wiley; see also, Clark Nardinelli, 'Industrial Revolution and the Standard of Living', https://www. econlib.org/library/Enc/IndustrialRevolutionandtheStandardofLiving. html#:~:text=The%20share%20of%20total%20income,unequal%20 between%201790%20and%201840.

10. See Simon Kuznets, 'Economic Growth and Income Inequality', 1955, *American Economic Review* 45, (March): 1–28*.

11. Thomas Piketty, *Capital in the Twenty-first Century*, Belknap Press, 2014.

12. Source: https://web.archive.org/web/20170715151421/http://www. cid.harvard.edu/cidtrade/issues/washington.html

13. C. Lopes, 'Economic Growth and Inequality: The New Post-Washington Consensus', United Nations Institute for Training and Research (UNITAR) COIMBRA RCCS 94, 2012.

14. See Joseph Stiglitz, 'Some Lessons from The East Asian Miracle', *The World Bank Research Observer*, 11 (2): pp. 151–177.

15. See for Instance Amartya Sen, *Inequality-re-examined*, Oxford University Press, 1995.

16. John Rawls, *A theory of Justice*, 1999.

17. See Martha Nussbaum, 'Capabilities as Fundamental Entitlements: Sen and Social Justice', *Feminist Economics, 2003*, 9 (2): 33; see also Martha Nussbaum, *Creating Capabilities: The Human Approach*, Cambridge, Massachusetts: Belknap Press of Harvard University Press, 2011.

18. Source: https://iep.utm.edu/sen-cap/#SH3c

19. Source: https://ourworldindata.org/human-development-index#: ~:text=The%20Human%20Development%20Index%20(HDI)%20 provides%20a%20single%20index%20measure,a%20long%20 and%20healthy%20life

20. Amartya Sen, *Inequality-re-examined*, Oxford University Press, 1995.

21. Oded Galor, 'Inequality, Human Capital Formation and the Process of Development', 2011, https://www.sciencedirect.com/science/article/abs/pii/B9780444534446000055

22. Anneleen Vandeplas, 'Education, (2021) Income, and Inequality in the European Union', in Georg Fischer and Robert Strauss (eds) *Europe's Income, Wealth, Consumption, and Inequality*, New York, Oxford Academic, 2011, https://doi.org/10.1093/oso/9780197545706.003.0009.

23. Source: https://voxeu.org/article/one-dollar-one-vote-explanation-welfare-state

24. World Inequality Report 2022.

25. World Inequality Report 2022. Introduction. See also Manavi Kapoor, 'Half of India is So Poor it Owns Almost Nothing', *Quartz India*, 8 December 2021, https://qz.com/india/2099957/world-inequality-report-says-india-is-poor-but-with-rich-elite/

26. Source: https://www.oecd.org/els/emp/Globalisation-Jobs-and-Wages-2007.pdf

27. See David H. Autor, David Dorn, and Gordon H. Hanson. 2013, 'The China Syndrome: Local Labor Market Effects of Import Competition in the United States', *American Economic Review*, 103 (6): 2121-68, which examines competition from China for the US local labour market and concludes that rising imports cause higher unemployment, lower labour-force participation and reduced wages in local labour markets.

28. I. Magyari, 'Firm Reorganization, Chinese Imports, and US Manufacturing Employment', US Census Bureau, Center for Economic Studies, 2017.

29. Wilfred J. Ethier, 'Globalization, Globalisation: Trade, Technology, and Wages', *International Review of Economics & Finance*, 2005, vol. 14, issue 3, pp. 237–258, https://doi.org/10.1016/j.iref.2004.12.001.

30. Thomas Piketty, *Capital in the Twenty-First Century*, Harvard University Press, 2014.

31. Thomas Piketty, 'About Capital in the Twenty-First Century', *American Economic Review*, Papers and Proceedings, 2014.

32. Chaudhuri et al, 'The Interaction of Ethnicity and Deprivation on COVID-19 Mortality Risk: A Retrospective Ecological Study',

Sci Rep **11**, 11555, 2021, https://doi.org/10.1038/s41598-021-91076-8

33. Source: https://www.reuters.com/business/healthcare-pharmaceuticals/who-warns-against-vaccine-hoarding-poor-countries-go-without-2021-12-09/

34. Zizek Slavoj, *Pandemic!: COVID-19 Shakes the World*, Polity, 5 June 2020.

35. Ibid. pp. 14-15.

36. 'Israel: Provide Vaccines to Occupied Palestinians', Human Rights Watch website, 17 January 2021, hrw.org

37. Angus Deaton, 'COVID-19 and Global Income Inequality', NBER working paper, 2021. Source: https://www.nber.org/papers/w28392

38. Narayan et al, 'World bank Report', retrieved from https://openknowledge.worldbank.org/bitstream/handle/10986/36848/COVID-19-and-Economic-Inequality-Short-Term-Impacts-with-Long-Term-Consequences.pdf?sequence=1&isAllowed=y

39. Source: https://www.worldbank.org/en/publication/human-capital#Data

40. 'COVID-19 Impact: Nobel laureate Abhijit Banerjee Warns of Growing Inequality in Education', *Business Today*, 25 November 2020, https://www.businesstoday.in/latest/economy-politics/story/covid-19-impact-nobel-laureate-abhijit-banerjee-warns-of-growing-inequality-in-education-279667-2020-11-25

41. Source: https://www.worldbank.org/en/news/press-release/2018/03/14/india-growth-story-since-1990s-remarkably-stable-resilient

42. Source: https://www.ideasforindia.in/topics/macroeconomics/india-s-service-led-economic-growth.html

43. See Chapter 2 of the 'State of Inequality in India Report', 2022.

44. C. Goldin, 'The U-Shaped Female Labor Force Function in Economic Development And Economic History', T.P. Schultz, (ed.), *Investment in Women's Human Capital and Economic Development*;
Chicago, IL, University of Chicago Press, 1995, pp. 61–90; see also, S. Kanwal, 'Rate of Female Labor Force Participation India 1990-2020', 16 March 2022, https://www.statista.com/statistics/983020/female-labor-force-participation-rate-india/#statisticContainer

45. Source: https://thewire.in/economy/india-world-inequality-report-poor-affluent-elite-progress

46. '*Climate Change and Wellbeing Around the World*', Gallup.

47. Dr Amit Kapoor, Jessica Duggal, 'The State of Inequality in India Report', Institute for Competitiveness, April 2022.

48. Surjit Bhalla, Karan Bhasin and Arvind Virmani, 'Pandemic, Poverty and Inequality: Evidence from India', IMF working paper, 2022, https://www.imf.org/en/Publications/WP/Issues/2022/04/05/Pandemic-Poverty-and-Inequality-Evidence-from-India-516155

49. See Mehrotra's piece in https://www.deccanherald.com/opinion/what-s-falling-poverty-or-quality-of-analysis-1111856.html

50. See Sinha Roy, Sutirtha; Van Der Weide, Roy, 'Poverty in India Has Declined over the Last Decade but Not as Much as Previously Thought', Policy Research Working Paper, 2022, 9994, World Bank, Washington, DC, World Bank, https://openknowledge.worldbank.org/handle/10986/37273 License: CC BY 3.0 IGO.

51. See for example, Grace Carswell and Geert De Neve, 'MGNREGA in Tamil Nadu: A Story of Success and Transformation? Journal Of Agrarian Change', 2014, 14 (4), pp. 564–585, DOI: 10.1111/joac.12054; for a non-technical summary of the national evidence see https://www.newsclick.in/MGNREGA-protects-poor-further-poverty-natural-calamities#:~:text=MGNREGA%20reduced%20poverty%20by%20up,5%20and%202011%2D12%20found.

52. See also Ministry of Micro, Small and Medium Enterprises, 2021, Prime Ministers Employment Generation Programme, PMEGP, https://msme.gov.in/11-prime-ministers-employment-generation-programme-pmegp; Ministry of Micro, Small and Medium Enterprises, 2021; Prime Ministers Employment Generation Programme, PMEGP, https://msme.gov.in/11-prime-ministers-employment-generation-programme-pmegp And Ministry of Statistics and Programme Implementation (MOSPI); 'Women and Men in India 2020', https://mospi.nic.in/publication/women-and-men-india-2020.

53. Government, society and markets, respectively.

54. The details up to this point in the section, are taken from Kim Elsesser, 'The Business Case for Diversity May Be Backfiring, A New Study Shows', *Forbes*, 20 June 2022.

55. Natasha Jamal and Teresa Tschida, '3 Actions for Leaders to Improve DEI in the Workplace', Gallup website, 27 April 2021, https://www.gallup.com/workplace/348266/actions-leaders-improve-dei-workplace.aspx
56. Corporate Social Responsibility Software Market Research Report 2021-2027, Market Statsville Group
57. Sachin P. Mampatta, 'India Inc's CSR Spends Over 1 Trillion Since Mandatory Law in FY15: Crisil', *Business Standard*, 24 August 2021, India Inc's CSR Spends Over 1 Trillion Since Mandatory Law in FY15: Crisil

CHAPTER 8

1. 'Global Burden of Disease Study', Institute of Health Metrics and Evaluation (IHME), https://ourworldindata.org/global-mental-health
2. Ibid.
3. Enterprise Resource Planning (ERP), Gartner website, https://www.gartner.com/en/information-technology/glossary/enterprise-resource-planning-erp
4. Data Science for Humanity, Stanford University, https://datascience.stanford.edu/research/research-areas/data-science-humanity
5. Bernard Marr, 'What Is the Difference Between Weak (Narrow) and Strong (General) Artificial Intelligence (AI)?', LinkedIn, 13 May 2021, https://www.linkedin.com/pulse/what-difference-between-weak-narrow-strong-general-artificial-marr; for a comprehensive discussion of the differences, see 'Web 3.0 vs. Metaverse: A Detailed comparison', Blockchain Council, https://www.blockchain-council.org/metaverse/web-3-0-vs-metaverse/#:~:text=The%20metaverse%20is%20a%203D,users%20can%20charge%20their%20creations.
6. Ayushi Abrol, 'Metaverse Vs Multiverse—What's The Difference?', Blockchain, https://www.blockchain-council.org/metaverse/metaverse-vs-multiverse/#:~:text=Basically%2C%20the%20metaverse%20is%20a,to%20its%20unified%20user%20interface.
7. Alyssa Ruiz, 'How Will the Higher Education Industry Adopt the Metaverse?', Investisdigital, 30 August 2022.

8. G. Riva, Ph.D. (1-2), Brenda K. Wiederhold PhD, MBA, 'What the Metaverse Is (really) and Why We Need to Know About It'; see also Ersin Dincellia and Alper Yaylab, 'Immersive Virtual Reality in the Age of the Metaverse: A Hybrid-narrative Review Based on the Technology Affordance Perspective', *The Journal of Strategic Information Systems*, vol. 31, issue 2, June 2022, 101717; Aleksi H. Syrjämäkia, Poika Isokoski, Veikko Surakka, Tytti P. Pasanen and Jari K. Hietanen, 'Eye Contact in Virtual Reality—A Psychophysiological Study', *Computers in Human Behavior*, Volume 112, November 2020, 106454.
9. Mkike Proulx, Julie Ask, Martha Bennett, J.P. Gownder and David Truog, 'There Is No Metaverse Today, But Be Prepared', *Forbes*, 29 March 2022, https://www.forrester.com/blogs/there-is-no-metaverse-today-but-be-prepared/
10. 'More than Seventy-Five Percent of US B2C Marketing Executives Plan to Invest in the "Metaverse" This Year, Despite Consumer Skepticism', Forrester, 30 March 2022, https://www.forrester.com/press-newsroom/forrester-metaverse-marketing-executives/
11. Arti, 'Pave the Way, "Father of Metaverse" Is Launching Blockchain', *Analytics Insight*, 10 June 2022, https://www.analyticsinsight.net/pave-the-way-father-of-metaverse-is-launching-blockchain/
12. Vijay Kumar, 'How Metaverse Is Gaining Ground in India', ET CIO.com, 3 March 2022, https://cio.economictimes.indiatimes.com/news/next-gen-technologies/how-metaverse-is-gaining-ground-in-india/89959772
13. 'Top 10 Trusted Metaverse Development Companies in India 2022', *The Hindu*, 8 March 2022, https://www.thehindu.com/brandhub/pr-release/top-10-trusted-metaverse-development-companies-in-india-2022/article65204298.ece
14. David Truog, 'Ten Principles for Designing the Metaverse', *Forbes*, 10 May 2022, https://www.forrester.com/blogs/designing-the-metaverse/
15. Apoorva Bellapu, 'Top 10 Attractive Metaverse Projects to Look Out for in 2022', *Analytics Insight*, 5 June 2022, https://www.analyticsinsight.net/top-10-attractive-metaverse-projects-to-lookout-for-in-2022/
16. Yessar Rosendar, 'Reliance's Jio Platforms Invests in Deep Tech Startup Two Platforms, Betting on The Metaverse', *Forbes*, 7 February

2022, https://www.forbes.com/sites/yessarrosendar/2022/02/07/reliances-jio-platforms-invests-in-deep-tech-startup-two-platforms-betting-on-the-metaverse/?sh=7fb3dece44c7

17. Vanshika Malhotra, 'Airtel Introduces India's First Multiplex in the Metaverse: Check It Out!' Beebom, https://beebom.com/airtel-multiplex-metaverse-introduced/

18. Shashank Bhardwaj, 'Indian Companies Storm the Metaverse and NFT space', *Forbes India*, https://www.forbesindia.com/article/crypto-made-easy/indian-companies-storm-the-metaverse-and-nft-space/75281/1, see also, 'Explained! How Indian tech giants Are Joining the Metaverse Bandwagon', CNBC, https://www.cnbctv18.com/cryptocurrency/explained-how-indian-tech-giants-are-joining-the-metaverse-bandwagon-12766032.htm

19. Hannah M. Mayer, 'The Future of The Metaverse: What 2022 Has in Store for The Immersive Digital World', *Forbes*, 24 January 2022, https://www.forbes.com/sites/hannahmayer/2022/01/24/the-future-of-the-metaverse-what-2022-has-in-store-for-the-immersive-digital-world/?sh=77d0aca8335a

20. David Truog, 'The Metaverse Must Be Deeply Human-Centric', *Forbes*, 7 June 2022, https://www.forrester.com/blogs/the-metaverse-must-be-deeply-human-centric/

21. Kathryn Hopkins, 'What Does Metaverse Mean for the Workforce of the Future?' CXC AMERICAS, 24 March 2022, https://www.cxcglobal.com/en-us/what-does-metaverse-mean-for-the-workforce-of-the-future

22. Poulomi Chatterjee, 'Accenture to Onboard 150,000 New Hires Using the Metaverse', *Analytics India Mag*azine, 19 April 2022, https://analyticsindiamag.com/accenture-announces-150000-new-hirings-to-work-from-metaverse/#:~:text=IT%20services%20consultant%20Accenture%20has,participate%20in%20immersive%-20learning%20experiences.

23. Mark Purdy, 'How the Metaverse Could Change Work', *Harvard Business Review*, 5 April 2022, https://hbr.org/2022/04/how-the-metaverse-could-change-work#:~:text=The%20metaverse%20could%20revolutionize%20training,training%20and%20with%20career%20advice.

410   Notes

24. Arti, 'Metaverse and the Future of Work: Are You Ready for the Change?', *Analytics Insight*, 21 March 2022, https://www.analyticsinsight.net/metaverse-and-the-future-of-work-are-you-ready-for-the-change/; See also 'Work in The Metaverse? How The Metaverse Is Shaping the Future of Work', Adecco Group website, 10 February 2022., https://www.adeccogroup.com/future-of-work/latest-insights/how-the-metaverse-is-shaping-the-future-of-work/; and 'The Advantages and Disadvantages of Working in the Metaverse', Adecco Group website, 4 April 2022, https://www.adeccogroup.com/future-of-work/latest-insights/the-advantages-and-disadvantages-of-working-in-the-metaverse/

25. Alexander Fernandez, 'The Metaverse: The Future of Work', *Forbes*, 18 March 2022, https://www.forbes.com/sites/forbesbusinesscouncil/2022/03/18/the-metaverse-the-future-of-work/?sh=2a6f9f274267

26. 'Metaverse and the Future of Marketing', Data Quest Online, 23 March 2022, https://www.dqindia.com/metaverse-and-the-future-of-marketing/; See also Geri Mileva, 'The State of the Metaverse 2022: Challenges & Opportunities', Influencer Marketing Hub, 21 January 2022, https://influencermarketinghub.com/state-of-the-metaverse/

27. Barry Po, 'Five Surprising Ways the Metaverse Meets the Future of Work', *Forbes*, 21 April 2022, https://www.forbes.com/sites/forbestechcouncil/2022/04/21/five-surprising-ways-the-metaverse-meets-the-future-of-work/?sh=34fb3313d1d4

28. David Rodeck and John Schmidt, 'What Is Blockchain?' *Forbes*, 25 March 2022, https://www.forbes.com/advisor/in/investing/what-is-blockchain/

29. 'What is Cryptocurrency and How Does it Work?', Kapersky, https://www.kaspersky.com/resource-center/definitions/what-is-cryptocurrency

30. 'The Pros and Cons of Cryptocurrency: A Guide for New Investors', N26, 17 January 2022, https://n26.com/en-eu/blog/pros-and-cons-of-cryptocurrency

31. Robyn Conti and John Schmidt, 'What Is an NFT? How Do NFTs Work?', *Forbes*, 25 March 2022, https://www.forbes.com/advisor/in/investing/what-is-an-nft-how-do-nfts-work/;   'Non-fungible

tokens (NFT)', Ethereum website, https://ethereum.org/en/nft/; Mitchell Clark, 'NFTs explained', The Verge, 6 June 2022, https://www.theverge.com/22310188/nft-explainer-what-is-blockchain-crypto-art-faq; Joshua Rodriguez, 'Non-Fungible Tokens (NFTs) Definition—Should You Invest in Digital Art?' MoneyCrashers, 14 September 2021, https://www.moneycrashers.com/non-fungible-tokens-nfts/

32. Thomas J. Brock, 'From the Experts: 8 Pros and Cons of Non-Fungible Tokens and How They Compare to Traditional Investments', 14 January 2022, https://www.annuity.org/2022/01/14/from-the-experts-8-pros-and-cons-of-nfts/; 'The Pros and Cons of Investing in NFTs', Fintra website, 30 May 2022, https://fintra.co.in/blog/pros-and-cons-of-investing-in-nfts

33. 'Perspectives: The Rise of Using Cryptocurrency in Business', Deloitte, https://www2.deloitte.com/us/en/pages/audit/articles/corporates-using-crypto.html

34. 'How Can Blockchain Power Industrial Manufacturing?', PwC Report, https://www.pwc.com/us/en/industrial-products/publications/assets/pwc-blockchain-in-manufacturing.pdf

35. 'Blockchain Use Cases and Applications', IBM Website, https://www.ibm.com/in-en/topics/what-is-blockchain; see also, Blockchain technology for Supply Chains—A Must or a Maybe?' McKinsey, 12 September 2017, https://www.mckinsey.com/business-functions/operations/our-insights/blockchain-technology-for-supply-chainsa-must-or-a-maybe

36. Aarti Chawla, 'The Future of Work Is Built on Blockchain', Datatech Vibe, 15 February 2022, https://datatechvibe.com/data/the-future-of-work-is-built-on-blockchain/

37. Daniel Lehewych, 'What Is Cryptocurrency's Role in The Future of Work?', Allwork website, 28 April 2022, https://allwork.space/2022/04/what-is-cryptocurrencys-role-in-the-future-of-work/

38. Dror Poleg, 'NFTs and the Future of Work', 25 March 2021, https://www.drorpoleg.com/nfts-and-the-future-of-work/ For other perspectives on the future of work, see 'Indian Workplace of 2022', PwC Paper, PricewaterhouseCoopers India, 2014; 'The Future of Work. New Perspectives on Disruption & Transformation',

PEGA; 'The Future of Work in India. Inclusion, Growth and Transformation', Observer Research Foundation.

39. The arguments in this section are taken from Avik Chanda and Meghana Srivatsav, 'What Leaders Need to Know About Honesty, Ethics and Integrity in the New Workplace', *Economic Times*, 29 October, 2021.

40. For a discussion on how such values and codes of conduct have evolved psychologically, see Robert Wright, 'The Moral Animal. Why We Are the Way We Are: The New Science of Evolutionary Psychology'.

41. Scott Stein, 'Microsoft Shutters Part of Its Social Metaverse for Safety Reasons', CNET.com, 16 February 2022, https://www.cnet.com/tech/computing/microsoft-shutters-part-of-its-social-metaverse-for-safety-reasons/

42. 'State of the Global Workplace 2022 Report', The Voice of the Employees, Gallup.

43. 'People and Culture First: Transformation Journey in the Future of Work', PwC report, February 2022; for a quick summary, see '50% of India Leaders Feel Unsure About the Future of Work: PwC India survey', https://www.pwc.in/press-releases/2022/50-percentage-of-india-leaders-feel-unsure-about-the-future-of-work-pwc-survey.html

44. T.R. Harish, 'Impact of New Labour Codes on Employee's Working Hours, Annual Leave', *Mint,* 22 June 2022, https://www.livemint.com/opinion/online-views/impact-of-new-labour-codes-on-employee-s-working-hours-annual-leave-11655904280353.html; 'New Labour Laws From July 1! How Working Hours, PF and In-hand Salary Will Change', DNA website, https://www.dnaindia.com/business/report-new-labour-laws-from-july-1-how-working-hours-pf-in-hand-salary-leaves-will-change-labour-codes-2959103; TR, H., 22 June 2022, 'Impact of New Labour Codes on Employee's Working Hours, Annual Leave', https://www.livemint.com/opinion/online-views/impact-of-new-labour-codes-on-employee-s-working-hours-annual-leave-11655904280353.html

45. 'Four-day Week "an overwhelming success" in Iceland', BBC News, 6 July 2021, https://www.bbc.com/news/business-57724779; Emma Simpson, 'The Workers Getting 100% Pay for 80% of the

Hours', BBC News, 6 June 2022,: https://www.bbc.com/news/business-61570021

46. As quoted by Eva Majercsik, 'What Does Your Workplace of The Future Look Like?', Forbes, 4 Aug 2021, https://www.forbes.com/sites/forbeshumanresourcescouncil/2021/08/04/what-does-your-workplace-of-the-future-look-like/?sh=4f170cff4317; the full report can be accessed through Prudential's website, https://news.prudential.com/presskits/pulse-american-worker-survey-is-this-working.htm

47. Quoted in the SHRM website article, 'What Will the Workplace Look Like in 2025?'. Source: https://www.shrm.org/hr-today/news/all-things-work/pages/the-workplace-in-2025.aspx; also see Dror Poleg, 'The Crypto Future of Work', 9 June 2021. Source: https://www.drorpoleg.com/the-crypto-future-of-work/

48. Daniel Davis, '5 Models for the Post-Pandemic Workplace', *Harvard Business Review*, 3 June 2021, https://hbr.org/2021/06/5-models-for-the-post-pandemic-workplace; See also Alpeyev, Pavel and Yuki Furukama, 'Pay Up to Stay Home is One Company's Approach to Remote Work', *Economic Times* (republished from Bloomberg), 2 July 2021, https://m.economictimes.com/news/international/business/pay-up-to-stay-home-is-one-companys-approach-to-remote-work/articleshow/83977868.cms Accessed 04 July 2021

49. Janet Pogue McLaurin, '5 Trends Driving the New Post-Pandemic Workplace', Gensler website, https://www.gensler.com/blog/5-trends-driving-the-new-post-pandemic-workplace

50. Jena McGregor, 'Two Years into The Pandemic, Almost Twice as Many Workers Prefer Hybrid Schedules to Fully Remote Work', *Forbes*, 16 March 2022.

51. J. Turner, '6 Ways the Workplace Will Change in the Next 10 Years', Gartner website, 20 August, 2019, https://www.gartner.com/smarterwithgartner/6-ways-the-workplace-will-change-in-the-next-10-years

52. 'The Future of Work after COVID-19 Report', McKinsey Global Institute (MGI), 18 February 2021; see also Gaurav Chattur, 'The Great talent Exodus and How Organizations Can Tackle it in 2021', PeopleMatters, 26 July 2021, https://www.peoplematters.in/article/

recruitment/the-great-talent-exodus-and-how-organizations-can-tackle-it-in-2021-30160

53. World Bank, 'World Development Report 2019: The Changing Nature of Work. Washington, DC: World Bank' doi:10.1596/978-1-4648-1328-3, License: Creative Commons Attribution CC BY 3.0 IGO.

54. 'Jobs of Tomorrow: The Triple Returns of Social Jobs in the Economic Recovery', World Economic Forum White Paper, in Collaboration with Accenture, May 2022; for a summary and other highlights of Davos 2022 meetings, see Kate Whiting, 'This is the future of work, according to experts at Davos 2022', World Economic Forum website, 26 May 2022. https://www.weforum.org/agenda/2022/05/future-work-jobs-davos-experts/

55. 'Now, Next & Beyond How Does Security Evolve from Bolted on to Built-in? Bridging the relationship gap to meet challenges posed by the new normal', EY Global Information Security Survey (GISS) 2019-20: India edition.

56. Sally Percy, 'Why Your Company Needs a Chief Philosophy Officer', *Forbes*, 9 March 2018, https://www.forbes.com/sites/sallypercy/2018/03/09/why-your-board-needs-a-chief-philosophy-officer/; see also Visty Banaji, 'You Need a "CPO" to Face the Future', People Matters, 10 June 2022, https://www.peoplematters.in/article/strategic-hr/you-need-a-cpo-to-face-the-future-34234

57. Ian Stewart and Myles Runham, 'After EI, DI? Chief Learning Officer';
'The Future of Work Arrives Early', SHRM, in collaboration with Oxford Economics and SAP Success Factors; see also, SHRM's Future Insights Top Trends Affecting the Workplace and the HR Profession According to SHRM Special Expertise Panels.

58. 'Building Workplaces and Workforces for the Future: The View from India', PwC report, April 2021.

59. Avik Chanda and Shubhabrata Roy, 'What Human-Centric Companies Prescribe for a Post-Covid World', *The Economic Times*, 19 May 2020. Source: https://economictimes.indiatimes.com/jobs/what-human-centric-companies-prescribe-for-a-post-covid-world/articleshow/75819868.cms; Avik Chanda, *Why Companies Need*

a Role-Based Model in the Covid-19 Paradigm', *Economic Times*, 14 April 2020; https://economictimes.indiatimes.com/jobs/why-companies-need-a-role-based-model-in-the-covid-19-paradigm/articleshow/75139253.cms

Bibliography

(2022). Retrieved from Literacy Rate in India 2022. Kerala and Bihar Literacy rate: https://www.theglobalstatistics.com/literacy-rate-in-india/

'A Look At Skill Gaps in the USA in 2022'. TC Global Website: https://tcglobal.com/a-look-at-skill-gaps-in-the-usa-in-2022/

Abraham, V., Cook, K., Keller, M., Pan, J., & Treharne, E. 'Data Science for Humanity'. Retrieved from Stanford University: https://datascience.stanford.edu/research/research-areas/data-science-humanity

Abrol, A. 'Metaverse Vs Multiverse – What's The Difference?' Retrieved from Blockchain Council;: https://www.blockchain-council.org/metaverse/metaverse-vs-multiverse/#:~:text=Basically%2C%20the%20metaverse%20is%20a,to%20its%20unified%20user%20interface

Accenture. 'Human Resilience What Your People Need now'. 'COVID-19: What to Do Now, What to Do Next'. https://www.accenture.com/_acnmedia/Thought-Leadership-Assets/PDF-2/Accenture-Human-Resilience-What-Your-People-Need-Now.pdf. Accessed on 9 February 2022.

Accenture. 'Rewire for Growth: Accelerating India's Economic Growth with Artificial Intelligence'. Published by Accenture Research, 2017.

Accenture. 'Rewire for Success: Boosting India's AIQ, Enabling Strong and Inclusive AI-Driven Economic Growth'. Published by Accenture Research, 2017.

Acemoglu, D., & Dell, M. 'Productivity Differences between and within Countries'. *American Economic Journal: Macroeconomics*, Vol. 2, No. 1 (2010): 169-188.

Acemoglu, D., & Restrepo, P. 'The Race between Man and Machine: Implications of Technology for Growth, Factor Shares, and Employment'. *American Economic Review*, Vol. 108, No. 6 (2018): 1488-1542.

Aetna website. 'Mindfulness and Meditation: 9 Stress-management Strategies to Consider in the Workplace'. https://www. aetnainternational.com/en/about-us/explore/fit-for-duty-corporate-wellness/mindfulness-meditation-9-stress-management-strategies-for-the-workplace.html. Accessed on 2 December 2021.

Agarwal, K. 'Why We Must Be Critical Of The New Education Policy 2020'. Feminism In India. 6 August 2020. https://feminisminindia. com/2020/08/06/new-education-policy-nep-2020-critical-analysis/.

Agarwal, Meha. 'How Artificial Intelligence Algorithms Are Changing India's Banking Industry? Inc42. 22 October 2019. https://inc42. com/features/how-artificial-intelligence-algorithms-are-changing-indias-banking-industry/. Accessed on 23 July 2021.

Agovino, T. 'What Will the Workplace Look Like in 2025?' Retrieved from shrm.org: https://www.shrm.org/hr-today/news/all-things-work/pages/the-workplace-in-2025.aspx.

Alawadhi, Neha. 'Amid WFH Burnout, Indian Professionals Want to Return to Office: Survey'. *Business Standard*. 15 September 2021. https://www.business-standard.com/article/economy-policy/amid-wfh-burnout-indian-professionals-want-to-return-to-office-survey-121091401055_1.html. Accessed on 16 February 2022.

Alpeyev, Pavel, and Yuki Furukama. 'Pay Up to Stay Home Is One Company's Approach to Remote Work'. *The Economic Times* (republished from Bloomberg). 2 July 2021. https://m.economictimes. com/news/international/business/pay-up-to-stay-home-is-one-companys-approach-to-remote-work/articleshow/83977868.cms. Accesed on 4 July 2021.

Ambaw, F. Mayston, R., Hanlon, C., & Alem, A. 'Incidence of Depression in People with Newly Diagnosed Tuberculosis in Ethiopia: A Cohort Study'. Cambridge: Cambridge University Press, 2021.

American Psychiatric Association. 'As Americans Begin to Return to the Office, Views on Workplace Mental Health Are Mixed'. 22

May 2021. https://www.psychiatry.org/newsroom/news-releases/as-americans-begin-to-return-to-the-office-views-on-workplace-mental-health-are-mixed. Accessed on 16 February 2022.

Analytics India Magazine. 'AI In Healthcare Is Challenging: What Can India Do?' 10 February 2021. https://analyticsindiamag.com/ai-in-healthcare-is-challenging-what-can-india-do/. Accessed on 23 July 2021.

Analytics India Magazine. 'How Surgical Robot Assistants Are Becoming a Reality in Indian Hospitals and Healthcare Sector'. 5 April 2019. https://analyticsindiamag.com/how-surgical-robot-assistants-are-becoming-a-reality-in-indian-hospitals-and-healthcare-sector. Accessed on 23 July 2021.

Analytics India Magazine. 'Impact on Jobs across Emerging Technologies During the Current Pandemic Crisis'. 4 August 2020. https://analyticsindiamag.com/impact-on-jobs-across-emerging-technologies-during-the-current-pandemic-crisis-by-aim-jigsaw-academy. Accessed on 23 July 2021.

Analytics India Magazine. 'Report: State of Artificial Intelligence in India—2020'. 8 September 2020. https://analyticsindiamag.com/report-state-of-artificial-intelligence-in-india-2020/. Accessed on 23 July 2021.

Analytics India Magazine. 'Top Robotics Companies to Look Forward to in 2021'. 2 January 2021. https://analyticsindiamag.com/top-robotics-companies-to-look-forward-to-in-2021/. Accessed 23 July 2021.

Analytics Jobs. 'Top 20 Start-ups in India revolutionizing Health-Care Industry with Artificial Intelligence'. https://analyticsjobs.in/latest-research/artificial-intelligence-in-healthcare. Accessed on 23 July 2021.

Anayi, L., Bloom, N., Bunn, P., Mizen, P., Oilonomou, M., Smietanka, P., & Thwaites, G. 'Which Firms and Industries Have Been Most Affected by Covid-19?' Retrieved from Economics Observatory. 5 May 2021. https://www.economicsobservatory.com/update-which-firms-and-industries-have-been-most-affected-by-covid-19

Anderson, R.J. and W.W. Sharrock. 'Ethical Algorithms: A Brief Comment on an Extensive Muddle'. Horizon Digital Economy, 2013.

Ariely, Dan. 'Payoff: The Hidden Logic that Shapes our Motivations'. New York: TED Books, Simon & Schuster, 2016.

Arti. 'Pave the Way, "Father of Metaverse" Is Launching Blockchain'. Retrieved from analyticsinsight.net. 10 June 2022. https://www.analyticsinsight.net/pave-the-way-father-of-metaverse-is-launching-blockchain/.

Arti. 'Metaverse and the Future of Work: Are You Ready for the Change? Retrieved from Analyticsindia.com. 21 March 2022. https://www.analyticsinsight.net/metaverse-and-the-future-of-work-are-you-ready-for-the-change/.

Asian Defence. '"Daksh" Bomb Disposal Robot Will Roll Out Soon for the Indian Army'. http://theasiandefence.blogspot.com/2009/08/bomb-disposal-robot-daksh-for-indian.html. Accessed 23 July 2021.

Asian Robotics. 'Industrial Robots & Cobots to 2025: Can Domestic Manufacturers Compete with Foreign Robots and Impact India's New Automation Market?' https://asianroboticsreview.com/home337-html. Accessed on 28 July 2021.

Autor, David H., David Dorn, and Gordon H. Hanson. 'The China Syndrome: Local Labor Market Effects of Import Competition in the United States'. *American Economic Review*, Vol. 103 (6) (2013): pp. 2121-2168.

Bandyopadhyay, Siddhartha, Anindya Banerjee and Kaustav Das. 'Algorithms in the Criminal Justice System and Healthcare: The Good, Bad and Ugly: Report'.

Banaji, V. 'You Need a "CPO" to Face the Future'. People Matters. 10 June 2022. https://www.peoplematters.in/article/strategic-hr/you-need-a-cpo-to-face-the-future-34234.

'Bangladesh: Female Labor Force Participation'. Retrieved from the Global Economy.com. https://www.theglobaleconomy.com/Bangladesh/Female_labor_force_participation/.

Barik, S. 'Funding Winter Sets in for Indian Startups, Staff Out in the Cold: Over 12K laid off'. Retrieved from *Indian Express*. 6 July 2022. https://indianexpress.com/article/business/indian-startups-funding-winter-lay-offs-8011194/.

Barkur, Gopalkrishna, Vibha, and Giridhar B. Kamatha. 'Sentiment Analysis of Nationwide Lockdown Due to COVID-19 Outbreak: Evidence from India'. *Asian Journal Psychiatry*, June 2020; 51: 102089.

Published online 12 Apr 2020. doi: 10.1016/j.ajp.2020.102089. https://www.ncbi.nlm.nih.gov/pmc/articles/PMC7152888/. Accessed on 16 February 2022.

Baruah, Ayushman. 'AI Applications in the Top 4 Indian Banks'. Emerj. 27 February 2020. https://emerj.com/ai-sector-overviews/ai-applications-in-the-top-4-indian-banks/. Accessed on 23 July 2021.

Basu, Sreeradha. 'HR Leaders Should Focus on "Wholistic Wellbeing", Use Data and Technology to Enhance Employee Wellbeing: Report'. *Economic Times*. 24 June 2021. https://economictimes.indiatimes.com/news/company/corporate-trends/hr-leaders-should-focus-on-wholistic-wellbeing-use-data-and-technology-to-enhance-employee-wellbeing-report/articleshow/83817697.cms?from=mdr. Accessed 4 July 2021.

BBC News. 'AlphaGo: Computer Defeat "painful" for Chinese Go Prodigy'. BBC. 27 May 2021. https://www.bbc.com/news/av/world-asia-china-40073960. Accessed on 6 October 2021.

Behera, S., and Behera, M. 'Gig Work and Platforms During the COVID-19 Pandemic in India'. *Economic and Political Weekly*, Vol. 55, Issue No. 45 (2020). pdf (epw.in).

Bellapu, A. 'Top 10 Attractive Metaverse Projects To Lookout For In 2022'. Analytics.insight.net. 5 June 2022. https://www.analyticsinsight.net/top-10-attractive-metaverse-projects-to-lookout-for-in-2022/.

Bernanke, Ben S., and Peter Olson. 'Are Americans Better Off than they Were a Decade or Two Ago?' Brookings. 19 October 2016. https://www.brookings.edu/blog/ben-bernanke/2016/10/19/are-americans-better-off-than-they-were-a-decade-or-two-ago/.

Bertram, V. M. 'STEM or STEAM? We're Missing the Point'. *Huffpost*. 6 December 2017. https://www.huffpost.com/entry/stem-of-steam-were-missin_b_5031895.

Bhaduri, Abhijit. 'What will Career 3.0 and Jobs 3.0 be like?' *Hindu BusinessLine*. 28 January 2019. https://www.thehindubusinessline.com/specials/businessline-25/what-will-career-30-and-jobs-30-be-like/article26105380.ece. Accessed on 05 October 2021.

Bhalla, Surjit, Bhasin Karan and Virmani Arvind. 'Pandemic, Poverty and Inequality: Evidence from India.' IMF working paper. 5 April 2022. Available on: https://www.imf.org/en/Publications/WP/

Issues/2022/04/05/Pandemic-Poverty-and-Inequality-Evidence-from-India-516155.

Bhalla, K. 'The Worst for Indian Startups Is yet to Come—Be Prepared for Layoffs, Unicorn Slowdown and Startup Shutdowns in 2022'. *Business Insider India*. 20 May 2022. https://www.businessinsider.in/business/startups/news/the-worst-for-indian-startups-is-yet-to-come-be-prepared-for-layoffs-unicorn-slowdown-and-startup-shutdowns-in-2022/articleshow/91681195.cms.

Bhardwaj, S. 'Indian Companies Storm the Metaverse and NFT Space'. *Forbes India*. https://www.forbesindia.com/article/crypto-made-easy/indian-companies-storm-the-metaverse-and-nft-space/75281/1.

Bhardwaj, Tarun. 'Technology-led Innovations Will Be the Mainstay of Future Healthcare in India: Mandeep Singh Kumar, VP&GM, Intuitive India'. *Financial Express*. 2 June 2021. https://www.financialexpress.com/lifestyle/health/technology-led-innovations-will-be-the-mainstay-of-future-healthcare-in-india-mandeep-kumar-singh-vpgm-intuitive-india/2263578/. Accessed on 23 Jul, 2021.

Biasi, B., and S. Ma. 'The Education-Innovation Gap'. *Journal of Economic Literature*, 2021.

Biswas-Diener, Robert (Ed.). *Positive Psychology as Social Change*. New York: Springer, 2011.

Blake, William. 'Milton a Poem, Copy B Object 2'. The William Blake Archive. Ed. Morris Eaves, Robert N. Essick, and Joseph Viscomi, 2012.

Alick, Knut, Alan Davies, Markus Leopoldsede, and Alex Niemeye. 'Blockchain Technology for Supply Chains—A Must or a Maybe?' McKinsey and Company. 12 September 2017. https://www.mckinsey.com/business-functions/operations/our-insights/blockchain-technology-for-supply-chainsa-must-or-a-maybe. Accessed on 20 February 2023.

BohatALA. 'Strategic Human Resource Activities at Apple Inc'. https://bohatala.com/strategic-human-resource-activities-at-apple-inc/. Accessed 2 December 2021.

Boobier, Tony. *Advanced Analytics and AI: Impact, Implementation and the Future of Work*. Wily Finance Series. Chichester, United Kingdom: John Wiley & Sons, 2018.

Bradberry, Travis and Jean Greaves. *Emotional Intelligence 2.0.* TalentSmart, 2009.

Brenner, P. S., & DeLamater, J. 'Lies, Damned Lies, and Survey Self-Reports? Identity as a Cause of Measurement Bias'. Social Psychology Quarterly. 79(4) (2016): 333-354. doi:10.1177/0190272516628298.

Bringsjord, Selmer. *Artificial Intelligence and Literary Creativity: Inside the Mind of BRUTUS, a Storytelling Machine.* New Jersey, London: Lawrence Erlbaum Associates, Publishers, 2000.

Brynjolfsson, Erik, and Andrew McAfee. *The Second Machine Age. Work, Progress and Prosperity in a Time of Brilliant Technologies.* New York and London: WW. Norton & Company, 2016.

Brock, T. J. 'From the Experts: 8 Pros and Cons of Non-Fungible Tokens and How They Compare to Traditional Investments'. Annuity.org. 14 January 2022. https://www.annuity.org/2022/01/14/from-the-experts-8-pros-and-cons-of-nfts/. Accessed on 20 February 2023

BusinessToday.in. 'India's Unemployment in 2020 at Worst Level in 29 Years, Shows Study'. 28 May 2021. https://www.businesstoday.in/jobs/story/india-unemployment-in-2020-at-worst-level-in-29-years-shows-study-297195-2021-05-28. Accessed on 5 October 2021.

Business Today.in. 'Covid-19 Impact: Nobel Laureate Abhijit Banerjee Warns of Growing Inequality in Education'. 25 November 2020. https://www.businesstoday.in/latest/economy-politics/story/covid-19-impact-nobel-laureate-abhijit-banerjee-warns-of-growing-inequality-in-education-279667-2020-11-25. Accessed on 28 September 2022.

Business Standard. 'India Inc's CSR Spends Over 1 Trillion Since Mandatory Law in FY15: Crisil.' 2021. https://www.business-standard.com/article/companies/india-inc-s-csr-spends-over-1-trillion-since-mandatory-law-in-fy15-crisil-121082401249_1.html Accessed on 20 February 2023.

C.A., Grant, L.M. Wallace, P.C. Spurgeon, C. Tramontano, and M. Charalampous. 'Construction and Initial Validation of the E-Work Life Scale to Measure Remote E-working'. *Employee Relations.* Vol. 41 No. 1 (2021): 16-33. https://doi.org/10.1108/ER-09-2017-0229.

Card, D., and O.C. Ashenfelter, *Handbook of Labour Economics*, North Holland, 1987.

Carr, Nicholas. *The Shallows: What the Internet is Doing to Our Brains.* New York, London: W.W. Norton & Company, 2010.

Carswell, Grace and De Neve, Geert (2014) 'MGNREGA in Tamil Nadu: A Story of Success and Transformation?' *Journal Of Agrarian Change.* 14 (4)(2014): 564-585. doi: https://doi.org/10.1111/joac.12054.

Carter, Matt. *Minds and Computers: An Introduction to the Philosophy of Artificial Intelligence.* Edinburgh: Edinburgh University Press, 2007.

Rathi, Ayush and Elonnai Hickok. '"Future of Work" in India's IT/IT-eS Sector'. Center for Internet and Society, January 2019.

Jujjavarapu, Geethanjali, Elonnai Hickock and Amber Sinha. 'AI and the Manufacturing and Services Industry in India'. Center for Internet and Society, 11 March 2018.

Chace, Calum. 'The Impact of Artificial Intelligence on Professional Services'. *Forbes.* 8 June 2020. https://www.forbes.com/sites/cognitiveworld/2020/06/08/the-impact-of-artificial-intelligence-on-professional-services/?sh=5abc56504732. Accessed on 28 July 2021.

Chadha, Amit. 'India's Healthcare Has a New Best Friend: Robots'. *Fortune India.* 13 January 2021. https://www.fortuneindia.com/opinion/indias-healthcare-has-a-new-best-friend-robots/105028. Accessed on 23 July 2021.

Chakraborty, Monomita. 'Top 10 Affordable Personal Robots to Buy in India This Year'. Analytics Insight. 17 May 2021. https://www.analyticsinsight.net/top-10-affordable-personal-robots-to-buy-in-india-this-year/. Accessed on 22 July 2021.

Chanda, Avik and Meghana Srivatsav. 'What Leaders Need to Know About Honesty, Ethics and Integrity in the New Workplace'. *Economic Times.* 29 October 2021.

Chanda, Avik, and Gautham Tummala. 'How "Conversational AI" Will Shape Future Workplace Interactions'. *Economic Times.* 15 January 2021. https://economictimes.indiatimes.com/jobs/how-conversational-ai-will-shape-future-workplace-interactions/articleshow/80284327.cms. Accessed on 9 October 2021.

Chanda, Avik, and Shubhabrata Roy. 'What Human-centric Companies Prescribe for a Post-COVID World'. *Economic Times.* 19 May 2020. https://economictimes.indiatimes.com/jobs/what-human-centric-companies-prescribe-for-a-post-covid-world/ articleshow/75819868.cms. Accessed 3 July 2021.

Chanda, Avik, and Suman Ghose. *From Command to Empathy: Using EQ in the Age of Disruption*. Harper Business, 2017.

Chanda, Avik. 'Millenials Will Look for Opportunities Despite Engagement'. Interview by Rajguru Tandon. BWBusinessWorld. 27 April 2018. http://www.businessworld. in/article/-Millenials-Will-Look-For-Opportunites-Despite-Engagement-/27-04-2018-147613/. Accessed 3 July 2021.

Chanda, Avik. 'From Resilience to Flourish, Through Positivity!' PeopleMatters. 10 Januar 2021. https://www.peoplematters.in/blog/ life-at-work/from-resilience-to-flourish-through-positivity-28110 Accessed 3 July 2021.

Chanda, Avik. 'How to Manage the "Internal Customer": India Inc Has a Serious Battle Looming'. ET Prime. 14 January 2020. https://economictimes.indiatimes.com/jobs/how-to-manage-the-internal-customer-india-inc-has-a-serious-battle-looming/ articleshow/73240738.cms. Accessed 03 July 2021.

Chanda, Avik. 'Kindness and Empathy Will Be Skills of the Future in India's Media and Publishing Industry'. *Quartz*. 15 June 2020. https://qz.com/india/1868170/how-indian-media-and-publishing-firms-can-survive-covid-19-slump/. Accessed on 09 February 2022.

Chanda, Avik. 'Resilience in Focus: Individuals, Teams and Processes'. PeopleMatters. 3 January 2021. https://www.peoplematters.in/ blog/life-at-work/resilience-in-focus-individuals-teams-and-processes-28033. Accessed 3 July 3, 2021.

Chanda, Avik. 'Sack, Furlough or Reskill? India Inc's Talent Dilemma'. *Economic Times*. 13 February 2020. https://economictimes. indiatimes.com/jobs/sack-furlough-or-reskill-india-incs-talent-dilemma/articleshow/74116053.cms. Accessed 3 July 2021.

Chanda, Avik. 'View: New Perspectives on Risk Management, for COVID times'. *Economic Times*, 15 April 2021. https:// economictimes.indiatimes.com/news/company/corporate-trends/ view-new-perspectives-on-risk-management-for-covid-times/ articleshow/82081508.cms. Accessed 3 July, 2021.

Chanda, Avik. 'Why Companies Need a Role-based Model in the COVID-19 Paradigm'. *Economic Times*. 14 April 2020. https://

economictimes.indiatimes.com/jobs/why-companies-need-a-role-based-model-in-the-covid-19-paradigm/articleshow/75139253. cms. Accessed 3 July 2021.

Chanda, Avik. Why HR leaders are betting high on behavioural skills. The Economic Times. 28 May, 2020. https://economictimes.indiatimes. com/jobs/why-hr-leaders-are-betting-high-on-behavioural-skills/ articleshow/76058842.cms Accessed 3 July 2021.

Chanda, Avik. 'Why India Inc Needs to Invest in Resilience'. *Economic Times*. 29 March 2020. https://economictimes.indiatimes.com/jobs/ why-india-inc-needs-to-invest-in-resilience/articleshow/74874387. cms. Accessed 3 July 2021.

Chanda, Avik. Why Investment in Human Capital Has Been Such a "Late Starter"'. PeopleMatters. 27 December 2020. https://www. peoplematters.in/blog/strategic-hr/why-investment-in-human-capital-has-been-such-a-late-starter-27997. Accessed 3 July 2021.

Chandan, J. S., T. Thomas, C. Bradbury-Jones, R. Russell, S. Bandyopadhyay, K. Nirantharakumar, and J. Taylor. 'Female Survivors of Intimate Partner Violence and Risk of Depression, Anxiety and Serious Mental Illness'. *The British Journal of Psychiatry*. 217(4) (2020):562-567. doi: 10.1192/bjp.2019.124. PMID: 31171045.

Chandan, J. S., Thomas, T., Gokhale, K. M., Bandyopadhyay, S., Taylor, J., & Nirantharakumar, K. 'The Burden of Mental Ill Health Associated with Childhood Maltreatment in the UK, Using the Health Improvement Network database: A Population-based Retrospective Cohort Study'. *The Lancet Psychiatry*, Vol. 6, Issue 11 (2019): 926-934.

Change2Crowd. Automation in the Tourism Industry. 21 August 2021. https://www.change2crowd.com/automation-in-the-tourism-industry/#:~:text=%20Automation%20in%20the%20Tourism%20 Industry%20%201,are%20now%20chatbots%20that%20can%20 answer...%20More%20. Accessed on 09 Oct, 2021.

Chapter 10: 'Social Infrastructure and Employment'. The Economic Survey of India, 2021-22, 365-374,. Government of India, Ministry of Finance Department of Economic Affairs Economic.

Charalampous, Maria, A. Christine A, Carlo Tramontano Grant and Evie Michailidis. 'Systematically Reviewing Remote E-workers' Well-being at Work: A Multidimensional Approach'. *European*

Journal of Work and Organizational Psychology Volume 28 (1)(2019), 51-73.

Charette, R. N. 'What Ever Happened to STEM Job Security?' IEEE Spectrum. 5 September 2013. https://spectrum.ieee.org/the-changing-pattern-of-stem-worker-employment. Accessed on 20 february 2023.

Chatham House. 'Artificial Intelligence for Healthcare: Insights from India'. 30 July 2020. https://www.chathamhouse.org/2020/07/artificial-intelligence-healthcare-insights-india-0/3-ai-healthcare-india-applications. Accessed on 23 July 2021.

Chatterjee, P. 'Accenture to Onboard 150,000 New Hires Using the Metaverse'. Analyticsindiamag.com. 19 April 2022. https://analyticsindiamag.com/accenture-announces-150000-new-hirings-to-work-from-metaverse/#:~:text=IT%20services%20consultant%20Accenture%20has,participate%20in%20immersive%-20learning%20experiences.

Chatterji, Sangeeta, Lotus McDougal, Nicole Johns, Mohan Ghule, Namratha Rao, and Anita Raj. 'COVID-19-Related Financial Hardship, Job Loss, and Mental Health Symptoms: Findings from a Cross-Sectional Study in a Rural Agrarian Community in India'. International Journal of Environmental Research and Public Health. 18(16): 8647. Published online August 2021. doi: 10.3390/ijerph18168647.

Chattur, Gaurav. 'The Great Talent Exodus and How Organizations Can Tackle it in 2021'. PeopleMatters. 26 July 2021. https://www.peoplematters.in/article/recruitment/the-great-talent-exodus-and-how-organizations-can-tackle-it-in-2021-30160. Accessed on 28 July 2021.

Chaudhuri, K., A. Chakrabarti, J.M. Lima, J.S. Chandan, and S. Bandyopadhyay. 'The Interaction of Ethnicity and Deprivation on COVID-19 Mortality Risk: A Retrospective Ecological Study'. *Scientific Reports*. 11(1)(2018): 1-8.

Chawla, A. 'The Future of Work Is Built On Blockchain'. Datatechvibe. 15 February 2022. https://datatechvibe.com/data/the-future-of-work-is-built-on-blockchain/. Accessed on 20 February 2023.

Chevalier, A., C. Harmon, I. Walker, and Y. Zhu. 'Does Education Raise Productivity, or Just Reflect it?' *The Economic Journal*, Vol. 114, Issue 499(2014): 499-517.

Chicago Booth: The Initiative of Global Market. 'Laffer Curve'. 26 June 2012. igmchicago.org. Accessed on 20 February 2023.

Christensen, Clayton. *The Innovator's Dilemma*. Harvard Business School Press, 1997.

Christensen, Nathan. 'Is there ROI In Empathy?' *Forbes*. 28 July 2021. https://www.forbes.com/sites/forbesbusinesscouncil/2021/07/28/is-there-roi-in-empathy/?sh=26f1f289ca3f. Accessed on 09 February 2022.

Ciment, Shoshy. 'Nike Continues to Emphasize Mental Health by Closing All Global Offices this Week to Give Employees a Break'. Footwear News. 25 August 2021. https://footwearnews.com/2021/business/news/nike-closes-global-offices-hq-mental-health-delta-1203171029/. Accessed 2 December 2021.

Clark, M. 'NFTs, Explained'. The Verge. 6 June 2022. https://www.theverge.com/22310188/nft-explainer-what-is-blockchain-crypto-art-faq Accessed on 20 February 2023.

Clifton, Jon, and Jim Harter. *Wellbeing at Work. How to Build Resilient and Thriving Teams*. Gallup Press. 10 June 2021.

CNBCTV18. 'How Indian Tech Giants Are Joining the Metaverse Bandwagon'. CNBCTV18. 23 April 2022. https://www.cnbctv18.com/cryptocurrency/explained-how-indian-tech-giantsare-joining-the-metaverse-bandwagon-12766032.htm. Accessed on 21 February 2023.

Conklin, H. The Skills Shortage is 2022's Biggest Threat: Here's How to Navigate Through'. Fortune. April 8 2022. https://fortune.com/2022/04/08/online-learning-workforce-training-digital-skills-gap/ Accessed on 20 February 2023.

Conti, R., & Schmidt, J. 'What Is an NFT? How Do NFTs Work?' *Forbes*. 25 March 2022. https://www.forbes.com/advisor/in/investing/what-is-an-nft-how-do-nfts-work/. Accessed on 20 February 2023.

Continuity Central. 'Strengthening Resilience Is the Key to Success in 2021: PwC Survey.' https://www.continuitycentral.com/index.php/news/resilience-news/6122-strengthening-resilience-is-the-key-to-success-in-2021-pwc-survey. Accessed on 9 February 2022.

Cooper, Cary L., Mustafa Sarkar and Thomas Curran. 'Resilience Training in the Workplace from 2003 to 2014: A Systematic

Review'. *Journal of Occupational and Organizational Psychology*. British Psychological Society. 25 April 2015.

Cornell University, INSEAD, and WIPO. 'The Global Innovation Index 2020: Who Will Finance Innovation?' Ithaca, Fontainebleau and Geneva, 2020.

'Covid Impact: 40% of Indian Start-Ups Hit, But Recovery Is Strong'. *Hindu BusinessLine*. 14 October 2020. https://www. thehindubusinessline.com/news/covid-impact-40-of-indian-start-ups-hit-but-recovery-is-strong-says-report/article62194590.ece. Accessed on 20 February 2023.

COVID-19 Mental Health and Wellbeing Surveillance: Report. Chapter 2, 'Important Findings'. Office for Health Improvement and Disparities, Government of United Kingdom, 2022.

Cribb, J. 'Intergenerational Differences in Income and Wealth: Evidence from Britain'. *FISCAL STUDIES*, vol. 0, no. 0 (2019), 1–25.

Csikszentmihalyi, Mihaly, and Isabella Selega Csikszentmihalyi (Eds.). *A Life Worth Living: Contributions to Positive Psychology*. New York: Oxford University Press, 2006.

Csikszentmihalyi, Mihaly. *Applications of Flow in Human Development and Education*. New York, London: Springer, 2014.

Csikszentmihalyi, Mihaly. *Flow: The Classic Work on how to Achieve Happiness*. Rider, 2002.

Csikszentmihalyi, Mihaly. *Good Business: Leadership, Flow and the Making of Meaning*. New York: Penguin Books, 2003.

Cygan-Rehm, K. 'Is Additional Schooling Worthless? Revising the Zero Returns to Compulsory Schooling in Germany'. VfS Annual Conference 2018. Freiburg, Breisgau: German Economic Association.

D'Monte, Leslie. 'Robots Are Coming For India's Shop Floors'. *Mint*. 10 September 2019. https://www.livemint.com/technology/tech-news/robots-are-coming-for-india-s-shop-floors-1568135022807. html. Accessed 22 July 2021.

Dadona, L. 'The Burden of Mental Disorders Across the States of India: The Global Burden of Disease Study 1990–2017'. The Lancet Psychiatry, Vol. 7, Issue 2 (2019): 148-161.

Davenport, Thomas H. *The AI Advantage: How to Put the Artificial Intelligence Revolution to Work*. Cambridge, Massachusetts: The MIT Press, 2018.

Davidson, Rita. 'How Google Employees Cope with Stress'. Trainingzone website. 27 June 2017. https://www.trainingzone. co.uk/community/blogs/rita-davis/how-google-employees-cope-with-stress?__cf_chl_jschl_tk__=pmd_DnPrwqN4YzLorr_DLXEax90c.dnIRjbKnKoDVRPRm8E-1634716983-0-gqNtZGzNAlCjcnBszQil. Accessed on 2 December 2021.

Davis, D. '5 Models for the Post-Pandemic Workplace'. *Harvard Business Review*. 3 June 2021. https://hbr.org/2021/06/5-models-for-the-post-pandemic-workplace. Accessed on 20 February 2023.

Deaton, A. 'Covid-19 and Global Income Inequality'. National Bureau of Economic Research (No. w28392), 2021.

Deloitte. 'Machines with Purpose: From Theory to Practice, Artificial intelligence in Professional Services'. Deloitte LLP, 2018.

Deloitte. 'From Survive to Thrive: The Future of Work in a Post-Pandemic World'. Deloitte Paper, 2021.

Deloitte. 'Mental Health and Well-being in the Workplace'. September 2022. https://www2.deloitte.com/in/en/pages/life-sciences-and-healthcare/articles/mental-health-2022.html?id=in:2os:3or:4in-mental-health:5:6lshc:20220908:dcom_home. Accessed on 25 September 2022.

DeSpain, Ben. 'Transforming a Work Culture During a Pandemic'. *Forbes*. 11 December 2020. https://www.forbes.com/sites/forbeshumanresourcescouncil/2020/12/11/transforming-a-work-culture-during-a-pandemic/. Accessed 4 July 2021.

'Despite Low Female Participation in the Workforce, Why More Women are Facing Unemployment In The Pandemic'. *Forbes*. 21 July 2021. https://www.firstpost.com/india/despite-low-female-participation-in-the-workforce-why-more-women-are-facing-unemployment-in-the-pandemic-explained-9825261.html. Accessed on 20 February 2023.

Diamandis, Peter, and Steven Kotler. *Abundance: The Future is Better than you Think*. New York: The Free Press, 2012.

Diener, Ed, John F. Helliwell and Daniel Kahneman. *International Differences in Well-Being: Positive Psychology Series*. Oxford: Oxford University Press, 2010.

Dilmegani, Cem. 'Top 12 AI Applications in Manufacturing in 2021'. 6 June 2021. https://research.aimultiple.com/manufacturing-ai/. Accessed on 28 Jul, 2021.

Dincelli, E., & Yayla, A. 'Immersive Virtual Reality in the Age of the Metaverse: A Hybrid-narrative Review Based on the Technology Affordance Perspective'. *The Journal of Strategic Information Systems*, Vol. 31, Issue 2 (2022).

Dirks, Brent. 'How to Use the Apple Watch Mindfulness App in watchOS 8'. Make Use Of. 31 August 2021. https://www.makeuseof.com/how-to-use-mindfulness-on-apple-watch/. Accessed on 2 December 2021.

Dore, B. 'In India's COVID-19 crisis, the Internet Is Both a Lifeline and a Barrier'. The New Humanitarian. 25 May 2021. https://www.thenewhumanitarian.org/news/2021/5/25/india-COVID-19-digital-divide-hampers-vaccine-and-healthcare-access. Accessed on 25 May 2021.

Duhigg, C. (2016, February 25). What Google Learned From Its Quest to Build the Perfect Team. Retrieved from The New York Times Magazine: https://www.nytimes.com/2016/02/28/magazine/what-google-learned-from-its-quest-to-build-the-perfect-team.html

Dweck, Carol. Mindset: Changing The Way You think To Fulfil Your Potential. Constable & Robinson, 2012.

Eckstein, O. (1966). Chapter 6. 'Perspectives on Employment under Technical Change'. In J. Stieber, *Employment Problems of Automation and Advanced Technology: An International Perspective* (pp. 86-104). Palgrave Macmillan.

Economic Times. Factory workers need to worry about automation more than techies. 28 Jun, 2017. https://economictimes.indiatimes.com/jobs/factory-workers-need-to-worry-about-automation-more-than-techies/articleshow/59356453.cms Accessed on 05 Oct, 2021.

ET Online. 'Poor Mental Health of Employees Costs Indian Employers $14 Billion Yearly: Deloitte survey'. *Economic Times*, 8 September 2022. https://economictimes.indiatimes.com/news/company/corporate-trends/poor-mental-health-of-employees-costs-indian-employers-14-billion-yearly-deloitte-survey/articleshow/94075801.cms. Accessed on 25 September 2022.

Edmondson, A. C. 'Managing the Risk of Learning: Psychological Safety in Work Teams'. *International Journal of Organizational Teamwork*.

Edmondson, A. C., and Z. Lei. 'Psychological Safety: The History, Renaissance, and Future of an Interpersonal Construct'. *Annual Review of Organizational Psychology and Organizational Behavior*, Vol. 1 (2014): 23-43.

Weildling, Anke and Engin Guven. 'The Future of Great Leadership Lies in Resilience: Parts I, I and III'. Egon Zehnder, 2020.

Elias, Jennifer. Google Is Tackling Mental Health Challenges Among Employees Through 'Resilience Training' Videos'. CNBC. 27 November 2020. https://www.cnbc.com/2020/11/27/google-tackling-mental-health-among-staff-with-resilience-training.html. Accessed on 2 December 2021.

Elsesser, Kim. 'The Business Case for Diversity May Be Backfiring, A New Study Shows'. *Forbes*, 20 June 2022. https://www.forbes.com/sites/kimelsesser/2022/06/20/the-business-case-for-diversity-is-backfiring/?sh=2b525103351d. Accessed on 23 September 2022.

Eqversity. 'Resilience Programming at Goldman Sachs'. https://eqversity.com/resilience-programming-at-goldman-sachs/#:~:text=Resilience%20Programming%20at%20Goldman%20Sachs%20At%20Goldman%20Sachs%2C,to%20avoid%20burnout%20and%20%E2%80%98stay%20in%20the%20game%E2%80%99. Accessed on 2 December 2021.

Ernst & Young. 'Future of Jobs in India: A 2022 Perspective'. Ernst & Young LLP, Published in India, 2017.

Ethier, Wilfred J. 'Globalization, Globalisation: Trade, Technology, and Wages'. *International Review of Economics & Finance*, Volume 14, Issue 3 (2005): 237-258, https://doi.org/10.1016/j.iref.2004.12.001.

EY. 'Intelligent Automation'. https://www.ey.com/en_in/intelligent-automation Accessed 22 July, 2021.

Fernandez, A. 'The Metaverse: The Future Of Work'. *Forbes*. 18 March 2022. https://www.forbes.com/sites/forbesbusinesscouncil/2022/03/18/the-metaverse-the-future-of-work/?sh=548dd5eb4267. Accessed on 21 February 2023.

Fix, B. 'The Trouble with Human Capital Theory'. *Real-World Economics Review*, Issue No. 86 (2018).

Ford, Martin. *Rise of the Robots: Technology and the Threat of a Jobless Future*, New York: Basic Books, 2015.

Ford, Martin. *The Lights in the Tunnel: Automation, Accelerating Technology and the Economy of the Future.* Acculant Publishing, 2009.

Forrester. 'More yhan Seventy-Five Percent of US B2C Marketing Executives Plan to Invest in the "Metaverse" this Year, Despite Consumer Skepticism'. Forrester. 30 March 2022. https://www.forrester.com/press-newsroom/forrester-metaverse-marketing-executives/. Accesed on 21 February 2023.

Forrester. 'European Edition: Predictions 2021'. Forrester. 2020. https://go.forrester.com/wp-content/uploads/2020/10/Forrester-Predictions-2021-EMEA-1.pdf. Accessed on 28 July 2021.

'Four-day week "an overwhelming success" in Iceland'. BBC. 6 July 2021. https://www.bbc.co.uk/news/business-57724779 Accessed on 21 February 2023.

Fredrickson, Barbara L. 'The Role of Positive Emotions in Positive Psychology: The Broaden-and-Build Theory of Positive Emotions'. *American Psychologist.* 2001;56: 218–226.

Frey, C. B., & Osborne, M. 'The Future of Employment: How Susceptible Are Jobs to Computerisation?' Oxford Martin Programme on Technology, 1-72 (2013).

Friedman, Thomas L. *The World is Flat: A Brief History of the Twenty-First Century.* New York: Farrar, Straus and Giroux, 2006.

From Public Spats To Feuding Founders: Gloomy 2022 For Indian Startups. (2022, June 12). Retrieved from Inc42: https://inc42.com/features/from-public-spats-to-feuding-founders-gloomy-2022-for-indian-startups/

'From Street to Screen Economy: How Has COVID-19 Accelerated Digital Transformation'. Inc42. 28 July 2021. https://timesofindia.indiatimes.com/business/india-business/from-street-to-screen-economy-how-has-covid-19-accelerated-digital-transformation/articleshow/84815847.cms. Accessed on 21 February 23

Fulcher, John. *Computational Intelligence and its Applications Series. Advances in Applied Artificial Intelligence.* Hershey, London, Melbourne, Singapore: Idea Group Publishing, 2006.

'Future Insights: Top Trends Affecting the Workplace and the HR Profession According to SHRM Special Expertise Panels'. SHRM.

Galor, Oded. 2011. 'Inequality, Human Capital Formation and the Process of Development'. *Handbook of the Economics of Education*, Elsevier, Vol. 4(2011): 441-493. https://www.sciencedirect.com/science/article/abs/pii/B9780444534446000055. Accessed on 21 February 23

Gallup: *How Millennials Want to Work and Live. The Six Big Changes Leaders have to make.*

Gallup: *Climate Change and Wellbeing Around the World.*

Gallup: *A Leader's Guide to Developing a Work-From-Home Strategy.*

Gallup: *Employee Engagement and Performance: Latest Insights From the World's Largest Study.*

Gallup: *Global Emotions Report 2022.*

Gallup: *State of the Global Workplace 2022 Report. The Voice of the Employees.*

Garbarino, James. *The Positive Psychology of Personal Transformation: Leveraging Resilience for Life Change.* New York: Springer, 2011.

Gartner. 'Three Steps to Hyperautomation'. 19 August 2020. https://www.gartner.com/doc/reprints?id=1-24ZGPCGB&ct=210105&st=sb. Accessed on 09 October 2021.

Gechert, Sebastian and Heimberger, Philipp. 'Do Corporate Tax Cuts Boost Economic Growth?', *European Economic Review*, Volume 147 (2022), https://doi.org/10.1016/j.euroecorev.2022.104157.

Gentle, S. 'UK Hiring Plans Up, While Skill Shortages Greater than Ever Before'. Onrec. 22 April 2022. Website: https://www.onrec.com/news/statistics/uk-hiring-plans-while-skill-shortages-greater-than-ever-says-new-monster-report. Accessed on 21 February 2023.

Gerretson, Isabel. 'Robots are Joining the Fight Against Coronavirus in India'. CNN Business. 21 July 2021. https://edition.cnn.com/2020/11/11/tech/robots-india-covid-spc-intl/index.html. Accessed on 23 July 2021.

Ghosh, M., & Chatterji, B. P. 'Mental health Insurance in India after COVID-19'. *The Lancet Psychiatry*, Vol. 7, Issue 12 (2020): 1016-1017.

Gilbertson, A., J. Dey, J, A. Deuchar, and N. Grills. 'India's COVID-19 Divide in Digital Learning, University of Melbourne'. 1 August 2021. https://pursuit.unimelb.edu.au/articles/india-s-covid-19-divide-in-digital-learning

'Global Health Data Exchange'. 2021. Retrieved from Institute for Health Metrics and Evaluation: http://ghdx.healthdata.org/gbd-results-tool. Accessed 21 February 2023.

Global Innovation Index 2021, 14th Edition: Executive Summary'. Geneva, Switzerland: World Intellectual Property Organization, 2021.

'Global Trade Negotiations Homepage'. April 2003. https://web.archive. org/web/20170715151421/http://www.cid.harvard.edu/cidtrade/ issues/washington.html. Accessed 21 February 2023.

Goertzel, Ben, and Cassio Pennachin (Eds.). *Artificial General Intelligence*. Berlin, Heidelberg: Springer Verlag, 2007.

Goldin, C. 'The U-Shaped Female Labor Force Function in Economic Development and Economic History'. In, Schultz, T. P. (ed.). *Investment in Women's Human Capital and Economic Development*. Chicago, IL: University of Chicago Press, 1995, 61–90.

Goldman Sachs. 'How Goldman Sachs Champions Wellness in the Workplace: A Recap of Our Global Resilience Series'. Goldman Sachs website. 9 August 2019. https://www.goldmansachs.com/ careers/blog/posts/global-resilience-recap-2019.html. Accessed on 02 December 2021.

Goldman Sachs. 'Diversity and Inclusion'. Goldman Sachs website. https://www.goldmansachs.com/our-commitments/diversity-and-inclusion/ Accessed on 2 December 2021.

Goled, S. 'The Tragic Twist in the Indian Startup Saga'. Analytics India Magazine. 13 June 2022. https://analyticsindiamag.com/the-tragic-twist-in-the-indian-startup-saga/. Accesed on 21 February 2023.

Goleman, Daniel. *Emotional Intelligence*. Bloomsbury Publishing India Private Limited, 2004.

Government of the United Kingdom. 'Coronavirus (COVID-19): Latest Updates and Guidance. Research and Analysis—Important findings'. Updated 18 November 2021. https://www.gov.uk/ government/publications/covid-19-mental-health-and-wellbeing-surveillance-report/2-important-findings-so-far. Accessed on 16 February 2022.

Gravity Flow. 'How Automated Workflow Tools Can Help the Travel Industry With Bookings'. https://gravityflow.io/articles/how-automated-workflow-tools-can-help-the-travel-industry-with-bookings/. Accessed on 9 October 2021.

Grover, Sandeep. 'Psychological Impact of COVID-19 Lockdown: An Online Survey from India'. *Indian Journal of Psychiatry*. July-August; 62(4)(July 2020): 354–362. doi: 10.4103/psychiatry. IndianJPsychiatry_427_20 https://www.ncbi.nlm.nih.gov/pmc/articles/PMC7597717/. Accessed on 16 February, 2022.

Gupta, Aviral. 'Reshaping the Hospitality Industry: New Technologies that Can Be Used to Enhance Services in the Post-COVID Era'. YourStory.12 November 2020. https://yourstory.com/2020/10/reshaping-hospitality-new-technologies-post-covid/amp. Accessed on 09 October 2021.

Hackernoon Website. 'Five Successful AI and ML Use Cases in Manufacturing'. 3 June 2020. https://hackernoon.com/five-successful-ai-and-ml-use-cases-in-manufacturing-ac3a30ol. Accessed on 28 July 2021.

Haidar, Faizan. '66% of Indian Employees Want to Work Completely from Home: Survey'. *Economic Times*. 27 November 2022. https://economictimes.indiatimes.com/news/company/corporate-trends/66-of-the-indian-employees-want-to-work-completely-from-home-survey/articleshow/79444498.cms?utm_source=contentofinterest&utm_medium=text&utm_campaign=cppst. Accessed on 16 February 2022.

Hanushek, E. A., G. Schwerdt, S. Wiederhold, and L. Woessmann. 'Returns to Skills Around the World: Evidence from PIAAC'. *European Economic Review*, Vol. 73 (2015): 103-130.

Harari, Yuval Noah. *21 Lessons for the 21st Century*. London: Jonathan Cape, 2018.

Harari, Yuval Noah. *Homo Deus – A Brief History of Tomorrow*. New York: Harvill Secker, 2015.

Harari, Yuval Noah. *Sapiens – A Brief History of Humankind*. New York: Harvill Secker, 2014.

Hariharan, S. 'Online Festive Shopping Attracts, Cyber Crime: Mcafee India Survey'. *Times of India*. 17 Novembe 2021. https://timesofindia.indiatimes.com/business/india-business/online-festive-shopping-attracts-cybercrime-mcafee-india-survey-finds/articleshow/79260351.cms . Accessed on 21 February 2023.

Harter, Jim. 'Manager Burnout Is Only Getting Worse'. Gallup. 18 November 2021. https://www.gallup.com/workplace/357404/ manager-burnout-getting-worse.aspx. Accessed on 25 September 2022.

Harter, Jim. 'Percent who Feel Employer Cares About their Wellbeing Plummets'. Gallup. 18 March 2022. https://www.gallup.com/ workplace/390776/percent-feel-employer-cares-wellbeing-plummets.aspx Accessed on 25 September 2022.

Harter, Jim. 'The First Step in Increasing Wellbeing Is Measuring it'. Business and Tech. https://www.futureofbusinessandtech.com/ employee-wellbeing/the-first-step-in-increasing-wellbeing-is-measuring-it/#. Accessed on 25 September 2022.

Hattori, Hiromitsu, Takahiro Kawamura, Tsuyoshi Ide, Makoto Yokoo, and Yohei Murakami (Eds.). *New Frontiers in Artificial Intelligence.* Berlin, Heidelberg: Springer Verlag, 2009.

Haugeland, John (Ed.) *Mind Design II. Philosophy Psychology Artificial Intelligence.* Revised and enlarged edition. Cambridge, Massachusetts, London, England: The MIT Press, 1997.

Haynes, John Michael, Gretchen Haynes and Larry Sun Fong. *Mediation: Positive Conflict Management.* SUNY Series in Transpersonal and Humanistic Psychology. Albany: State University of New York Press, 2004.

He, Laura. 'Google's Secrets of Innovation: Empowering its Employees'. *Forbes.* 29 March 2013. https://www.forbes.com/sites/ laurahe/2013/03/29/googles-secrets-of-innovation-empowering-its-employees/?sh=72afd4cb57e7. Accessed on 2 December 2021.

Hefferon, Kate, and Ilona Boniwell. *Positive Psychology: Theory, Research and Applications.* New York: Open University Press, 2011.

Heimberger, Phillipp. 'Does Economic Globalisation Affect Income Inequality? A Meta-analysis'. *World Economy.* Vol. 43(2020): 2960–2982. https://doi.org/10.1111/twec.13007.

Henderson, Harry. *Milestones in Discovery and Invention: Artificial Intelligence. Mirrors for the Mind.* New York: Chelsea House, 2007.

'Here Are the 42 Indian Startups that Entered the Unicorn Club in 2021'. 29 December 2021. Team Inc42: https://inc42.com/buzz/ indian-startups-that-entered-the-unicorn-club-in-2021-in-india/. Accessed on 21 February 2023.

HFS. 'Automation to Impact 750,000 Low Skilled Indian Jobs, but Create 300,000 Mid-high Skilled Jobs by 2022'. https://www.hfsresearch. com/cognitive-computing/jobs-impact-automation_083017/ Accessed on 6 October 2021.

Hobsbawm, E. J. 'The Standard of Living during the Industrial Revolution: A Discussion'. *The Economic History Review*, New Series, Vol. 16, No. 1 (1963): 119- 134.

Hope, David and Limberg, Julian (2022). 'The Economic Consequences of Major Tax Cuts for the Rich'. *Socio-Economic Review*, Volume 20, Issue 2 (2022): 539–559. https://doi.org/10.1093/ser/ mwab061.

Hopkins, K. 'What Does Metaverse Mean for the Workforce of the Future?' CXC AMERICAS. 24 March 2022. https://www. cxcglobal.com/en-us/what-does-metaverse-mean-for-the-workforce-of-the-future . Accessed 21 February 2023.

HotelTechReport. 'How to Think About Automation's Impact on Hospitality'. Hotel Tech Report website. 28 May 2021. https:// hoteltechreport.com/news/automation-in-hospitality. Accessed on 09 October 2021.

'How COVID-19 Has Pushed Companies Over the Technology Tipping Point and Transformed Business Forver'. McKinsey website. 5 October 2020. https://www.mckinsey.com/business-functions/strategy-and-corporate-finance/our-insights/how-covid-19-has-pushed-companies-over-the-technology-tipping-point-and-transformed-business-forever. Accessed 21 February 2023.

Human Rights Watch. 'Israel: Provide Vaccines to Occupied Palestinians'. 2021. https://www.hrw.org/news/2021/01/17/israel-provide-vaccines-occupied-palestinians#:%7E:text=(Jerusalem)%20 %E2%80%93%20Israeli%20authorities%20should,Human%20 Rights%20Watch%20said%20today. Accessed 21 February 2023.

Hunter, Lawrence (Ed.). *Artificial Intelligence and Molecular Biology*. Cambridge, Massachusetts: The MIT Press, 1993.

IBM. 'AI Is Reshaping the Supply Chain'. https://www.ibm. com/thought-leadership/institute-business-value/report/ cognitivesupplychain. Accessed on 14 October 2021.

IBM. 'Overview of IT Automation'. https://www.ibm.com/topics/ automation. Accessed on 9 October 2021.

Idea to Value. 'Why I Have a Problem with the Global Innovation Index'. Idea to Value website. September 2016. https://www.ideatovalue. com/inno/nickskillicorn/2016/09/problem-global-innovation-index/. Accessed on 21 February 2023.

Ideas For India. 'India's Service-led Economic Growth'. 2021. https://www.ideasforindia.in/topics/macroeconomics/india-s-service-led-economic-growth.html. Accessed on 21 February 2023.

IndiaAI. 'AI Is Being Used by the UP Police to Catch Criminals'. India AI website. 16 August 2019. https://indiaai.gov.in/case-study/ai-is-being-used-by-the-up-police-to-catch-criminals. Accessed on 23 Jul, 2021.

IndiaAI. 'IIT-D Launches New Lab on AI for Judiciary'. India AI website. 16 July 2021. https://indiaai.gov.in/news/iit-d-launches-new-lab-on-ai-for-judiciary. Accessed on 23 July 2021.

IndiaAI. 'Indian Researchers Use ML to Create Mortality Prediction Model for COVID-19 Patients'. 12 May 2021. https://indiaai. gov.in/case-study/indian-researchers-use-ml-to-create-mortality-prediction-model-for-covid-19-patients. Accessed on 23 July 2021.

IndiaAI. 'This AI-powered Backpack Helps the Visually Impaired Navigate World'. 30 April 2021. https://indiaai.gov.in/case-study/this-ai-powered-backpack-helps-the-visually-impaired-navigate-world Accessed on 23 July 2021.

Infosys. 'Leadership in the Age of AI: Adapting, Investing and Reskilling to Work Alongside AI'. Published by Infosys, 2018.

Infosys. 'Role of AI in Travel and Hospitality Industry'. Published by Infosys, 2018. https://www.infosys.com/industries/travel-hospitality/documents/ai-travel-hospitality.pdf#:~:text=To%20personalize%20customer%20service%2C%20the%20Travel%20and%20Hospitality,patterns%20and%20predict%20guest%20preferences%20with%20increasing%20accuracy. Accessed on 9 October 2021.

InnoHealth Magazine. 'India's Top Artificial Intelligence Organizations in Healthcare'. InnoHealth Magazine website. https://innohealthmagazine.com/2020/innovation/top-artificial-intelligence-organizations-in-healthcare-in-india/. Accessed on 23 July 2021.

Kapoor, Amir and Jessica Duggal. 'The State of Inequality Report'. Institute for Competitiveness, 2022.

Institute of Health Metrics & Evaluation (IHME). 'Global Burden of Disease Study'. Our Data in World website. https://ourworldindata.org/global-mental-health. Accessed on 1 February 2022.

'Global Health Data Exchange' http://ghdx.healthdata.org/gbd-results-tool. Accessed on 16 February 2022.

International Federation of Robotics. 'World Robotics Report 2020'. https://ifr.org/ifr-press-releases/news/record-2.7-million-robots-work-in-factories-around-the-globe. IFR Press Conference, Frankfurt, 24 September 2020. https://ifr.org/downloads/press2018/Presentation_WR_2020.pdf Accessed 22 July 2021.

International Labour Organization. 'Global Commission on the Future of Work: Work for a Better Future'. ILO website. 22 January 2019. https://www.ilo.org/global/publications/books/WCMS_662410/lang--en/index.htm. Accessed 10 June 2021.

International Labour Organization. 'ILO Research Paper Series: Working Time and the Future of Work'. ILO website. 7 November 2018. https://www.ilo.org/wcmsp5/groups/public/---dgreports/---cabinet/documents/publication/wcms_649907.pdf. Accessed 10 June 2021.

International Labour Organization. Research Department Working Paper no 29. 'The Future of Work: A Literature Review'. ILO website. 17 April 2018. https://www.ilo.org/global/research/publications/working-papers/WCMS_625866/lang--en/index.htm Accessed 10 June 2021.

International Labour Organization. 'The Future of Work We Want: A Global Dialogue'. ILO website. 7 April2017. https://www.ilo.org/wcmsp5/groups/public/---dgreports/---cabinet/documents/publication/wcms_570282.pdf. Accessed 10 June 2021.

International Labour Organization, UNDP. 'Employment, Lives and Social Protection Guide for Recovery Implementation'. 2021.

International Monetary Fund. 'Automation, Skills and the Future of Work: What do Workers Think?' IMF website. 20 December 2019. https://www.imf.org/en/Publications/WP/Issues/2019/12/20/Automation-Skills-and-the-Future-of-Work-What-do-Workers-Think-48791. Accessed 10 June 2021.

International Monetary Fund. 'Group of Twenty: Future of Work: Measurement and Policy Changes'. IMF 18 July 2018. https://

www.imf.org/external/np/g20/pdf/2018/071818a.pdf.   Accessed 10 June 2021.

International Monetary Fund. 'Rethinking the World of Work'. IMF website. 2 December 2020. https://www.imf.org/external/pubs/ft/fandd/2020/12/pdf/rethinking-the-world-of-work-dewan.pdf Accessed 10 June 2021.

International Monetary Fund. 'Technology and the Future of Work'. IMF website. 18 July 2018. https://www.imf.org/external/np/g20/pdf/2018/041118.pdf. Accessed 10 June 2021.

International Organization for Standardization (ISO). ISO 45003:2021(en). 'Occupational Health and Safety Management — Psychological Health and Safety at Work — Guidelines for Managing Psychosocial Risks'.

Jacobs, Tina. 'Artificial Intelligence in Supply Chain & Logistics'. Throughput Inc. 23 January 2020. https://throughput.world/blog/topic/ai-in-supply-chain-and-logistics/. Accessed on 14 October 2021.

Jamal, Natasha and Teresa Tschida. '3 Actions for Leaders to Improve DEI in the Workplace' Gallup. 27 April 2021. https://www.gallup.com/workplace/348266/actions-leaders-improve-dei-workplace.aspx. Accessed on 25 September 2022.

World Economic Forum. 'Jobs of Tomorrow: The Triple Returns of Social Jobs in the Economic Recovery'. WEF website. May 2022. https://www3.weforum.org/docs/WEF_Jobs_of_Tomorrow_2022.pdf. Accessed on 21 February 23.

Journals of India. 'Robotics in India'. 28 February 2020. https://journalsofindia.com/robotics-in-india/ Accessed on 22 July 2021.

Kabat-Zinn, Jon. *Full Catastrophe Living: Using the Wisdom of Your Body and Mind to Face Stress, Pain, and Illness.* New York: Bantam Books, 1990.

Kabat-Zinn, Jon. *Mindfulness Meditation.* Nightingale Conant, 1995.

Kabat-Zinn, Jon. *Mindfulness Wherever You Go, There You Are: Mindfulness Meditation in Everyday Life.* Hyperion, 10th Edition, 2005.

Kaku, Michio. *Physics of the Future: How Science Will Shape Human Destiny and Our Daily Lives by the Year 2100.* New York: Doubleday, 2011.

Kampelmann, S., F. Rycx, Y. Saks, and I. Tojerow. 'Does Education Raise Productivity and Wages Equally? The Moderating Role of Age and Gender'. *IZA Journal of Labour Economics 7*, 1 (2018).

Kanal, L.N., and A. Rosenfeld. *Machine Intelligence and Pattern Recognition. Volume 9.* Amsterdam, New York, Oxford, Tokyo: North Holland, 1990.

Kanwal, S. (2022, March 16). 'Rate of Female Labor Force Participation India 1990-2020'. Statista. March 16 2022. https://www.statista.com/statistics/983020/female-labor-force-participation-rate-india/#statisticContainer. Accessed on 21 February 2023.

Kapoor, Manavi. 'Half of India Is so Poor it Owns Almost Nothing', *Quartz India.* 8 December 2021. https://qz.com/india/2099957/world-inequality-report-says-india-is-poor-but-with-rich-elite/. Accessed on 28 September 2022.

Kaplan, Jerry. *Humans Need Not Apply: A Guide to Wealth and Work in the Age of Artificial Intelligence.* New Haven, Connecticut: Yale University Press, 2015.

Karbrough, K. 'These Are the Sectors Where Green Jobs Are Growing in Demand'. WEF Website. 23 September 2021: https://www.weforum.org/agenda/2021/09/sectors-where-green-jobs-are-growing-in-demand/. Accessed 21 February 2023.

Kawabata, Yasunari. *The Master of Go.* New York: Penguin Random House, 1996.

Kelly, Alex. '3 Ways AI Is Revolutionizing Professional Services'. Enterprise AI. 11 June 2021. https://www.enterpriseai.news/2021/06/11/3-ways-ai-is-revolutionizing-professional-services/ Accessed on 28 July 2021.

Kennedy, John F. 'Remarks in Heber Springs, Arkansas, at the Dedication of Greers Ferry Dam'. (October 1963). Online by Gerhard Peters and John T. Woolley, The American Presidency Project. https://www.presidency.ucsb.edu/node/236260. Accessed 21 February 2023.

Knoddle, Richard. 'Working Culture: We can't Afford to Ignore Mental Health'. Goldman Sachs website. 10 September 2019. https://www.goldmansachs.com/citizenship/goldman-sachs-gives/meet-the-grantees/mentally-healthy-universities.html. Accessed on 2 December 2021.

Knoop, Hans Henrik, and Antonella Della Fave (Eds.). 'Well-Being and Cultures: Perspectives from Positive Psychology'. *Cross Cultural Advancements in Positive Psychology.* Volume 3. Dordrecht: Springer, 2013.

Kochhar, A. S., R. Bhasin, G.K. Kochhar, H. Dadlani, V.V. Mehta, R. Kaur, C.K. Bhasin. 'Lockdown of 1.3 Billion People in India During Covid-19 Pandemic: A survey of its Impact on Mental health'. *Asian Journal of Psychiatry*, Vol. 54 (2020).

Kochhar, Anuraj Singh. 'Lockdown of 1.3 Billion People in India During Covid-19 pandemic: A survey of its Impact on Mental Health. *Asian Journal Psychiatry*. 54: 102213 (18 June 2020). doi: 10.1016/j.ajp.2020.102213. https://www.ncbi.nlm.nih.gov/pmc/articles/PMC7301781/. Accessed on 16 February 2022.

Konings, J., and S. Vanormelingan. 'The Impact of Training on Productivity and Wages: Firm-Level Evidence'. *The Review of Economics and Statistics*. Vol. 97, Issue 2 (2015): 485-497.

Kotler, Steven. *The Habit of Ferocity. Peak Performance Primer*. Amazon Publishing, 2018.

Kotler, Steven. Tomorrowland. *Our Journey from Science Fiction to Science Fact*. Amazon Publishing, 2015.

Kotwal, A., Ramaswami, B., & Wadhwa, W. 'Economic Liberalization and Indian Economic Growth: What's the Evidence?' *Journal of Economic Literature*, Vol. 49, No. 4 (2011): 1152-1199.

Kumar, Chetan. 'India Doubles Number of Industrial Robots in 5 Years'. *Times of India*. 30 September 2020. https://timesofindia.indiatimes.com/india/india-doubles-number-of-industrial-robots-in-5-years/articleshow/78407600.cms. Accessed on 22 July 2021.

Kumar, V. 'How Metaverse Is Gaining Ground in India'. ET CIO. com. 3 March 2020. https://cio.economictimes.indiatimes.com/news/next-gen-technologies/how-metaverse-is-gaining-ground-in-india/89959772?redirect=1. Accesed on 21 February 2023.

Kumar, Vivek. 'Banking of Tomorrow: Top Indian Banks Using Artificial Intelligence'. Analytics Insight. 3 February 2021. https://www.analyticsinsight.net/banking-of-tomorrow-top-indian-banks-using-artificial-intelligence/. Accessed on 23 July 2021.

Kurzweil, Ray. *The Singularity is Near. When Humans Transcend Biology*. New York: Viking Penguin, 2005.

Kuznets, Simon. 'Economic Growth and Income Inequality'. *American Economic Review* Vol. 45 No. 1 (1955): 1–28.

Langer, Ellen. *Counterclockwise: Mindful Health and the Power of Possibility*. Ballantine Books, 2009.

Langer, Ellen. *Mindfulness*. 25th Anniversary Edition. With a New Preface by the Author. Boston: Da Capo Press, 2014.

Langer, Ellen. *The Art of Noticing*. Boston: The Langer Mindfulness Institute, 2014.

Langer, Ellen. *The Power of Mindful Learning*. Da Capo Books, Reprint Edition, 2016.

Lehewych, D. 'What Is Cryptocurrency's Role In The Future Of Work?' Allwork. 28 April 2022. https://allwork.space/2022/04/what-is-cryptocurrencys-role-in-the-future-of-work/ . 21 February 2023.

Levine, Marvin. *The Positive Psychology of Buddhism and Yoga: Paths to a Mature Happiness. With a Special Application to Handling Anger*. New Jersey, London: Lawrence Elbaum Associates, Publishers, 2000.

Lewis, Sarah. *Positive Psychology at Work: How Positive Leadership and Appreciative Inquiry Create Inspiring Organizations*. Chichester, United Kingdom: John Wiley & Sons, 2011.

LinkedIn. 'Future of Skills Report, 2019'. Retrieved from https://business.linkedin.com/talent-solutions/recruiting-tips/future-of-skills-for-asia-pacific-2019. Accessed 19 June 2021.

Liu, Jenny JW, Natalie Ein, Julia i, Mira Battaion, Maureen Reed, and Kristin Vickers. 'Comprehensive Meta-analysis of Resilience Interventions'. Clinical Psychology Review. December 2020.

Lopez, Shane J. *Positive Psychology: Exploring the Best in People. Volume 1, Discovering Human Strengths*. Westport, Connecticut and London: Praeger, 2008.

Lopes, Carlos. 'Economic Growth and Inequality: The New Post-Washington Consensus'. *RCCS Annual Review*. 2012. URL: http://journals.openedition.org/rccsar/426; DOI: https://doi.org/10.4000/rccsar.426. Accessed on 21 February 2023.

Lorenz, Konrad. *On Aggression*. London and New York: Routledge, 2002.

Lucas Jr., R. E. 'On the Mechanics of Economic Development'. *Journal of Monetary Economics*, Vol. 22, No. 1 (1988): 3-42.

Lucas Jr., R. E. 'Why Doesn't Capital Flow from Rich to Poor Countries'. *American Economic Association*, Vol. 80, No. 2 (1990): 92-96.

Lucas Jr., R. E. 'Supply-Side Economics: An Analytical Review'. *Oxford Economic Papers*, Vol 42, Issue 2 (1990): 293–316, https://doi.org/10.1093/oxfordjournals.oep.a041948.

McCabe, Laurie. 'How AI and ML Will Revolutionize Professional Services'. Laurie McCabe's Blog. 13 November 2020. https://lauriemccabe.com/2020/11/13/how-ai-and-ml-will-revolutionizeprofessional-services/. Accessed on 28 July 2021.

McGregor, Jena. 'Two Years Into The Pandemic, Almost Twice as Many Workers Prefer Hybrid Schedules to Fully Remote Work'. *Forbes*. 16 March 2022. https://www.forbes.com/sites/jenamcgregor/2022/03/15/two-years-into-the-pandemic-almost-twice-as-many-workers-prefer-hybrid-schedules-to-fully-remote-work/?sh=38d5e04177ec. Accessed on 25 September 2022.

Magyari, I. 'Firm Reorganization, Chinese Imports, and us Manufacturing Employment'. Columbia University, 2017.

Mahapatra, Dwarikanath. 'Overview of AI in Indian Healthcare'. Ai4bharat.org. https://ai4bharat.org/articles/overview-of-ai-in-indian-healthcare/. Accessed on 23 July 2021.

Majercsik, E. (2021, August 4). 'What Does Your Workplace of the Future Look Like?' *Forbes*. 4 August 2021. https://www.forbes.com/sites/forbeshumanresourcescouncil/2021/08/04/what-does-your-workplace-of-the-future-look-like/?sh=69de3fb4317f. Accessed 21 February 2023.

Malhotra, V. (2022, June 14). 'Airtel Introduces India's First Multiplex in the Metaverse; Check it Out!' Beebom. 14 June 2022. https://beebom.com/airtel-multiplex-metaverse-introduced/. Accessed on February 2023.

Marcuse, Herbert. *One-Dimensional Man. Studies in the Ideology of Advanced Industrial Society. 2nd Edition.* London and New York: Routledge Classics, 2002.

Market Stats Ville. 'Corporate Social Responsibility Software Market 2021: Industry Size, Regions, Emerging Trends, Growth Insights, Opportunities, and Forecast By 2027'. Market Statsville Group Website. 2021. https://www.marketstatsville.com/request-sample/corporate-social-responsibility-software-market. Accessed on 21 February 2022.

Marr, Bernard. 'What Is the Difference Between Weak (Narrow) and Strong (General) Artificial Intelligence (AI)? LinkedIn. 13 May 2021. https://www.linkedin.com/pulse/what-difference-between-weak-narrow-strong-general-artificial-marr. Accessed 4 July 2021.

Martin, Charles Patrick, Kai Olav Ellefsen, and Jim Torresen. 'Deep Predictive Models in Interactive Music'. Cornell University. 21 January 2018. https://arxiv.org/abs/1801.10492.

Martis, Lily. '7 companies with Epic Wellness Programs'. Monster. https://www.monster.com/career-advice/article/companies-good-wellness-programs. Accessed 2 December 2021.

Marx, Karl. Grundrisse. *Foundations of the Critique of Political Economy* (rough draft). Translated by Martin Nicolaus. Penguin Books, in association with the New Left Review, 1973.

Mayer, H. M. 'The Future Of The Metaverse: What 2022 Has in Store for the Immersive Digital World'. *Forbes*. 24 January 2022: https://www.forbes.com/sites/hannahmayer/2022/01/24/the-future-of-the-metaverse-what-2022-has-in-store-for-the-immersive-digital-world/?sh=2ec1685e335a. Accessed 21 February 2023.

McKinsey & Company. 'National Surveys Reveal Disconnect Between Employees and Employers Around Mental Health Need'. 21 April 2021.

McKinsey & Company. 'Returning to Work: Keys to a Psychologically Safer Workplace'. McKinsey website. 15 July 2021. https://www.mckinsey.com/industries/healthcare-systems-and-services/our-insights/returning-to-work-keys-to-a-psychologically-safer-workplace?cid=other-eml-alt-mcq-mck&hdpid=15c23ed2-92ab-4e36-9dec-02bc66306a29&hctky=12810559&hlkid=baf5ac2d32044875a970a33f8fa088a0. Accessed on 28 Jul, 2021.

McKinsey & Company. 'Succeeding in the AI Supply-chain Revolution'. McKinsey website. 20 April 2021. https://www.mckinsey.com/industries/metals-and-mining/our-insights/succeeding-in-the-ai-supply-chain-revolution . Accessed on 14 October 2021.

McKinsey Global Institute. 'Jobs lost; Jobs gained: Workforce Transitions in a time of Automation 2017'. McKinsey website. https://www.mckinsey.com/featured-insights/future-of-work/jobs-lost-jobs-gained-what-the-future-of-work-will-mean-for-jobs-skills-and-wages . Accessed 26 June 2021.

McKinsey Global Institute (MGI). 'The Future of Work after Covid-19'. McKinsey website. 18 February 2021. https://www.mckinsey.com/featured-insights/future-of-work/the-future-of-work-after-covid-19. Accessed 4 July 2021).

McKinsey Quarterly. 'Overcoming Stigma: Three Strategies Toward Better Mental Health in the Workplace'. McKinsey website. 23 July 2021. https://www.mckinsey.com/industries/healthcare-systems-and-services/our-insights/overcoming-stigma-three-strategies-toward-better-mental-health-in-the-workplace?cid=other-eml-alt-mcq-mck&hdpid=15c23ed2-92ab-4e36-9dec-02bc66306a29&hctky=12810559&hlkid=4701bf4f0c034af2974eb850a5914021. Accessed on 28 July 2021.

McLaurin, J. P. '5 Trends Driving the New Post-Pandemic Workplace'. Gensler: https://www.gensler.com/blog/5-trends-driving-the-new-post-pandemic-workplace. Accessed on 21 February 2023.

Medhi, Trisha. 'These Made-in-India Robots Are Helping Health Workers Fight COVID-19'. YourStory. 5 August 2020. https://yourstory.com/2020/08/made-in-india-robots-coronavirus-aatmanirbhar-bharat/amp. Accessed on 23 July 2021.

Mehra, Samiksha. 'Conversations: How IIT-H Is Decoding the AI Black Box with Research on XAI'. IndiaAI. 15 July 2021. https://indiaai.gov.in/article/how-iit-h-is-decoding-the-ai-black-box-with-research-on-xai. Accessed on 23 July 2021.

'Mental Health Matters'. *The Lancet* Vol. 8, Issue 11, E1352, November 2020.

'Metaverse and the Future of Marketing'. Dataquest. 23 March 2020. https://www.dqindia.com/metaverse-and-the-future-of-marketing/. Accessed on 21 February 2023.

Mehotra, Santosh. 'What's Falling: Poverty or Quality of Analysis. Deccan Herald. 23 May 2022. https://www.deccanherald.com/opinion/what-s-falling-poverty-or-quality-ofanalysis-1111856.html. Accessed on 20 February 2023.

Mileva, G. (2022, January 21). 'The State of the Metaverse 2022: Challenges and Opportunities.' Influencer MarketingHub. 21 January 2022. https://influencermarketinghub.com/state-of-the-metaverse/. Accessed 21 February 2023.

Miller, Chance. 'Apple Reportedly Scales Back Ambitious "HealthHabit" Project for Transforming Healthcare'. 9to5mac.com. 19 August 2021. https://9to5mac.com/2021/08/19/apple-reportedly-scales-back-ambitious-healthhabit-project-for-transforming-healthcare/. Accessed on 2 December 2021.

Ministry of Human Resource Development, Government of India. 'National Education Policy 2020'. https://www.education.gov.in/sites/upload_files/mhrd/files/NEP_Final_English_0.pdf. Accessed 14 June 2021.

Ministry of Micro, Small and Medium Enterprises. 'Prime Ministers Employment Generation Programme, PMEGP'. 2021. https://msme.gov.in/11-prime-ministers-employment-generation-programme-pmegp. Accessed 10 July 2021.

Ministry of Statistics and Programme Implementation (MOSPI). 'Women and Men in India 2020'. https://mospi.nic.in/publication/women-and-men-india-2020. Accessed 2 July 2021.

Mint. 'AI to Play a Key Role in India's Growth in Agriculture: Nasscom EY Report'. Livemint. 25 March 2021. https://www.livemint.com/technology/tech-news/ai-to-play-a-key-role-in-india-s-growth-in-agriculture-nasscom-ey-report-11616681716106.html. Accessed on 23 July 2021.

Mishel, L., & Bivens, J. Identifying the Policy Levers Generating Wage Suppression and Wage Inequality. Economic Policy Institute. 13 May 2021. https://www.epi.org/unequalpower/publications/wage-suppression-inequality/ . Accesed on 21 February 2023.

Misra, S. S., and T. Patel. 'The Inequality Virus-India Supplement 2021'. Oxfam India. 22 January 2021. https://www.oxfamindia.org/press-release/inequality-virus-india-supplement-2021. Accessed 21 February 2023.

Mitter, Swasti (Ed.) 'Computer-aided Manufacturing and Women's Employment: The Clothing Industry in Four EC Countries'. London: Springer-Verlag Limited, 1992.

Mordor Intelligence. 'Robotics Market – Growth, Trends, COVID-19 Impact, and Forecasts (2021-2026)'. Mordor Intelligence website. https://www.mordorintelligence.com/industry-reports/robotics-market Accessed on 22 July 2021.

Most Productive Countries 2022. World Population Review: worldpopulationreview.com.

Mousteri, Victoria, Michael Daly, and Liam Delaney. 'The Scarring Effect of Unemployment on Psychological Well-Being Across Europe'. *Social Science Research*. Volume 72 (2018): 146-169.

Mruk, Christopher J. 'Self Esteem – Research, Theory and Practice. Towards a Positive Psychology of Self-Esteem. Third Edition'. New York: Springer Publishing Company, 2006.

Mulcahy, D. 'The Gig Economy: The Complete Guide to Getting Better Work, Taking More Time Off, and Financing the Life You Want'. AMACOM, 2016

Munshi, K., and M. Rosenzwig. 'Networks and Misallocation: Insurance, Migration, and the Rural-Urban Wage Gap'. *American Economic Review*, 106(1), 46-98. https://www.repository.cam.ac.uk/bitstream/handle/1810/254304/Munshi%20&%20Rosenzweig%202015%20American%20Economic%20Review.pdf?sequence=1

Nair, Krishnaprasad S. 'Impact of Robots in the Financial Sector'. *IOSR Journal of Business and Management*. 2018 (72-76). International Management Research Conference 2018. http://www.iosrjournals.org/iosr-jbm/papers/Conf.ADMIFMS1808-2018/Volume-1/11.%2072-76.pdf Accessed on 23 July 2021.

Narayan, A., A. Cojocaru, S. Agrawal, T. Bundervoet, M. Davalos, N. Garcia, C. Lakner, D.G. Mahler, V.M. Talledo, A. Ten, and N. Yonzan. 'COVID-19 and Economic Inequality Short-Term Impacts with Long-Term Consequences'. World Bank Group. 2022. Policy research working paper, 9902.

Nardinelli, Clark. 'Industrial Revolution and the Standard of Living'. Econlib. https://www.econlib.org/library/Enc/IndustrialRevolutionandtheStandardofLiving.html. Accessed 21 February 2023.

National Skill development Corporation (NSDC). 'Pradhan Mantri Kaushal Vikas Yojana 2021'. https://pmkvyofficial.org/. Accessed 30 June 2021.

National Skill development Corporation (NSDC). 'Pradhan Mantri Kaushal Kendra 2021'. https://nsdcindia.org/pmkk. Accessed 30 June 2021.

National Statistical Office. Per Capita Net State Domestic Product. Reserve Bank of India. 24 November 2021. https://m.rbi.org.in/scripts/PublicationsView.aspx?id=20676. Accessed 21 February 2023.

NCSDE. 'Skill Gap in India'. Retrieved from https://www.ncsde.in/skill-gap-in-india/.

NextRembrandt. 'Can the Great Master be Brought Back to Create One More Painting? https://www.nextrembrandt.com/. Accessed on 5 October 2021.

Nhất Hạnh, Thích. *Being Peace*. Hind Pocket Books, 2004.

Nhất Hạnh, Thích. *Living Buddha, Living Christ*. Rider, First Edition, 1996.

Nhất Hạnh, Thích. *No Death, No Fear*. RHUK, 2002.

Nhất Hạnh, Thích. *The Heart of Understanding*. Full Circle Publishing, 2017.

Nhất Hạnh, Thích. *The Miracle of Mindfulness*. RHUK, 2008.

Nhất Hạnh, Thích. *Zen Keys*. Anchor Books, 1974.

Nike News. 'Nike Headspace Partnership Mindfulness Training'. Nike News website. 1 March 2018. https://news.nike.com/news/nike-headspace-partnership. Accessed 2 December 2021.

Non-fungible tokens (NFT). Retrieved from ethereum.org: https://ethereum.org/en/nft/

EY Global. 'How Does Security Evolve from Bolted on to Built-in?' EY. 18 February 2020. https://www.ey.com/en_gl/consulting/how-does-security-evolve-from-bolted-on-to-built-in. Accessed 21 February 2023.

Nussbaum, Martha. 'Capabilities as Fundamental Entitlements: Sen and Social Justice'. *Feminist Economics*. Vol. 9 (2-3)(2008): 33-59.

Nussbaum, Martha. *Creating Capabilities: The Human Approach*. Cambridge, Massachusetts: Belknap Press of Harvard University Press, 2011.

Nuvolari, Alessandro. 'The "Machine Breakers" and the Industrial Revolution'. Working Paper 00.11. Eindhoven Centre for Innovation Studies (ECIS). Paper prepared for the Eighth International Joseph A. Schumpeter Society Conference, Manchester, UK, 28 June-1 July 2000.

O'Donovan, Roisin, D.V. Dun, and E. McAuliffe, E. 'Measuring Psychological Safety in Healthcare Teams: Developing an Oservational Measure to Complement Survey Methods'. *BMC Medical Research Medology 20*, Article No.. 203, 2020.

O'Neil, Cathy. *Weapons of Math Destruction: How Big Data Increases Inequality and Threatens Democracy*. New York: Crown, 2016.

O'Rourke, Kevin H., Ahmed S. Rahman and Alan M. Taylor. 'Luddites, the Industrial Revolution, and the Demographic Transition'. *Journal of Economic Literature*. June 2011.

Observer Research Foundation. 'The Future of Work in India. Inclusion, Growth and Transformation'. October 2018.

Open Culture. 'Jules Verne Accurately Predicts What the 20th Century Will Look Like in His Lost Novel, Paris in the Twentieth Century (1863)'. Open Culture website. 25 January 2016. https://www.openculture.com/2016/01/jules-verne-accurately-predicts-what-the-20th-century-will-look-like.html Accessed on 7 October 2021.

Organisation for Economic Corporation and Development (OECD). 'Globalisation, Jobs and Wages'. OECD website. 2007. 0020071P-1p4.indd (oecd.org). Accessed on 21 February 2023.

Our World in Data. 'Human Development Index'. 2014. https://ourworldindata.org/human-development-index#:~:text=The%20Human%20Development%20Index%20(HDI)%20provides%20a%20single%20index%20measure,a%20long%20and%20healthy%20life

Page, J. 'The East Asian Miracle and Development Policy: A Twenty-Year Retrospective. Japan's Development Assistance'. Palgrave Macmillan, UK, 2016.

Pandey, Srishti. 'TCS, Infosys, Wipro, Cognizant, HCL, Tech Mahindra, Other IT Firms to Lay Off 30 Lakh Employees by 2022!' Daily Blog. 17 June 2021. https://dailyblogday.online/tcs-infosys-wipro-cognizant-hcl-tech-mahindra-other-it-firms-to-lay-off 30-lakh-employees/. Accessed 4 July 2021.

Parcerisa, Christin. 'Tips from Google's Resilience Expert on Avoiding Burnout'. The Keyword. 27 April 2021. https://blog.google/inside-google/life-at-google/tips-from-googles-resilience-expert-on-avoiding-burnout/. Accessed on 2 December 2021.

Parmar, Belinda. 'The Most Empathetic Companies, 2016'. *Harvard Business Review*. 1 December 2016. https://hbr.org/2016/12/the-most-and-least-empathetic-companies-2016. Accessed on 9 February 2022.

Pateman, Ema. 'Mindfulness at work – insights from early adopters'. Shine. 1 December 2019. https://www.shineworkplacewellbeing.com/mindfulness-at-work/. Accessed on 2 December 2021.

Pathak, Kalpana. 'Freshers in India Have Better Opportunities: TeamLease EdTech'. *Mint*. 21 September 2021. https://www.livemint.com/news/india/freshers-in-india-have-better-opportunities-teamlease-edtech-11632203446407.html. Accessed on 5 October 2021.

Pathak, Kalpana. 'Pandemic Pushes Firms to Hire More Temp Staff'. *Mint*. 18 June 2021. https://www.livemint.com/industry/human-resource/pandemic-pushes-firms-to-hire-more-temp-staff-11623955094524.html. Accessed 04 July 2021.

PEGA. 'The Future of Work. New Perspectives on Disruption & Transformation'. Pegasystems, 2020. https://www.pega.com/system/files/resources/2021-04/pega-future-of-work-report.pdf?_rid=YToxOntzOjM6Im5pZCI7czo1OiI5OTAxNiI7fQ--&utm_source=google&utm_content=pcrid|482226397594|pkw|kwd-20061192138|pmt|b|pdv|m|&utm_medium=cpc&utm_campaign=G_India_NonBrand_AI_EN. Accessed on 28 Jul, 2021.

Percy, S. 'Why Your Board Needs A Chief Philosophy Officer'. *Forbes*. 9 March 2018. https://www.forbes.com/sites/sallypercy/2018/03/09/why-your-board-needs-a-chief-philosophy-officer/?sh=bdb7e9f42e3d. Accessed on 21 February 2023.

Perel, Esther. 'How the Growing Identity Economy is Reshaping the Future of Work'. FastCompany. 13 May 2021. https://www.fastcompany.com/90635838/how-the-growing-identity-economy-is-reshaping-the-future-of-work. Accessed on 5 October 2021.

'Periodic Labour Force Survey (PLFS) Quarterly Bulletin'. New Delhi: Ministry of Statistic and Programme Implementation, National Statistical Office, Government of India, 2021.

'Perspectives: The Rise of Using Cryptocurrency in Business'. Deloitte.com. https://www2.deloitte.com/us/en/pages/audit/articles/corporates-using-crypto.html. Accessed on 21 February 2023.

Peterson, Christopher, and Martin E.P. Seligman. *Character Strengths and Virtues: A Handbook and Classification*. New York: Published by American Psychological Association and Oxford University Press, 2004.

Peterson, Christopher. *Pursuing the Good Life: 100 Reflections on Positive Psychology*. New York: Oxford University Press, 2013.

Photopoulos, Julianna. 'Fighting Algorithmic Bias in Artificial Intelligence'. Physicsworld. 4 May 2021. https://physicsworld.com/a/fighting-algorithmic-bias-in-artificial-intelligence/. Accessed 4 July 2021.

Pierce, Justin. 'Insights, How COVID-19 Has Sped up Hospitality Technology'. eHotelier Website. 11 February 2021. https://insights.

ehotelier.com/insights/2021/02/11/how-covid-19-has-sped-up-hospitality-technology/. Accessed on 9 October 2021.

Piketty, Thomas. *Capital in the Twenty-first Century*. Cambridge: Belknap Press, 2014.

Pink, Daniel H. *A Whole New Mind: Why Right-Brainers Will Rule the Future*. New York: Riverhead Books, Penguin, 2006.

Po, B. Five Surprising Ways the Metaverse Meets the Future Of Work. *Forbes*. 21 April 2022. https://www.forbes.com/sites/forbestechcouncil/2022/04/21/five-surprising-ways-the-metaverse-meets-the-future-of-work/?sh=6171716d3d1d. Accessed on 21 February 2023.

Poleg, D. 'The Crypto Future of Work'. Drorpoleg.com. 9 June 2021. https://www.drorpoleg.com/the-crypto-future-of-work/. Accessed on 21 February 2023.

Poleg, D. 'NFTs and the Future of Work'. Drorpoleg.com. 25 March 2021. https://www.drorpoleg.com/nfts-and-the-future-of-work/. Accessed on 21 February 2023.

Polyani, Karl. *The Great Transformation*. Boston, Massachusetts: Beacon Press, 2001.

PricewaterhouseCoopers India and Bengal Chamber of Commerce and Industry (BCCI). 'Reimagining the Possible in the Indian Healthcare Ecosystem with Emerging Technologies'. PwC Publication, 2018.

PricewaterhouseCoopers India. 'Artificial intelligence in India—Hype or Reality: Impact of Artificial Intelligence Across Industries and User Groups'. PwC Publication. February 2018. https://www.pwc.in/assets/pdfs/consulting/technology/data-and-analytics/artificial-intelligence-in-india-hype-or-reality/artificial-intelligence-in-india-hype-or-reality.pdf. Accessed on 23 July 2021.

PricewaterhouseCoopers India. 'Indian Workplace of 2022'. PwC Paper, 2014.

PricewaterhouseCoopers India. 'PwC's Global Crisis Survey 2021: India Insights'. September 2021.

PricewaterhouseCoopers Report. 'How can blockchain Power iIndustrial Manufacturing?' https://www.pwc.com/us/en/industrial-products/publications/assets/pwc-blockchain-in-manufacturing.pdf. Accessed on 21 February 2023.

PricewaterhouseCoopers. '50% of India Leaders Feel Unsure About the Future of Work: PwC India survey'. PwC website. 23 February 2020. https://www.pwc.in/press-releases/2022/50-percentage-of-india-leaders-feel-unsure-about-the-future-of-work-pwc-survey.html. Accesed on 21 February 2023.

Proulx, M., J. Ask, M. Bennett, J. Gownder and D. Truog. 'There Is No Metaverse Today, But Be Prepared'. Forrester. 29 March 2022. https://www.forrester.com/blogs/there-is-no-metaverse-today-but-be-prepared/ . Accessed 21 February 2023.

Prummer, A. (2020). 'Micro-targeting and Polarization'. *Journal of Public Economics*, Vol. 188.

Prudential Newsroom. 'Pulse of the American Worker Survey: Is this Working?' Prudential. https://news.prudential.com/presskits/pulse-american-worker-survey-is-this-working.htm. Accessed on 21 February 2023.

Purdy, M. (2022, April 5). 'How the Metaverse Could Change Work'. *Harvard Business Review*. 5 April 2022. https://hbr.org/2022/04/how-the-metaverse-could-change-work#:~:text=The%20metaverse%20could%20revolutionize%20training,training%20and%20with%20career%20advice. Accessed on 21 February 2023.

Quah, D. T. 'The Weightless Developing Economy'. UNI-WIDER: https://www.wider.unu.edu/publication/weightless-developing-economy. Accessed on 21 February 2023.

Radhakrishnan, Rajiv and Chittaranjan Andrade. 'Suicide: An Indian perspective'. Indian Journal Psychiatry. 54(4)(October-December 2012): 304–319. doi: 10.4103/0019-5545.104793.

Radjou, N., J.C. Prabhu, and S. Ahuja. *Jugaad Innovation: Think Frugal, Be Flexible, Generate Breakthrough Growth*. India: Wiley, 2012.

Rao, Dattaraj. *Role of Artificial Intelligence in the Indian Manufacturing Environment*. Persistent website. 20 May 2019. https://www.persistent.com/blogs/role-of-artificial-intelligence-in-the-indian-manufacturing-environment/. Accessed on 28 July 2021.

Rath, Tom and Jim Harter. *The Five Essential Elements of Well-Being*. Gallup Website. 4 May 2010.

https://www.gallup.com/workplace/237020/five-essential-elements.aspx. Accessed on 25 September 2022.

Rath, Tom and Jim Harter. *Wellbeing: The Five Essential Elements.* Deckle Edge, May 2010.

Rawls, John. *A Theory of Justice.* Harvard University Press, Belknap Press, 1999, xvii–xxii. https://doi.org/10.2307/j.ctvkjb25m.4.

Raza, Muhammad. 'IT Automation Trends to Watch in 2021'. BMC Blogs. 28 October 2020. https://www.bmc.com/blogs/it-automation-trends/#. Accessed on 9 October 2021.

Reinhart, Carmen M. and Kenneth S. Rogoff. 'This Time is Different: A Panoramic View of Eight Centuries of Financial Crises'. NBER Working Paper Series. Cambridge, Massachusetts: National Bureau of Economic Research, March 2008.

Reuters. 'WHO Warns Against Vaccine Hoarding as Poorer Countries Go Without'. 2021. https://www.reuters.com/business/healthcare-pharmaceuticals/who-warns-against-vaccine-hoarding-poor-countries-go-without-2021-12-09/. Accessed on 21 February 2023.

ReviewPro. 'Why Hotel Automation is the Next Big Thing in Hospitality'. ReviewPro blog. 23 June 2021. https://www.reviewpro.com/blog/hotel-automation-next-big-thing/. Accessed on 9 October 2021.

Rifkin, Jeremy. *The End of Work: The Decline of the Global Labor Force and the Dawn of the Post-Market Era.* New York: G.P. Putnam's Sons, 1995.

Riva, G. and B.K. Wiederhold, B. K., 'What the Metaverse Is (Really) and Why We Need to Know About It'. *Cyberpsychology, Behaviour, and Social Networking*, Vol. 25, No.6 (2022).

Robinson, Adam. 'The Top 5 Impacts of Artificial Intelligence (AI) in Logistics: Supply Chain Game Changer'. Supply Chain Game Changer. 13 September 2021. https://supplychaingamechanger.com/the-top-5-impacts-of-artificial-intelligence-ai-in-logistics/. Accessed on 14 October 2021.

Rodeck, D., & Schmidt, J. (2022, March 25). 'What Is Blockchain?' *Forbes.* 25 March 2022. https://www.forbes.com/advisor/in/investing/what-is-blockchain/. Accessed on 21 February 2023.

Rodriguez, J. 'Non-Fungible Tokens (NFTs) Definition – Should You Invest in Digital Art?' Money Crashers. 14 September 2021. https://www.moneycrashers.com/non-fungible-tokens-nfts/. Accesed on 21 February 2023.

Roos, J. 'Build STEM Skills, but Don't Neglect the Humanities'. *Harvard Business Review*. 24 June 2015. https://hbr.org/2015/06/build-stem-skills-but-dont-neglect-the-humanities. Accesed on 21 February 21, 2023.

Rosender, Y. (2022, February 7). 'Reliance's Jio Platforms Invests in Deep Tech Startup Two Platforms, Betting on the Metaverse'. *Forbes*. 7 February 2022. https://www.forbes.com/sites/yessarrosendar/2022/02/07/reliances-jio-platforms-invests-in-deep-tech-startup-two-platforms-betting-on-the-metaverse/?sh=6fcc7be44c7e . Accessed on 21 February 2023.

Rowland, Christine. 'Intel's Organizational Culture for Business Resilience (an Analysis)'. Panmore Institute website. 19 April 2017. http://panmore.com/intel-organizational-culture-business-resilience-analysis. Accessed on 2 December 2021.

Ruiz, Alyssa. 'How Will the Higher Education Industry Adopt the Metaverse?' Investisdigital. 30 August 2022. https://www.investisdigital.com/blog/technology/will-higher-education-adopt-the-metaverse. Accessed on 25 September 2022.

Sanskriti University. 'Machine Learning, AI & Big Data Analytics in Travel and Hospitality Industry'. Sanskriti website. 4 October 2021. https://sanskriti.edu.in/blog/machine-learning-ai-big-data-analytics-travel-hospitality-industry. Accessed on 9 October 2021.

Sardeshmukh, Shruti R., Dheeraj Sharma, Timothy D. Golden. 'Impact of Telework on Exhaustion and Job Engagement: A Job Demands and Job Resources Model. New Technology, Work and Employment.' Wiley Online Library. 26 October 2012.

Say, Jean-Baptiste. *A Treatise on Political Economy: Or the Production, Distribution And Consumption Of Wealth*. Translated from the Fourth Edition of the French by C.R. Prinsep, M.A. Philadelphia: Grigg & Elliott, 1834.

Schaffrik, Bernhard. 'The Forrester Wave™: Robotic Process Automation, Q1 2021. The 14 Providers That Matter Most and How they Stack Up'. Forrester, 15 March, 2021.

Schumpeter, J. (2008). *Capitalism, Socialism and Democracy. Harper Perennial Modern Thought*. 3rd Edition, Paperback.

Schwab, Klaus, and Thierry Malleret. *COVID-19: The Great Reset*. Forum Publishing, 2020.

Schwab, Klaus. 'The Fourth Industrial Revolution'. World Economic Forum, 2016.

Schwanauer, Stephan, and David A. Levitt (Eds.). *Machine Models of Music*. Cambridge, Massachusetts, and London, England: The MIT Press, 1993.

Seebo. 'Machine Learning and AI in Manufacturing: A Quick Guide to the Fundamentals'. Seebo Website. https://www.seebo.com/machine-learning-ai-manufacturing/. Accessed on 28 July 2021.

Seligman, Martin E.P. *Authentic Happiness: Using the New Positive Psychology to Realize Your Potential for Lasting Fulfillment*. New York: Atria Paperback (Simon and Schuster), 2002.

Seligman, Martin E.P. Flourish. *A Visionary New Understanding of Happiness and Well-being*. New York: Free Press, 2011.

Seligman, Martin E.P. *Learned Optimism. How to Change Your Mind and Your Life*. New York: Vintage Books, 2006.

Sen, Amartya. *Inequality Re-examined*. Oxford University Press, 1995.

Sharma, Y. S. (2022, March 8). 'Despite Policy Support, Labour Participation by Women Still Low'. *Economic Times*. 8 March 2022. https://economictimes.indiatimes.com/jobs/despite-policy-support-labour-participation-by-women-still-low/articleshow/90061223.cms Accessed on 21 February 2023.

Silway, Rebecca. 'AI in Travel and Hospitality Market Industry Analysis 2021–031'. Industrial Forecast Report, 28 September 2021. https://industrialforecastreport.home.blog/2021/09/28/ai-in-travel-and-hospitality-market-industry-analysis-2021-2031/. Accessed on 9 October 2021.

Simpson, E. 'The Workers Getting 100% Pay for 80% of the Hours'. BBC. 6 June 2022. https://www.bbc.co.uk/news/business-61570021. Accessed on 21 February 2023.

Singh, A.J. 'Impact of COVID-19 on the Hospitality Industry and Implication for Operations and Asset Management'. Boston Hospitality Review. 31 May 2021. https://www.bu.edu/bhr/2021/05/31/impact-of-covid-19-on-the-hospitality-industry-and-implication-for-operations-and-asset-management/ Accessed on 9 October 2021.

Singh, Ashish Pratap. 'Artificial Intelligence in India 2021 (Strategy of AI in India)'. TechGecs. 19 January 2021. https://www.techgecs.in/2020/08/artificial-intelligence-in-india.html?m=1. Accessed on 23 July 2021.

Sinha Roy, Sutirtha, Van Der Weide, Roy. Poverty in India Has Declined Over the Last Decade but Not as Much as Previously Thought. Policy Research Working Paper; 9994, 2020. World Bank, Washington, DC. World Bank. https://openknowledge.worldbank.org/handle/10986/37273   License: CC   BY 3.0 IGO,

Skelley, Jeffrey. 'Trump Supporters Aren't "Shy", but Polls Could Still Be Missing Some of Them'. FiveThirtyEight. 23 September 2020. https://fivethirtyeight.com/features/trump-supporters-arent-shy-but-polls-could-still-be-missing-some-of-them/. Accessed on 16 February 2022.

Smith, Adam. *An Inquiry into the Nature and Causes of the Wealth of Nations*. Indianapolis, Indiana: Liberty Classics/ Oxford University Press, 1979.

Spence, M. 'Job Market Signaling'. *The Quarterly Journal of Economics*, Vol. 87, No. 3 (1973), 355-374.

Spence, M. (1979). 'Investment Strategy and Growth in a New Market'. *Bell Journal of Economics*, Vol. 10, Issue 1 (1979): 1-19.

Sreekumar, V., P. R. David, and P. Deb. India's Startup Explosion: More Pitfalls than Promise?' LSE 11 May 2022. https://blogs.lse.ac.uk/businessreview/2022/05/11/indias-startup-explosion-more-pitfalls-than-promise/. Accessed on 21 February 2023.

Global Economy. 'Sri Lanka: Female Labor Force Participation'. *Global Economy.com*. https://www.theglobaleconomy.com/Sri-Lanka/Female_labor_force_participation/. Accessed on 21 February 2023.

Srinivas, R. 'India Facing Shortage of Engineers in S&T: DRDO DG'. *Hindu*. 29 January 2013. https://www.thehindu.com/news/cities/Vijayawada/india-facing-shortage-of-engineers-in-st-drdo-dg/article4356570.ece. Accessed on 21 February 2023.

Srivastava, Smriti. 'Top Robotics Companies Redefining Indian Automation Industry'. Analytics Insight. 23 May 2020. https://www.analyticsinsight.net/top-robotics-companies-redefining-indian-automation-industry/. Accessed on 28 July 2021.

Stein, S. 'Microsoft Shutters Part of its Social Metaverse for Safety Reasons'. CNET. 16 February 2022. https://www.cnet.com/tech/computing/microsoft-shutters-part-of-its-social-metaverse-for-safety-reasons/. Accessed on 28 July 21.

Stewart, Henry. 'Five Big Companies Who Swear By Mindfulness'. LinkedIn post. 17 August 2015.

Stewart, Ian, and Myles Runham. 'After EI, DI? Chief Learning Officer'. Chief Learning Officer. 29 June 2021. https://www.chieflearningofficer. com/2021/06/29/after-ei-di/. Accessed 4 July 2021.

Stieber, Jack (Ed.). *Employment Problems of Automation and Advanced Technology: An International Perspective. Proceedings of a Conference held at Geneva by the International Institute for Labour Studies.* London: Macmillan and Company Limited, 1966.

Stiglitz, J. *Globalization and its Discontents.* W.W. Norton & Company, 2002.

Stiglitz, Joseph. Some Lessons from The East Asian Miracle. *The World Bank Research Observer.* Vol. 11 No. 2 (2016): 151–177

Syrjamaki, A. H., P. Isokoski, V. Surakka, T,P. Pasanen, and J.K Hietanen. 'Eye Contact in Virtual Reality— A Psychophysiological Study'. *Computers in Human Behaviour,* Vol. 112 (1996).

Tandon, R. 'India's Street Typists Heading for a Final Full-stop'. BBC News. January 2014. https://www.bbc.com/news/business-25620755. Accessed on 21 February 2023.

Team, D. W. 'New Labour Laws from July 1! How Working Hours, PF and in-hand Salary Will Change'. dnaindia.com. 9 June, 2022. https://www.dnaindia.com/business/report-new-labour-laws-from-july-1-how-working-hours-pf-in-hand-salary-leaves-will-change-labour-codes-2959103. Accessed on 21 February 2023.

Tegmark, Max. *Life 3.0: Being Human in the Age of Artificial Intelligence.* New York: Alfred A. Knopf, 2017.

Teitelbaum, M. S. 'The Myth of the Science and Engineering Shortage'. *The Atlantic.* 19 March 2014. https://www.theatlantic. com/education/archive/2014/03/the-myth-of-the-science-and-engineering-shortage/284359/. Accessed on 21 February 2023.

Tharamangalam, J. 'The Perils Of Social Development Without Economic Growth: The Development Debacle of Kerala, India'. Bulletin of Concerned Asian Scolars, 30:1 (1988): 23-34.

Adecco Group. 'The Advantages and Disadvantages of Working in the Metaverse'. Adecco Group websiter. 4 April 2022. https://www.adeccogroup.com/future-of-work/latest-insights/the-advantages-and-disadvantages-of-working-in-the-metaverse/. Accessed on 21 February 2023.

SHRM. 'The Future of Work Arrives Early'. shrm.org. https://www.shrm.org/hr-today/trends-and-forecasting/research-and-surveys/pages/the-future-of-work-arrives-early.aspx. Accessed on 21 February 2023.

Hindu Business Line Bureau. 'Top 5 Robotic Start-ups Pushing Boundaries in India.' *Hindu Business Line.* 1 June 2020. https://www.thehindubusinessline.com/info-tech/other-gadgets/top-5-robotic-start-ups-pushing-boundaries-in-india/article31720944.ece. Accessed on 22 July 2021.

The Lancet Global Health. 'Mental Health Matters'. *The Lancet.* November 2020. doi:https://doi.org/10.1016/S2214-109X(20)30432-0.

The Lancet Psychiatry. The Burden of Mental Disorders Across the States of India: The Global Burden of Disease Study 1990–2017. Articles| Volume 7, Issue 2, P148-161, 1 February 2020.

Chen, Brian X. 'Inside Apple's Internal Training Program'. *New York Times.* https://www.nytimes.com/2014/08/11/technology/-inside-apples-internal-training-program-.html Accessed on 2 December 2021.

McKinsey. The Postpandemic Economy: The Future of Work after COVID-19.' McKinsey website. February 2022. https://www.mckinsey.com/~/media/mckinsey/featured%20insights/future%20of%20organizations/the%20future%20of%20work%20after%20covid%2019/the-future-of-work-after-covid-19-report-vf.pdf. Accessed on 21 February 2023.

N26. 'The Pros and Cons of Cryptocurrency: A Guide for New Investors'. N26 website. 17 January 2022. https://n26.com/en-eu/blog/pros-and-cons-of-cryptocurrency. Accessed on 21 February 2023.

Fintra. 'The Pros and Cons of Investing in NFTs'. Fintra. 30 May 2022. https://fintra.co.in/blog/pros-and-cons-of-investing-in-nfts. Accessed on 21 February 2023.

Ghosh, Jayati. 'Poor Country with Affluent Elite, India is Going Nowhere'. The Wire. 22 January 2020. https://thewire.in/economy/

india-world-inequality-report-poor-affluent-elite-progress. Accessed on 21 February 2023.

Thomas, Mike. '11 Robotics Applications in Banking and Finance'. BuiltIn Beta. 10 April 2020. https://builtin.com/robotics/robo-banking-robotics-applications-banking-and-finance. Accessed on 23 July 2021.

Thomson, E. P., *The Making of the English Working Class* (Penguin Modern Classics). American Historical Review, 1963.

Toffler, Alvin. *Future Shock*. 15th Printing. New York: Bantam, 1971.

Tony Blair Institute for Global Change. 'The Hidden Pandemic: Long Covid'.https://institute.global/policy/hidden-pandemic-long-covid. Accessed on 1 February 2022.

re: Work. 'Tool: Foster Psychological Safety'. re:Work website. https://rework.withgoogle.com/guides/understanding-team-effectiveness/steps/foster-psychological-safety/. Accessed on 21 February 2023.

Hindu. 'Top 10 Trusted Metaverse Development Companies in India 2022'. *Hindu*. 8 March 2022. https://www.thehindu.com/brandhub/pr-release/top-10-trusted-metaverse-development-companies-in-india-2022/article65204298.ece. Accessed on 21 February 2023.

TR, H. 'Impact of New Labour Codes on Employee's Working Hours, Annual Leave'. *Mint*. 22 June 2022. https://www.livemint.com/opinion/online-views/impact-of-new-labour-codes-on-employee-s-working-hours-annual-leave-11655904280353.html. Accessed on 21 February 2023.

Tracxn. 'AI in Healthcare Startups in India'. Tracxn website. 18 July 2021. https://tracxn.com/explore/AI-in-Healthcare-Startups-in-India. Accessed on 23 July 2021.

Triparthi, K., Robertson, S., & Cooper, C. A Brief Report on Older People's Experience of Cybercrime Victimisation In Mumbai, India'. *Journal of Elder Abuse & Neglect*, Vol. 31, Issues 4-5(2019): 437-447. https://discovery.ucl.ac.uk/id/eprint/10084093/1/Cooper%20AAM%20Brief%20report.pdf.

Truog, D. 'The Metaverse Must Be Deeply Human-Centric'. Forrester. 7 June 2022. https://www.forrester.com/blogs/the-metaverse-must-be-deeply-human-centric/. Accessed on 21 February 2023.

Truog, D. 'Ten Principles for Designing the Metaverse'. Forrester. 10 May 2022. https://www.forrester.com/blogs/designing-the-metaverse/. Accessed on 21 Febraury 2023.

Tuck, Jay. 'Evolution Without Us.' Jaytuck.com. https://www.jaytuck. com/images/Tuck%20-%20EvolutionWithoutUs%20-%20 Excerpts.pdf Accessed on 25 June 2021.

Turner, J. '6 Ways the Workplace Will Change in the Next 10 Years'. Gartner. 6 July 2022. https://www.gartner.com/smarterwithgartner/6-ways-the-workplace-will-change-in-the-next-10-years . Accessed on 21 February 2023.

Boston Consulting Group. 'Unlocking the Potential of the Gig Economic in India'. Boston Consulting Group website: https://media-publications.bcg.com/India-Gig-Economy-Report.pdf. Accessed on 21 February 2023.

Vaillant, George E. *Adaptation to Life*. Cambridge, Massachussets, London, England: Harvard University Press, 1977.

Valier, Kat. 'HR's Guide to Cultivating Workforce Resilience'. HR Factorial website. 8 October 2021. https://factorialhr.com/blog/workforce-resilience/. Accessed on 2 December 2021.

Van Harmelen, Frank, Vladimir Lifschitz, and Bruce Porter (Eds.). *Handbook of Knowledge Representation. Foundations of Artificial Intelligence.* Amsterdam, Elsevier, 2008.

Vandeplas, Anneleen. *Education, Income, and Inequality in the European Union, in Georg Fischer, and Robert Strauss (eds) Europe's Income, Wealth, Consumption, and Inequality New York.* xford University Press, 2021. doi: https://doi.org/10.1093/oso/9780197545706.003.0009

Varma, V. 'High on Literacy, Low on Workforce: Why are Kerala's Women not Making it Work?' Indian Express. 1 August 2022. https://indianexpress.com/article/gender/high-on-literacy-low-on-workforce-why-are-keralas-women-not-making-it-to-work/. Accessed on 21 February 2023.

Verma Rahul and Ankita Barthwal. 'Lockdown Boosted Family Life, but India's Young Face Anxiety, WFH Fatigue'. *Mint.* 4 January 2021. https://www.livemint.com/news/india/lockdown-boosted-family-life-but-india-s-young-face-anxiety-wfh-fatigue-11609506992201. html. Accessed on 16 February 2022.

Verma, Sandeep. 'Advanced Guide to Marketing Automation for Travel Industry'. Aritic PinPoint. 16 July 2021. https://aritic.com/blog/aritic-pinpoint/marketing-automation-for-travel-industry/. Accessed on 9 October 2021.

Vijai, Dr. C. 'Artificial Intelligence in Indian Banking Sector: Challenges and Opportunities.' *International Journal of Advanced Research*. 7(5) (April 2019): 1581-1587.

VoxEU. 'A "One Dollar, One Vote" Explanation of the Welfare State'. 2010. https://doi.org/10.1093/oso/9780197545706.003.0009

Walker, Dr. Rob F. 'Artificial Intelligence in Business: Balancing Risk and Reward'. A PEGA Whitepaper. Pegasystems, Inc. 2017.

Weeden, K. A. 'Why Do Some Occupations Pay More than Others? Social Closure and Earnings Inequality in the United States'. *American Journal of Sociology*, Vol. 108(1) (2002): 55-101.

Wei, X., X. Liu, and J. Sha. 'How Does the Entrepreneurship Education Influence the Students' Innovation? Testing on the Multiple Mediation Model'. *Frontiers in Psychology*, Vol. 10 (2019): 1-10.

Weller, Chris, and Andrea Derler. 'How Microsoft Overhauled its Approach to Growth Mindset'. Neuroleadership. 22 November 2018. https://neuroleadership.com/your-brain-at-work/microsoft-growth-mindset-transformation. Accessed on 2 December 2021.

Weller, Chris. 'We Talked to 20 Orgs About Growth Mindset—Here Are Our 7 Biggest Findings.' Neuroleadership website. https://neuroleadership.com/your-brain-at-work/microsoft-growth-mindset-transformation. 18 October 2018. Accessed on 2 December 2021.

West, Daniel M. *The Future of Work: Robots, AI and Automation*. Washington, DC: Brookings Institution Press, 2018.

'What is Blockchain Technology?' IBM.com. https://www.ibm.com/in-en/topics/what-is-blockchain. Accessed on 21 February 2023.

'What is Cryptocurrency and How Does it Work?' Kaspersky: https://www.kaspersky.com/resource-center/definitions/what-is-cryptocurrency. Accessed on 21 February 2023.

Whiting, K. 'This is the Future of Work, According to Experts at Davos 2022'. World Economic Forum. 26 May 2022. https://www.weforum.org/agenda/2022/05/future-work-jobs-davos-experts/. Accessed on 21 February 2023.

'Why Companies like Intel, Aetna and Google are Investing in Mindfulness Training Programs'. Y website. 6 January 2021. https://www.offyoga.com/blog/2021/1/6/why-companies-invest-in-mindfulness-training-programs. Accessed on 2 December 2021.

Wilds, Chris. 'Robotics in Banking with 4 RPA Use Case Examples + 3 Bank Bot Use Case Videos'. The Lab Knowledge Work Factory. https://thelabconsulting.com/robotics-in-banking-with-4-rpa-use-case-examples/. Accessed on 23 July 2021.

Wilson, Allan R. 'One-Dimensional Society Revisited: An Analysis of Herbert Marcuse's One-Dimensional Man, 34 Years Later'. A Thesis Submitted to the Faculty of Education of the University of Lethbridge in Partial Fulfilment of the requirements for the Degree Master of Education. Lethbridge, Alberta, April, 1998.

Wells, Thomas, 'The Internet Encyclopedia of Philosophy: Sen's Capability Approach'. https://iep.utm.edu/sen-cap/#SH3c.

Winter 2022 Fortune/Deloitte CEO Survey. 'CEOs Eye 2022 with Optimism and a Dash of Uncertainity'. Deloitte website. https://www2.deloitte.com/us/en/pages/about-deloitte/articles/press-releases/ceos-eye-2022-with-optimism-and-a-dash-of-uncertainty.html. Accessed 21 February 2023.

Winterbotham, M., G. Kik, S. Selner and S. Whittaker. UK Employer Skills Survey 2019: Summary Report, November 2020.

'Work in the Metaverse? How The Metaverse Is Shaping the Future Of Work'. The Adecco Group. 10 Fenruary 2022. https://www.adeccogroup.com/future-of-work/latest-insights/how-the-metaverse-is-shaping-the-future-of-work/. Accessed on 21 February 2023.

World Bank Group. 'Framing the Future of Work'. 18 October 2018. World Bank. https://documents.worldbank.org/en/publication/documents-reports/documentdetail/806971539845535746/framing-the-future-of-work. Accessed 10 June 2021.

World Bank Group. Raja, Siddhartha; Christiaensen, Luc. The Future of Work Requires More, Not Less Technology in Developing Countries. Jobs Notes; No. 2. World Bank, Washington, DC. © World Bank. 2017. https://openknowledge.worldbank.org/handle/10986/27934 License: CC BY 3.0 IGO. Accessed 10 June, 2021.

World Bank. 2018. India's Growth Story Since the 1990s Remarkably Stable and Resilient India's Growth Story Since the 1990s Remarkably Stable and Resilient (worldbank.org)

World Bank Group. World Development Report 2019. The Changing Nature of Work. 2019. https://www.worldbank.org/en/publication/wdr2019 Accessed 10 June, 2021.

World Bank Group. World Development Report 2021. Data for Better Lives. Washington, DC: 2021. https://www.worldbank.org/en/publication/wdr2021 Accessed 10 June, 2021.

World Development Report 2019 : The Changing Nature of Work. (2019). Washington, DC: World Bank. https://documents1.worldbank.org/curated/en/816281518818814423/pdf/2019-WDR-Report.pdf

World Economic Forum. Digital Culture: The Driving Force of Digital Transformation. June 2021. https://www.weforum.org/reports/digital-culture-the-driving-force-of-digital-transformation Accessed 04 July, 2021.

World Economic Forum. Disrupting Unemployment. WEF website. 17 February 2015. https://www.weforum.org/reports/disrupting-unemployment. Accessed on 10 June 2021.

World Economic Forum. 'Jobs of Tomorrow: Mapping Opportunity in the New Economy'. WEF website. 3 January 2020. http://www3.weforum.org/docs/WEF_Jobs_of_Tomorrow_2020.pdf. Accessed 10 June 2021.

World Economic Forum. Reskilling the Workforce, One Person at a Lifetime. 20 October 2020. 28 June 2021. WEF website. https://www.weforum.org/agenda/2021/06/reskilling-the-workforce-lifelong-learning/. Accessed 4 July 2021.

World Economic Forum. 'Strategies for the New Economy: Skills as the Currency of the Labour Market'. WEF website. 22 January 2019. https://www.weforum.org/whitepapers/strategies-for-the-new-economy-skills-as-the-currency-of-the-labour-market. Accessed 10 June 2021.

World Economic Forum. 'The Future of Jobs Report 2018'. WEF website. 17 September 2018. https://www.weforum.org/reports/the-future-of-jobs-report-2018. Accessed 10 June 2021.

World Economic Forum. 'The Future of Jobs Report 2020'. WEF website. 20 October 2020. https://www.weforum.org/reports/the-future-of-jobs-report-2020. Accessed 10 June 2021.

'World Employment and Social Outlook- Trends 2021' ILO Website: https://www.ilo.org/global/research/global-reports/weso/trends2021/lang--en/index.htm. Accessed 21 February 2023.

World Health Organization (WHO). 'Fact Sheets/Detail/ Mental Disorders'. WHO website. 28 November 2019. https://www.who.int/news-room/fact-sheets/detail/mental-disorders. Accessed on 16 February 2022.

WorldSkills India. 2021. https://worldskillsindia.co.in/worldskill/about.php#section2. Accessed on 10 July 2021.

World Inequality Report. 2022. https://wir2022.wid.world/. Accessed on 21 February 2023

Wright, Robert. *The Moral Animal: Why We Are the Way We Are: The New Science of Evolutionary Psychology*. New York: Pantheon Books, 1994.

Young, Justin. Nike Inc. 'Organizational Culture Characteristics: An Analysis'. Panmore Institute. 7 February 2017.

Nike Inc. Organizational Culture Characteristics: An Analysis - Panmore Institute Accessed 2 December 2021. http://panmore.com/nike-inc-organizational-culture-characteristics-analysis. Accessed on 21 February 2023.

Zeldin, Theodore. *An Intimate History of Humanity*. New York: Harper Perennial, 1996.

Zizek, Slavoj. *Pandemic! Covid-19 Shakes the World*. United Kingdom: Polity, 2020.